Management Techniques for a Diverse and Cross-Cultural Workforce

Naman Sharma
Amity University, India

Vinod Kumar Singh
Gurkul Kangri University, India

Swati Pathak
Invertis University, India

A volume in the Advances in Logistics, Operations, and Management Science (ALOMS) Book Series

Published in the United States of America by
	IGI Global
	Business Science Reference (an imprint of IGI Global)
	701 E. Chocolate Avenue
	Hershey PA, USA 17033
	Tel: 717-533-8845
	Fax: 717-533-8661
	E-mail: cust@igi-global.com
	Web site: http://www.igi-global.com

Copyright © 2018 by IGI Global. All rights reserved. No part of this publication may be reproduced, stored or distributed in any form or by any means, electronic or mechanical, including photocopying, without written permission from the publisher.
Product or company names used in this set are for identification purposes only. Inclusion of the names of the products or companies does not indicate a claim of ownership by IGI Global of the trademark or registered trademark.

Library of Congress Cataloging-in-Publication Data

Names: Sharma, Naman, 1986- editor. | Singh, V. K. (Vinod Kumar), 1969-
   editor. | Pathak, Swati, 1986- editor.
Title: Management techniques for a diverse and cross-cultural workforce /
   Naman Sharma, Vinod Kumar Singh, and Swati Pathak, editors.
Description: Hershey : Business Science Reference, [2018]
Identifiers: LCCN 2017032932| ISBN 9781522549338 (hardcover) | ISBN
   9781522549345 (ebook)
Subjects: LCSH: Diversity in the workplace--Management. | Industrial
   management--Cross-cultural studies. | Multiculturalism. | Intercultural
   communication.
Classification: LCC HF5549.5.M5 M3296 2018 | DDC 658.3008--dc23 LC record available at https://lccn.loc.gov/2017032932

This book is published in the IGI Global book series Advances in Logistics, Operations, and Management Science (ALOMS) (ISSN: 2327-350X; eISSN: 2327-3518)

British Cataloguing in Publication Data
A Cataloguing in Publication record for this book is available from the British Library.

All work contributed to this book is new, previously-unpublished material.
The views expressed in this book are those of the authors, but not necessarily of the publisher.

For electronic access to this publication, please contact: eresources@igi-global.com.

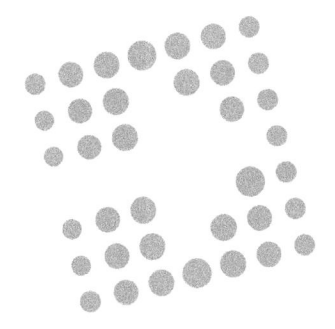

Advances in Logistics, Operations, and Management Science (ALOMS) Book Series

ISSN:2327-350X
EISSN:2327-3518

Editor-in-Chief: John Wang, Montclair State University, USA

MISSION

Operations research and management science continue to influence business processes, administration, and management information systems, particularly in covering the application methods for decision-making processes. New case studies and applications on management science, operations management, social sciences, and other behavioral sciences have been incorporated into business and organizations real-world objectives.

The **Advances in Logistics, Operations, and Management Science (ALOMS) Book Series** provides a collection of reference publications on the current trends, applications, theories, and practices in the management science field. Providing relevant and current research, this series and its individual publications would be useful for academics, researchers, scholars, and practitioners interested in improving decision making models and business functions.

COVERAGE

- Production management
- Organizational behavior
- Information management
- Risk Management
- Operations management
- Networks
- Finance
- Computing and information technologies
- Political science
- Marketing engineering

> IGI Global is currently accepting manuscripts for publication within this series. To submit a proposal for a volume in this series, please contact our Acquisition Editors at Acquisitions@igi-global.com or visit: http://www.igi-global.com/publish/.

The Advances in Logistics, Operations, and Management Science (ALOMS) Book Series (ISSN 2327-350X) is published by IGI Global, 701 E. Chocolate Avenue, Hershey, PA 17033-1240, USA, www.igi-global.com. This series is composed of titles available for purchase individually; each title is edited to be contextually exclusive from any other title within the series. For pricing and ordering information please visit http://www.igi-global.com/book-series/advances-logistics-operations-management-science/37170. Postmaster: Send all address changes to above address. Copyright © 2018 IGI Global. All rights, including translation in other languages reserved by the publisher. No part of this series may be reproduced or used in any form or by any means – graphics, electronic, or mechanical, including photocopying, recording, taping, or information and retrieval systems – without written permission from the publisher, except for non commercial, educational use, including classroom teaching purposes. The views expressed in this series are those of the authors, but not necessarily of IGI Global.

Titles in this Series

For a list of additional titles in this series, please visit:
https://www.igi-global.com/book-series/advances-logistics-operations-management-science/37170

Motivationally Intelligent Leadership Emerging Research and Opportunities
Michael A. Brown Sr. (Florida International University, USA)
Business Science Reference • ©2018 • 139pp • H/C (ISBN: 9781522537465) •US $155.00

Novel Six Sigma Approaches to Risk Assessment and Management
Vojo Bubevski (Independent Researcher, UK)
Business Science Reference • ©2018 • 251pp • H/C (ISBN: 9781522527039) • US $200.00

Enterprise Resiliency in the Continuum of Change Emerging Research and Opportunities
Raj Kumar Bhattarai (Tribhuvan University, Nepal)
Business Science Reference • ©2018 • 186pp • H/C (ISBN: 9781522526278) • US $150.00

Examining Cultural Influences on Leadership Styles and Learning ...
Valerie Zhu (Xi'an University of Science and Technology, China)
Business Science Reference • ©2017 • 207pp • H/C (ISBN: 9781522522775) • US $125.00

Globalization and the Ethical Responsibilities of Multinational Corporations ...
Tarnue Johnson (Argosy University - Chicago, USA)
Business Science Reference • ©2017 • 110pp • H/C (ISBN: 9781522525349) • US $125.00

Multi-Criteria Decision Making for the Management of Complex Systems
Albert Voronin (National Aviation University of Ukraine, Ukraine)
Business Science Reference • ©2017 • 201pp • H/C (ISBN: 9781522525097) • US $175.00

Handbook of Research on Manufacturing Process Modeling and Optimization Strategies
Raja Das (VIT University, India) and Mohan Pradhan (Maulana Azad National Institute of Technology, Bhopal, India)
Business Science Reference • ©2017 • 530pp • H/C (ISBN: 9781522524403) • US $285.00

Managerial Strategies and Green Solutions for Project Sustainability
Gilman C.K. Tam (Independent Researcher, China)
Business Science Reference • ©2017 • 255pp • H/C (ISBN: 9781522523710) • US $180.00

For an enitre list of titles in this series, please visit:
https://www.igi-global.com/book-series/advances-logistics-operations-management-science/37170

IGI Global
DISSEMINATOR OF KNOWLEDGE

701 East Chocolate Avenue, Hershey, PA 17033, USA
Tel: 717-533-8845 x100 • Fax: 717-533-8661
E-Mail: cust@igi-global.com • www.igi-global.com

Editorial Advisory Board

Omvir Gautam, *Lovely Professional University, India*
Ruchi Jain, *Amity School of Business, India*
Jugal Kishor, *Central University of Rajasthan, India*
Anand Kumar, *Union Bank of India (UK) Ltd., UK*
Pankaj Madan, *Gurukul Kangri University, India*
B. K. Punia, *MDU, India*
S. C. Sharma, *Manipal University, India*
Swati Sharma, *Amity University Rajasthan, India*
M. K. Singh, *VBU, India*
Rajan Singh, *Texplas, India*
Vivek Singh, *Tata Motors, India*
Yogesh Upadhyay, *Jiwaji University, India*
Sedat Yuksel, *MOHE, Oman*

List of Reviewers

Pooja Agarwal, *Lovely Professional University, India*
Savita Malik, *Arya (PG) College, India*
Deeksha Sharma, *National (PG) College, India*
Dipti Raj Sharma, *Invertis University, India*
Himani Singhal, *G. L. Bajaj Institute of Management, India*
Preeti Yadav, *Amity University Rajasthan, India*
Priya Yadav, *Gurukul Kangri University, India*

Table of Contents

Foreword xvii

Preface xix

Acknowledgment xxv

Section 1
Workforce and Diversity: An Introduction

Chapter 1
Diversity Management: A New Perspective 1
    Srishty Mehra, Lovely Professional University, India
    Karan Sharma, Lovely Professional University, India

Chapter 2
Gender Diversity in Board of Directors: A Content Analysis From Turkey –
Women's Presence Level in Turkey's Boards 20
    Meltem Akca, Istanbul University, Turkey
    Burcu Özge Özaslan Çalışkan, Istanbul University, Turkey

Chapter 3
Workforce Trends and Challenges: A Peek Into the Future 39
    Mihir Joshi, Gurukula Kangri Vishwavidyalaya, India

Section 2
Organizational Culture and Cross-Cultural Issues

Chapter 4
The Elements of Work Environment: Organizational Culture, Organizational
Climate, and Job Satisfaction 55
    Nebojsa Pavlovic, University of Kragujevac, Serbia

Chapter 5
Cross-Cultural Conflicts: Concept, Causes, and Elucidations 79
    Narendra Singh Chaudhary, Symbiosis International University, India
    Radha Yadav, Jaipuria School of Business, India

Section 3
Management Techniques for Cultural Issues and Diversity

Chapter 6
Thinking Globally, Leading Locally: Defining Leadership in Diverse Workforce 98
    Gursimranjit Singh, I. K. Gujral Punjab Technical University, India
    Priyanka Singh, I. K. Gujral Punjab Technical University, India
    Maninder Singh, Amritsar College of Engineering and Technology, India

Chapter 7
An Overview of Employer Branding With Special Reference to Indian Organizations 116
    Shikha Rana, IMS Unison University, India
    Ravindra Sharma, Swami Rama Himalayan University, India

Chapter 8
Antecedents and Consequences of Employee Engagement for a Diverse Workforce 132
    Shampy Kamboj, Amity University, India
    Bijoylaxmi Sarmah, North-Eastern Regional Institute of Science and Technology, India

Chapter 9
Diversity and Inclusion Management: A Focus on Employee Engagement 149
    Urmila Itam, REVA University, India
    Bagali M. M., REVA University, India

Chapter 10
Relationship Between Empowerment and Organizational Commitment: An Empirical Study of IT Industry 172
    Bhanu Priya, Gurukul Kangri University, India
    Vandana Singh, Gurukul Kangri University, India

Chapter 11
Role of Team Climate in Improving Team Functioning and Team Empowerment 186
    Alpa D. Parmar, The Maharaja Sayajirao University of Baroda, India
    Chhaya Patel, The Maharaja Sayajirao University of Baroda, India

Chapter 12
Workplace Discrimination: The Most Critical Issue in Managing Diversity 206
    Shikha Sharma, Punjabi University, India
    Nimarta Mann, Punjabi University, India

Chapter 13
Developing Strategic Leadership in the Indian Context: Leadership 224
    Minisha Gupta, IMS Unison University, India

Chapter 14
Relativity Applies to Physics, Not Ethics 236
    Purna Prabhakar Nandamuri, IFHE University, India
    Mukesh Kumar Mishra, IFHE University, India
    Gowthami Ch, ITM Business School, India

Chapter 15
Performance Appraisal Techniques Across Various Sectors in India................259
    Shikha Rana, IMS Unison University, India

Chapter 16
Exploring the Relationship Between Organizational Culture and WLB 280
    Smita Singh, University of Lucknow, India

Chapter 17
Human Resource Management in Indian Microfinance Institutions 297
    Richa Das, IMS Unison University, India

Related References 312

Compilation of References 327

Index 379

Detailed Table of Contents

Foreword xvii

Preface xix

Acknowledgment xxv

Section 1
Workforce and Diversity: An Introduction

Chapter 1
Diversity Management: A New Perspective 1
Srishty Mehra, Lovely Professional University, India
Karan Sharma, Lovely Professional University, India

The subject of workplace diversity came to the consideration of the academic and business world in the 1990s. "Variety is the spice of life." Everyone would agree with the need for diversity, so the issue is not with the concept, but in how we make use of this concept at work, especially when there is polarization between people who are working together, leading to conflict and disharmony. Diversity management emphasizes valuing and building on individual differences in order for all employees to reach their maximum potential and represents an important step away from the legal compliance-oriented equal employment opportunity. Since the current literature reveals that these practices often result in backlash and that minority employees tend to feel excluded at the workplace, a necessity emerges to investigate individual level factors of LMs that may influence these processes.

Chapter 2
Gender Diversity in Board of Directors: A Content Analysis From Turkey –
Women's Presence Level in Turkey's Boards 20
    Meltem Akca, Istanbul University, Turkey
    Burcu Özge Özaslan Çalışkan, Istanbul University, Turkey

Gender diversity in corporate governance is a popular topic in management environment studies. One of the most significant components of this concept is women in boards. Due to the inequalities of women in boards there are a number of academic studies on women in top management. This chapter explains gender diversification problem in boards. Furthermore, reasons for workforce diversity in decision-making levels are determined. The role and critical mass of women members in different cultures are discussed. Finally, it introduces the representation levels of women in the boards of BIST 100 companies in Turkey. Data is obtained from annual reports, websites, and related documents of companies.

Chapter 3
Workforce Trends and Challenges: A Peek Into the Future................................39
    Mihir Joshi, Gurukula Kangri Vishwavidyalaya, India

In this chapter, the author has reviewed the human workforce of the previous generations by taking into account the features and characteristics of the workforce, which is getting older. The purpose of this chapter is to evaluate the future of the current workforce. The future generation is still unexplored, but it is clear that the coming generation will be a blend of advanced technology and ultra-advanced simulations. The coming years will introduce more advanced artificial intelligence into the workforce that will not just be cognitively intelligent in a retrospective way but also emotionally intelligent. The future human workforce will face a challenge to maintain the requisite skill sets to cope with the constant change.

Section 2
Organizational Culture and Cross-Cultural Issues

Chapter 4
The Elements of Work Environment: Organizational Culture, Organizational
Climate, and Job Satisfaction...55
    Nebojsa Pavlovic, University of Kragujevac, Serbia

One of the biggest issues facing every organization is how to keep and recruit skilled employees. This chapter deals with work environment because there is a widespread belief that it is one of the most significant factors affecting the development of job satisfaction. The goal of this chapter is to dig deeper into the important factors that exert influence on a positive work environment. The author uses meta-analysis to assesses primary sources, which are believed to contain necessary information about certain terms that describe work environment. The results of the research indicate that a positive work environment is closely connected to employee satisfaction. It is incumbent upon managers and leaders to intensively work on improving a workplace for every employee. Further research is necessary because of the dynamics of organizational structure and inevitable, rapid technological changes. This means that managers have to put in an enormous effort so as to produce in-depth analyses of their work environments and to determine how to improve them.

Chapter 5
Cross-Cultural Conflicts: Concept, Causes, and Elucidations 79
    Narendra Singh Chaudhary, Symbiosis International University, India
    Radha Yadav, Jaipuria School of Business, India

The authors discuss in detail the meaning of conflict, cross-cultural conflict, the reasons for the conflicts, and its impact on overall organization performance and productivity. The authors also highlight and discuss the various strategies that can be worked out to reduce and resolve conflicts amicably and how to use conflicts for the betterment of the organization. The authors also focus upon the various issues and concerns that need to be taken care of while handling the conflicts and resolving them effectively. The authors have also drawn attention towards the future research perspectives, which will help organisations and management to address the cross-cultural conflicts and utilizing them for the betterment of the organisation in a constructive manner.

Section 3
Management Techniques for Cultural Issues and Diversity

Chapter 6
Thinking Globally, Leading Locally: Defining Leadership in Diverse Workforce...98
    Gursimranjit Singh, I. K. Gujral Punjab Technical University, India
    Priyanka Singh, I. K. Gujral Punjab Technical University, India
    Maninder Singh, Amritsar College of Engineering and Technology, India

Global leadership effectiveness has become one of the major issues in human resource management. It is very important for cross cultural managers to take into consideration the paradigm shift in the business world, keeping in mind the opportunity for organizational growth and individual development. The key issue that the present corporate leaders have to face is to formulate action plans to tackle diversity in the workforce covering the broader spectrum of dimensions, vis-à-vis, ethnicity, age, gender, educational background, economic status, marital status, and skill sets. Since the corporate environment is greatly accelerated by the globalization and advancements in technology, global leaders need to attain a set of competencies that would facilitate them to realize their vision and thus enhance their performance efficiency and competitiveness. The chapter deals with the specific paradigms of the leadership styles and the management of workforce diversity so as to establish the linkages between leadership style and diversity management.

Chapter 7
An Overview of Employer Branding With Special Reference to Indian Organizations 116
    Shikha Rana, IMS Unison University, India
    Ravindra Sharma, Swami Rama Himalayan University, India

Talent acquisition is the most crucial activity an organization goes through. The reasons for its criticality are not just confined to the cost and time involved in recruiting talent but also matching the right incumbents at the right place and at the right time along with the organizational fit are the most essential factors to deal with. Nowadays, organizations are working in VUCA (volatile, uncertainty, complexity, and ambiguity) environment that seeks a lot in terms of employee performance. Employer branding was initiated by Ambler and Barrow with an aim to attract and retain the best talent through various activities, and the contemporary research has proven that if branding of the organization is done in an effective manner then it retains the best talent; further, it enhances job engagement and motivation. The present chapter elaborates the concept of employer branding, benefits, and importance of employer branding. Recent surveys and trends of employer branding in Indian organizations have also been discussed.

Chapter 8
Antecedents and Consequences of Employee Engagement for a Diverse Workforce..132
    Shampy Kamboj, Amity University, India
    Bijoylaxmi Sarmah, North-Eastern Regional Institute of Science and
        Technology, India

In the recent years, employee engagement has become a hot topic of discussion among popular business press and consulting firms. This topic has created interest in various stakeholder groups ranging from scholarly human resource practitioners to policy makers or government agencies. The interest in employee engagement has progressively increased, however, in academic literature: the concept of employee engagement has been studied rarely and comparatively less is known regarding its antecedents and consequences. Recently, a number of researchers have argued that the challenge of engaging the employees is mounting. Although it seems to conceptually overlap with existing constructs, for instance, job involvement, organizational commitment, still some empirical research confirms that engagement is a separate construct. Therefore, this chapter aims (a) to shed some light in this respect by assessing the association between workforce diversity, specifically in terms of their age and employee engagement, and (b) to provide a variety of precursors and outcomes of employee engagement.

Chapter 9
Diversity and Inclusion Management: A Focus on Employee Engagement 149
Urmila Itam, REVA University, India
Bagali M. M., REVA University, India

Diversity and inclusion have been increasingly recognized and are the most utilized organizational resources over the last three decades. However, research has demonstrated that many organizations may not have the requisite diversity in their midst. Research further highlights that employees might feel that few of their components of their social identities may be valued and included, leaving them feeling excluded. These attitudes may influence employee behaviors, leading to low morale, high absenteeism, low job satisfaction, negative word of mouth, and so on, which will eventually make the estranged employee leave the job/organization. Understanding the impact of diversity and inclusion on individual, group, and organizations performance is analyzed through employee engagement by developing a framework. To develop a framework that provides rigorous theoretical evidence for its ability to determine whether an organization has indeed engendered an inclusive and engaging environment for its employees is the goal of the chapter.

Chapter 10
Relationship Between Empowerment and Organizational Commitment: An
Empirical Study of IT Industry 172
Bhanu Priya, Gurukul Kangri University, India
Vandana Singh, Gurukul Kangri University, India

This study was done to examine the relationship between empowerment and organizational commitment in the employees of IT sector. Data were collected from 70 employees of IT sector. The study used questionnaire method for the purpose of data collection. Two questionnaires, namely empowerment and organizational commitment, were used to collect the data for the study. SPSS software was used for data operation. The results of correlation showed a significant positive relationship between employees' empowerment and their commitment to organizations. Analyses also revealed a significant positive relationship between the employees' empowerment dimensions (i.e., meaning, competence, self-determination, and impact) and their organization commitment.

Chapter 11
Role of Team Climate in Improving Team Functioning and Team
Empowerment 186
    Alpa D. Parmar, The Maharaja Sayajirao University of Baroda, India
    Chhaya Patel, The Maharaja Sayajirao University of Baroda, India

The changing work force dynamics have great impact on organisation effectiveness as it requires proper and deep understanding of organisation structure and working patterns. The organisations are changing their workgroups into teams and that requires deep understanding of how teams are functioning and how they work within the organisation. The social climate plays a significant role in the improvement of the team climate, which provides shared belief amongst the team member of organisations and leads to the development of positive team climate. This chapter refers to the theory of team climate and provides a different perspective that reflects the difference between team climate and organisational climate. The changing work force diversity and pattern of organisation structure really needs understanding of team climate and how it can contribute to developing conducive team climate for learning within the organisation. Further, the chapter emphasises role of team climate in terms of team functioning and team empowerment.

Chapter 12
Workplace Discrimination: The Most Critical Issue in Managing Diversity 206
    Shikha Sharma, Punjabi University, India
    Nimarta Mann, Punjabi University, India

Diverse workforce is now a global phenomenon. The quality of interaction between people of diversified cultures in the organization has significant association with the marketing, managing, as well as human resource functions. The majority organizations are indulging in diversity management programmes so that they can benefit from the varied skills. But discriminatory behaviour against people of different backgrounds than majorities in the workplace act as a hindrance in taking full advantage of workplace diversity. This chapter reveals different forms in which discrimination can arise in a discrimination-free environment. The organizational as well as individual factors that cause discrimination at the workplace are discussed. The aftereffects that are related to discriminatory behavior at work, which render both employees as well as organization at disadvantage, are also highlighted. The chapter will help by highlighting the issue faced by thousands of employees every year and suggesting steps that need to be undertaken to remove discrimination from the workplace settings.

Chapter 13
Developing Strategic Leadership in the Indian Context: Leadership 224
    Minisha Gupta, IMS Unison University, India

With intense competition, it has become quite challenging for organizations to continuously create and innovate. Since leadership has been identified as an effective key factor in attaining sustainable competitive edge, there remains a lack of research to assess the role of leadership most likely to cause creativity and innovation. This chapter tries to conceptualize the impact of developing strategic leadership in Indian organizations. This has a significant impact on organizational creativity and innovation. Firms facing recession need to develop their leaders as strategic leaders who can generate a positive wave in the organization, provide direction to employees, generate genuine interest among employees to learn and grow. Strategic leaders develop commitment among employees by providing a vision and goal to them. They think strategically and frame policies as per employees' needs and expectations. This study demonstrates the impact of strategic leadership style to generate creativity and innovation among their subordinates.

Chapter 14
Relativity Applies to Physics, Not Ethics 236
    Purna Prabhakar Nandamuri, IFHE University, India
    Mukesh Kumar Mishra, IFHE University, India
    Gowthami Ch, ITM Business School, India

Ethical relativism is the most prevalent philosophical sub discipline. Ethical relativism represents that there is no moral right or wrong, asserting that morals evolve and change with social norms over a period of time. As the businesses have been growing transnational, this has become a burden rather than advantage, leading to confusion about whether to follow the host country or the home country cultural standards. Adopting the host country cultural values might end up with contradictory and inconsistent practices in the same organization whereas strictly believing in the home country culture might lead to rigidity and chaos in respective markets, forfeiting the opportunities. Thus, overcoming the mindset of ethical relativism has become a big burden on multinational businesses. Eventually, there lies a great hope for ethical universalism rather than relativism in the context of cross-cultural and diverse businesses.

Chapter 15
Performance Appraisal Techniques Across Various Sectors in India................259
    Shikha Rana, IMS Unison University, India

In recent times competitive and outperforming employees are of the utmost requirement for the success and sustenance of any organization. Organizations hire employees to achieve long-term and short-term goals so that they can get an edge over competitors and can meet the challenges posed by the continuously changing environment. Therefore, employees strive hard and give their level best to the organization and prove their worth by showing exemplary performance. At this juncture it becomes really important for the employers to know the exact level of employee performance as every employee differs in skills, abilities, and competence. This chapter discusses the concept, development of performance appraisal, and techniques of performance appraisal that are used across various sectors in India.

Chapter 16
Exploring the Relationship Between Organizational Culture and WLB 280
Smita Singh, University of Lucknow, India

The objective of the chapter is to investigate the relationship between organisational culture and work-life balance Questionnaires for organisational culture and work-life balance were developed and tested and the relationship between the two explored. The main findings were 1) organisational culture has a significant impact on work-life balance, and 2) more than rewards, it is support in terms of resources, roles, and empathy that have a significant impact on WLB of an individual. It is the prevailing culture that determines whether an employee does or does not take the benefit of existing family-friendly or work/life policies. While the organization may include policies related to work/life in its human resource manual, it is the culture of the organization that instills confidence in the individual to make use of the offered options. The chapter highlights the issues arising when organisational culture lacks empathy.

Chapter 17
Human Resource Management in Indian Microfinance Institutions 297
Richa Das, IMS Unison University, India

Over the years, microfinance has assumed a great importance all over the world. The reason behind the increasing importance of microfinance in poverty alleviation is considered a prime objective in all developing and underdeveloped countries. Traditionally, MFIs did not have a defined HR policy or structure, since the size of the organization was always very small. The last few years have seen an upswing in the size of the organizations and also in the margins generated by MFIs. The purpose of this chapter is to analyze the human resource management issues and challenges faced in microfinance industry in India.

Related References 312

Compilation of References 327

Index 379

Foreword

'परस्परं भावयन्तः श्रेयः परम अवप्स्यथ'

(Parasparam Bhavayantah Sreyah Param Avapsyatha)

- Bhagavad Gita (3.11: Karma-Yoga)

By mutual co-operation, togetherness, respect and fellow feeling, we will all may enjoy the highest good, both material and spiritual. Keeping in mind the above teaching from our ancient scripture, organizations today have to create a balance of power and harmony between their diverse and culturally vibrant workforce. India has emerged as a global powerhouse for human resources and its citizens are known all over the world for spreading the message of peace and harmony.

In context of businesses and management, organizations today have a diverse and culturally distinguished workforce which at times may result in advent to certain issues. Understanding these issues and knowing how to convert them into organizational strength is imperative to use diversity as a competitive advantage in contemporary times of cut-throat competition. Unfortunately, these organizational issues derived from global workforce today lacks sufficient attention of all the stake holders belonging to Academia as well as Industry and due to which both individual as well organizational performance has been adversely affected.

Upon reviewing the literature provided in the book *Management Techniques for a Diverse and Cross-Cultural Workforce*, its reader may find enough premise to reflect progressively on the concerned subject. The book has different sections for addressing issues related to diverse workforce and the issues concerning cultural differences. The book further dedicated a separate section on various innovative management techniques that can be used to enhance organizational performance by optimizing this unique workforce with in the confinements of their strengths and limitations. Each chapter takes up a unique human resources related issue like employee engagement, performance appraisal, work-life balance or discrimination and further highlights a wide variety of considerations, theoretical and practical implications that are relevant for management today in global organizations.

This text is very rightly timed and hopefully it will engage a wide variety of practitioners as well as researchers to improve organizational functioning. The editors Prof. (Dr.) Vinod Kumar Singh, Dr. Naman Sharma and Swati Pathak have made a sincere attempt to cover various facets of workforce diversity at organizations envisioned by practitioners. Valuable insights can be found by reading the whole book which is appreciable.

I compliment editors, authors and publisher for this wonderful academic venture and wholeheartedly wish this book a great success and believe it will serve as a valuable resource to academicians, researchers and policy makers in this field.

Shri Trivendra Singh Rawat
Chief Minister of Uttarakhand, India

Preface

With each passing day, organizations and their cultures are increasingly turning more and more diverse in nature. The credit for this change goes to the contemporary workforce that is made up of unique set of individuals having different backgrounds and approach towards their work. With the advent of global and multinational operations, organizations and its management can no longer take this diverse workforce for granted and only the ones which know how to manage this diverse workforce are likely to sustain in future.

Organizational cultures attempt to acknowledge individual differences and try to balance them as well but still many of times inequalities persists leading to issues and decline productivity. Extant researches have established that inappropriate policies and poor implementation by management has led to dissatisfied employees, poor productivity, talent loss, injustice and biasness among individuals etc.

This book is an exhaustive text aiming to provide theoretical and empirical insights to both researchers and practitioners related to management of diverse workforce in organizations. There has been a huge research gap in the above-referred area and this book is a sincere attempt to bridge this gap. The book discusses the basics of diversity, its need and challenges and then elaborate on various management techniques that are either used or can be used by the organizations to take the maximum benefits of workforce diversity for productivity.

This project is published keeping in view the needs of policy makers, academicians, researchers, management practitioners and consultants in order to enhance their understanding on the subject and to help them identify and implement right strategies to counter the issues related to diversity at workplace in an effective manner. This book provides both theoretical as well as empirical research findings related to workforce diversity and management techniques that can be utilized to optimize and get the best use of diversity in the organizations. In this way the book contributes substantially to the Academia as well as industry with respect to workforce diversity and its management.

ORGANIZATION OF THE BOOK

The book is organized into three sections. Each section addresses a distinct concept related to the subject of the book. The details of three sections are as follows:

- **Section 1:** Workforce and Diversity – An Introduction
- **Section 2:** Organizational Culture and Cross-Cultural Issues
- **Section 3:** Management Techniques for Cultural Issues and Diversity

A total of 17 chapters cover these three sections justifying the purpose and objectives of the book. A brief description of each chapter follows:

First section of the book discusses about issues related to workforce and diversity and contains three chapters. First chapter, 'Diversity Management: A New Perspective', introduces the concept and features of diversity in workforce today. The chapter discusses the various factors such as HR strategies, leadership, occupational backgrounds, psychographic and demographic factors that affect diversity management in organizations. The chapter further discusses that various outcomes of organizational diversity these days. In a nutshell, this chapter engages its readers with the basics of workplace diversity and diversity management.

Second chapter of the book titled 'Gender Diversity in Board of Directors: A Content Analysis from Turkey – Women Presence Level in Turkey's Boards' discuss the issues related to women representation for key positions (boardrooms) in organizations across countries like Norway, Australia, United Kingdom, United States of America, European Union, Turkey and some other regions. This chapter with the help of secondary data highlights the relationship between women employees and performance relations. Through discussing gender diversity and related issues, this chapter contributes significantly in the context of book. The regional representation of women in organizations can be used by future research to develop customized strategies for the organizations.

The third and the last chapter of first section titled 'Workforce Trends and Challenges: A Peek Into Future' discuss the past, present and future of the workforce as we know it. In particular the chapter stressed on the advent and future of AI workforce. Examples such as that of Unilever create the awareness in the minds of readers about the arrival and application of AI workforce in the organizations. The chapter may help the researchers pertaining to the field of HR/OB as well as big data analysts to broaden their research work and include new variables to make their research more meaningful. It also encourages the students, practitioners and academicians to ponder upon the diversity equation that will be present in the organizations in coming years due to interaction between human and AI workforce.

Preface

Second section of the book is dedicated to organizational and cross-cultural issues prevalent today. There are two chapters that cover these topics. Chapter 4, 'The Elements of Work Environment, Organizational Culture, Organizational Climate, and Job Satisfaction: Work Environment', stresses on the concept of positive work environment. It begins with the discussion on elements of work environment and defines various key terms including organizational culture, organizational climate and job satisfaction etc. It laid down the importance of communication with the employees and also discusses how a change in work environment may motivate the employees. It also discusses briefly about certain management techniques such as flexible working hours and how they can be used to create a positive and productive work environment. The chapter successfully covers other elements of work environment and conclude on the lines of necessary cautions and steps that an organization must take to foster such environment in their premise.

Chapter 5 of this book is dedicated to the issues related to cross cultural conflicts that exists in organizations today. This chapter titled as 'Cross Cultural Conflicts-Concept, Causes and Elucidations' covers the basics of cross cultural conflicts, why such conflicts arise in an organization, what are the implications of these conflicts and how these conflicts can be managed by the management. The chapter highlighted 'Thomas Kilmann Conflict Mode Instrument' which can be used to handle such conflicts in the organization. This chapter can be used as a guide by the organizations which are currently dealing with such issues and it may also be used by researchers as a starting point for developing their own research in this area.

Section 3 of this book elaborates on the various management techniques that are used/can be used by the organizations to effectively used its workforce diversity to its advantage. A total of 12 chapters are covered in this section. Chapter 6 titled 'Thinking Globally, Leading Locally: Defining Leadership in Diverse Workforce' discuss the concept of global leadership styles. The chapter initiates with the brush up on diversity and how it is affecting the world. It then builds this premise to discuss the various leadership styles and the problems faced by global leaders today. It further discusses some of the leadership skills for successful global leaders and shares some industry examples in this regard. It also discusses relevant managerial implications in this regard and provide insights to both managers as well the future researchers on the subject.

In Chapter 7, 'An Overview of Employer Branding With special reference to Indian Organizations', authors have discussed the concept and practice of employee branding by organizations these days. Based on the secondary data, this chapter presents examples from different companies such as Hindustan Unilever, Infosys and Whirlpool etc. and hence provides excellent reference for both industry and academia. This chapter highlights the importance of branding that is required by organizations today to retain talented employees also discusses the development of employee branding strategy. It suggests that employee branding is an appropriate technique to improve employee engagement for the organization.

Chapter 8 links the employee engagement with workforce diversity. This review chapter titled 'Antecedents and Consequences of Employee Engagement for Diverse Workforce' discusses the predictors as well as the outcomes of employee engagement in light of diverse workforce that organizations have today. This chapter focus on Job demands-resource model which describes the development of employee work environment. The chapter discuss in detail both individual as well organizational antecedents of employee engagement hence providing an insight to managers on how they can foster better engagement for their employees. The consequences of employee engagement are largely positive in nature and hence chapter suggests to implement such techniques by the management to ensure better engagement for their employees.

Chapter 9 of the book acts as an extension to chapter eight. It links diversity and inclusion management with employee engagement in the organizations. It suggests that any organization can achieve excellence in its goal if it can master the diversity-inclusiveness for its employees. The chapter includes cases of organizations such as Apple and Starbucks to explain how these organizations maintain and include their diverse workforce in achieving their organizational objectives. Chapter further discusses various techniques to value diversity and inclusion management by the organizations. It lays down the various ways in which diversity and inclusion management helps companies to achieve better employee engagement and recommend research objectives for future studies in this area.

Chapter 10 contain an empirical research on 'Relationship Between Empowerment and Organizational Commitment: An Empirical Study of IT Industry'. A study conducted on 70 IT sector employees provides an insight on employee empowerment. The study concludes that by creating a sense of competence and self-determination in employees, an organization can cement their commitment towards organizational objectives and overall mission and vision of the organization.

Chapter 11 as per its title 'Role of Team Climate in Improving Team Functioning and Team Empowerment' discusses the team climate in the organization and how it can be used for organizational productivity. The chapter discusses both team as well as organizational climate and how it affects the functioning of individuals as well as teams in the organization. Relevant examples such as that of TCL has been taken to bring clarity to the subject and various implications have been discussed on the matter in an effective manner. This chapter would be resourceful to the students and beginners on the subject to understand the basics of team climate and team empowerment.

Chapter 12 took up the serious issue of workplace discrimination prevalent in organizations these days. Titled 'Workplace Discrimination: The Most Critical

Preface

Issue in Managing Diversity', this chapter discusses the pre-employment and post-employment discrimination against employees in the organizations. Various such types of workplace discrimination are discussed in detail to sensitize the students on this matter also the consequences of such discriminatory actions are discussed in details. In the end of the chapter suggestions are given to tackle or avoid such discriminatory acts at workplace.

Chapter 13 the issues related to strategic leadership especially in context of India has been taken up and discussed in detail. This chapter titled as 'Developing Strategic Leadership in Indian Context: Leadership' begins on the note of various challenges which are present in developing strategic leadership in the organizations. It also highlights the importance of strategic leadership in the performance of an enterprise. In conclusion this study suggests that strategic leadership is something that is vital and needs to be developed in Indian leaders in order to their organizations to achieve competitive advantage.

'Relativity Applies to Physics, Not Ethics' is Chapter 14 in this book. This chapter has a unique approach in discussing and detailing the moral responsibilities, ethics and duties that should be performed with in the organizations. This exhaustive review text presents the arguments and essence of past studies to conclude the difference in moral standards in different organizations based on individual and organizational notions. The unethical steps or poor implementation of moral standards affect an organization in a long run and the same has been discussed in this chapter in great detail. This chapter can be used by both managers as well as researchers to decipher the functioning of the organizations within certain moral boundaries.

Chapter 15 covers the concept of performance appraisal techniques used in different sectors of India. This chapter contributes extensively by presenting, differentiating and even to an extent correlating the performance appraisal techniques used in Indian industries. This chapter is significant because performance appraisal is crucial to reward and retain talented employees in the organization. In today's dynamic work environment, performance appraisal is one of very few techniques that can be generalized in an organization for its diverse workforce. This chapter fills the research gap in this area and provides insights for future research.

Chapter 16, 'Exploring the Relationship Between Organizational Culture and WLB', discusses one of the most widely research topics of human resource management/organizational behavior. The relationship between organizational culture and work life balance is considered essential to study as different employees have different needs and organization has to develop a sustainable culture that can support all these individual needs in a balanced manner to keep its workforce motivated and engaged towards organizational goals. This chapter discuss these issues in detail and caters to needs of management as well as academia.

The final chapter, Chapter 17, highlights human resource management practices in Indian micro finance institutions. This chapter is focused to micro finance institution of India which are considered backbone of small scale business and development of economy in rural parts of India. These institutions have their unique workforce related challenges which makes them different from other organizations. Through this chapter, this unique workforce has been bought into light and HR practices of these organizations are discussed to build premise for future research in these organizations.

In totality, the book attempts to cover the various facets of workplace diversity today in the organizations. We hope that this book would serve insights and motivation to practitioners, researchers, academicians and students of human resource/ organizational to further study and contribute in this field.

Naman Sharma
Amity University, India

Vinod Kumar Singh
Gurukul Kangri University, India

Swati Pathak
Invertis University, India

Acknowledgment

We would like to acknowledge a number of people associated with this book project specially the authors, editorial board members and reviewers. Without their constant support and cooperation, this book could have never been completed.

Most of all, we would like to thank the contributors for this book. All seventeen chapters are special and this book would always be incomplete if even one of them is not there. Some of the authors also served as reviewers for the book. We sincerely appreciate their extra efforts in improving the quality of the book. We are also grateful to all our editorial board members and reviewers who took out valuable time from their busy schedules to help us improve the quality of the content included in the book.

In the end, we are truly grateful to our families for their understanding and never dying support to us in completion of this book on time.

Naman Sharma
Amity University, India

Vinod Kumar Singh
Gurukul Kangri University, India

Swati Pathak
Invertis University, India

Section 1
Workforce and Diversity:
An Introduction

Chapter 1
Diversity Management:
A New Perspective

Srishty Mehra
Lovely Professional University, India

Karan Sharma
Lovely Professional University, India

ABSTRACT

The subject of workplace diversity came to the consideration of the academic and business world in the 1990s. "Variety is the spice of life." Everyone would agree with the need for diversity, so the issue is not with the concept, but in how we make use of this concept at work, especially when there is polarization between people who are working together, leading to conflict and disharmony. Diversity management emphasizes valuing and building on individual differences in order for all employees to reach their maximum potential and represents an important step away from the legal compliance-oriented equal employment opportunity. Since the current literature reveals that these practices often result in backlash and that minority employees tend to feel excluded at the workplace, a necessity emerges to investigate individual level factors of LMs that may influence these processes.

INTRODUCTION

As there is global marketplace for goods and services, businesses use diversity in their product brands as well as in their human resources leading to conditions for human capital to freely transferable from one nation to another but Simply having a diverse employee population is not sufficient, hence for a company to make a mark

DOI: 10.4018/978-1-5225-4933-8.ch001

in today's challenging economy, it has to utilize the multifaceted marketplace, with respect for different cultures, ideas and philosophies.

Thus it leads to a Quote that "Variety is the spice of life." Hence the need for diversity cannot be denied, so the issue is not with the concept, but in how we make use of this concept at work, especially when there is polarization between people who are working together, leading to conflict and disharmony.

The subject of workplace diversity came to the consideration of the academic and business world from the beginning of the 1990s until today (De Meuse & Hostager, 2001; Jansen, Otten, & van der Zee, 2016). A diverse workforce reflects a multitude of beliefs, understandings, values, views of the world and unique information (Guillaume, Dawson, Otaye-Ebede, Woods, & West, 2015; Harrison, Price, & Bell, 1998; Repeckiene, Kvedaraite, &Jankauskiene, 2011; Shen et al., 2009).

Thus diversity management emerged as new concept to manage the diversity in the organization and use diversity as a tool for increasing the productivity of the organization and reduce the various problems and differences countered by the presence of diverse workforce in business.

OBJECTIVES

- Understanding the various categories of diversity present in the organization.
- To Know the Contributions and coordination of diversity in achieving organizational mission and goals;
- To eliminate the institutional racism and social non-acceptance of all forms;
- Evaluate the difference in perceptions & diverse cultures in decisions making;
- Forming such management practices & policies that promote inclusive participation of different people at the workplace;
- To minimize the conflicts created due to presence of difference in values and perceptions.

MANAGING DIVERSITY AT WORK

1. Finding opportunity out of opinions to expand the thinking and, challenging to expand perspectives and perception, and always results in a better outcome.
2. Considering different opinions, views and attitudes as a way to learn and understand their perspectives that's how you will be able to develop yourself completely.
3. Keeping Open mindset to accept difference in the views of others and trying to see things from their point of view to enlarge the scope of discussion.

4. Critically analyzing the body language and actions of others to learn about their attitude and feelings hence Listening has more importance than speaking.
5. Softly dealing in case of conflicts arising out of difference in the viewpoints of the group to maintain the harmony and create congenial work culture.

Diversity Management emphasizes valuing and building on the individual differences in order for all employees to reach their maximum potential and represents an important step away from the legal compliance-oriented equal employment opportunity (EEO) (Shen et al., 2009). The term refers to the process of creating and maintaining a workplace without discrimination, where stakeholders (e.g., employees, customers, investors, suppliers and individuals from the local or global community) feel supported and included regardless of their differences (such as gender, religion, culture, personality, expertise etc.) (Roberge, Lewicki, Hietapelto, &Abdyldaeva, 2011). The basic objectives mainly include creativity, flexibility, employee attraction, employee retention, as well as better marketing capabilities.

Both diversity research and general human resource (HR) management literature have highlighted that organisational leaders (Kalev, Dobbin, & Kelly, 2006; Ng & Sears, 2012) and line managers (LMs) (Nishii & Mayer, 2009; Purcell & Hutchinson, 2007) are crucial for effective diversity management (DM) and policy implementation to be successful. For the purpose of this study, LMs are defined as lower-level managers with direct supervisory responsibility. Hence, immediate LMs are closer to the subordinates on a day-to-day basis than the organisation itself (Kuvaas & Dysvik, 2010), entailing that their engagement in the implementation process of HR diversity practices and, thus, DM on the line is crucial.

Hence, despite a number of HR DM programmes and initiatives throughout the years, discrimination that is based on race, age, ethnicity and gender of employees is still alive and well (Germain, Herzog, & Hamilton, 2012; Harcourt, Lam, Harcourt, & Flynn, 2008; King, Dawson, Kravitz, & Gulick, 2012; Mor Barak, Cherin, &Berkman, 1998; Shen et al., 2009). Thus, it is necessary to find appropriate solutions to the obstacles a diverse workforce is facing (Roberge et al., 2011). Accordingly, for the purpose of this study, effective DM on the line is defined as LMs' support of HR diversity practices (Shore et al., 2011) and an environment where "employees from all demographic backgrounds feel included" (Chrobot Mason & Aramovich, 2013, p. 660) Since the current literature reveals that these practices often result in backlash (Kidder et al., 2004) and that minority employees tend to feel excluded at the workplace (Mor Barak & Levin, 2002), a necessity emerges to investigate individual level factors of LMs that may influence these processes (Nishii, 2013). It has been attempted to identify the input and process factors which have the most significant impact on organizational diversity and the output factors which were most often used to measure organizational diversity.

CONCEPTUAL MODEL

Conceptual model of diversity management is shown in Figure 1.

CONCEPTUAL FRAMEWORK

Based on the existing literature, a conceptual model has been developed (Figure 1) which examines the proposed relationship and also explains the relationship between diversity management & its factors and the various outcomes of diversity management. The factors effecting diversity includes all the important aspects of the business such as occupational backgrounds, demographic factors etc. while the outcomes from diversity like communications and problem solving etc. have direct effects on the working of the organization. Hence this framework attempts to include all necessary concepts that have direct or indirect relation to the organizational diversity and this provide a clear view that an organization should adhere and enhance organizational diversity to improve employees' productivity and hence the growth of the organization with a great vision to achieve satisfaction on part of both employee as well as employer.

FACTORS AFFECTING ORGANISATIONAL DIVERSITY

Diversity and HR Strategies

Some organizations design HR diversity programmes either to comply with legal requirements or to achieve flexibility, better marketing capabilities and employee

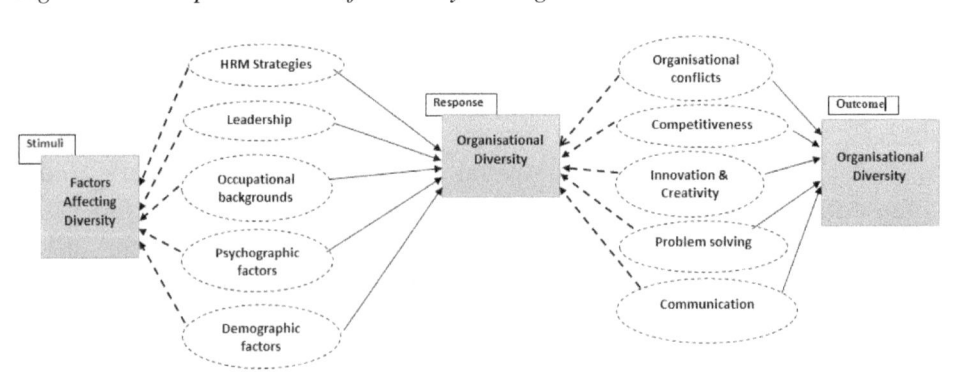

Figure 1. Conceptual model of diversity management

Figure 2. Factors affecting diversity management

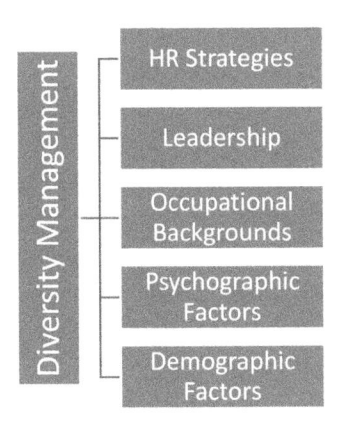

Diversity Management:
- HR Strategies
- Leadership
- Occupational Backgrounds
- Psychographic Factors
- Demographic Factors

retention; however, not all of these programmes manage to increase diversity (Kulik, 2014; Shen et al., 2009). Some diversity practices are focused on recruitment and higher representation of diversity in numbers, while others target management of a diverse workforce and efforts to `ensure retention of minority employees (Groeneveld&Verbeek, 2012; Kulik, 2014).

A large body of research has acknowledged that effective DM requires appropriate HR policies and practices (Dass& Parker, 1999; Roberge et al., 2011; Shen et al., 2009). Namely, through effective HR practices and procedures, DM leads to positive outcomes (Shen et al., 2009). Strategic managerial and HR practices are also regarded as important moderators of the relationship between diversity and organisational performance (Roberge et al., 2011).

There are different types of HR diversity practices in organisations, while perceptions of these practices often vary within the same organisation (Fink, Pastore, &Riemer, 2003)

Therefore, this process requires complete attention and dedication of LMs toward the implementation (Kuvaas et al., 2014; McConville, 2006) that should increase organisational performance over time and provide a number of positive diversity outcomes.

The theory of self-concern (Miller, 1999), social identity (Tajfel, 1982) and perceived fairness (Grover, 1991) may be applied in order to advance the concept of LMs' role in the implementation process of HR diversity practices.

1. The theory of self-concern, as explained by Miller (1999), implies that people pursue their self-interest through actions conforming to the structures of neoclassical economic theory. Namely, it entails that individuals who would benefit materially from the implementation of a certain practice will be more

likely to have positive attitudes towards that practice than individuals who would not (Miller, 1999). Both scholars and people in general often assume that self-concern is an extremely important, if not the only, motivator of behaviour (Gerbasi & Prentice, 2013).Classic models of motivation and behaviour suggest that people will engage in deliberative cognitive processing with the aim to maximise their own self-interests or outcomes (Meglino & Korsgaard, 2004).

2. Social identity theory (Tajfel, 1982) suggests that a social category to which an individual belongs and perceives to belong provides a definition of their identity in terms of the defining characteristics of the specific category. This social categorisation leads to 22 accentuation of intracategory similarities, implying that one of the principal attributes of intergroup behaviour and attitudes is the tendency for members of an in-group to consider members of the out-group in a relatively uniform manner – "undifferentiated items in a unified social category" (Tajfel, 1982, p. 21).

3. The theory of perceived fairness (Deutsch, 1975) proposes that there are three specific principles determining perceptions of resource allocation situations – equity, equality and need. More specifically, equity concerns whether resources are allocated proportionally to inputs or contributions; equality concerns whether people are rewarded equally, implying that everybody should receive the same or have the same opportunity to benefit, while need concerns whether people are rewarded based on their level of need or deprivation (Conlon, Porter, & Parks, 2004).

Thus, organisations are using various HR diversity programmes in an attempt to integrate these individuals, while the final responsibility for implementation of these programmes relies on LMs (e.g., Konrad & Linnehan, 1995; Purcell & Hutchinson, 2007).

Diversity and Leadership

Though diversity poses many challenges to the leadership in organization as it may prove difficult to lead to with the people with different set of beliefs, religion, caste and needs adjustment in the group dynamics but a capable leadership will channelize the energy of the diverse team with appropriate tactics and keep the problems arising out of differences at minimum. The leadership has to maintain a balance in the diverse composition of employees.

Cultural awareness and competence are essential for effective leadership in the context of diversity. Some authors suggest that cultural intelligence is central to understanding effective global leadership. Cultural intelligence is the ability to behave appropriately in cross-cultural settings, an ability that encompasses cognitive (knowledge), emotional (motivational, mindfulness), and behavioral dimensions (Blasco, Feldt, &Jakobsen, 2012). It is referred as "a system of interacting knowledge and skills, linked by cultural metacognition that allows people to adapt to, select, and shape the cultural aspects of their environment,"

Cultural Intelligence is hypothesized to be linked to effective intercultural interactions, including interpersonal relationships and task performance (Thomas et al., 2008). Some studies found that cultural intelligence allows leaders to share knowledge and information within their organizations, to facilitate active research and to enhance team learning during cross-cultural interactions (e.g., Groves & Feyerherm, 2011; Ng, Van Dyne, &Ang, 2009; Rockstuhl, Seiler, Ang, Van Dyne, & Annen, 2011)

Diversity and Occupational Backgrounds

Workforce came from various backgrounds with variety in experience, qualifications, know how etc. join an organization and such differences provide diversity in the organization.

Diversity in backgrounds may be having peculiar demands and expectations from the organization they join like some employees prefer stability and routine amount of work while there may be some who are ambitious and expect growth in the organization thus the diversity of such occupational backgrounds may give rise to some problems but proper coordination and synchronization will help them to work and ultimately achieve goals of organization.

For Example, a person coming from marketing background earlier joining administrative role in the organization will be having more persuasiveness and target achieving capability than persons with other backgrounds and such background differences help others in the work groups to learn new things and ways to perform in the organization.

Diversity and Psychographic Factors

Psychographics factors includes the personality, values, opinions, attitudes, interests, and lifestyles of persons. These factors lead to the difference in the interpretations of the same situation by the people.

Organizational innovation requires the generation of novel ideas that address the current organizational situation. Novel ideas result from "the process of merging thought categories, or mental images, either across or within domains, in ways that have not been done before, in order to develop an original and appropriate solution situation or problem" (Kilgour, 2006, p. 82). Hence, one foundation of creativity is the "generative process" (Leung, Maddux, Galinsky, & Chiù, 2008) that results in a wider set of options.

For Example, two persons climbing the same mountain in their own different manner, will be having different perspectives about that mountain. Only when a person reaches the top of the mountain, he or she can have a view of the whole and analyze all sides of any issue.

Psychographics are built by the family backgrounds, conditions and environment, social circles of the person. Thus a person with cooperative family and grown in congenial environment will be more socially adjustable than any other person having difficult family situations and exploitative environment.

The work culture and rules & regulations followed in organization affects the psychographics of the employees and may focus the interests and attitudes of employees towards the goal fulfillment of the organization but individual psychographics diversity will determine their level of performance of the employees in the organization.

Diversity and Demographic Factors

Demographic factors such as age, gender, ethnicity, and nationality are considered to be readily diversifiable in a organization because there are people working in business with different age groups, genders, nationalities thus there is surely difference in the their opinions and attitudes.

According to Pelled (1996) each variable can be classified according to its level of visibility and job relatedness and the visibility relates to the observation of the variable by group members and job relatedness refers to the extent of variable shaping perceptions and skills related to the cognitive tasks.

Hence cognitive diversity is associated with cognitive diversity which is useful collectively as a broader range of cognitive perspectives will influence a team access to information along with its capacity to solve problems and recognize strategic opportunities (Roberson, 2006).

At organizational level, research has shown that organizations with access to a wider variety of knowledge resources more effective innovators (Rodan & Galunic, 2004) and are better able to develop and assimilate new processes their ongoing operations (Fichman & Kemerer, 1997). Although some researchers have discounted the possibility that demographic composition can affect task outcomes in organizations (Joshi & Roh, 2009), others emphasized that differences in values, attitudes, experiences, perspectives, and cultures between gender and racial racioethnic groups have the potential to increase the number of thought categories and mental images available organization (Earley, 1989; Feingold, 1994; Frink et al., 2003; Kashima, Hamaguchi, Kim, Choi, Gelfand, & Yuki, 1995; Konrad, Ritchie, Lieb, & Corrigall, 2000; Richard, 2000; Stedham & Yamamura, 2004).

The demographic mix of employees in the organization may sometimes lead to disagreements between the working teams due to different perceptions and interests.

Like Senior employees will not approve frequent changes in the organization as they may find it difficult to adapt with changes and regard such changes causing instability in future but young workforce will readily accept the dynamic environment and consider them as opportunity. Similarly male employees have different areas of interests than female employees in the organization.

MAIN FOCUS

First, it is argued that HR diversity practices are different from other HR practices and necessary requirements for their implementation are elaborated. Second, due to ability of intergroup contact to overcome challenges postulated by social identity theory (Tajfel, 1982), such as prejudice, social categorisation, in-group favouritism and intergroup bias, intergroup contact theory is reviewed, as one of the main theoretical frameworks in this dissertation, followed by the role of diversity values in effective DM on the line. Third, LMs' orientations are elaborated as one of the crucial factors for successful HR diversity practices' implementation and effective management of diverse workgroups. Fourth, challenges faced by individuals from an immigrant background and women at the workplace are elaborated. Fifth, employee outcomes reflecting effective DM on the line are discussed. Sixth, research questions of this dissertation are presented, identifying three gaps in the existing DM and HRM literature addressed in the studies. Hence, the main purpose of present dissertation is to contribute to an increased understanding of the role of LMs' experiences and traits in effective DM on the line.

Within HRM strategy, LMs are given HR practices to implement and it is these enacted HR practices that employee perceive and react to (Purcell & Hutchinson, 2007). The manner in which the purpose of such practices is communicated is one of the very important factors for success of this implementation process (Guest, 2011). From the HR literature, there is large variation between individual LMs regarding the quality and consistency of implemented practices (Kuvaas et al., 2014; McGovern et al., 1997; Purcell & Hutchinson, 2007). Several studies have emphasised that LMs' values and beliefs are pivotal for these practices to become properly implemented (Guest, 2011; Herdman & McMillan-Capehart, 2010). Similarly, a large body of research has underlined that LMs are far more engaged in the implementation process when they perceive such practices to be in accordance with their own interests and values (Harris, 2001; Harrison et al., 2006; Kuvaas & Dysvik, 2010; Purcell & Hutchinson, 2007).

The necessity to investigate the conditions under which diversity is effectively managed and HR diversity practices successfully implemented emerges from two streams of research. Namely, one stream shows that the overall impact of diversity is beneficial (Cox & Blake, 1991; Ely, 2004; Ely & Thomas, 2001; Richard, 2000), while the other indicates that it may be detrimental (Chatman & Flynn, 2001; Foldy, 2004; Pelled, Ledford, & Mohrman, 1999).

Observing the impact of diversity on organisational outcomes, strategic managerial and HR practices are seen as crucial 25 moderators of this relationship (Roberge et al., 2011), where the primary aim of most diversity practices is to recruit, promote and retain diverse employees (Esen, 2005).

OUTCOMES OF ORGANISATIONAL DIVERSITY

Relationship Between Diversity and Organisational Conflicts

Sometimes the outcomes are not happy. A state of discord caused by the actual or perceived opposition of needs, values and interests between people working together. There is the inevitable clash between formal authority and power, it also affects the groups related with them. There can be lots of reasons of organizational disputes related with diversity like how the work should be done, it may have different answers by the workers coming from different cultures and backgrounds. Other forms of conflicts can be rivalries, jealousies, personality clashes, unacceptability of different opinions, mutual disagreements, competitiveness among employees, various

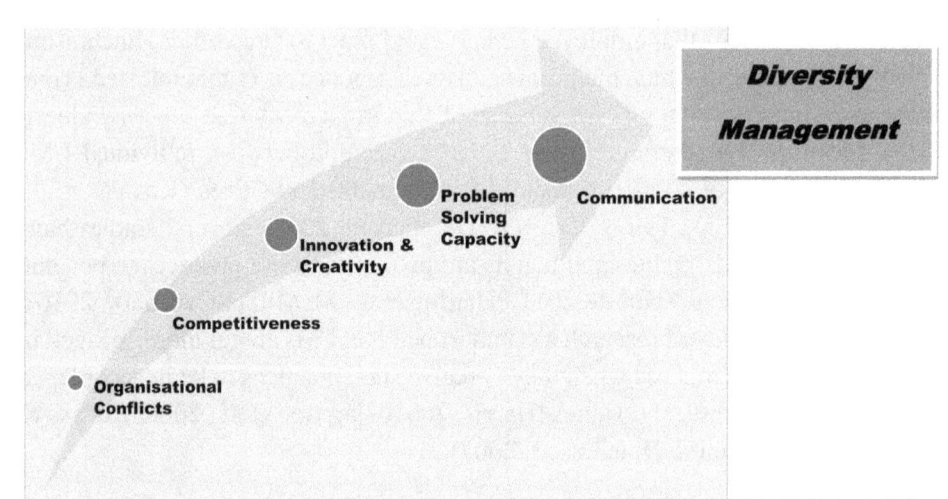

Figure 3. Outcomes of organisational diversity

status provided, insecurities. It also includes the social conflicts like interpersonal, intragroup, intergroup etc. Unresolved conflicts in the workplace will ultimately lead to miscommunication resulting from confusion or refusal to cooperate, quality issues, missed deadlines, increase in organizational stress, disruption to work flow, decreased job satisfaction.

Relationship Between Diversity, Imaginativeness, Innovation and Competitiveness

Diversity has direct relationship with the three concepts of imaginativeness, innovation and competitiveness because diversity provides heterogeneity in the organization that give rise to more combinations of the workforce and encourages the variety in the talent.

In the present dynamic world, the businesses have to remain sustainable and retain their competitiveness and to survive in such conditions there is a need for providing more value to their products and this could be done through innovation and product development. The process of making enhanced or new product requires a large pool of ideas and skills. Such requirements can be fulfilled by employing a uniform workforce. Hence, adding people having diversity will provide more talent and acknowledging their specialty set of skills.

The employee involvement perspective has the potential to provide the diversity management field with a coherent set of organizational practices for fostering intergroup contact and improving intergroup relations. Specifically, Allport's contact hypothesis (1954) argues that four features of a contact situation can effectively reduce intergroup prejudice, namely, equal status between the groups in the contact situation; common goals; intergroup cooperation; and institutional support (e.g., authorities, laws, or custom). A recent meta-analysis research in this field suggests that these conditions are not essential and mere contact can reduce intergroup prejudice (Pettigrew & Tropp, 2)

Relationship Between Diversity Management and Problem-Solving Capacity

The increasing popularity of team-based organizational structures reflects the widely shared belief that teamwork offers the potential to achieve outcomes that could not be achieved by individuals working in isolation.

To succeed in increasingly competitive domestic and global markets, many organizations are pursuing new business strategies that emphasize the development of innovative products & services and responsiveness to customers who may be interested in a broad range of products & services offered by a firm. Achieving these new objectives requires coordination among employees who have dissimilar technical backgrounds and perspectives, so many organizations now are incorporating multidisciplinary teams as a basic form of organizing. For example, in the telecommunications and electronics industries, multidisciplinary R&D teams bring together experts with a variety of knowledge backgrounds, with the expectation that such teams will be more likely to generate innovative ideas for new products and services.

For service delivery, multidisciplinary teams often are designed to ensure that all of a customer's potential needs can be met by a single team. Regardless of whether the customer is a medical patient being served by a multidisciplinary medical team, or an insurance policy holder who holds many different types of insurance policies, multidisciplinary service teams simplify the customer-organization interface and may improve the service received.

The composition of multidisciplinary teams is shown to have implications for problem-solving and decision-making processes, the development of status hierarchies, patterns of participation and communication, the development of cohesiveness, team performance, and, in the longer term, both the stability of the team and its ability to learn and develop over time.

Readily detected attributes can be determined quickly and consensually with only brief exposure to a target person. Generally, they are immutable. Readily detected task-related attributes include organizational and team tenure, department or unit membership, formal credentials and education level. Readily detected relations-oriented attributes include gender, race, ethnicity, national origin and age.

Task-related underlying attributes include physical skills and abilities as well as cognitive knowledge, skills, abilities and job experience; relations oriented underlying attributes include social status, attitudes, values and personality.

For example, an automotive design team that is occupationally diverse (e.g. a purchasing manager, a market researcher, an R&D engineer and a foreman from the manufacturing plant) would be expected to make better design decisions than a more homogeneous team because of the diversity of task-relevant knowledge, skills, and abilities they presumably would bring to the task.

CONCLUSION

With the increase in globalization, the need to become more diverse in nature has become the need of the hour as the business of the companies is now no more restricted to a particular country. As a result, diversity has increasingly become a "hot-button" issue in political, legal, corporate and educational arenas. Workforce diversity acknowledges the reality that people differ in many ways, visible or invisible, mainly age, gender, marital status, social status, disability, sexual orientation, religion, personality, ethnicity and culture (Kossek, Lobel and Brown 2005). With an attempt to develop a conceptual framework which establish relationship between organizational diversity & various factors affecting diversity and went further with the effects of diversity on business management hence mandating the management to create policies to manage diversity effectively.

It has been observed that some factors given in the model have more influence on the diversity management than other factors such as psychographics and demographic factors contributes more towards the organizational diversity while it can also be seen that the diversity further have effects on various areas including communication, competitiveness etc. hence the main aim of diversity management is to observe and maintain a balance between the pros and cons of organizational diversity in the efficient working of the business.

REFERENCES

Allen, R. S., Dawson, G., Wheatley, K., & White, C. S. (2007). Perceived diversity and organisational performance. *Employee Relations*, *30*(1), 20–33. doi:10.1108/01425450810835392

Bennett, R. J., & Robinson, S. L. (2000). Development of a measure of workplace deviance. *The Journal of Applied Psychology*, *85*(3), 349–360. doi:10.1037/0021-9010.85.3.349 PMID:10900810

Bezrukova, K., Jehn, K. A., & Spell, C. S. (2012). Reviewing diversity training: Where we have been and where we should go. *Academy of Management Learning & Education*, *11*(2), 207–227. doi:10.5465/amle.2008.0090

Blasco, M., Feldt, L. E., & Jakobsen, M. (2012). If only cultural chameleons could fly too: A critical discussion of the concept of cultural intelligence. *International Journal of Cross Cultural Management*, *12*(2), 229–245. doi:10.1177/1470595812439872

Bozionelos, N., & Nikolaou, I. (2010). Does treating the permanent workforce well matter to temporary employees? *The Academy of Management Perspectives*, *24*(1), 84–86. doi:10.5465/AMP.2010.50304422

Chatman, J. A., & Flynn, F. J. (2001). The influence of demographic heterogeneity on the emergence and consequences of cooperative norms in work teams. *Academy of Management Journal*, *44*(5), 956–974. doi:10.2307/3069440

Chrobot-Mason, D., & Aramovich, N. P. (2013). The psychological benefits of creating an affirming climate for workplace diversity. *Group & Organization Management, 38*(6), 659–689. doi:10.1177/1059601113509835

Conlon, D. E., Porter, C. O., & Parks, J. M. (2004). The fairness of decision rules. *Journal of Management, 30*(3), 329–349.

Cox, T. H., & Blake, S. (1991). Managing cultural diversity: Implications for organizational competitiveness. *The Executive*, 45-56.

Cummins, P. G., & O'Boyle, I. (2014, Fall). Leading through others: Social identity theory in the organisational setting. *Organization Development Journal*.

Cunningham, G. B. (2009). The moderating effect of diversity strategy on the relationship between racial diversity and organisational performance. *Journal of Applied Social Psychology, 39*(6), 1445–1460. doi:10.1111/j.1559-1816.2009.00490.x

Dass, P., & Parker, B. (1999). Strategies for managing human resource diversity: From resistance to learning. *The Academy of Management Executive*.

De Meuse, K. P., & Hostager, T. J. (2001). Developing an instrument for measuring attitudes toward and perceptions of workplace diversity: An initial report. *Human Resource Development Quarterly, 12*(1), 33–51. doi:10.1002/1532-1096(200101/02)12:1<33::AID-HRDQ4>3.0.CO;2-P

DeChurch, L. A., Hiller, N. J., Murase, T., Doty, D., & Salas, E. (2010). Leadership across levels: Levels of leaders and their levels of impact. *The Leadership Quarterly, 21*(6), 1069–1085. doi:10.1016/j.leaqua.2010.10.009

Ely, R. J. (2004). A field study by group diversity, participation in diversity education programmes, and performance. *Journal of Organizational Behavior, 25*(6), 755–780. doi:10.1002/job.268

Ely, R. J., & Thomas, D. A. (2001). Cultural diversity at work: The effects of diversity perspectives on work group processes and outcomes. *Administrative Science Quarterly*, 46.

Fink, J. S., Pastore, D. L., & Riemer, H. A. (2003). Managing employee diversity: Perceived practices and organisational outcomes in NCAA Division III athletic departments. *Sport Management Review, 6*(2), 147–168. doi:10.1016/S1441-3523(03)70057-6

Gerbasi, M. E., & Prentice, D. A. (2013). The Self-and Other-Interest Inventory. *Journal of Personality and Social Psychology, 105*(3), 495–514. doi:10.1037/a0033483 PMID:23795908

Germain, M. L., Herzog, M. J. R., & Hamilton, P. R. (2012). Women employed in male-dominated industries: Lessons learned from female aircraft pilots, pilots-in-training and mixed-gender flight instructors. *Human Resource Development International, 15*(4), 435–453. doi:10.1080/13678868.2012.707528

Gilliland, S. W. (1993). The perceived fairness of selection systems: An organizational justice perspective. *Academy of Management Review, 18*(4), 694–734.

Godwin, K. (2005). Promoting diversity – The role of line managers. *Equal Opportunities Review.*

Gonzalez, J. A., & Denisi, A. S. (2009). Cross-level effects of demography and diversity climate on organisational attachment and firm effectiveness. *Journal of Organizational Behavior.*

Groeneveld, S., & Verbeek, S. (2012). Diversity policies in public and private sector organisations: An empirical comparison of incidence and effectiveness. *Review of Public Personnel Administration.* doi:10.1177/0734371X11421497

Grover, S. L. (1991). Predicting the perceived fairness of parental leave policies. *The Journal of Applied Psychology, 76*(2), 247–255. doi:10.1037/0021-9010.76.2.247

Groves, K. S., & Feyerherm, A. E. (2011). Leader cultural intelligence in context: Testing the moderating effects of team cultural diversity on leader and team performance. *Group & Organization Management, 36*(5), 535–566.

Guillaume, Y. R., Dawson, J. F., Otaye-Ebede, L., Woods, S. A., & West, M. A. (2017). Harnessing demographic differences in organizations: What moderates the effects of workplace diversity? *Journal of Organizational Behavior, 38*(2), 276–303. doi:10.1002/job.2040 PMID:28239234

Harcourt, M., Lam, H., Harcourt, S., & Flynn, M. (2008). Discrimination in hiring against immigrants and ethnic minorities: The effect of unionization. *International Journal of Human Resource Management, 19*(1), 98–115. doi:10.1080/09585190701763958

Harrison, D. A., Price, K. H., & Bell, M. P. (1998). Beyond relational demography: Time and the effects of surface- and deep-level diversity on work group cohesion. *Academy of Management Journal, 41*(1), 96–107. doi:10.2307/256901

Harrison, D. A., Price, K. H., Gavin, J. H., & Florey, A. T. (2002). Time, teams, and task performance: Changing effects of surface- and deep-level diversity on group functioning. *Academy of Management Journal.*

Herdman, A. O., & McMillan-Capehart, A. (2010). Establishing a diversity program is not enough: Exploring the determinants of diversity climate. *Journal of Business and Psychology, 25*(1), 39–53. doi:10.1007/s10869-009-9133-1

Homan, A. C., van Knippenberg, D., Van Kleef, G. A., & De Dreu, C. K. W. (2007). Bridging faultlines by valuing diversity: Diversity beliefs, information elaboration, and performance in diverse work groups. *The Journal of Applied Psychology, 92*(5), 1189–1199. doi:10.1037/0021-9010.92.5.1189 PMID:17845079

Hope Pelled, L., Ledford Jr, G. E., & Albers Mohrman, S. (1999). Demographic dissimilarity and workplace inclusion. *Journal of Management Studies, 36*(7), 1013–1031. doi:10.1111/1467-6486.00168

Jansen, W. S., Otten, S., & van der Zee, K. I. (2015). Being part of diversity: The effects of an all-inclusive multicultural diversity approach on majority members' perceived inclusion and support for organisational diversity efforts. *Group Processes & Intergroup Relations, 18*(6), 817–832. doi:10.1177/1368430214566892

Jansen, W. S., Otten, S., & van der Zee, K. I. (2016). Being different at work: How gender dissimilarity relates to social inclusion and absenteeism. *Group Processes & Intergroup Relations.*

Jansen, W. S., Vos, M. W., Otten, S., Podsiadlowski, A., & van der Zee, K. I. (2016). Colorblind or colorful? How diversity approaches affect cultural majority and minority employees. *Journal of Applied Social Psychology, 46*(2), 81–93. doi:10.1111/jasp.12332

Kilgour, M. (2006). Improving the creative process: Analysis of the effects of divergent thinking techniques and domain specific knowledge on creativity. *International Journal of Business and Society, 7*(2), 79.

King, E. B., Dawson, J. F., Kravitz, D. A., & Gulick, L. (2012). A multilevel study of the relationships between diversity training, ethnic discrimination and satisfaction in organizations. *Journal of Organizational Behavior, 33*(1), 5–20. doi:10.1002/job.728

Konrad, A. M., & Linnehan, F. (1995). Formalized HRM structures: Coordinating equal employment opportunity or concealing organizational practices? *Academy of Management Journal, 38*(3), 787–820. doi:10.2307/256746

Kossek, E. E., Lobel, S. A., & Brown, A. J. (2005). Human Resource Strategies to Manage Workforce Diversity. In Handbook of Workplace Diversity. Academic Press.

Kulik, C. T. (2014). Working below and above the line: The research–practice gap in diversity management. *Human Resource Management Journal, 24*(2), 129–144. doi:10.1111/1748-8583.12038

Kvedaraitė, N., & Jankauskienė, V. (2011). Intercultural competence as precondition for cultural diversity management. *Economics & Management, 16*.

McKay, P. F., Avery, D. R., Tonidandel, S., Morris, M. A., Hernandez, M., & Hebl, M. R. (2007). Racial differences in employee retention: Are diversity climate perceptions the key? *Personnel Psychology, 60*(1), 35–62. doi:10.1111/j.1744-6570.2007.00064.x

Meglino, B. M., & Korsgaard, A. (2004). Considering rational self-interest as a disposition: Organizational implications of other orientation. *The Journal of Applied Psychology, 89*(6), 946–959. doi:10.1037/0021-9010.89.6.946 PMID:15584834

Miller, D. T. (1999). The norm of self-interest. *The American Psychologist, 54*(12), 1053–1060. doi:10.1037/0003-066X.54.12.1053 PMID:15332526

Mor Barak, M. E. (2014). *Managing diversity: Toward a globally inclusive workplace* (3rd ed.). Thousand Oaks, CA: Sage.

Mor Barak, M. E. (2015). *Inclusion is the key to diversity management, but what is inclusion? Human Service Organisations: Management, Leadership & Governance*.

Mor Barak, M. E., Cherin, D. A., & Berkman, S. (1998). Organizational and personal dimensions in diversity climate: Ethnic and gender differences in employee perceptions. *The Journal of Applied Behavioral Science, 34*(1), 82–104. doi:10.1177/0021886398341006

Nakui, T., Paulus, P. B., & van der Zee, K. I. (2011). The role of attitudes in reactions toward diversity in workgroups. *Journal of Applied Social Psychology, 41*(10), 2327–2351. doi:10.1111/j.1559-1816.2011.00818.x

Ng, E. S., & Sears, G. J. (2012). CEO leadership styles and the implementation of organizational diversity practices: Moderating effects of social values and age. *Journal of Business Ethics, 105*(1), 41–52. doi:10.1007/s10551-011-0933-7

Nishii, L. H., & Mayer, D. M. (2009). Do inclusive leaders help to reduce turnover in diverse groups? The moderating role of leader-member exchange in the diversity to turnover relationship. *The Journal of Applied Psychology, 94*(6), 1412–1426. doi:10.1037/a0017190 PMID:19916652

Nkomo, S. M., & Cox, T., Jr. (1996). Diverse identities in organisations. In S. R. Clegg, C. Hardy, & W. R. Nord (Eds.), *Handbook of organisation studies*. Academic Press.

Olsen, J. E., & Martins, L. L. (2012). Understanding organisational diversity management programmes: A theoretical framework and directions for future research. *Journal of Organizational Behavior, 33*(8), 1168–1187. doi:10.1002/job.1792

Purcell, J., & Hutchinson, S. (2007). Front-line managers as agents in the HRM-performance causal chain: Theory, analysis and evidence. *Human Resource Management Journal, 17*(1), 3–20. doi:10.1111/j.1748-8583.2007.00022.x

Roberge, M. É., Lewicki, R. J., Hietapelto, A., & Abdyldaeva, A. (2011). From theory to practice: Recommending supportive diversity practices. *Journal of Diversity Management, 6*(2), 1. doi:10.19030/jdm.v6i2.5481

Roberson, Q. M. (2006). Disentangling the meanings of diversity and inclusion in organizations. *Group & Organization Management, 31*(2), 212–236. doi:10.1177/1059601104273064

Rodan, S., & Galunic, C. (2004). More than network structure: How knowledge heterogeneity influences managerial performance and innovativeness. *Strategic Management Journal, 25*(6), 541–562. doi:10.1002/smj.398

Soulat, A., & Nasir, N. (2017). Examining the Role of Employee Diversity Management and Employee Involvement Variation on Organizational Innovation: A Study from Pakistan. *Singaporean Journal of Business. Economics and Management Studies, 5*(9), 62–69.

Turner, J., & Tajfel, H. (1982). *Social identity and intergroup relations.* Academic Press.

KEY TERMS AND DEFINITIONS

Competitiveness: Ability of a business to offer superior quality products and services to other competitors in the market.
Conflicts: The disagreement between individuals or groups within the organization on issues ranging from resource allocation and divisions of responsibility to the overall direction of the organization.
Cultural Differences: The existence of a multiplicity of sub-cultures and different value systems in an organisation.
Demographic: This is area concerned with the elements of size and composition of a population such age, gender, preferences, etc.
Ethnicity: The state of belonging to a social group that has a common national or cultural tradition in an organisation.

Imaginativeness: It is the ability to create new and better things with the imagination and finding solutions for business problems in new way.

Psychographics: These are any attributes relating to personality, values, attitudes, interests, or lifestyles of the people in organisation.

Socio-Economic Diversity: It means having representation from a variety of social classes, not necessarily dependent on race or gender in a business.

Values and Beliefs: These are principles and ideals which form the foundation of ethics and culture of a business.

Work Culture: It is environment comprising beliefs, thought processes, attitudes of the employees in combination with ideologies and principles of the organization.

Workplace: It is the physical setting of the business where the employees are employed to perform their day to day duties.

Chapter 2

Gender Diversity in Board of Directors:
A Content Analysis From Turkey – Women's Presence Level in Turkey's Boards

Meltem Akca
Istanbul University, Turkey

Burcu Özge Özaslan Çalışkan
Istanbul University, Turkey

ABSTRACT

Gender diversity in corporate governance is a popular topic in management environment studies. One of the most significant components of this concept is women in boards. Due to the inequalities of women in boards there are a number of academic studies on women in top management. This chapter explains gender diversification problem in boards. Furthermore, reasons for workforce diversity in decision-making levels are determined. The role and critical mass of women members in different cultures are discussed. Finally, it introduces the representation levels of women in the boards of BIST 100 companies in Turkey. Data is obtained from annual reports, websites, and related documents of companies.

DOI: 10.4018/978-1-5225-4933-8.ch002

INTRODUCTION

Major scandals (Enron, WorldCom, Imclone, and Adelphia) have a role in the development of corporate governance mentality around the world. In general, the concept of corporate governance can be defined as a regular management approach that involves all stakeholders benefits. One of the most important purpose of corporate governance is to minimise company corruptions which are related with unfair practices. Corporate governance deals with employment policies, boardroom structures, stakeholders rights (Burke, 2003). Transparency, trust, equality, protection of legal rights and personal liabilities are also some domains of corporate governance model. From this point of view customers', employees' and stakeholders' satisfaction is very important for corporate governance philosophy. However, corporate governance related applications in companies have become popular around the women employment in senior positions has not reached the desired levels worldwide. In other words, unfair employment issues like lack of women in boards is significant matter that corporate governance management mentality ever conflict. In recent years, the concept of women employment in board of directors as a member has received growing interest in the academia. Boards are substantial decision making areas in companies. Board's main tasks are discussed as controlling company operations, leading internal and external environmental relations and managing corporational operations. Board members are responsible managers who need to achieve organisational aims with their decisions. Therefore, structure of the board has a vital influence over the company's operational, financial and reputational performance. It is agreeable that a well-structured board includes one main aim: Minimising gender, race, age, religious and political discrimination. When the board member's characteristics are analysed, it is seen that most of them are white men over 50 years old. In other words, men dominated the companies' boards worldwide. Uniformity and similarities of board members in all characteristics can influence the board's structure and its functionality. Corporate governance model advises companies to decrease differentness discrimination. The development of corporate governance approach around the world is focused more diverse and balanced workforce in organizations. Everyday thousands of women are participating in the workforce however only little percentage of them have seats on senior positions. Gender discrimination in boards damages boards' structure. If women have the same opportunities with men in boards gender discrimination issue will disappear. Fair-minded companies are generally managed with conscientious decision makers. Equality and diversity mentality of boards will spread over the company with butterfly effect and some of the corporate governance practices will be provided easily. In well-structured boards it is expected to minimise performance defaults and influence shareholder's perspective to have a different and strategic view by having more woman in boards (Burke, 2003).

This chapter aims to demonstrate women employment on boards in Turkey. Besides, authors have touched women issue in boards around the world. Consequently, results are expounded with the perspective of corporate governance approach.

BENEFITS OF WOMEN REPRESENTATION ON BOARDS

Women employment on boards gains importance day by day with the related academic theories. Resource dependency theory clarifies that woman board members will play a boundary spanning role at boards. According to human capital theory, woman board member's job experience and skills bring a different perspective to the company. Agency theory also maintains that boards are better controlled with the development of boards' diversity. Social psychological theory approaches diversity in boards with 2 main perspective: to minimise groupthink failures, impress shareholders (Carter, D'Souza, Simkins, & Simpson, 2010). Reference to literature review, positive impacts of women employment as a boards member determines why boards are required to have women inside. Besides, employment policies started to expand women in boards to prevent corruptions and confusions. Although there are many advisory studies about women on boards, there are some non-visible mechanisms which prevent women career trends in "Chief" and "Senior" levels at working life. This syndrome is called glass ceiling in scientific literature. Being a "woman" can cause this ceiling as a glass. The concept of glass ceiling finds women insufficient and push women into the background of career trend. This push-back steps are also observed in the boardrooms. However, studies about women have been examined since 1970, women representation rate in boards is under the desired levels in our day. Women employment in boards make little progress due to some barriers for women career development. The feminine factors (maternity, childcare, housework), lack of education and foreign language are some barriers for women's career stages (Vinnicombe & Singh, 2003). Burke (1996) also explained obstacles of women employment in boards as listed below:

- Lack of high-class, skilled women board member candidates,
- Preconceived options about women capabilities as a board member,
- To have a low opinion of gender diversity at boardrooms,
- No legal penalty for lack of gender diversification at boardrooms.

It is well known that board member's duties are so significant that they need to be furnished with advanced skills to generate board functions over the company's operations. They generally control managers and observe their operations. In addition to that, they play a boundary spanning role between company and environment. Members provide information and analyse company's situation. They are responsible from adaptation of laws and rules over the operations (Carter, D'Souza, Simkins, & Simpson, 2010). These tasks can be actualized with qualified members. For this reason, appointment requirements make easier of women's staffing at boardrooms. Burke (1996) stated the importance of having some qualifications like academic experience or international practise for woman candidates.

If considered from the beneficial view point, fresh perspective of women may have positive impact over the board mechanism and decision making process. Increasing woman member seats in boards may also improve male's behaviour and work environment. Diversity in boards can expedite the problem solving time with increased productivity. Additively, women skills are also helpful to minimise dichotomies between members (Adams & Ferreira, 2009). Moreover, diversification in boards decreases group-thinking failures (European Commission, 2011). In addition to that, experiences, attitudes, skills and willingness behaviours of women can keep alive boards. After all, information flow, dynamism, and newfangleness of boardrooms come into prominence with woman members (Stephenson, 2004). Woman board members may easily understand problems of working women. They will be role model for woman employees (Jónsdóttir et al., 2008). Woman board members also make easier to suffer skillful women labour force to the company (Stephenson, 2004).

However, companies hold one or two women in the boards to demonstrate shareholders that they are sensitive in women employment issue, they actually do not like women's attendance in decision making. Although woman members' provide a different experiment to the board which is comprised of political, cultural and social factors, they are generally accepted as undesirable members (Rosenborg, 2008).

"Critical mass" is an another woman related issue in the boards. Company size, company culture, leadership style, company industry can affect the board's structure and number of woman board members. Generally, woman members have seats in large scaled companies instead of medium and small ones. Companies whose products are related with women intend to have woman board members. Woman managers and board members are generally work in senior positions at cosmetic, chemical, service and banking industries(Harrigan,1981). Kramer, Konrad, Erkut and Hooper, (2006) indicated that number of woman member seats have secret meanings. According to the researchers, just one woman member in the boardroom will feel isolated and may not be so successful as two woman board members' activity. It should not be forgotten that if two woman board member do not like each other, boardroom will be grouped and this situation will influence the enacting performance. Finally, if there are more than three woman in the boardroom they will be accepted as a "manager" instead of "woman". At that rate, they will have the power to change inflexible politics to increase productivity. Critical majority of women will provide more stable, successful and dynamic boardroom structure. Schwartz-Ziv (2013) also identified that woman members should have at least three seats in boards to have a sustainable company performance.

WOMEN MEMBER AND PERFORMANCE RELATIONS

Boards are formed to control company operation for performance rise. Members generally discuss company profitability methods in boards. They usually focus performance concept with the perspective of corporate governance. Men board members intensify on financial performance standards while women are emphasise over social and humane performance factors. Woman members ordinarily give consequence to corporate social responsibility (Huse, Nielsen & Hagen, 2009) Williams (2003) indicated that companies who have woman members are more charitable, social, artistic, cultural, and communal.

Diversification in board's structure enable members to make better controlling and monitoring board operations for decreasing operational risks and increasing performance. According to the literature, women employment in boards and performance relations have been investigated for years. Results of these studies revealed that women impact over performance is possible but not necessarily. Financial performance, social performance, reputational performance, sustainable corporate governance performance are some of performance elements which were studied in the literature. Some of these studies found positive relations between variables, however some of them were negative. Although in this chapter it is not focused over the performance relations, authors decided to summarize some of related articles.

Buchwald and Hottenrott (2015) worked over fifteen European countries' companies which were listed in the stock markets between 2003-2011. After their analyses, they found that woman members representation has positive impacts over boardrooms outcomes like reduced turnover. In another study, researchers investigated 140 related article. In this meta analyse it was obtained that women representation in boards is positively related with financial outcomes. In addition to these results, it was underlined that, in countries which powerfully protect shareholders rights and have a strong gender equality, women generally have a critical mass in boards to have a better organisational outcomes. Egalitarian societies are more likely to represent women members in their boards (Joshi, Neely, Emrich, Griffiths, & George, 2015). Similarly, Sarkar and Selarka (2015) examined that there is a positive interaction between woman members in boards and corporational value. They used 10218 Indian companies data-set between 2005 and 2014. They also emphasised that this positive impact may diminish in the companies which are managed with family members. Likewise, Noland, Moran and Kotschwar (2016) investigated 21980 companies data-set over 91 countries around the world. They determined that women employment in senior levels like a board member enhances company performance.

On the other hand, Adams and Ferreira's (2009) research results demonstrated that there is a negative relation between gender diversification with company performance. It is believed that gender quotas which are obligated by government may decrease the companies value. Rose (2015) also found similar results. Study was realised over 39 German companies board characteristics structure. Reference to results, there is not a relationship between gender diversification and financial performance. According to Ahern and Dittmar (2012) quotas for women employment on the board can trigger decreasing of Norwegian companies stock market performance. Mınguez-Vera and Martin (2011) explained the negative impacts of women in boards as a common 2 issue: Women generally do not like to take risks and women capabilities are not appropriate for the member's job. Authors think that boards are involved woman members just for legal obligations or quotas. Therefore it was stated in the article that there is not an objective relation between company performance and women presence.

According to literature review, women employment related studies use companies which are listed in the stock markets. "Women" related studies in management area have enlarged its framework with corporate governance notion since 1990. Open to public companies data are generally explored in the related financial platforms. Therefore, it is easy to obtain detailed data for these companies. One of the main reason of investigating open to public company (Vinnicombe & Singh, 2003). In this study it is aimed to use same method like literature review while generating research sample. Before analysis of Turkey's boards, it should be better to give some cases from the world about woman members and their places in boards.

REPRESENTATION OF THE WOMEN AT BOARDROOMS

Women representation in the world boards are an issue since 1970s. Increased employment of women in parliament has triggered gender balanced policies for women workforce in senior levels. As it is known, governments need to take some precautions to have more women on boards. Although, governments advise companies to have equitable practices for women employment in boards, woman seats have not reached the desired levels at boards. For this reason, governmental policies started to be more hard. With legislations and acts, new methods have been used to pick up women employment in decision making areas.

Quotas are one of the most popular method for women presence in boards. Percentage for women employment in boards to minimise discrimination is called as quota. Quotas are generally used to increase woman member's seats in boards. It means that, boards are required to have woman members in a specific ratio. Besides, quotas can be beneficial for women career development (European Commission, 2014). Quato practices around the world intend to rise up women staffing as a board member. Quato practices also have three common aims: to clear off glass ceiling syndrome in business career, to enhance women education level and to increase women labour in all positions at business pattern. Governmental authorities, local and international associations support these development practises to employ woman members in the boardrooms. It is also expected with quota practices that high skilled women will take seats in senior levels to increase herself and organizational capabilities. If considered from a role model perspective more women in boards can be helpful for women workforce inside the company. In addition to that, woman members may introduce new working policies for women employees (Bertrand, Black, Jensen, & Lleras-Muney, 2014). They will adjust working schedules or work environment features for woman employees to solve work-life conflicts of women (Comi, Grasseni, Origo & Pagani, 2016). Finally, woman employees performance will rise with woman members equitable and clean approaches over the woman employees' working conditions.

On the contrary view, to make a gender equality in boards with obligations (quotas) may damage the objective diversification aims. In the opposite views, it is believed that quotas will pick up unskilled woman members boost due to the legal restrictions. Despite all explanations, some countries prefer to use quota practices while some of them are not related with quotas. In some countries there are hard and mandatory quotas which may criticised by researchers. On the other side, some governments advise soft quota methods for companies to have a balance in boards (Konrad, Kramer, & Erkut, 2008). Although women employment problem in senior levels has been discussed more than 40 years, women representation has not reached the expected levels. Lack of willingness for women employment in boards triggered quota practices for companies. By these paces, what is expected from quotas will be seen in coming years.

In this chapter it is aimed to discuss about most popular country's practices about women representation at boards. According to the literature, it is seen that Norway is the first country who intended to have gender equality. After this approach, Norwegian model has spread around the world. Countries started to adjust Norwegian model on their boards according to their cultural and structural features. In this chapter, authors considered appropriate to mention about sample practices in some countries like Australia, United Kingdom, European Union Members, United States of America and other countries.

Norway

Women employment and women place in work life have a great significance in Scandinavian countries. Norway is a nova for the both women representation at boardrooms and women employment. Norway's employment policies reinforce to women developments in the work life to have a sustainable success. Norway's government put a rule for boardrooms (some featured companies) to have a woman members as a stated percentage by 2007. Government imposed a quota practice for boardrooms to have %40 percentage woman members inside. Norway caught the world's eyes on it with this pioneer equitable behaviour. It is expressed that quota applications started with public related boardrooms and then applied private company boardrooms (Smith, Smith, & Verner, 2006). Women representation in boardrooms was %6 in 2000 at Norway. During the improvement works, this percentage approached the %40 levels. In countries which have qualified women workforce and strong gender equality strain, quota practices will cover the expected purposes (Comi, Grasseni, Origo & Pagani, 2016a). While some experts love the Norway's attitude for boardroom structures, some of them criticize the quotas. Assailers explained criticism reasons in two main cliché: 1) Companies can appoint woman as a board member, who is not competent for this position, 2) These appointments in boards due to the quota obligations prevent the major aim of the women employment mission (Churchard,2011). Even though there have been still critics for quota practises, it is seen a partial improvement with these steps for women representation in worldwide.

Australia

Australia is a transoceanic country but it takes a significant role for gender diversification at employment researches and studies which are supported with the women entrepreneur's associations and related government departments. Although there are various studies for gender equality in work force, women representation in boards is less than the world average. Sheridan and Milgate (2003) demonstrated that there were only 251 woman members where men had 6409 chairs in Australian Stock Exchange 200 (ASX200) companies' boards. More than ten years later, it was observed that woman members took part less than %15 of the total board seats in 2015. With normative oppressions of the stock exchange offices and capital market boards, it is aimed to increase woman members in the boardrooms. Last reports of capital market board and related associations' publications have recommended companies, whose stocks are traded in the ASX200, to have at least two woman members in the boards. In addition to these advisory approaches, the Australian Council of Superannuation Investors (ACSI) and the Australian Institute of Company Directors (AICD) collaborate to have more women members in boards. Forenamed authorities in the country also aim to increase women seats to %30 by 2018 (BlackRock, 2015).

United Kingdom

The level of woman board members in the United Kingdom was not sufficient for one of the most developed country in the world. In recent years, business-led and voluntary activities have speeded up the women employment in boards. A study for woman members in the London Stock Exchange companies (FTSE) reported that women had only %10 seats in 2010. Therefore, it was targeted to increase woman board member employment in FTSE companies in coming years. Some associations and institutions have worked together to remark the people's attention over this topic. These working groups and organisations studies, which were supported with governmental authorities, resulted with higher women presence on boards. By the %25 quota practices for listed companies (quota is limited with some specific objectivities of companies) woman member appointments have raised up. Women have % 26 of all seats in in FTSE-100 companies while in FTSE-350 companies this percentage is only %19 at the end of 2016. In FTSE-100 companies there were at least one women member in 2016. Although, there were 152 company without a woman member inside the FTSE-250 companies in 2011, this number decreased to 15 in 2016. It is observed that governmental bureaucrats in the UK expected to have more woman members in the boardrooms. They advise FTSE 350 companies' boards to have at least %33 woman members by 2020 (Davies, 2015) (Seierstad, Warner-Søderholm, Torchia, & Huse, 2017).

United States of America

USA is called as a locomotive of the world economy however its boardrooms do not have enough women members. Women members' representation level in Fortune-500 companies was %12 in 2001. This ratio increased %15 in 2010. Although scandals of big companies took place in USA and corporate governance generation speeded up here the percentage of women board members has not reached the desired levels yet (Dalton and Dalton, 2009). There were 12 women CEO in Fortune 500 companies in 2011 while Fortune 501-1000 companies had 14 at the same year (Catalyst, 2011). Reference to Branson (2007) %35 of the MBA graduated people and %50 of the mid- level managers in the USA are women. Despite the skilled women labour, there is not woman board member at one third of the all companies. It means that there is a prejudice about women career development for senior levels (Branson, 2007). American Stock Exchange Board established regulations in 2010 to have a gender diversified boards. Regulations are related with boardroom member's appointment procedures. They invited companies to explain appointment procedures to shareholders to provide principle of transparency. It is expected to provide clean diversity of boardroom structures with these regulations. After these steps some organisations who support for women employment in boards has created awareness on this topic. During these developments, women presence in boards increased to %18,7 in 2015. Women Corporate Directors Association which was founded to support women members, aimed to increase the percentage of women members to %20 by 2020 in USA's companies. However, in some states of America quotas are used for companies, there is not a general practice over the whole USA. According to final works for women representation, it is also expected to have at least %30 women members in S&P companies (Deloitte, 2015).

European Union

There are various developed countries inside the European Union. However, this, EU has not intervened in gender diversification initially. EU did not stand idle by evolvement of women employment discrimination and concentrated on this topic. EU published reports to improve women employment in the member countries. "Strategy for Equality between Women and Men 2010-2015",which was adopted by European Commission, has expedited woman members related studies development in the region. In the above named report it is aimed to have gender equality in boards. After this report, in 2012, a procedural quota practices were established to reach at least %40 member presence for each gender by 2020.(European Commission, 2011). Instead of establishing fixed and mandatory quota applications, European Commission submitted a soft rule for companies to behave transparency and equitable for woman candidates appointments. In other words, this approached is called as procedural quota for companies (Christiansen, Lin, Pereira, Topalova, & Turk, 2016). According to these improvement steps the average percentage of woman members in Europe rose up nearly to %20 (Rose,2015). Women have started to play a part one fourth of board seats in Sweden, France, Italy, Germany and Denmark (Comi, Grasseni, Origo & Pagani, 2016a).

In Germany, normative pressures of DAX 100 stock market point out the importance of governmental precautions for the presentation of woman in the boardrooms. German companies, which are listed in the German Exchange Market, are proposed to have minimum %30 woman members and %50 by the end of 2018. Besides, Spain explained to impose a quota for boardrooms to prevent gender diversification. By 2015, the companies who have more than 250 employees (other necessities for quota) required to have at least %40 woman board members. In addition to Spain, Iceland goaled to impose quota practices for open to public companies who have more than 50 employees. It is expected to increase woman members ratio to %40 in coming years. Due to the pressures and attempts of Finland government to involve at least one woman and quota (%40) practices in boards, women's applications have increased. In Holland, government also clarified to impose %30 quota for boardrooms but they stated that certain determinations for implementation will be shared with the public opinion by 2016 (Rose, 2015). Finally, in France, authorities and associations started to study on women representation at boardrooms by popularizing of quota practices in EU. It is intended to raise the ratio of women members in boards to %40 by 2016 at companies who have quota necessities. With this judgement, women managers and board members staffing in CAC 40 companies picked up. These companies caused competition in the business environment to obtain skilful and experienced women to obey the rules (Noland, Moran & Kotschwar, 2016).

Turkey

Turkey took a step last decade rapidly. Economic growth, European Union adaptation process improvements, increased infrastructures raised up the Turkey's value. These developments have been enhanced the Turkey's reputation around the world. Foreign investors have started to interest with Turkey's companies and its stocks. In this process, it is aimed to attract the foreign investor's attention to Turkey's Stock Exchange Market. Turkey's Stock Exchange Market was restructured with new rules to be more transparent, accountability and fairy. In the perspective of corporate governance, it is tried to provide an equitable system with legislations. Stock Exchange Commission and the related governmental authorities work together to ensure corporate governance adaptation for companies. Besides, governmental commissions established regulations for companies. The focal point of these obligations is to bring Turkey's corporate governance level as emerged economies. According to corporate governance approach, women issue in boards can be solved with Stock Exchange Commissions and the relevant departments. Turkey's Stock Exchange Commission ruled some regulations for the companies who are listed in the stock exchange market. In 2011 at the statement of 57 numbered "f" item, it was emphasised that there should be at least one woman member in the boardroom. It was an advisory approach and tried to make a normative pressure on companies. After this practice, Stock Exchange Commission set up new rules for companies, who are listed in the stock market, to have at least %25 woman members in 2014. In addition to that, companies are released to determine %25 quota practice program on their organisational aims. They are hold liable to explain "woman member policies" on their annual reports. In generally it is understood that government and related authorities aimed to increase woman members at boards in Turkey. Therefore, companies are obligated to have at least %25 woman members in soonest time. However, authorities give the free options to achieve this quota timing. For example, ABYXX is a company which is listed in the Turkey's Stock Market. Although there are some advisory rules for women members, ABYXX company is just responsible from 1) to explain company's policy about woman members in the annual reports, 2) to determine a time to reach a woman members quota which must be at least %25. Even though Turkey's quota approach is softer than other countries it is expected to increase women employment in boards and senior levels with these new practices. Finally, with "Apply or explain" attitude it is considered to raise the women seats in the boardroom. These precautions and advices aimed to enhance women labour force at decision making process of Turkey's companies. According to Sabancı University Report between 2012 and 2015, number of woman members in boards increased. In 2015, there were 2916 members in BIST-400 boards. 293 of the 2916 members were women. In 143 company there were one woman member in boards while in 64 company there were two. In 26 company women had three seats and in 4 company there were four woman board members. Only in two company women had the critical mass of members with five seats. Women members' presence level was %11,9 in 2014 and %11,35 in 2015. There were 26 chairwoman in BIST 400 companies in the same year. However most of these chairwoman were family members and only five of them were professional manager without family membership. In BIST-100, 62 company at least had one woman member in their boards while there were not a woman member in 38 company boards. Critical mass of woman employment is seen in administrative, service, finance and manufacturing sectors (Ararat, Alkan & Aytekin, 2016).

Other Regions

Countries as Israel, South America and Brazil have intended to impose quota practices for women presentation at boardrooms. In this context, it was planned to implement quota practices firstly in public related companies and then private ones (Hillman, Shropshire & Cannella, 2007). Although these improvement plans, women representation level was near %20 in Israel's TA-10 companies last year. Unfortunately, women presence average has not passed %5-6 levels in South America. For example, in Brazil woman member seats are comprised of only %6 of all board positions. By this unpleasant results, governmental authorities mentioned to have at least %40 quota practices by 2022 (Deloitte,2015), (African Development Bank, 2015).

In Asian and Far Eastern countries, even though women employment is higher than world average, the presence of women in boards has a little percentage. Women in these regions are generally employed at low level jobs. In East Asia women have only six percent of board seats however per capita is high here. Women managers presence in Japan is %2,5 while this percent seen as %13,5 in China (Noland, Moran & Kotschwar,2016). There is not an established quota practises in China and Japan. Woman members have %8,5 of all seats in China however this ratio is just %2,4 in Japan. On the other side, Malaysia has quota practices to reach more women in boards. It is expected to have at least %30 woman members in boards for coming years while women presence in boards was more than %10 by 2015(Deloitte,2015).

According to available estimates, while the %36 of labour force in India comprise women, only %5 of them have account for senior management positions. Besides, women presence level was %7,7 in boards where woman CEO's had only %2,7 of all chairs in 2015(Deloitte,2015). Indian government establish a regulation in 2015 which forced companies to have at least one woman member. The main purpose of these precautions is to balance gender diversity at boards.

Employment of women in Arabian and Middle East countries is not sufficient and the level of women deploy in all positions below the world average degree. Traditional and environmental factors affect the women staffing in this region. It is hoped that women sources as an employee in these regions will rise with the coming years.

In Canada women organisations are belong to have gender balance in boards. There are various active association groups in Canada who are connected with each other and work together to increase woman members level in boards. Woman member presence in Canada is nearly %15 and it is targeted to have firstly %30 and then %40 within the next years (Deloitte,2015)

Around 12 countries of Africa, women presence ratio is %12.7. While world average percentage is taken as %17, Africa's average for woman board members is pleasing for local authorities. In these countries one third of boards has no woman member, other one third of boards has one woman member while residual one of three has two or three woman members. Kenya has the leadership position for women representation at boards. Women presence percentage is %19,8 in Kenya. South Africa is the second country with %17,4 percentage. Respectively other countries and their women presence ratios are as; Botswana (16.9), Zambia (15.9), Ghana (15.7), Tanzania (14.3), Uganda (12.9), Nigeria (11.5), Egypt (8.2), Tunisia (7.9), Morocco (5.9), Cote D'ivoire (5.1).

RESULTS OF THE STUDY

In this chapter, it is aimed to demonstrate women representation level in Turkey. Borsa Istanbul (Istanbul Stock Exchage-BIST 100) companies' boards were investigated for the study. Besides that, boardroom structures were analysed with the gender diversification perspective. Reports and website information of companies were researched to examine boardroom's structures. In addition to these works, authors worked over the Public Disclosure Platform reports and database. The survey was actualised in 2017. Consequently, it is revealed that women representation level is not sufficient for a developing country.

According to the analysis of BIST-100 companies;

- Women representation level in boardrooms is %11,2.
- In BIST-100 companies there are 848 board members in total. There are just 95 woman seats. It means that BIST-100 companies boards' seats are filled with 753 men members.
- 17 of the 95 woman member are independent members. It means that approximately %18 of the woman members are independent. 17 independent woman members are worked in the 16 different companies' boards. Inside the total 848 BIST-100 members, independence woman member ratio is less than %1.
- There is not any woman in 38 BIST-100 companies' boards. In other words, BIST 100 companies are under the control of only men. In a colloquial manner, these companies are managed with "old boys".
- In 40 companies, there is just one woman member at boards. These companies follow the advisory rules of governmental authorities.
- There are two woman members in 15 companies. There are three woman members in four companies. There are four women members in two companies' boardroom. Likewise, there are five woman members in just one company. It goes without saying that most of woman members are insider and familiar.
- In addition to these, there are six chairwoman in BIST-100 companies. In the old boys' club, there are six women boss in Turkey. Although, most of them are family members in family holdings we would like to announce them as a woman leaders. In four different companies there are woman vice presidents one for each. In three companies there are deputy chairwoman one for each.
- Finally, when it is analysed woman members' occupations, it is observed that sectoral diversification may influence member's career. Woman members

occupations can be arranged as; engineer, lawyer, financer, economist, business woman, academician and manager. Furthermore, it is found that woman members take place in the early detection of risk committee, corporate governance committee, appointment committee and audit committee.

CONCLUSION

Gender diversification related issues put forward the woman board member's presence problem across the worldwide. Corporate governance management model also focuses on gender balanced and fair employment policies in organisations. Besides, "women" (managers, organisations, groups) addressed the women issue and put a spot line on this topic across the globe. It is expected to promote women employment in the strategic levels to have a successful organizational performance. Women employment perspective should take part in both boards and other positions in companies.

Reference to the literature, it is estimated that women control more than %80 of household consumption expenditure in universal. For this reason, they desire to work in strategic positions of companies. To enrich the business life, corporate prestige, sustainable reputation and performance it should be sign out the women role in the boardrooms and senior levels at companies. When women come into women's own in boards or senior levels, at least as men, it is expected to increase world business value.

Deregulations, privatisation, increased welfare of society, raise of foreign trade operations, economic stabilisation, innovations, generation of regional operations have triggered the whole sector's improvement in Turkey. Turkey's EU harmonization process also expedites all components of Turkey's industries evolution. However, women employment is a major problem in Turkey. Although it is aimed to increase women staffing in all positions, results show that there is a long way to reach the equality in employment issue. As it is mentioned in upper paragraphs, Turkey try to balance board structures. In this regard, Turkey formed a soft quota practices for listed companies and let them free to reach the expectant level. Only by necessity, it is ruled to determine women employment policy per year on companies annual reports. With this approach, it is aimed to see companies' intention about women employment. It is also targeted to provide gender-balanced and fair appointment opportunities with in Turkey.

Women employment in parliament also has picked up last years in Turkey. Women in parliament always keep warm "women" issues. Women education, women employment, women development in all positions are some of these current topics. It is planned to have more women senior managers in state-owned companies also.

In addition to these plans girls are educated to developed their skills and capabilities. Governmental improvement steps will go on until to have fair and clean board characteristics in companies.

In this chapter, it is emphasized woman board members' representations. In addition to this, new precautions, implementations, legal obligations, quota practices about the gender diversification in management levels are considered. Women members presence level of Turkey's listed companies are investigated in the gender perspective. In this way, it is found that women representation level is %11.2 in BIST-100. However, most of women in boards are insiders or family members. It is also observed that women employment in boards is enhancing day by day with new juridical regulations. With procedural quota practices in Turkey it is planned to have a gender-balance boards inch by inch.

Next researches for women employment in boards will focus on the relationship between boards traits and organisational characteristics. In addition to that, it should be analysed the impact of working conditions on woman members performance in boards. Although women staffing at senior levels have been studying for 40 years, women presence level related reports determine that it is required a long time for balance at boards.

REFERENCES

Adams, R. B., & Ferreira, D. (2009). Women in the boardroom and their impact on governance and performance. *Journal of Financial Economics*, *94*(2), 291–309.

African Development Bank. (2015). *Where are the women:Inclusive Boardrooms in Africa'stop listed companies?* Author.

Ahern, K. R., & Dittmar, A. K. (2012). The changing of the boards: The impact on firm valuation of mandated female board representation. *The Quarterly Journal of Economics*, *127*(1), 137–197. doi:10.1093/qje/qjr049

Ararat, M., Alkan, S., & Aytekin, B. (2016). *Women on Board Turkey*. doi:10.5900/SU_SOM_WP.2016.29132

Bertrand, M., Black, S. E., Jensen, S., & Lleras-Muney, A. (2014). *Breaking the glass ceiling? The effect of board quotas on female labor market outcomes in Norway*. National Bureau of Economic Research. Retrieved from http://www.nber.org/papers/w20256

BlackRock. (2015). *Achieving Gender Diversity in Australia: The Ugly*. The Bad and The Good.

Branson, D. M. (2006). *No seat at the table: How corporate governance and law keep women out of the boardroom*. New York: NYU Press.

Brieger, S. A., Francoeur, C., Welzel, C., & Ben-Amar, W. (2017). Empowering Women: The Role of Emancipative Forces in Board Gender Diversity. *Journal of Business Ethics*, 1–17.

Buchwald, A., & Hottenrott, H. (2015). Women on the Board and Executive Duration–Evidence for European Listed Firms. *ZEW, 178*. Retrieved from https://ssrn.com/abstract=2580776

Burke, R. J. (1996). Why aren't more women on corporate boards?: Views of women directors. *Psychological Reports, 79*(3), 840–842. doi:10.2466/pr0.1996.79.3.840

Burke, R. J. (2003). Women on corporate boards of directors: The timing is right. *Women in Management Review, 18*(7), 346–348. doi:10.1108/09649420310498966

Carter, D. A., D'Souza, F., Simkins, B. J., & Simpson, W. G. (2010). The gender and ethnic diversity of US boards and board committees and financial performance. *Corporate Governance, 18*(5), 396–414. doi:10.1111/j.1467-8683.2010.00809.x

Catalyst. (2011). *2011 Catalyst Census: Fortune 500 Women Board Directors*. Author.

Christiansen, L., Lin, H., Pereira, J., Topalova, P. B., & Turk, R. (2016). Gender diversity in senior positions and firm performance: Evidence from Europe. *IMF Working Papers*, 1-29.

Churchard, C. (2011). Boardroom quotas fail to convince senior women. *People Management*, 6.

Comi, S., Grasseni, M., Origo, F., & Pagani, L. (2016, September 30). Quotas have led to more women on corporate boards in Europe. *LSE Business Review*. Retrieved from http://blogs.lse.ac.uk

Comi, S., Grasseni, M., Origo, F., & Pagani, L. (2016a). *Where Women Make the Difference. The Effects of Corporate Board Gender-Quotas on Firms' Performance Across Europe*. ESPE. Retrieved from https://editorialexpress.com

Dalton, D. R., & Dalton, C. M. (2008). On the progress of corporate women: less a glass ceiling than a bottleneck? In S. Vinnicombe, V. Singh, R. J. Burke, D. Bilimoria, & M. Huse (Eds.), *Women on Corporate Board of Directors International Research and Practice* (pp. 184–197). Cheltenham, UK: Edward Elgar. doi:10.4337/9781848445192.00025

Deloitte. (2015). *Women in the boardroom A global perspective.* Deloitte Touche Tohmatsu Limited.

European Commission. (2011). Strategy for equality between women and men 2010-2015. Author.

European Commission. (2014). *Gender balance on corporate boards: Europe is cracking the glass ceiling.* Author.

Harrigan, K. R. (1981). Numbers and positions of women elected to corporate boards. *Academy of Management Journal, 24*(3), 619–625. doi:10.2307/255580

Hillman, A. J., Shropshire, C., & Cannella, A. A. (2007). Organizational predictors of women on corporate boards. *Academy of Management Journal, 50*(4), 941–952. doi:10.5465/AMJ.2007.26279222

Huse, M., Nielsen, S. T., & Hagen, I. M. (2009). Women and employee-elected board members, and their contributions to board control tasks. *Journal of Business Ethics, 89*(4), 581–597. doi:10.1007/s10551-008-0018-4

Jónsdóttir, T., Vinnicombe, S., Singh, V., Burke, R., Bilimoria, D., & Huse, M. (2008). Women on corporate boards of directors: The Icelandic perspective. *Women on corporate boards of directors: International Research and Practice,* 88-95.

Joshi, A., Neely, B., Emrich, C., Griffiths, D., & George, G. (2015). Gender research in AMJ: An overview of five decades of empirical research and calls to action thematic issue on gender in management research. *Academy of Management Journal, 58*(5), 1459–1475. doi:10.5465/amj.2015.4011

Konrad, A. M., Kramer, V., & Erkut, S. (2008). Critical Mass: The Impact of Three or More Women on Corporate Boards. *Organizational Dynamics, 37*(2), 145–164. doi:10.1016/j.orgdyn.2008.02.005

Kramer, V. W., Konrad, A. M., Erkut, S., & Hooper, M. J. (2006). *Critical mass on corporate boards: Why three or more women enhance governance.* Wellesley, MA: Wellesley Centers for Women.

Mínguez-Vera, A., & Martin, A. (2011). Gender and management on Spanish SMEs: An empirical analysis. *International Journal of Human Resource Management, 22*(14), 2852–2873. doi:10.1080/09585192.2011.599948

Noland, M., Moran, T., & Kotschwar, B. R. (2016). *Is gender diversity profitable? Evidence from a global survey.* Peterson Institute for International Economics Working Paper. Retrieved from 10.2139/ssrn.2729348

Rose, M. (2015). *The impact of board diversity in board compositions on firm financial performance of organizations in Germany*. Paper presented at the fifth IBA Bachelor Thesis Conference, Enschede, The Netherlands.

Rosenberg, S. Z. (2008, April 8). Why Aren't There More Women on Boards? Moving past tokenism and box checking opens doors to more diversity. *Bloomberg*. Retrieved from https://www.bloomberg.com

Sarkar, J., & Selarka, E. (2015). Women on board and performance of family firms: Evidence from India. *IGIDR*, 1-50.

Schwartz-Ziv, M. (2013). Does the gender of directors matter? *Edmond J. Safra Working Papers, 8*.

Seierstad, C., Warner-Søderholm, G., Torchia, M., & Huse, M. (2017). Increasing the number of women on boards: The role of actors and processes. *Journal of Business Ethics, 141*(2), 289–315. doi:10.1007/s10551-015-2715-0

Sheridan, A., & Milgate, G. (2003). "She says, he says": Women's and men's views of the composition of boards. *Women in Management Review, 18*(3), 147–154. doi:10.1108/09649420310471109

Smith, N., Smith, V., & Verner, M. (2006). Do women in top management affect firm performance? A panel study of 2,500 Danish firms. *International Journal of Productivity and Performance Management, 55*(7), 569–593. doi:10.1108/17410400610702160

Stephenson, C. (2004). Leveraging diversity to maximum advantage: The business case for appointing more women to boards. *Ivey Business Journal, 69*(1), 1–5.

Terjesen, S., Sealy, R., & Singh, V. (2009). Women directors on corporate boards: A review and research agenda. *Corporate Governance, 17*(3), 320–337. doi:10.1111/j.1467-8683.2009.00742.x

Vinnicombe, S., & Singh, V. (2003). Locks and keys to the boardroom. *Women in Management Review, 18*(6), 325–333. doi:10.1108/09649420310491495

Williams, R. J. (2003). Women on corporate boards of directors and their influence on corporate philanthropy. *Journal of Business Ethics, 42*(1), 1–10. doi:10.1023/A:1021626024014

Chapter 3
Workforce Trends and Challenges:
A Peek Into the Future

Mihir Joshi
Gurukula Kangri Vishwavidyalaya, India

ABSTRACT

In this chapter, the author has reviewed the human workforce of the previous generations by taking into account the features and characteristics of the workforce, which is getting older. The purpose of this chapter is to evaluate the future of the current workforce. The future generation is still unexplored, but it is clear that the coming generation will be a blend of advanced technology and ultra-advanced simulations. The coming years will introduce more advanced artificial intelligence into the workforce that will not just be cognitively intelligent in a retrospective way but also emotionally intelligent. The future human workforce will face a challenge to maintain the requisite skill sets to cope with the constant change.

I like being in the workforce; it keeps me grounded.

INTRODUCTION

World War II was a cataclysm that bombarded the world with its virulent events that changed the visage of mankind. But metamorphosis is constant and the species which speedily progresses with it, survives. The years succeeding 1946 bought the transformational times. 69 years since then, the world has seen different generations: Baby Boomers, Generation X, Generation Y and the future generation. In a simple

DOI: 10.4018/978-1-5225-4933-8.ch003

Copyright © 2018, IGI Global. Copying or distributing in print or electronic forms without written permission of IGI Global is prohibited.

dictionary word Workforce is defined as the people engaged in work or are available for work. But doesn't just being available for work means that it is the potential labor.

The Baby Boomers born between 1946 -1964 and after the World War II are the workaholics who have actually established the grounds for the economic development in world. This group of people likes to focus more on the job and value a well settled job. To this generation working hard on an objective brings solace. World Wide boomer generation managers work more number of hours than their successor generations. However, on the verge of retirement this generation is optimistic motivator and true guides.

The Generation X (1965-1980) crafted the steps to electronic age. This generation not only tries to maintain the work life balance but also enjoys liberty. In contrast to their predecessors people in this generation are more self-reliant, love facing new challenges and move on to new endeavours.

The Generation Y or the Millennials (1981-2000) has been completely wired with technology. This generation seeks constant and rapid change which therefore, shows that this generation is not afraid to shift jobs or even careers. This generation is constantly work driven with high confidence. In this era, women as an integral part of workforce also came into focus. As per PWC, by 2016 working women in the enterprises will comprise of 80% of the millennial women. Besides containing a feeling to be responsible to maintain work life balance, getting more socialized, this generation is what could be the last to communicate with people both face to face and through social networking.

The future generation is still unexplored but it is clear that the coming generation will be a blend of advance technology and ultra-advance simulations. The coming years will introduce more advance artificial intelligence workforce that will not just be cognitively intelligent in a retrospective way but also emotionally intelligent. The future human workforce will face a challenge in context to maintaining the requisite skill sets to cope up with the constant change. The change here signifies the advancements in technology, infrastructure and the machine-human interface. As per the current trend, the future represented in motion pictures is no longer a dream. Countries around the globe have started experiencing the need and volatility of the new workforce.

It is imperative to understand the future of the working class in developing nations such as India where the very definitions of numerous business terms have a completely different meaning. Indian youth is this country's major strength to economic and social development which creates extremely high competition among individuals. By 2026 Indian workforce will constitute of age group 15-64 years and so India will amass huge human capital pool. Additionally, the large amount of youth in India and other countries with higher youth population will face strong employability challenge. The coming decades will also bring challenges in the field of talent management for developed nations. It is forecasted that by 2020 countries in the world might face an acute shortage of talent. The shortage of talent in USA, UK and Canada can be fulfilled by surplus amounts of supply from developing nations and the artificial intelligence (BCG, 2016).

This chapter will discuss the challenges that are at the door step of future generations besides exploring the possibilities for skill enhancement of today's workforce. This chapter will also take into consideration the lessons learnt from the past generations.

The Work Force

Just who would have thought that the idea of RoboCop motion picture (1987) by Edward Neumeier will come true, 30 years later, with the induction of a RoboCop in Dubai Police. If the RoboCop developed by Barcelona based PAL Robotics stands successful then, by 2030 Dubai Police will comprise of more than 25% RoboCops. This has created a new dimension for the employment world and a new challenge for the human workforce. In near future the world will be known by these two types of workforces: Human and Artificial Workforce. Let's take into consideration the Human workforce first that has been the reason for both chaos and Karma.

Human Workforce

The Human workforce is technically known as Human Resource, a term used for the first time in history by economist John R. Commons in 1893. However, it was publicized by another economist of 19th century E.Wight Bakke in 1958. Any work in an organization that involves the use of human strength, ability (physical and emotional) or special set of skills that complete a specific task is Human Workforce. It is synonymous to what Human Resource or Human capital means but from a broader perspective. The Human workforce is effected by the changing times and economic situations.

The modern industrial world faced two major world wars of which the Second World War was more fierce and catastrophic. The events succeeding the end of war laid the foundation for a new era in which the human life was valued; living standards were enhanced and technological advancements led to an increase in research and development. In a way the society became more aware of the surroundings, socially citizen became more cooperative. This strengthening of society subsequently created large number of social and organizational groups.

After the Great War ended the process of transfiguration began with the rise in number of infants and that what came to be known as *Baby Boom*. This generation saw several social and political reformers (Martin Luther King) who further bonded the society. Baby boomers ousted the traditional customs and created their own.

In USA the average birth till 1940s was 2.3 to 2.8 million infants per year that significantly rose to 3.46 million in 1946. During late 1950s the birth average reached the pinnacle with 4.3 million. The rapid growth in population increased the demand of consumer products, real estate, automobiles and services. The baby boomer generation grew without the advance technology and therefore, is considered to be the most hardworking generation of all. As of now this generation is on the verge of retirement and ready to be taken over by the generation Xers. Past decades have seen rapid changes in demographic patterns and cultural influences (Sharit & Czaja, 1994).

Generation X, refers to those persons who took birth between 1965 and 1977. People of this generation were named as Generation X after the Douglas Coupland marked them by this name in his novel Generation X:Tales for an Accelerated Culture published in 1991. Members of Generation X are generally hesitant to take risks and play safe .Some of the characteristics that provide more clear understanding about this group are Pessimism, Media-Savvy and Self- Reliance. They also have a feeling of unfriendliness as they are the first generation that was effected by the parental divorce. Generation X members consider themself superior to others and are more addicted to caffeine intake. This generation is also effected by the Cold War termination. There exist various names by which Generation X people are called namely, Baby Busters, Brash Pack, No Income Kids With Education(NIKES), Young Individualistic freedom minded few(YIFFIES),Fun loving youth en-route to success(FLYERS),Indifferent generation, Invisible generation. Some more synonyms of Generation X are Post boomers, Generation 2000, slackers and the MTV generation. Members of Generation are considered more loyal towards brands or products they buy or use.

Generation Y are those individuals born between the year 1977-1988 (Chowdhury and Coulter 2006). Generation Y has been regarded as as less cynical, more optimistic, more idealistic, more deviated to values, both traditional and non-traditional. Generation Y, consists of 60 million individuals and are bit similar to Generation X but with many differences. Generation Y is also known as Echo Boom Generation or iGeneration. They have been explained as the individuals who are edgy, urban focused and idealistic. This generation is a very practical or rational thinker and have learned from their predecessors that how an opportunity is grasped and created. After years of service the generation before the Y lost their jobs to rising group culture. Generation Y after working for two to three years in an organization moved to different firm for a better opportunity. As compared to Generation X, generation Y do more and frequent job changes to move to a better position. Since the baby boom Generation Y as some demographers, believe those born between 1979 and 1994, are the biggest workforce recorded till date with more than 60 million individuals. This group however, has been affected by the radicalism, terrorism, rise of technology and conflicts of Gulf. Generation is addressed by several names that they have gained in short duration or with the shrinkage of world by social networking as Echo Boomers or Millennium Generation. The term Generation Y was first devised in 1993 by Advertising age as the generation that came into this world at the end of twentieth century. Generation Y is docile to more Internet use than the previous generation, equal to Generation X in its interest in volunteerism and its work orientation, and is less brand loyal and less risk averse than Generation X. Members of Generation Y have greater satisfaction with the Internet than members of Generation X.

As per the corporates each of the generation is a blend of hard work, creativity, passion, tech savvy and socially aware. Therefore, making these generations work in a single place is both a challenge and opportunity. However, every manager has to forge a path where this diverse workforce can coordinate and achieve common targets. It is essential for every manager to understand the factors that motivate each of these work force so that tasks can be managed with better efficiency. Generation Y may require proper training and who could better guide them than the Baby boomers and Generation X. Moreover, it gives a manager a chance to deduce the individual competence of the workforce. David McClelland introduced the idea of 'competency' with a view to reframe the selection procedure. The Harvard psychologist rejected the traditional methods of testing the on job performance of employees. His study pointed to the competency mapping of employees on the basis of interpersonal sensitivity, cross-cultural relation and skill differentiation. Thus, this process can help concentrate on the individual and group based gaps and help eliminate the gap.

Artificial Workforce

Living forever is not possible, not at least when human tissues have no ability to regenerate. Even if so happens and the stem cell research achieves new paradigm, life of any natural organism is finite. So, here enters the artificial intelligence, artificial neural networks and ultimately the artificial workforce. A worker who will never require sleep, rest or no exasperations related to job and no hierarchy of needs. It's a frightening thought that human reign might come to an end at the very hands of the machines that we have created. Right from bookkeeping till food preparation the process has become fully automated. In automobile sector the creation of a chasis till final assembling of the automobile takes minimal human effort. At BMW most of the complex and serious assembling of parts at the body shop is done by robots however, individuals possessing very high qualification supervise this process. The question is for how long will the human presence be there? John Maynard Keynes envisaged that "there will come a time when in order to make work more economical companies will derive new ways to ornament the use of labour."

After the Second World War the prime focus of every economy was on building technological milestones. United States created several benchmarks in the field of Nuclear energy (besides 1054 nuclear tests performed between 1945 till 1992 and others undisclosed), space technology, medicine etc and gained super power status. Artificial Intelligence came into existence in 1956 at a workshop conducted by Herbert Simon and Marvin who became the pioneers of this field. The start of 2017 saw a leading software company releasing more than 9000 employees due to the development of an artificial intelligent system. Wipro, a leading Indian software firm has developed an artificial intelligence system known as *Holmes* and has cut down new recruitments for lower end jobs. Wipro has laid-off 3200 employees in the beginning of the year 2017 and plans to achieve 4500 target by the end of 2017-18 fiscal year (Eluvangal, 2017).

Companies employing AI systems claim that an AI can do any work in minutes what humans can do in days or months. Infosys has trained more than 490 employees in machine learning and artificial intelligence to develop ultra-advance systems that will cut more jobs in future. Infosys claims that the equipment required for establishing AI have lessened in cost and that the process has become bit simple to meet the needs of clients (Das, 2017). What will companies achieve of it and why hire when you are ultimately going to fire the individual? Several such questions arise. A high end official at a leading software company says that company can add to the operating margins and meet higher end goals. The purpose here is to resolve more client issues efficiently, swiftly and with zero errors.

Had there been no workforce to work, growth would not have been possible. Researchers report that the rise in the use of automated or computer operated equipment has increased human unemployment besides, showing growth in several sectors (Brynjolfsson and McAfee, 2011). Objectives that can be fulfilled by using a unique set of algorithms do not require manual labour for sensitive works. Owing to this decline in labour intensive jobs the middle level workers are moving gradually to lower level services sector. The reason behind this is that the jobs requiring special human touch are less prone to computerization. Such jobs require more human attention with affective responses towards the consumer. Therefore, the jobs requiring cognitive responses are more vulnerable to become automated as compared to the works requiring flexibility. Scholars deduce that jobs requiring problem solving skills, development of highly sophisticated technology that require very high level of skills give a competitive advantage to individuals with such capabilities. As per Goos & Manning (2007), work requiring high skills for complex cognitive tasks that represent high income group and the work where very low cognitive ability is required hold a major part of the employment today. Moreover, individuals having high level skills create new technologies that in turn drive out more middle level jobs.

The process of technological advancements is a constant process and the pace with which it is moving leaves no doubt that AI will one day create its space like that of an Android phone. Today the skills learned and achieved by any worker become obsolete in no time. This is indeed due to technical innovations which is infinite and has no borders. A technical creation that originates in one continent continues to grow and inspire other continents. A simple example is of fully automated cars at Google. At some point in time it was asserted that an automated system designed to drive in traffic would be complex. But when Google converted several Priuses into fully automated cars a new facet was created.

Few scholars believe that AI will not completely take over human jobs. However, in coming decades more than one-third of the jobs could be taken over by AI. This process is slow but steady as can be observed by the changes made in several sectors. At Memorial Sloan-Kettering Cancer Centre the oncologists are making use of IBM's Watson computer to provide prolonged care and cancer diagnostics. Thus replacing the health care employees involved in making diagnostics. Similarly, with the availability of Big Data several chunks of unprocessed data can be visualized and made available to predict the next step. Big Data aids to the working of not just one sector of the industry but covers all cognitive tasks. There are several such examples that point in the direction of the arrival of AI age. A website that helps its users create their own website and provides personalized domain called wix.com uses an AI. This AI system just requires few attributes and data to be applied on the website and few clicks, that's it. The user has to just sit back, relax and wait before the website is created.

Artificial Workforce in Industry

At Unilever the process of recruitment has changed and taken a step closer to what future will look like. Meet the new HR at Unilever, an AI. The Dutch-British consumer goods giant Unilever has been using artificial intelligence to hire entry-level employees, and as per the company it has vividly increased assortment and cost effectiveness. Unilever has ventured with digital HR service providers HireVue and Pymetrics to perform the AI screening process. It has radicalized their recruitment process and has given an edge over competitors. The company no longer has to send HRs to universities, collect and scrutinize resumes and do all other conventional activities for the step one. The candidates move to the next round only if they pass the AI screening for an in-person interview. Candidates get information about the job opportunities through Facebook or LinkedIn and only have to submit their LinkedIn profiles.

Pymetrics has created a platform where each and every candidate plays 12 neuroscience based games for approximately 20 minutes. Further if the results of candidates match with the required profile for a specific position they are interviewed by HireVue where they are given a schedule to respond upon. AI analyzes the gestures, postures, eyeball movement and vocal modulation for the hiring manager. After these successful two steps the candidate is called at the Unilever office where they are given a real life situation for the final assessment. Unilever "hired their most diverse class to date." There was a 10% increase in hires of non-white applicants and an increase from 840 to 2,600 universities represented. The average time for a candidate to be hired went from four months to four weeks, with a cumulative saving of 50,000 hours of candidates' time. Recruiter's time spent on applications was decreased by 75%. The rate of offers to candidates who made it to the final round increased from 63% to 80%, and the acceptance rate of these offers increased from 64% to 82%. The completion rate of the 12 Pymetrics games was 98%. The average score of the overall process was rated 4.1 out of 5.0, based on the 25,000 applicants who took a survey. Games test traits like ability to focus, memory, relationship to risk, and ability to read emotional versus contextual cues. For example, the game that tests risk gives users three minutes to collect as much "money" as possible using the following system: clicking "pump" inflates a balloon by $0.05; at any point the user can click "collect money; if the balloon pops from over-inflation, the user receives no money. The user is presented with balloons until the timer runs out.

Another field that may get affected due to the rising number of AI based systems is the education. Numerous amounts of e-learning websites have created a web of Knowledge Park. These sites provide certificates or diplomas in subjects that enhance individual skills. These courses are developed in coordination with companies having presence throughout the globe and by experts from some of the world's elite Universities and Institutions like MIT and Harvard. The gigantic amount of study material is available online then, why to invest in extremely expensive brick and mortar based education? Experts are of the view that students throughout the world are looking for the courses that help them to groom themselves and in short time period grant them a good job opportunity. In coming years students will focus more on distance education and so online portals are developing advance systems that will guide students on the basis of their high school grades. Big Data network will give students immediate feedback related to the popularity of the course and future scope. The syllabus will be hence developed by keeping in view the activities around the globe. A research conducted on 700 different occupations shows that the white collar jobs in these sectors are most likely to be taken over by the AI.

Surveyors, judicial law clerks, cost estimators, market research analysts and marketing specialists, civil engineering technicians, electrical and electronics drafters, medical transcriptionists, technical writers, human resource assistants, tax examiners, collectors, and revenue agents, accountants and auditors, paralegals and legal assistants, gaming dealers, cashiers, file clerks, credit authorizers, checkers, and clerks, claims adjusters, examiners, and investigators, credit analysts, loan officers, data entry keyers, and insurance underwriters (Chelliah, 2017).

Big Data is a huge set of complex data that may be real time data. Big Data captures every data type right from digital text to jpg. It also includes the digital signatures left over by any end user over any website or digital platform. Social networking sites like Facebook or microblogging sites like twitter have become a mine of digital text. It creates trends and the things go viral. All this is happening through the complex algorithms designed for this purpose. Several non-routine

Cognitive tasks have become digitized. The primary assessment of information is done through these algorithms. Gauging or scalability of performing humongous computations is achieved better with the advance algorithms as compared to the manual labor. It is no longer a hidden process that spending time over Zettabytes of computation can be done through an algorithm or machine networking (Campbell-Kelly, 2009). Pattern detection can only be done by the Machine Learning algorithms that can detect patterns what human eye cannot and all this on the internet. As per Cisco systems around 1 Zettabytes (1×10^{21} bytes) was analyzed in 2016. In the sections where Big Data is new the ML algorithms assist in deducing similarities and differences between the past and present data. This analysis helps to digitize or computerize the tasks associated with the data. Therefore, the computerization or digitization of data is not just confined to tasks that are preset on the basis of software but it can even go around. So, wherever the Big Data lies the nature of task does not matter it could be a systemized task or an un-systemized task (Brynjolfsson and McAfee, 2011; Frey & Osborne, 2013).

Algorithms also fulfill one highly important gap that has influenced many decisions in a negative manner and has questioned the human emotional state, called as human bias. An AI can analyse the complete scenario and act on the basis of it that aids to the cognitive task. An algorithm can be designed to make a decision that algorithm will carry out without any biasness. As compared to AIs the tendency of humans to get affected by the mood, affective responses or varying emotional states is a common phenomenon. It can also include occupational hazard, job burn outs or in some cases certain necessities that may affect the decision. In court cases the phenonmenon of biasness is commonly observed and in developing countries AI can bring revolutionary changes to the judicial system where hundred thousand cases are stagnant owing to due dates (Frey & Osborne, 2013). Core and complex algorithms are being designed to perform a number of tasks that were done previously by lawyers or paralegals. Also legal documents and evidences are scanned and incidents are tested through pre-trials over the analyses. A commonly mentioned example is of Clearance system designed and developed by Symantec that understands the concepts using the language analysis module and presents results graphically and can sort more than five hundred thousand documents. Another field that requires AI is Fraud detection which essentially needs both impartial decision making and the ability to detect trends in big data. Additionally, data sensing and modulation techniques have improvised and become an efficient source of information processing. These sensors can be deployed in tasks where condition monitoring and detection has to be performed such as observing patients where a small mistake can adversely influence a life. This gives an opportunity to detect anomalies in the system; irrational elements causing biasedness are avoided and removed. Machine Learning has increased exponentially since the decline in the costs of digitization and is able to successfully perform procedures related to monitoring, aircrafts, water quality and water flow, supply chain, detecting moisture content in the farms (MGI, 2013; Frey & Osborne, 2013). Several corporations in cities like Beijing, São Paulo are using sensors on pipes and water suppliers to manage water loss and water quality besides managing the supply infrastructure. It has significantly reduced the water loss. In not too distant future it is expected that other nations and cities will follow the same type of sensors so as to manage electricity theft, water loss and even the loss of public property to thefts. In cities like Indore the traffic police in coordination with a technological institute have installed a 'Robocop' to handle traffic management (HT, 2017). This robot uses scanners to detect automobile speed, untimely crossing of traffic lights and can also send the fines or challans to the respective addresses for which it utilizes police department databases. If successfully operated, several such Robocops will be employed to reduce the work pressure on human traffic police who have tough time managing traffic in extreme heat or pollution.

For quite some time now the financial sector has been utilizing the services of AI. These systems designed on the basis of ML algorithms offer a better analysis of the financial data, press declarations and information related to the financial trading (Mims, 2010). Companies that offer financial safety and portfolio management like Future Advisor utilize AI based financial advise from abroad prospect and at a reasonable cost. Further-more, the work of software engineers is also on the verge of being taken over by the AIs. The algorithms that are designed by the programmers can be created at a more sophisticated and can address root levels of the programming through an AI interface. AI interface gives a wide range of design options that can be employed through an algorithm. Another department under the software development is software testing that is the reason behind the rejection and acceptance of any software. Algorithms thus, designed for the purpose of detecting bugs can easily take over a software tester work. The bug detection will be done without any anomalies that a human coder may leave as an error (Livshits and Zimmermann, 2005; Kim, et al., 2008). The Big Data offers a wide range of codes that an algorithm can understand and improvise to fulfill the client needs (or the end user). This methodology will ominously improvise the human programs along with the compilation process. An AI can compile an efficient program better and similar to the way any program is written on the platform. An AI on the other hand can create and detect the code errors while creating it only if the errors occur. This way the man-made compilers are way below the level of the AI optimized compilers.

Future of Artificial Workforce

As per MGI, 2013 the higher order algorithms are due to take over more than 140 million jobs globally. The report further informs that globally the costs of robots and robotic equipment is falling by 10 percent rate and this rate is due to increase year by year. A robot with industrial features like high precision and machine vision currently cost around 100,000 to 150,000 USD will cost even less than 50,000 to 75,000 USD in coming decades. A Chinese i-phone assembler company Foxconn is investing heavily on gaining more robot based labour as compared to human labour that saves cost and time. The net sales of robots have increased by 50% in the forbidden kingdom and 40% globally since, 2011 and are due to increase further on annual basis.

In future as the technology further advances and the cost of machines decreases the role of robots will become greater as compared to present. More number of tasks will be assigned to the robots as their assignments in construction, maintenance, packing and agriculture expands. The role of robots today could be seen in small jobs such as lawn mowing, vacuum cleaning and gutter cleaning etc. and is increasing at a pace of 20% annually. Additional roles of robots can be observed in health care sector, service marketing and elderly care (MGI, 2013; Robotics-VO, 2013). In USA the low wage based lower level jobs might get taken over completely by robots in coming times as the costs of the robotic equipment and technology become cheaper (Autor and Dorn, 2013).

CONCLUSION

Technological advancements in every industrial sector are imperative to the development of civilization. Past has seen it and present knows it but it's the future which needs clarity of vision. The changes in present workforce do not imply that humans will lose all their jobs in future because the jobs have yet not been divided on the basis of automation and non-automation (Green, 2012, Pieffer & Suphan, 2015). Instead the human and machine coordination will become of utmost importance in future. For an artificial intelligence system achieving self-consciousness, self-awareness, perceiving of emotions, understanding and managing of emotions is quite far. Teaching an AI about understanding the human nature will be a complex cognitive process, but not impossible. However, reaching a level where AI will not require teaching is interesting and by far most challenging. As per Arntz et al.,

(2016) only a few selected tasks in a job are currently automated like in OECD countries only 9% of the jobs are automatable, 6% in Estonia and Korea and 12% in Austria and Germany. The researchers followed a task based approach to assess the association between the automatibility of jobs and worker's task and found an over estimation in the study by Frey & Osborne (2013) that 47% of the jobs in US will become automated.

Research also shows that although, at global level jobs in several sectors could become automated but at the same time technological advancements will create new jobs (Arntz et al., 2016). It is not so that the jobs will not get influenced by the process of automation but the jobs of future will become highly competitive and demanding. Workers will require matching with the skills required in the changing environment. In such scenarios workers having higher set of skills will need not to be flushed out of the workplace. Since, the very creators of the advance technology will require handling of the machine and its maintenance. Thus, the new prospect for workers or employees will be to actually complement the artificial intelligence. According to Arntz et al., (2016), the total jobs created between the year 1999 and 2010 by the IT sector and during the IT boom were 11.6 million which shows that as the technological progressions take place so does the nature of jobs change but these advancements did not wipe out the human workforce. The development of technology will increase the complexity of job specifically for those into the research and development field, software development and advance robotics or mechatronics. As the nature of technology changes so does the type of product and services and their demand. The increase in the demand for the product and services will need higher productivity rate from the workers which means more working hours and more salary/compensation (Gregory et al., 2015; Graetz & Michaels, 2015; Arntz et al., 2016). Moreover, the adoption of automation in sectors such as manufacturing is very low like at 4-10% in Germany which implies that for the developing nations such as China and India automation process of industries will take a decade to affect the working culture. The ideology of Arntz et al., (2016) and Frey & Osborne, (2013) are two ends of the advance technology continuum and leaves with the question that what type of change will this new era of artificial intelligence will bring is unpredictable. Will it jeopardize the human workforce or create new opportunities? The reason for such skepticism is simple that where will the civilization go from here since, the technological advancements like computerization, advance robotics, improved mobile phone technology, improved medical equipment and highly advance human interactive systems such as SIRI or CORTANA did not directly influence the nature of work a human does. A simple example is of carrying out a surgery where an AI might replace a surgeon and offer more precise and accurate surgery as compared to a human surgeon. And as far as the compassion, understanding of human emotions and managing of emotions is concerned, an artificial intelligence system can be equipped with an emotionally intelligent brain that can help it understand the different situations such as shock, trauma and empathize at the same time. Emotional Intelligence, *the ability to perceive, facilitate, understand and manage emotions*, will become important in an AI in future (Mclean, 2017). Precisely, it means that human and AI interaction is important as in future humans will be attracted to an AI for their human ways. The interaction between an AI and human is necessary to create a socialized environment for in future AI will need human recognition and societal acceptance (Reeves & Nass, 1996; Picard, 2004).

REFERENCES

Arntz, M., Gregory, T., & Zierahn, U. (2016). *The Risk of Automation for Jobs in OECD Countries: A Comparative Analysis*. OECD Social, Employment and Migration Working Papers, 189. OECD Publishing. 10.1787/5jlz9h56dvq7-en

Brynjolfsson, E., & McAfee, A. (2011). *Race against the machine: How the digital revolution is accelerating innovation, driving productivity, and irreversibly transforming employment and the economy*. Lexington, MA: Digital Frontier Press.

Campbell-Kelly, M. (2009). Origin of computing. *Scientific American Magazine*, *301*(3), 62–69. doi:10.1038/scientificamerican0909-62 PMID:19708529

Chelliah, J., & Chelliah, J. (2017). Will artificial intelligence usurp white collar jobs? *Human Resource Management International Digest*, *25*(3), 1–3. doi:10.1108/HRMID-11-2016-0152

Chowdhury, T. G., & Coulter, R. A. (2006). Getting a "sense" of financial security for generation Y. *Marketing Theory and Applications*, 191-192.

Das, A. (2017). *Infosys releases 9,000 employees with automation in 2016*. Retrieved on August 13, 2017 from http://timesofindia.indiatimes.com/companies/infosys-releases-9000-employees-with-automation-in-2016/articleshow/56680094.cms

David, H., & Dorn, D. (2013). The growth of low-skill service jobs and the polarization of the US labor market. *The American Economic Review*, *103*(5), 1553–1597. doi:10.1257/aer.103.5.1553

Eluvangal, S. (2014). *Bots cut Wipro employee strength by 12,000*. Retrieved on August 13, 2017 from https://ultra.news/s-e/30972/bots-help-wipro-cut-employee-strength-12000

Frey, C. B., & Osborne, M. A. (2017). The future of employment: How susceptible are jobs to computerisation? *Technological Forecasting and Social Change, 114*, 254–280. doi:10.1016/j.techfore.2016.08.019

Goos, M., & Manning, A. (2007). Lousy and lovely jobs: The rising polarization of work in Britain. *The Review of Economics and Statistics, 89*(1), 118–133. doi:10.1162/rest.89.1.118

Green, F. (2012). Employee involvement, technology and evolution in job skills: A task-based analysis. *Industrial & Labor Relations Review, 65*(1), 36–67. doi:10.1177/001979391206500103

Kim, S., Whitehead, E. J., & Zhang, Y. (2008). Classifying software changes: Clean or buggy? *Software Engineering. IEEE Transactions, 34*(2), 181–196.

Livshits, B., & Zimmermann, T. (2005). DynaMine: finding common error patterns by mining software revision histories. ACM SIGSOFT Software Engineering Notes, 30(5), 296-305. doi:10.1145/1081706.1081754

Mclean, A. (2017, February 20). Emotional intelligence is the future of artificial intelligence: Fjord. *Zdnet.com*. Retrieved August 13, 2017, from http://www.zdnet.com/article/emotional-intelligence-is-the-future-of-artificial-intelligence-fjord/

MGI. (2013). *Disruptive technologies: Advances that will transform life, business, and the global economy.* Tech. Rep., McKinsey Global Institute. Retrieved on August 13, 2017 from http://www.mckinsey.com/business-functions/digital-mckinsey/our-insights/disruptive-technologies

Mims, C. (2010). AI that picks stocks better than the pros. *MIT Technology Review.* Retrieved on August 13, 2017 from https://www.technologyreview.com/s/419341/ai-that-picks-stocks-better-than-the-pros/

Mitra, P. P. (2017, June 20). Watch: A 14-feet robocop directs traffic in Indore, makes commuters obey rules. *Hindustan Times*. Retrieved June 28, 2017, from http://www.hindustantimes.com/india-news/watch-a-14-feet-robocop-directs-traffic-in-indore-makes-commuters-obey-rules/story-rStGTxxsfCQgTOJV8kUzlO.html

Pfeiffer, S., & Suphan, A. (2015). *The Labouring Capacity Index: Living Labouring Capacity and Experience as Resources on the Road to Industry 4.0.* Retrieved on August 13, 2017 from https://www.sabine-pfeiffer.de/files/downloads/2015-Pfeiffer-Suphan-EN.pdf

Picard, R. W. (2004). Toward Machines with Emotional Intelligence. In *ICINCO (Invited Speakers)* (pp. 29-30). Retrieved on August 13, 2017 from https://dam-prod.media.mit.edu/x/files/pdfs/07.picard-EI-chapter.pdf

Reeves, B., & Nass, C. (1996). *The Media Equation*. New York, NY: Cambridge University Press.

Robotics-VO. (2013). *A Roadmap for US Robotics: From Internet to Robotics*. Retrieved on August 13, 2017 from http://www.roboticscaucus.org/Schedule/2013/20March2013/2013%20Robotics%20Roadmap-rs.pdf

Sharit, J., & Czaja, S. J. (1994). Ageing, computer-based task performance, and stress: Issues and challenges. *Ergonomics*, *37*(4), 559–577. doi:10.1080/00140139408963674 PMID:8187745

Section 2
Organizational Culture and Cross-Cultural Issues

Chapter 4
The Elements of Work Environment:
Organizational Culture, Organizational Climate, and Job Satisfaction

Nebojsa Pavlovic
University of Kragujevac, Serbia

ABSTRACT

One of the biggest issues facing every organization is how to keep and recruit skilled employees. This chapter deals with work environment because there is a widespread belief that it is one of the most significant factors affecting the development of job satisfaction. The goal of this chapter is to dig deeper into the important factors that exert influence on a positive work environment. The author uses meta-analysis to assesses primary sources, which are believed to contain necessary information about certain terms that describe work environment. The results of the research indicate that a positive work environment is closely connected to employee satisfaction. It is incumbent upon managers and leaders to intensively work on improving a workplace for every employee. Further research is necessary because of the dynamics of organizational structure and inevitable, rapid technological changes. This means that managers have to put in an enormous effort so as to produce in-depth analyses of their work environments and to determine how to improve them.

DOI: 10.4018/978-1-5225-4933-8.ch004

Copyright © 2018, IGI Global. Copying or distributing in print or electronic forms without written permission of IGI Global is prohibited.

INTRODUCTION

Apart from numerous advantages, the dynamic and rapid development of organizations has also brought about a myriad of issues. One of the biggest issues has been the loss of skilled employees. Managers are now forced to improve working conditions in order to persuade their employees to continue to work for them. The question is: will pleasant and positive work environment convince people to continue to work for a certain organization? Will this kind of environment persuade some skilled employees from other organizations to change their work environment?

In order to create a positive work environment, one has to be acquainted with its basic elements, as well as with how and to what extent those elements affect employee satisfaction.

The subject matter of the section on a positive work environment would be the introduction to positive work environment. Also, this paper will present its elements and the positive and negative characteristics that can either attract or repel those individuals who are interested in a certain organization.

The goal of this section is to acquaint the reader with a positive work environment and its decisive elements.

Numerous research has indicated that the key to the success and good results of an organization is a positive work environment. The question is whether a positive work environment serves as a catalyst to produce impressive results?

The results of every organization depend heavily on a positive work environment. Many authors dealing with organizational design and culture have reached this unique conclusion (Robbins & Coulter, 2009). A manager who is in charge of creating an organizational design, which will enable a positive work environment, has the leading role in an organization. Firstly, a positive work environment should form its basic element – organizational culture, which will enable employees to be satisfied with their work.

There is a widespread belief that the creation of positive environment is an expensive and lengthy process. That process can be long if a manager does not put in considerable effort to change organizational culture in favor of the organization. A manager sets an example for his employees with his work ethic and behavior. If a leader does not have enough strength to lead his employees then he will serve as a weak example for them and there will be no changes. As we will see in this paper, numerous research has shown that one will achieve great results if one starts gradually introducing the changes.

The second section analyzes important elements of a positive work environment.

Today, the creation of a positive work environment, which is supposed to bring about employee satisfaction and thus better results, has been causing issues to the researchers (Aronson, 2013). Those issues arise because it is difficult to highlight all factors and elements which bring about positive work environment. Thus, the author is aware that this section can be expanded. The topic has been narrowed down to include several factors which are under the influence of managers. Therefore, those factors are paramount when it comes to the creation of a positive work environment. The technological influence on the attitudes towards positive work environment is only mentioned in passing. However, technology exerts enormous influence on the whole workplace in real life. The author was aware that the lack of practical examples could be detrimental to the understanding of this topic. However, the author hopes that the mentioned sources will be of help to the readers.

THE ELEMENTS OF WORK ENVIRONMENT

When discussing the elements of work environment our starting point should be the role of managers and leaders in its creation. Management is by far the most important part of every organization; it is in charge of planning, organizing, managing and controlling. Management and leadership decide about the goals, making sure that they are in accordance with the vision and mission of an organization.

Organizational culture and organizational climate take first place because they are closely connected to the organization's identity. The changes made in organizational climate and culture can improve the work environment.

One of the most important elements – which will be discussed later – is communication because employee relations depend on it.

Respecting ethical and moral principles is a growing need for organizations. If an organization disrespects those principles, it will be faced with a severe penalty for its unethical behavior and people will be dissuaded from conducting business with it.

The majority of people think that an organization provides security to them and their families. Apart from giving salaries and providing a sense of security, an organization makes sure that its employees are not exposed to any abuse or discrimination.

The teamwork is something that comes naturally to human beings. Apart from the fact that it is easier to work in a group, the teamwork is proven to be the most effective way to organize things in order to achieve specific goals.

A positive work environment harbors respect. In these kinds of organizations, it is customary to award your employees for their effort, loyalty, and good results.

A healthy work environment brings about the feelings of cosines and comfort in an organization. It is essential to equip a workplace with state-of-the-art equipment (e.g. with air-conditioners that have heating and cooling options; ergonomic chairs; wall colors; right lightning; pens, papers, notebooks; computer, the internet and mobile connection, etc). Managers take care of their employees. It is paramount to ensure that there is a chance for self-management, decision-making, training, improvement, and self-development of every employee. Apart from this, employees will be happy and satisfied if they have a chance to move up the career ladder. They need motivation and encouragement from their manager for this and in turn, they will achieve their life goals.

Defining Work Environment

A work environment is a place where a task is performed. A workplace includes a location, i.e. a business building. The work environment can also include other factors which are connected to the workplace, such as air quality, noise levels, free parking space, food and coffee supply.

The environment can be static or dynamic. The static environment implies that organizational culture never changes and that an organization maintains the status quo. The dynamic environment always changes which in turn changes organizational culture. The changes can bring about two things: employees can either feel the improvement or they can feel that the work environment is not improving their job satisfaction.

A work environment is a very complex term. It is composed of numerous elements which exert influence on it. Those elements can transform a positive work environment into a negative one. The scope of this paper does not allow room for writing about every aspect of work environment. Thus, the author focuses on those factors in which employees have leading roles. Employee satisfaction determines whether a work environment will be positive or negative (Aronson, 2013). According to Robbins (2008), the main elements to determine whether a work environment will be positive or negative are: organizational climate, organizational culture, and job satisfaction.

Both organizational climate and culture are narrower terms than work environment, although they are sometimes closely connected to it. Job satisfaction is an attitude which is thought to be an important factor in the study of organizational behavior (Aronson, 2013).

The reason for researching these three factors is the crucial influence that a manager has on them (Dessler, 2015). According to Dessler, apart from having a conscious influence, a manager also has a subconscious one. A manager indicates how an employee should behave. According to Schein (2010), managers have a crucial role in the process of creating organizational culture and climate. Thus, they will exert influence on job satisfaction. Their attitude will determine whether a work environment is positive or negative.

Organizational Culture

There is a widespread agreement among researchers that organizational culture exists. Thus, it plays a key role in shaping work environment and it exerts major influence on employee behavior. However, they haven't reached an agreement about what organizational culture truly is (Watkins, 2013).

The most common definition of organizational culture is the one given by Deal and Kennedy (1982). They state that organizational culture is the way in which employees (in a specific work environment) work. Similarly, Watkins has a short definition: Organizational culture is the organization's immune system (Watkins, 2013).

Reilly's definition is also popular; it states that organizational culture has strong, widely shared core values. Regardless of which definition we talk about, they share three common elements (Moorhead & Griffin, 1989):

1. All the definitions refer to the set of values held by individuals in an organization. These values define good or acceptable behaviors and bad or unacceptable behavior.
2. The values are taken for granted; an employee discovers them in an organization. They are basic assumptions made by employees.
3. The emphasis is placed on the symbolic means through which the values in an organization's culture are communicated (examples, stories, myths).

Based on these elements, one can provide a definition of organizational culture as the set of shared values that are taken for granted. Those shared values help people in an organization understand which actions are thought to be acceptable, and which unacceptable. The values are communicated through the use of stories and other symbolic means (Robbins & Coulter, 2008).

Organizational culture, together with its elements, holds an organization together and creates a unique identity. There is no such thing as two identical organizational cultures, and organizations differ in this respect. An employee can immediately discover an organization's identity. Just by setting foot in an organization one can perceive its organizational culture.

More importantly, organizational culture shapes both the positive and negative work environment. Namely, if we have a positive organizational culture, we will have a positive work environment and vice versa.

One of the most important researchers into organizational culture, Schein, states that the connection between organizational culture and work environment is easily explained. He argues that organizational culture is the basic and the most important factor that decides whether a work environment is positive or negative (Schein, 2010).

This is why it is paramount to strive to preserve a positive culture or to change it if it's negative. As previously mentioned, the employees are representatives of organizational culture, thus they will aspire to preserve it. However, they are against any kind of changes in cultural patterns. The main task of a manager would be to change the organizational culture by persuading employees that that is the best solution. In this case, a manager employs his leadership abilities. It is a very difficult task and only a handful of managers are able to change organizational culture.

Katzenbach et al. (2017) discuss the steps a manager has to take in order to improve, i.e. change, organizational culture. He states that organizational culture is not necessarily made up of only bad elements. Also, after a detailed analysis, one can commence work on changing those parts which are thought to be bad. Firstly, one should start from critical types of behavior that are detrimental to the organization's existence. The managers should do the "right thing" and set an example by showing how to behave in certain situations. If the instructions are written in a book, they will not bring about changes. If someone wants a different culture, he has to prove it. If a manager has leadership abilities, he can influence employees to accept his patterns of behavior. The unofficial leaders in an organization can prove to be of help to the managers. Every group has them. The leader has to acknowledge them and communicate the need for changes in behavior through them. The formal leaders have to put in extra effort to improve their behavior and work. They shouldn't demand that their employees behave in a way they do not. If a manager is late for work, there is a strong chance that his employees will also be late.

While changing the organizational culture one must expect evolution, nor revolution. It is difficult for the changes to become effective immediately. The process of changing behavioral patterns is a long-term one and it yields patience and cooperation of every employee.

Organizational Climate

Organizational climate has only two factors which govern people's behavior: personality and environment. This is a state of psychosocial relation among employees and their attitude towards their organization. Organizational climate has a major influence on employee satisfaction, attitudes, and behavior.

Organizational climate in an organization can be authoritative, democratic, and one that disintegrates interpersonal relationships. The democratic climate ensures a positive work environment. It is characterized by participative management, collaboration, good communication, responsibility, trust between managers and employees. Also, by showing respect for client's needs (Bojanovic, 1999).

A favorable organizational climate for a positive work environment exists when every employee feels like he is a part of some organization. In addition, he must believe that he is useful and important. Apart from that, he must feel like he is expected to help the organization achieve its goals and results on the market (Vujic, 2008). The future of an organization does not only depend on the knowledge of whether its environment is positive or negative, but also on the results.

Job Satisfaction

Researchers into organizational behavior have discovered that job satisfaction is one of the most important things when evaluating a positive environment. In the organizational effectiveness model, specifically in the continuity strategy model and integrative model, job satisfaction is believed to be a basic criterion for effectiveness (Judge et al., 2001).

Researchers have reached an agreement that job satisfaction is one of the most important criterions for evaluating organization's effectiveness.

Job satisfaction is defined as a positive feeling about one's job resulting from an evaluation of its characteristics (Robbins & Judge, 2009). Satisfaction is not a behavior but rather an employee attitude in some organization. There is a close connection between job satisfaction and organization's success. Research indicates that an organization achieves better results when its employees are satisfied with their job than when they are not (Buckingham & Coffiman, 2003).

There is a simple solution: it is only necessary for the employees to be satisfied with their work. But what makes employees satisfied with their work? Researchers have found that salary is not paramount for job satisfaction and that it does not take first place. Job satisfaction is achieved when jobs are interesting, diverse, and independent. Additionally, when they do not involve strict control and supervision and when there are training programs which help employees improve. A good relationship with colleagues is also paramount. After all of these elements, salary is listed as important for job satisfaction (Diener et al., 1993).

It is important to stress that only satisfied and happy employees are productive. The managers have begun to put in considerable efforts to make their employees happier and more satisfied. They are focusing on job conditions and positive work environment (Laffaldano & Muchinsky, 1985).

Two Types of Work Environment: Positive and Negative

A work environment can be both positive and negative. A positive work environment is the one that motivates employees to put in extra effort in order to achieve good results. According to Rowe and Howell (2014), the positive performances in a work environment are the science of success. A positive work environment brings about happiness, satisfied smiles. Something people experienced in their childhood.

A negative work environment compels employees to work less, achieve bad results and to leave an organization. Fostering negative organizational culture is the best way to lose the most valuable human resources in a company (Rowe & Howell, 2014).

What Brings About a Positive Work Environment?

A positive work environment strives to provide good and quality working conditions for employees (Robbins & Judge, 2009).

The employees are the most important part of every organization. Therefore, every organization wants to employ the right people, but that can turn out to be a difficult task. The distinctive characteristic of a successful organization is the amount of effort they devote to the process of recruiting and preserving skilled employees by providing a good work environment.

One of the most important characteristics of a positive work environment is freedom and workers' self-management. This refers to giving a possibility to employees to equally participate in decision-making regarding important issues in an organization. Employees need to feel joy in their workplace. This is only possible if one respects their integrity, and if there are respect and social responsibility. A positive communication entails a lot of time and resources today. Employees stress the importance of good communication when deciding where they are going to work. The managers often end their conversations by assigning tasks and issuing instructions. The modern communication in the organization includes feedback which is provided to the employee as an award and a sign of respect for his finished task. The employees actually want to be a part of organization's vision and its success. If organizational culture disregards respect, the employees will not be satisfied with their work. The employees demand humor and entertainment in the workplace, which means that they want to love what they do and not find it dull. The managers are required to adjust both organizational climate and culture to the needs of their employees. The good managers are ready to change organizational culture in order to bring about a positive work environment. The employees working in a positive work environment will: work on improving their productivity, be proud of their work, share knowledge and experience with other employees, and enjoy going to work and be happier and more satisfied (Cridland, 2014).

People tend to forget that interior design is paramount for a positive work environment. A myriad of agencies tackle the issue of workplace design. The websites are filled with tips on what to do in order to make your employees feel pleasant. . Also, they describe how to encourage employees to achieve what you expect of them.

When someone mentions interior design we immediately think about the office, lighting, and heating. It is of paramount importance to have the best lighting insofar as it exerts influence on the mood of your employees and their performance. Those concerned with health believe that workplaces should resemble the outdoors. Therefore, they demand a vast number of windows and natural lightning. Also, one should always set the ideal temperature by using heating and cooling systems in the workplace.

Also, architectural plans are being changed. Employees want the so-called "open space", where they can communicate among themselves and collaborate together. According to the magazine Inc., a myriad of employers are taking necessary measures to create an open space in order to have a positive work environment (Heibutzki, 2017).

If we follow certain advices a workplace organization can bring about both positive results and a positive work environment (Kuleto, 2017).

It is said that the office reflects those working in it. This is why it is important to take care of the workplace and offices. We should not think that thirty minutes is a lot of time to spend cleaning the space that we visit every day. It is necessary to remove the things which we do not use in the workplace. Everything we need should be within arm's reach. A person can waste a lot of time trying to find the necessary material. This also refers to the computers. It should always be accessible and it should not contain unnecessary files. We should name the files we are using. It should be noted that it is time consuming to search for missing files. It is advisable to devote one day to clean the office. The unnecessary papers should not be strewn on the table. If we are in dire need of them, then the best thing to do is to arrange them in a pile. If we do not need them, then they should be thrown away. Therefore, an office should include shelves on which we could store things – they should be functional, and not decorative. The employees, on their part, should always check whether their employer can find a certain message or some important file after returning from a vacation. The recent research has shown that family photos or religious relics do not send a good message to your colleagues or to your boss. They might think that you would rather be at home than working (Kuleto, 2017).

One of the most important elements of work environment is the macroergonomic approach (Taghipur, 2015). Taylor was the first scientist to deal with the problem of ergonomics insofar as he improved the employee performance by adjusting materials to their abilities. That was how Taylor, after observing and analyzing the movement of employees, reached the best solutions, which in turn gave the best results (Williams, 2010). Since then, the science of ergonomics has been advancing, but its goal has remained the same: adjusting the workplace so that an employee can achieve efficiency and effectiveness in the workplace.

The employees are increasingly starting to decorate their workplace following the old rules. Those old rules include Chinese culture that relies on the work-life balance – feng shui. The five elements that are important for feng shui are: metal, water, tree, fire, and earth. By combining them and choosing the appropriate place to display them in our office, we achieve energy balance which is transferred to our employees.

The adherents of these rules claim that employees, who follow these rules, feel successful, diligent, and energetic. The rules of feng shui are strict and they have to be respected in order to achieve results (Sator, 2011).

As previously mentioned, the environment brings about the positive feelings within an organization. According to Valden (2017), the attractive and comfortable design causes a burst of energy. Thus, this energy increases productivity and success. Having a lot of windows means that your employees will be exposed to the sunlight and vitamin D, both of which put them in a good mood. It has been proven that windows actually stimulate creativity and the ability to come up with some new ideas. The employees can focus on their tasks if there is no noise. Even communication is improved when there in an open environment, which does not occur when the offices are cramped, according to Valden.

Motivating Your Employees by Changing the Nature of Their Work Environment

Motivation is an inner driving force which provides energy and driving force to people so that they can achieve goals, satisfy their needs and, most importantly, fulfill their tasks.

It is easy to conclude that motivation is closely connected to employee satisfaction. Motivated employees are satisfied with their work environment. Dissatisfied employees usually need motivation in order to carry out their work.

Research has shown that interior design and decoration exert influence on employee's effort and motivation, as well as on their results. One of the best-known theories in the field of motivation (developed in 1943) is Maslow's theory (2004). According to this theory on of the most important needs is self-actualization. Hackman and Oldham (1976) used this need to explain how the workplace should be organized so that an employee could prove that he is capable of solving the most creative problems and tasks, applying his acquired and learned skills.

Jobs in which an employee is expected to perform his duty for eight hours per day are thought to be monotonous. In addition, they will not motivate employees like those jobs which require talent and creative thinking.

The employees who are motivated by various types of duties are willing to learn and improve themselves by acquiring new skills. Research has indicated that salary is not crucial in determining employee satisfaction, but the actual work. The managers have to take this information into consideration and try to combat boredom in the workplace as it leads to bad results.

Also, a manager has to have in mind the abilities of an employee when entrusting him with a task. The employees enjoy performing those tasks that entail creativity. For instance, a shoemaker would probably love to work on a new collection, rather than just perform the same task each and every day. When an employee is entrusted with a task that he can perform, then he demonstrates his exceptional abilities. Thus, he is motivated and puts in a considerable effort.

An employee feels motivated when a manager stresses the importance of his position and tasks. Of course, not all tasks within an organization are important. However, a successful manager is marked by his ability to present each task as important for the success of his organization. Employees should be able to relate to their work and results. The success is increased when an employee starts to talk about his organization outside the working hours. This is a sign that he has adopted an organizational culture of the organization he works in.

Autonomy means that employees have the freedom to execute tasks in their own way. Discretion is paramount when motivating employees. Also, they are motivated when they have an opportunity to decide for themselves. Research has shown that employees act more responsible when they are given complete control over their tasks than when they feel that someone imposed a task on them. By delegating tasks and decreasing control, the managers achieve really good results. According to Drucker (2004), this makes the employees feel extremely motivated.

Also, feedback can serve as a good motivation (Carosell, 2014). Employees are motivated when there is a constant communication between them and managers about their tasks. The employees who do not get any feedback feel like their job is not valuable and that anyone can perform it. The managers are aware of this and, thus, they use feedback as a powerful work motivation factor . Therefore, an employee sees that his job is important and that an organization would not operate without him.

If the workplaces are not designed carefully and they do not generate motivation and employee satisfaction, a manager can do the following: redesign the workplace by rotating the desks, enrich the workplace and introduce the flexible working hours.

Refresher or how it was once called – retraining – is to periodically allocate different tasks to an employee. A manager can note that certain tasks are too mundane to an employee just by listening to him. The employee might leave the organization and start working for another one as a consequence of his dissatisfaction, regardless of the salary and compensations. It has been already mentioned that research has shown that job satisfaction is the most important factor in deciding where to work (Gangestand & Snyder, 2000).

To broaden the scope of a job is to increase the number of tasks performed by an individual. This will result in a diverse workplace. People find this kind of a workplace to be more challenging and acceptable than that which involves boring routine jobs. More than 100 years ago, Taylor proved that employees were more likely to accept a workplace that entailed a myriad of tasks than the one in which they would perform the same task every day, regardless of the salary (Williams, 2010).

Job enrichment involves vertical expansion of activities which increase the ability of employees to control planning, execution, and evaluation of a performance. It is derived from Herzberg's two-factor theory (Herzberg, 1987). An employee is responsible for his performance in job enrichment. A manager is in charge of giving feedback about his performance so that an employee can correct his mistakes (Hackman & Oldham, 1980).

Work sharing is a new trend in the business world. It is a process which enables two or more people to divide the number of working hours (40 hours per week) among themselves. This means that one employee can work in the morning and the other in the afternoon. They could also work on alternate days or one could work one week, and the other the next. This allows the employees to have more than one job, which does not only include a higher salary, but also a chance to make connections and boost their salaries. Research indicates that in the USA more than 30% of big organizations offer these opportunities to their employees. Both the organization and the employees gain from work sharing. An organization can employ more employees with different levels of competence and skills, and employee gains the workplace flexibility (Dawson, 2001).

Many people find that working from home is an ideal job. It does not involve commuting, working hours are flexible and employees can decide how and when to work. Also, an employee is free and his colleagues are not bothering him. One can perform routine jobs from home, including: information processing (analyst). Also, one can perform complicated jobs which seek knowledge (such as: writers, professors). Also, the organizations profit from this kind of work. Firstly, they do not need to provide office supplies which mean that the organizations would save money. However, the disadvantages are the lack of supervision and control. This is why organizations allocate tasks which do not need any supervision but only require the employee's devotion (Davenport & Pearlson, 1998).

Communication Is an Important Element of Work Environment

Communication is an important part of the work environment. While the employees might feel accepted in one workplace, they might feel rejected in the other. It all depends on communication. The transparent and open communication will motivate employees to put in extra effort in their work and achieve better results. Two-way communication is fostered, as well as face-to-face communication. If an organization promotes a favorable climate for communication, employees will not be reluctant to suggest ideas for improving the workplace and changing organizational culture.

We, of course, communicate by speaking, but there is also non-verbal communication where words aren't necessary. Research has shown that non-verbal communication is more important (Lehman & Dufrene, 2015). As it has been already mentioned, the most important element is organizational culture. It is manifested through symbols that have certain meaning only in one organization. Other organizations find those symbols incomprehensible and they carry no meaning to them. It is paramount to establish a communication which will enable the employees to transmit messages and information with little noise and no barriers.

According to Wren and Voich (1994) communication is a means with which we convince, inform, motivate and lead individuals towards organization's goal. The essence of organizational effort is communication.

More precisely, Lehman and Dufrene (2015) define communication as a process of exchanging information and meaning among individuals through a common system of symbols, signs, and behavior.

There are numerous obstacles which are detrimental to good communication. Firstly, the sender transfers messages. He wants to hide something or to manipulate the process of decoding a message. Similarly, we have a selective perception of the receiver. The receiver can, for various reasons, interpret the message in his own way.

The overflow of information is common today. Also, it can get in the way of receiving a message. More often than not one "can't see the forest for the trees".

Emotions are the constant obstacles when it comes to interpreting messages. Different people may interpret a message differently – some may find it worrisome, while others may interpret it as plain.

Language can be the biggest obstacle. It is not enough to just know the foreign language. One must be acquainted with the culture of the sender.

People also fear communication and that can lead to bigger problems. It is not uncommon for some managers to be petrified of talking in front of a bigger group of people or to be scared of presentations. If a manager avoids meetings then he will do more harm than good.

When it comes to modern problems in communication, we should stress the communication issues arising between men and women. Also, intercultural communication which occurs between two people or two organizations from different cultures. For instance, research conducted by Tannen (1995) indicates that women use the language in order to make a connection. However, men use the language to highlight their power and independence.

Technology has changed the process of communication. Mobile phones have especially advanced communication. Today everyone is available no matter where they are. One only needs a signal in order to communicate. Also, there is the ability to use video which enables organizations to hold video-conferences . This means that people do not have to travel in order to be present in a meeting.

When it comes to the relationship between communication and a positive work environment, research has shown that job satisfaction will increase if there is communication between people. This in turn brings about a positive work environment. (Lehman & Dufrene, 2015).

Furthermore, if an organization strives to have no obstacles and barriers in communication then the employees will understand the messages they receive. Also, a manager will then be able to provide feedback.

A perfect communication does not exist. However, if one chooses the right channel and removes the barriers and noises on time, then there will be a positive work environment.

The Influence of Dissatisfied and Satisfied Employees on Work Environment

The term job satisfaction is often defined as a positive feeling about a job resulting from an evaluation of its characteristics (Robbins & Judge, 2009).

Researchers have already established that satisfied employees will achieve better results in the workplace (Spector, 1992). The interesting part is that the salary does not take first place when it comes to job satisfaction. Job satisfaction is more important that salary. The choice of colleagues, who and how supervises his work is also more important. The results of this research came as a surprise.

The research used a questionnaire made by Spector and it was composed of 36 questions . Those questions focused on the nature of the job, supervision, salary, benefits, chances for promotion, and the relationship with colleagues. The results were like those obtained from the second questionnaire, which posed this question: Are you satisfied with your job? According to the researchers, it is possible to measure job satisfaction with only one question. Although "satisfaction" is a complex and broad term, that question presents the essence of job satisfaction (Wanous et al., 1997).

The consequences might arise if employees are not satisfied with their work environment. Firstly, the employees will want to leave an organization which has organizational culture that does not suit them. Secondly, the employees will come together and create a (pre)conflict and express their disagreement with the managers (there is a possibility of including unions). Thirdly, they will show disloyalty to the company. Lastly, employees will be neglectful of their work and obligations (Robins, Judge, 2009).

Job satisfaction and satisfaction with work environment have positive effects:

- On work performance,
- On civic behavior of employees,

- On satisfaction of clients,
- It decreases the number of people leaving the organization,
- It decreases the number of people who are late to work,
- It decreases the number of deviant behavior and conflicts in the workplace.

The feelings of employees affect job satisfaction. Job satisfaction, as we have already seen, exerts a major influence on a positive work environment. This is why the managers devote special attention to the feelings of their employees and they solve problems on time. Robbins & Judge (2009) list 4 factors that bring about the increase in job satisfaction:

1. Intellectually challenging work.
2. Equal awards.
3. Working conditions which support the employees and
4. Colleagues who give their full support.

Let's take a look at the new organizational designs that should increase employee satisfaction: flexible working hours and family-friendly work.

Flexible Working Hours

The data collected through research show that employees demand flexible working hours – especially those having a desk job. However, the managers are not willing to accept these working hours. One of the main reasons is the lack of time and insufficient number of employees. If the flexible working hours are introduced, then the managers will have to create new organizational designs in order to achieve positive results (Rodgers, 1993).

Family-Friendly Work

It is paramount to establish a family-friendly work where parents can bring up their children in good conditions. The companies will create a better workplace if they establish a family-friendly work, where the parents are encouraged to perform their roles. An ideal environment for child development is created when the parents are given the necessary help and protection (Unicef, 2017).

The recent research in the field of social psychology might lower the influence of managers on job satisfaction (Mesmer-Magnus & Viswesvaran, 2006). These researches show that genetic factors exert influence on job satisfaction. Also, they state that employees can be happy or unhappy, satisfied or dissatisfied depending on their genetics (Arvey et al., 1994). The genetic factors influence up to 80% of people. Although we have these new information, a manager is the one who chooses whether he will hire those who are energetic or those who find little pleasure in working. Those employees will not achieve good results.

Connecting Employees to Work Environment (Adjusting Them to Organizational Culture)

It is paramount to adjust organizational cultures of every employee to that of the company. Also, the employees should adjust their behavior to the company's values (Certo & Certo, 2008). This is necessary if one wants to avoid conflicts and have a successful teamwork. If the environment is positive, then an employee will accept the existing organizational culture. A negative work environment would compel employees to change organizational culture or to leave the organization and find a suitable organizational culture (Drucker, 2004).

An organization needs to learn if it wants to have employees who will adjust to its organizational culture (Pavlovic, 2013).

An organization that learns is the one that has developed the ability to constantly learn, adjust and change (Robbins & Coulter, 2008).

An organization that learns has the following characteristics (Pavlovic, 2015):

- There are no limits to the organizational design. The employees are given authority and a manager allocates tasks to them. They work in a team that is not closely supervised and controlled, but that is responsible for certain tasks.
- An Organizational culture that fosters interpersonal relations, concern for an organization and its goals. Lastly, trust between employees, as well as that between employees and managers is important in these organizations. Communication is two-way.
- Communication is open and effective. Information is delivered on time. Feedback is required.
- The leadership is based on collaboration and exchange of visions with all employees.

Those organizations that have the characteristics of an organization that learns have a positive work environment that attracts people to work for and conduct business with them (Liedtka, 1996).

The Impact of Technology on Work Environment

This section answers the question connected to technology and changes within it. The impact of technology cannot be neglected. A vast number of research indicate this. Today, technology has a bigger role than the manager himself (Robbins, 2008). Therefore this section deals with the following questions:

- How does technology influence employees and can technology change work environment?
- Do managers encourage their employees to introduce innovations in their performance? Do they encourage them to create those innovations? Are employees awarded for that?
- How important is to create organizations that learn and that are prepared to adjust to new situations? How important are the changes of organizational culture for a work environment?

One of the most significant influences of globalization has been the technological advances made in most countries. Those developments would not be possible without globalization. The most important are the developments in computer science, satellite and telecommunications equipment (Marjoribanks, 2000). That process always starts in the developed countries and continues to the underdeveloped ones. The reasons behind the technological development of the underdeveloped countries are twofold. The first reason was to introduce modern technology so that the global companies could relocate to the underdeveloped countries. Therefore, they were able to use both human and material resources under favorable conditions. The second reason was to attract talented and educated workforce from the poor parts of the world. Regardless of the reasons, information now flows swiftly from one part of the world to the other. People are now informed . Thus, they can choose for themselves and they can secure a positive work experience and the environment.

In the future, it is expected that technology will exert a bigger influence on the performance of every organization. The aforementioned flexible working hours are just one of the elements that will be incorporated. The flexible working hours will create virtual teams that will increase the performance and results of an organization (Townesend, 2017). The advantage of the flexible working hours and virtual teams is that one can employ people from all over the world. There will be no need for administration. The contracts will be signed swiftly, using a digital signature. This is a crucial part in introducing technology in the workplace. Also, your employees will be able to work not only for one organization but for several. They will work only in good working conditions. On the other hand, the organizations can employ anyone, especially the best experts because they will be available to them. The question is: Have we given the best offer and have we provided the best working conditions? The employers will probably have to match the working conditions of other organizations. This all will improve working conditions and create a positive work environment. The employees will then choose: the organization, their colleagues and, most importantly, their job.

Malhotra et al. (2017) discuss what is needed in order to create a positive work environment through virtual teams. Firstly, one has to develop trust. Of course, diversity is inevitable, but it is crucial that the members of the virtual teams accept and respect each other. In addition, they mention that it is paramount to organize and manage meetings, monitor work progress, enhance visibility of members in and out of the organizations, and provide benefits to the members.

Artificial intelligence is a recurring topic. Albanese (2017) mentions a number of advantages, such as: better communication, improved satisfaction of the clients, control of the objects and better planning. However, artificial intelligence has its drawbacks. These include: privacy violation, looking for solutions that are not practical for everyone, mistakes that might occur on hardware and that might lead to even bigger damages. People are also against it because it is dehumanizing the brand.

The use of artificial intelligence is expected to increase by over 500%. It is necessary to analyze whether artificial intelligence will improve the position of employees. Also, whether this kind of "help" will lead to a positive work environment.

The Unequal Power in Work Environment

The notion of power is significant in understanding discrimination and abuse. According to the researchers, the unequal power is brought about by the boss-employee relationship and that power is transformed into discrimination and abuse (Cortina & Wast, 2005). The unequal power is created by the fact that a boss can supervise, control, award, and discipline his employees. The unequal power can turn the employees into victims, and bosses into people who reach unethical decisions.

One cannot talk about a positive work environment if there is inequality expressed through discrimination, abuse or disrespect of ethical principles. This section deals with how the unequal power in an organization can influence a positive work environment.

As it can be seen, individuals are trying to decrease the power of managers by using different terms for the same position. They are often called associates, instructors, or helpers. The pay gaps are concealed by not clearly stating the responsibilities of a manager. The employees are given the opportunity to decide, and managers allocate their tasks to their employees. Apart from the roles given to them by their managers, the employees are also forced to take responsibility for the results. The question is: does control over certain tasks create a positive work environment? Black & Holden (1998) have conducted a research into this.

According to Aronson, discrimination is a stereotypical belief. He describes it as an unjustified, negative and harmful behavior towards a member of some organization just because he belongs to a different organization (Aronson et al., 2013).

Dessler's definition states that discrimination is the unfair treatment and unequal influence (Dessler, 2015). The unfair treatment would refer to the intentional discrimination. This type of discrimination arises when a person is being treated differently because of his race, religion, sex, or ethnicity. There are a vast number of examples. For instance, an employer refuses to hire a woman because he thinks she might neglect her job because of her family. Also, there is age discrimination. An employer does not want to hire people who are age 50 or older because he thinks the younger employee will be more efficient and productive in the workplace.

The unequal impact arises when an employer demands that a candidate gives him something which he knows that the candidate does not have or cannot obtain in such a short notice. For instance, when an employer knows in advance who he will hire. He will demand that the other candidates hold certain qualifications, or possess some skills or competences that are not important for that workplace. Today, there are numerous complaints because of this discrimination.

There is discrimination on the basis of disability, compensation, education, religion, race, sex, color, national origin or ethnicity, religious or political beliefs, gender identity, sexual orientation, family status, birth, genetic, health, marital status, criminal conviction, age, appearance, political party affiliation and membership in certain organizations. It is difficult to list all discriminations.

The most common manifestations of discrimination are:

- Violation of equal rights and obligations,
- Abuse and unfair treatment, and
- Hate speech

Even though there are certain laws, it is difficult to establish equality.

There are two basic types of discrimination. The first one is direct, while the second one is indirect, i.e. discrimination which is not visible.

Indirect discrimination occurs when, because of some reason, a person or a group are treated unfairly. For instance, indirect discrimination is when someone does not have to pay for something – women do not have to pay entry fee when going to a club, while men have to.

Direct discrimination occurs when someone does not respect equality. For instance, direct discrimination is when an employer demands that his candidates prove that they had attended public schools, not private, or vice versa.

Apart from discrimination which can directly create a negative work environment, ethical issues also lead to consequences that can harm an organization (Pavlovic, 2016).

According to Schumann (2004), ethics is a set of behavior guidelines that govern certain individuals or groups. People conform to these norms when deciding how they should behave. Therefore, ethics is both normative and moral.

The employees are always confronted with ethical issues. They sometimes wonder whether it is right to use a photocopier for private purposes. Also, is it right to report a colleague who plays computer games or visits social networks during working hours?

Ethical behavior is determined by a manager with his behavior and an employee who supports it. A strict moral law is brought about by pressures and a code of conduct. It is important that employees have ethical behavior. When moral laws are accepted in an organization then an employee will say that he is a moral person because: that is who I truly am! (Robbins, 2015).

In order to improve ethical behavior, HR managers often use the following measures: selection, ethics training program, work efficiency evaluation, rewards and incentives system, ethics management and ensuring that there is fair treatment. How to achieve the best results in ethics? The best answer is to hire ethical people (Krohe, 1997).

A positive work environment and respect is caused by adhering to moral laws. If organizations do not follow moral principles, they will violate employee rights and cause problems in communication. A negative work environment is created because of this. Usually, the employees strive to leave this kind of an environment.

CONCLUSION

Positive work environment is a solution for keeping and recruiting skilled people in every organization. It is important to carefully work on creating a positive work environment. The employees are the most valuable resource every organization has and their working conditions are significant to them. It is important to adjust those conditions to their needs. A manager has to analyze organizational culture as it is the most important part of the work environment. He should retain it if it is efficient, and change it if it is detrimental to the organization's development.

A manager can create a positive work environment only if he includes his employees in the process. They will share a positive experience. The managers will feel good. Their employees will be satisfied with the changes made and they will feel like a significant part of the organization as they are involved in creating and achieving goals.

In the future, the biggest concern will not be how to recruit skilled employees, but how to keep them. A positive work environment is the first step to employee satisfaction. The constant work on improving the elements of work environment will create an environment that will inspire employees to work harder and be more productive. Also, it will not compel them to leave their organization.

REFERENCES

Albanese, J. (2017). *What You Need to Know About AL in the Workplace*. Retrieved April, 2017, from http//:www.inc.org

Aronson, E., Vilson, T., & Akert, R. (2013). *Socijalna psihologija, peto izdanje*. Zagreb: Mate.

Arvey, R., McCall, T., & Bouchard, T. (1997). Genetic Influences on Job Satisfaction and Work Values. *Personality and Individual Differences*, 7(2).

Black, B., & Holden, W. (1998). The Impact of gender on Productivity and Satisfaction Among Medical School Psychologist. *Journal of Clinical Psychology in Medical Settings*, 3(1).

Bojanović, R. (1999). *Psihologija međuljudskih odnosa*. Centar za primenjenu psihologiju.

Buckingham, M., & Coffiman, C. (2003). *First, Break All the Rules: What the Worlds Greates managers Do Differentialy*. New York: Simon & Schuster.

Caroselli, M. (2015). *Leadership Skills For Managers*. Zagreb: Mate.

Certo, S., & Certo, T. (2008). *Modern management* (10th ed.). MATE.

Cortina, M., & Wasti, S. (2005). Profiles in Coping: Responses to Sexual Harassment Across Persons, Organizations and Cultures. *The Journal of Applied Psychology*, 2(8).

Cridland, C. (2014). *How You Can Build a Positive Workplace Culture*. Retrieved April, 2017, from http//:www.mindfulmeditation.com

Davenport, T., & Pearlson, K. (1998). Two cheers for the Virtual Office. *Sloan Management Review*, 2(1).

Dawson, C. (2001). Japan: Work-Sharing Will Prolong the pain. *Business Week*, 12(3).

Deal, T., & Kennedy, A. (1982). *Corporate Cultures*. Reading, MA: Addison-Wesley.

Dessler, G. (2015). *Human Resource Management (12th ed.)*. Zagreb: MATE.

Diener, E., Sandvik, E., Seidlitz, L., & Diener, M. (1993). The Relationship between Income and Subjective Well-Being: Relative or Absolute? *Social Indicators Research*, *28*(1).

Drucker, P. (2004). *The Daily Drucker*. Harper Collins Publishers.

Gangestand, S., & Snyder, M. (2000). Self-monitoring: Appraisal and Reappraisal. *Psychological Bulletin*, *4*(5). PMID:10900995

Hackman, J., & Okdham, G. (1976). Motivation through thr Design of Work: Test od a Theory. *Organizational Behavior and Human Performance*, *8*(1).

Hackman, J., & Okdham, G. (1980). *Work Redesign*. Reading, MA: Adison Wesley.

Heibutzki, R. (2017). *God Working Conditions for Workers*. Retrieved April, 2017, from http//:www.inc.com

Herzberg, F. (1987). One time: How do you motivate employees? *Harvard Business Review*, *5*(1).

Judge, T., Thoresen, C., Bono, E., & Patton, G. (2001). The Job Satisfaction-Job Performance Realationship: A Qualitative and Quantitative Review. *Psychological Bulletin*, *27*(1). PMID:11393302

Katzenbach, J., Oeischlegel, C., & Thomas, J. (2017). *Principles of Organizational Culture*. Retrieved April, 2017, from http//:www.strategy-business.com

Krohe, J. (1997). The Big Business Ethics, Across The Board. *Human Resource Management Review*, *16*(10).

Kuleto, V. (2017). *Organizacija radnog mesta*. Retrieved April, 2017, from http//www.valentinculeto.com

Laffaldano, M., & Muchinski, M. (1985). Job Satisfaction and Job performance: A meta-analysis. *Psychological Bulletin*, *3*(1).

Lehman, C., & DuFrene, D. (2015). *Poslovna komunikacija*. Beograd: BCOM, DataStatus.

Liedtka, M. (1996). Collaborating across Lines of Business for Competitive Advantage. *The Academy of Management Executive*, *4*(1).

Malhotra, A., Majchzak, A., & Rosen, B.(2007). Leading Virtual Teams. *Perspectives*, *21*(1).

Marjoribanks, T. (2000). *News Corporation, Tehnology and the workplace*. Cambridge University Press. doi:10.1017/CBO9780511552137

Maslow, A. (2004). *Psychology in Management*. Adizes.

Mesmer-Magnus, J., & Viswesvaran, C. (2006). How family-friendly work enviroments affect work/family conflict: A Meta-analytic examination. *Journal of Labor Research, 27*(4).

Pavlović, N. (2013). *Kriza u društvu znanja,Ključne kompetencije u obrazovanju odraslih, Zbornik radova;Međunarodna konferencija u Hrvatskoj*. Vodice.

Pavlović, N. (2013). *Savremene koncepcije liderstva i organizacione kulture,Srednja škola „Đura Jakšić*. Rača.

Pavlović, N. (2015). *Nove uloge menadžmenta ljudskih resursa, SŠ Đura Jakšić*. Rača.

Pavlovic, N. (2016). *Poslovna kultura i etika, Univerzitet u Kragujevcu, Fakultet za hotelijerstvo I turizam u Vrnjačkoj Banji*. Vrnjačka Banja.

Pavlović, N., & Krstić, J. (2016). *Preduzetništvo i menadžment. Univerzitet u Kragujevcu, Fakultet za hotelijerstvo i turizam u Vrnjačkoj Banji*. Vrnjačka Banja.

Robbins, S., & Coulter, M. (2008). *Management* (8th ed.). Belgrade: DataStatus.

Robbins, S., & Judge, T. (2009). *Organizacijsko ponašanje (12th ed.)*. Zagreb: MATE.

Rodgers, C. (1993). The Flexible Workplace: What have We Learned? *Human Resource Management, 31*(1).

Rowe, K., & Howell, P. (2014). *The positive work place*. ASTD, Human Capital Community. Retrieved April, 2017, from http//:www.td.org/publication

Šator, G. (2011). *Harmonia zivota a byvania (2nd ed.)*. Bratislava: IKAR.

Schein, E. (2010). *Organizational Culture and leadership* (4th ed.). San Francisco, CA: Jossey-Bass.

Schumann, P. (2004). A Moral Principles Framework for Human Resource Management Ethics. *Human Resource Mangement RE:view, 11*(1).

Spector, E. (1997). *Job Satisfaction:Aplication, Assessment, Causes and Consequences*. Thousand Oaks, CA: SAGE.

Taghıpur, M., Mahboobi, M., Nikoefair, A., & Mowloodi, E. (2015). Analysing the Effect of Physical Conditions of the Workpalce on Employees Productivity. *International Journal of Environmental Protection and Policy, 3*(4).

Tannen, D. (1995). *You Just Do not Understand: Women and Men in Conversation*. New York: Ballantine Books.

Townsend, A., DeMarie, S., & Hendrickson, A. (2017). *Virtual teams: Technology and the workplace of the future*. Retrieved April, 2017, from http//www.amp.aom.or/content

Unicef CSR. (2017). Retrieved April, 2017, from http//:www.unicef.com/csr/235.htm

Vujić, D. (2008). Menadžment ljudskih resursa i kvalitet. Centar za primenjenu psihologiju.

Walden, M. (2017). *How Important is Your Work Environment?* ICS Insights. Retrieved April, 2017, from http//:www.infinity-cs.com

Wanous, J., & Reichers, E., & Hudy. (1997). Overall Job Satisfaction: How good Are Single-Item Measures? *The Journal of Applied Psychology, 4*(2). PMID:9109282

Watkins, M. (2013). What is Organizational Culture? And Why Should We care? *Harvard Business Review, 5*(10).

Williams, C. (2010). *Principi menadžmenta*. Beograd: DataStatus.

Chapter 5
Cross-Cultural Conflicts:
Concept, Causes, and Elucidations

Narendra Singh Chaudhary
Symbiosis International University, India

Radha Yadav
Jaipuria School of Business, India

ABSTRACT

The authors discuss in detail the meaning of conflict, cross-cultural conflict, the reasons for the conflicts, and its impact on overall organization performance and productivity. The authors also highlight and discuss the various strategies that can be worked out to reduce and resolve conflicts amicably and how to use conflicts for the betterment of the organization. The authors also focus upon the various issues and concerns that need to be taken care of while handling the conflicts and resolving them effectively. The authors have also drawn attention towards the future research perspectives, which will help organisations and management to address the cross-cultural conflicts and utilizing them for the betterment of the organisation in a constructive manner.

INTRODUCTION

As the world is progressing in this era of globalization, business world is making a move beyond their domestic territories to expand their businesses in the foreign land. The business world is now focusing on the geocentric approach to get the best person to carry out the job. The changed approach of the corporate world has now opened the job avenues for the potential talent giving them opportunity to experience and get exposed to the different opportunities and make best out of their competencies.

DOI: 10.4018/978-1-5225-4933-8.ch005

Copyright © 2018, IGI Global. Copying or distributing in print or electronic forms without written permission of IGI Global is prohibited.

People are now coming out of their closet and accepting assignments in the foreign land with a hope to learn and grow in their respective careers. As geographical distances are diminishing with people from various destinations are landing in the same workplace. With the growing dominance of the Multinationals Corporations in the business world, predominant cultures of the organizations are fading away, giving way to cultural mix giving acceptance to individuals from various origins and faith.

The popular organizations ranging from big corporate giants like Apple, Microsoft, Google or any other conglomerates like TATA, Reliance, Proctor and Gamble, HUL etc. are addressing the diversity at their workplace with a motive to reap out the benefits of the same. The workplace diversity has helped to channelize the potential of diversity and helped these organizations to grow and prosper and make a mark in the business world.

On one hand, where the diversity in the workforce is bringing its paybacks for the organizations on the other hand it is also giving rise to the conflicts originating from the diversity itself. It becomes essential for the organizations to give due consideration to the conflicts which arises owing to the existing cross cultural diversity at workplace.

Cross cultural diversity which nowadays is being treated as a boon may turn into bane if not handled carefully. Although, diversity embraces the individual differences based upon age, gender, race, ethnicity, value systems and personality but also provide the unexpected challenges. The challenges may range from cultural clash augmented with differing value systems hampering the overall work environment and disturbing the synergy at workplace. Chua (2013), is his research concluded that intercultural tensions and conflicts are inevitable in the global workplace and ambient culture disharmony disrupts creativity. The authors in the chapter will be discussing the definitions, concept of cross cultural conflicts and list out the probable causes responsible for occurrence of the conflicts and have also suggested the various methods through which conflicts could be brought down to create harmony and peace at work place which contributes to overall increase in the performance and productivity of the business firm/organisations.

Definition of Cross Cultural Conflict

The term "Cultural Conflict" was firstly used in year 1949.Cultural conflict is defined as "differences in values and beliefs that creates a disagreement between two parties". In terms of Culture, conflict relates to unharmonious or contradictory norms, values, priorities and motives.

In today's world, Business has been spreading all over the world to assure high sustainability and complete with their competitors. The time has come where Human

Resource from worldwide work under the one roof with holding the different culture of their country. 194 countries in the world with the 6500 spoken languages, it creates cross-cultural conflict at work place.

Cross-cultural conflict is defined as the most acute way to resolve significant socio-cultural and ethnic inconsistencies that arise in the course of intercultural interaction, which consists in counteraction of the subjects of conflict and is usually accompanied by negative emotions towards the representatives of another cultural group (Hurn & Tomalin, 2013; Weaver, 2001; Avruch et al., 1998).

There are lots of similarities and differences among the cultures. It is a possible link between the individualistic and collectivistic cultural values and their preferred styles of conflict resolution (Markus & Kitayama, 1991). One of the researchers notified in his research that culture is acquired and inculcated set of values and norms and not inherited from the past, (Alas, 2006). Famous researcher of culture studies, defined "culture as the sharing of the motives, values, beliefs, identities and interpretation from the common experience of group to the other generation" (Hofstede, 2001; Pachuki & Breiger, 2010; Morris et al., 1998) emphasized that "members of the same culture are likely to share a set of values acquired in the process of socialization – values that represent the acceptable modes of conduct in a particular society. When the shared values from the different culture are not acceptable by an individual, it creates culture conflict".

For e.g. India is a culturally diversified country with the 29 states, 22 official languages and different religions. Each state has its own values and beliefs; which creates intercultural conflict at the work place when people from other states come in the organisation.

Cultural Conflict is all about the expectations of an individual i.e. when individual's expectation of a certain behavior from individuals coming from different cultural backgrounds is not met (Grewe, 2005). It becomes difficult to resolve the parties' conflict, when it starts getting reflected in politics, especially at a macro level.

In the end, we can summarize that conflict is a confrontation or divergence of interests. This can be understood by two most widely used approaches. First approach, defines conflict as a clash of parties, opinions, strengths, etc. (Avruch et al., 1998). While second approach understands the conflict as a clash of opposing goals, interests, attitudes and worldviews of opponents or the subjects of interaction (Weaver, 2001). It is inevitable and occurs in organization every day to get better ideas or to make the point in front of management for the successful business.

Why Conflicts Arise?

Afzalur (2010) states that "conflict can arise between members of the same group, known as intergroup conflict, or it can occur between members of two or more groups, and involve violence, interpersonal discord, and psychological tension, known as intergroup conflict".

Conflict is as "the internal discord that results from differences in ideas, values, or feelings between two or more people" (Marquis & Huston, 1996). A conflict exists in an individual as well as in groups and organizations. A conflict arises, when there is a clash of opposite personalities and varied interests of the parties involved.

The conflicts can also be attributed to the opposing value systems and ethical judgments. It is obvious for the people to disagree and confront anything which they perceives will act as an obstruction in their way. The other caused can be dedicated to differing attitudes of the people, norms and rituals followed by them. As individual needs varies from person to person ranging from their goals and interests, differentiating them from each other, relying on their perception of self and others. However, common themes with different aims and viewpoints create a discord between individuals and groups or organization.

For Example: The cross cultural issues or conflicts which exist across cultures can be attributed to many factors ranging from language to perceptual mismatches. For instance, conflicts between Western and Asian cultures and their perspectives can be attributed to language; the first and obvious reason. Asians want that foreigners should pay respect and must put efforts to command the local language, whereas natives from Western culture treat English as a universal language which they feel everyone should observe as a primary medium of communication in the modern world.

Similarly, some cross-cultural issues/conflicts ascend out of the distinct perception of concepts of individualism and collectivism. On one hand, Asians rely on strong sense of collective viewpoint which makes them more inclined to work in groups followed by reliance upon other's group members for decision-making and pay high regards for cooperation and team work. They treat it as a best way to abate risks and reduce individual responsibilities. While on the other hand, Westerners are more independent in terms of their approach, actions and decisions to wards work and personal relationships due to existence of strong sense of individualistic attitude in them.

When it comes to risk aversion, both cultures adapt to varied styles of uncertainty avoidance. Asians are found trying more to avoid risks more in comparison to their Western counterparts like Americans. Asians in terms of risk taking feel it is better to be assured and save face/ personal repute than to face embarrassment, whereas in the similar situation natives from the Western world are seen more willing to chase risks due to their independent nature.

When the question arise regarding addressing conflicts, Asians have more upon trust their personal affiliations and depends highly on indirect manner to resolve conflicts. And, treat negotiation and compromise as best methods for conflict resolution. On the contrary, citizens of the Western world are more open and believe in direct confrontation and like to settle down things/issues through rational viewpoint, direct clarifications based upon evidences.

Researchers DuPraw and Axner 1996 have explored six major attributes leading to cultural differences – the means through which cultures, tends to differentiate from one another. These elucidations point out some of the frequent causes of cross-cultural conflicts (DuPraw & Axner, 1996)

1. Different Styles of Communication

The way people communicate varied across cultures. The use of language, particular words and sayings are different as per societal norms and acceptance. The degree of importance awarded to nonverbal communication involving facial expressions and gestures along with seating arrangements, personal space, and urgency of time. Even the difference in the observation of magnitude of assertiveness across cultures may also augment cross cultural misunderstandings.

2. Distinct Attitudes Toward Conflict

The way conflict is perceived by the individuals vary across the existing cultures, wherein some view conflict as positive while others treat it as negative thing which should be avoided. Like most of the people in eastern countries, perceive open conflict inappropriate and have a feeling of embarrassment and humiliation prefer to work out differences quietly. Written exchange is considered as preferential mode to resolve conflicts. On contrary, residents of western countries like USA, generally don't desire to have conflicts but people are often motivated to deal directly with conflicts that do arise. In fact, face-to-face interfaces are appreciated way to address whatever problems exist.

3. Different Approaches to Completing Tasks

The way people proceeds towards completion of tasks differentiate across the cultures. The prominent factors which segregate them includes uncommon access to resources, unlike verdicts of the incentives associated with task completion, different notions of time, and various thoughts about task orientation and work-relationship building should go hand in hand.

When the question arrives regarding working collectively on a task, cultures variation plays a dominant role in deciding establishment of relationships prior collaboration. This means the people from different cultural backgrounds pursue and move differently when it comes to forming relationships or accomplishing task.

4. Different of Styles Decision-Making

The styles of decision-making among individuals vary widely across cultures. For instance, in U.S., responsibilities are frequently delegated by senior colleagues for a particular task to a subordinate and practice prompt decision-making. But, in India decision making responsibilities lies mainly with Superior and great emphasis is placed on the hierarchy who takes final decisions. When decisions are to be taken in a group of people, going with majority is an accepted practice in the U.S., while in Japan more weightage is given to consensus mode. It has to be noted that expectation of an individuals' about their own roles in shaping a decision may got influenced by their cultural frame of reference.

5. Different Attitudes Toward Disclosure

All cultures have different approach towards disclosure of the information. Some are frank enough to talk about their emotions while some shows reluctance, about the causes behind conflict or a clash or any other personal information. You have to be cautious enough while dealing with conflict and be aware that people may differ in what they feel comfortable revealing. The things which seem natural to you-Why conflict arise? What was your involvement in it? How it occurs,-may seem intrusive to others. The disparities among cultures and attitude towards revelation need to be looked upon before giving concluding remarks about people based upon your views and experiences.

6. Different Approaches to Knowing

We can find notable differences occurring among cultural sets when it comes to epistemologies – that is, the means people come to know things. Like, Asian cultures' epistemologies tend to emphasize more upon the validity of knowledge gained through endeavoring toward transcendence whereas African cultures' rely more on symbolic imagery and rhythm as affective ways of knowing things. On the contrary, European cultures focus more on cognitive means like counting and measuring and treat it as a more valid approach to gain knowledge and know things.

Implications of the Cross Cultural Conflict Management

Cross Cultural conflicts can bring in serious implications to the business organisations, if not dealt carefully. It needs proactive approach to address the issues right before hand, it becomes grave and uncontrollable and starts impacting business negatively.

"Managing cultural conflict in your organization not only creates a more harmonious workplace. It also ensures that you reap the creative benefits of multiculturalism" (Blanding, 2013). The statement very much clarifies and highlights the necessity of the smooth harmonious relationships at work and also point out towards the repercussions that business may supposed to face due rise of conflicts.

As cross cultural diversity is the reality of the today's world with people of various nationalities working together under one roof with diverse intentions and expectations. No one can deny the fact that on one hand cross cultural diversity brings in talent pool which augments and enhance the profitability and overall wellbeing of the organisations.

The organisations which are able to embrace its diversity by recognizing the cultural and perceptual differences reap the benefit of its talent team by using cooperative conflict management styles otherwise face the tough situation in handling its multicultural workforce leading to conflicts and affecting the motivational levels of the employees and their morale negatively. In a research study conducted by (Chen et al., 2005) where they interviewed 111 Chinese employees in Shanghai and found that a cooperative conflict management approach positively pays to work productivity and relationships among foreign managers and Chinese employees, whereas a competitive or avoidance approach is negatively associated to work productivity and relationships. The cross cultural conflicts can lead to serious implications on the overall organisation functioning with low performance and financial losses to the organisation.

Exhibit 1: Culture Clash at Pharmacia and Upjohn

'Despite being part of the same advanced, industrialized world, Kalamazoo (Michigan, United States), Stockholm (Sweden), and Milan (Italy) are worlds apart in many important ways. Senior managers leading the merger between two pharmaceutical firms, Upjohn Company of the United States and Pharmacia AB of Sweden (with operations in Italy), came to realize how significant these differences were after the merger took place in 1995.

Swedes take off most of the month of July for their annual vacation, Italians take off most of August. Not knowing this, US executives scheduled meetings in the summer only to have to cancel many because their European counterparts were at the beach. As the more dominant US firm began to impose its way of doing things on the newly acquired European organizations, international relationships became increasingly strained.

Neither the Swedes nor the Italians were happy with impositions such as the drug and alcohol testing policy brought in by Upjohn, or the office smoking ban. These clashed with local ways of doing things and the more informal work environment that these cultures prefer. Although

Upjohn later relaxed many of these work rules, allowing some local practices and preferences to prevail, ill-feeling and a degree of resistance had already developed among European colleagues.

The additional bureaucracy and the command-and control style imposed by the Americans created more significant problems for the 34,000 employees and managers in Pharmacia and Upjohn Company. The Swedes were used to an open, team-based style of management where responsibilities are devolved; managers are trusted and not strictly monitored or closely managed. Swedish executives also tend to build up a consensus behind big decisions, "getting everyone in the same boat" (alla aer i baten) rather than handing orders down the hierarchy. As a traditional US multinational, however, Upjohn was more used to strong leadership and a centralized command-and control structure. Its CEO, Dr. John Zabriskie, quickly created a strict reporting system, tight budget control, and frequent staffing updates, which clashed with the Swedish organization style. Swedish managers would leave meetings disgruntled, having been overruled by US executives keen to push their vision of the merged company.

The Swedes' own ways of doing things had already clashed with the Italian style of management, following the takeover of Farmitalia (part of Montedison) by Pharmacia in 1993. Italians are used to a distinctive division between workers (and their strong unions) and managers. Their steeper hierarchies contrast the more egalitarian Swedes. Italians also place a high value on families and will leave work to tend to sick relatives or help with childcare, which the Swedes frown upon. The addition of the Americans from Upjohn to this mix created further cultural confusion. Communication problems, beyond the obvious language differences, became a real barrier to honest dialogue. "You go there thinking you're going to streamline the place," said American Mark H. Corrigan, Pharmacia and Upjohn Vice President for Clinical Development, "and you leave just having added five pounds from some wonderful meals."

These differences, many of them small but important at the local level, quickly began to have an impact on the overall performance of the merged company. In the months and years following the merger unforeseen inefficiencies and added costs began to undermine the potential synergies of bringing together two such companies in the *first place. At one level the problems amounted to things like canceled meetings, new organization demands (such as monthly report writing), and a general decline in staff morale. There were also unexpected difficulties integrating the IT systems across the various parts of the merged organization. These and other changes added an estimated $200 million to the predicted costs of the restructuring, taking the total cost to $800 million. Even more seriously, for a pharmaceutical company heavily reliant on its new drugs pipeline to survive, delayed product launches and the loss of key staff (including the head of R&D at Pharmacia) had a longer-term impact. "There was probably an under-appreciation ... of these cultural differences," says Art Atkinson, former Vice President for Clinical Research and Development.*

Particular problems resulted from the restructuring of the firm's global R&D structure. Prior to the merger Upjohn owned well-known names such as Rogaine and Motrin and had annual sales of around $3.5 billion, but had a weak new product pipeline and slow sales growth compared to its larger competitors. Similar-sized Pharmacia had a more promising pipeline but weak distribution and sales in the US market, the world's largest. These amounted to a strong rationale for the merger. Together they could challenge the financial power and the larger R&D programs of their competitors. However, integrating and refocusing the various parts of the new R&D structure became a major problem. Rather than place the R&D headquarters in the United States, Sweden, or Milan, a decision was made to establish a new and neutral London based center for the R&D function. This simply added a layer of management and a more complex matrix reporting structure, which further alienated key R&D personnel.

In 1997, after the stock price of the merged corporation had fallen significantly, CEO John Zabriskie resigned. Swede Jan Ekberg, the former head of Pharmacia, took over temporarily and began to rebuild aspects of the merged organization.

After acquiring a major part of Monsanto in 2000, Pharmacia and Upjohn became Pharmacia, which was then itself acquired by the US giant Pfizer in April 2003.

This made Pfizer, according to its own Annual Report, the "number one pharmaceutical company in every region of the World."

All this proves is that going global is hard work. Not all of these problems could have been foreseen, but a real lack of awareness of cultural differences did lead to many of the organization difficulties and people problems with a real impact on the bottom line.'

Sources: (Frank & Burton, 1997; Thomas, 2000; Pfizer, 2003 as cited in International Culture, 2008)

How to Manage the Cross-Cultural Conflict Management

Cross-cultural management is an art to manage the behavior of the employees in a cross-cultural context. It is an essential part of the organization to understand and articulate the common values and beliefs among the organization's members. Managers and top management need to play an active role to recognize the behaviors and perceptions of the employees at the situation of the cross-cultural issues and should take proactive steps to avoid the same.

The three important points that should be recalled to manage the cross-cultural conflicts are: Adaptability, Understanding and Communication- Where adaptability refers to the term respect for each other's values, traditions and beliefs. It is highly appreciated notion; if diverse workforce understands that they have to work collectively to attain the objectives of the organization, which in turn leads them to realize their specified personal goals.

Understanding depicts the feeling, empathy, compassion and concern of the employees at the work place. Here, understanding is to understand the each other's feelings and respond accordingly. Communication states exchange or sharing of information and clarifying misunderstandings with the concerned person before it converts into grievances due to involvement of ego or self-respect and promotes cordial relationships at work.

In this era of globalization, companies have been using global communication technologies across boundaries to solve the cross-cultural conflicts and gain the benefits of the cultural diversity. By accepting, conflict as inevitable part of life, organisations can make the most of every situation and can be used as a learning opportunity. This can be further utilized as a prospect to transform the situation into something better. Researchers have proposed the typology of five behavioral styles that helps to resolve the cross-cultural conflicts. The (Thomas & Kilmann, 1974) Conflict Mode Instrument is widely used for handling conflict given in figure 1. The five behavioral styles are named as: Competing style, Avoiding style, compromising style, Accommodating style and Collaborating style. These five behavioral styles are encircled by the two approaches; one is active style and another passive style.

The Thomas Kilmann Conflict Mode Instrument is a model for handling conflict (Figure 1).

Collaborating style and competing style follows the active style in which there is a (Win-Win) and (Win-Lose) situation respectively, while on the other hand,

Figure 1. Thomas Kilmann conflict mode instrument

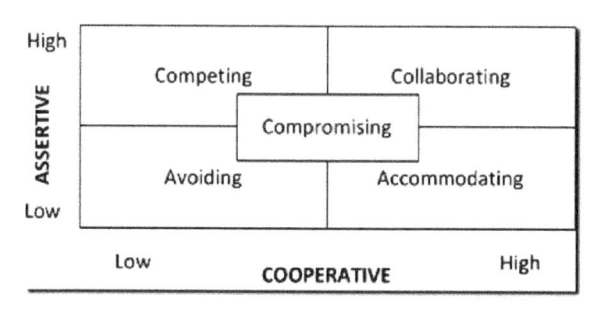

avoiding style results in lose-lose, compromising leads to (I Lose /Win Some–You Lose/ Win Some) followed by (I lose-You win) situation in the accommodating style to resolve the cross-cultural conflicts. (Hurn & Tomalin, 2013; Avruch et al., 1998; Song et al., 2009). For Example: - In a study significant cultural differences were being observed in the Australian and Chinese countries, wherein Australians prefer active behavioural styles to resolve the cross-cultural conflicts whereas Chinese inclined more towards passive behavioral styles of conflict management (Leung & Chan, 1999). It shows that Australians believe in win-lose and win-win approach and Chinese aspire for more harmonious and compassionate approach (Hurn & Tomalin, 2013).

Researchers have put forwarded their argument that face act as an explanatory mechanism for conflicting behaviour in varied cultural groups during development of face negotiation theory (Toomey & Kurogi,1988). The theory suggested three major variables, .i.e. cultural, individual and situational. These three variables influence a person's choice of given set of face concerns over others. Consequently, the selection of diverse sets of face concerns affects the use of various face works and conflict management strategies in social encounters.

Researcher further pointed out that "conflict management style" is a culturally accepted notion, which displays that culture play's an influential role, in an individual's preference for conflict management styles (Toomey, 2006). In a similar, study carried out by (Weaver, 2001) also depicted the similar results that conflict resolution style depends upon the culture of the concerned parties. People from the same culture would apprehend and accept each other's approach in handling conflicts much easier than those from other cultures. Further, studies have shown that organizational problems become greater than before in the culturally diverse workplace because of the difference in the workers' cultural values, attitudes, and work styles (Chan & Goto, 2003; Leung & Chan, 1999; Sauceda, 2003).

Strategies to Reduce Conflicts

Cross Cultural diversity is very much appreciated at workplace as it pools the talent at one place, but it can lead to several cultural clashes. Conflicts which may vary from opposing viewpoints to diverse styles of communication can stimulate the climate of distrust and negativity, there by harming the overall productivity and the bottom line of the organisation. It is therefore essential to reduce the conflicts and promote synergy at workplace and utilize the available talent at workplace to its fullest. Few strategies that can be used to minimize the cross cultural conflicts are listed below.

1. Promotion of Cultural Awareness

Cultural awareness is a vital component to resolve conflicts in multicultural workplaces. The awareness can be generated through diversity training sessions and workshops, lectures and key note speeches, discussions and participation in conferences. Although, cross cultural conflicts cannot not be avoided completely but can be minimized to great extent through extending awareness with strategies to resolve the issues when they do arise.

Cultural awareness helps the people at workplace to understand the complexities of various cultural traditions and behaviours which influence the employee interactions. Better understanding of the culture by the employees represented at workplace leads to fewer clashes and leads to greater respect for their peers and their cultural sentiments. The quote cited below says it all- "If we are going to live with our deepest differences then we must learn about one another." —— Deborah J. Levine, Matrix Model Management System: Guide to Cross Cultural Wisdom

2. Modify Communication Styles

Communication styles should be altered as per the requirement of the prevailing cross cultural environments. Changes should be proposed on the basis of the cultures which are more prominent at workplace. A good example from the article written by Toegel and Barsoux (2016):

Norms of Participation differs significantly across cultures. Team members from more democratic and individualistic nations, such as the U.S. or Australia, may be adapted to voicing their unfiltered opinions and ideas, while those from more graded cultures, such as India, tend to speak up only after more senior colleagues have expressed their views. People from some cultures may feel shy to contribute because they worry about coming across as superficial or foolish; Finns, for example, favor a "think before you speak" approach, in stark contrast to the "shoot from the hip" attitude that is more prevalent among Americans.

3. Introducing Fundamental Vagaries Reflecting Workplace Diversity

A conflict generally arises at workplace due to reflection of only one culture when following structural procedures. If structural norms are blamable for workplace conflict, they must be addressed by the top management well in time. A mediator should be roped in to assess the situation and suggest conflict resolution techniques by recommending systemic changes that can be implemented to avoid future problems.

For example, if confrontation is operationally built into workplace meetings and other congregations, it may be wise to phase this out, especially if cultures opposed to heavy confrontation are well represented in the workplace.

Moreover, precise processes must be put in place for communications with outsourced employees in diverse countries, because already significant cultural conflicts can be intensified by digital communication.

4. Identifying Cultural Conflicts

Identification of the signs of cultural conflicts should be done well in time. It would prove helpful in reducing cultural conflicts or tensions. Thus, it is essential to be culturally sensitive in a workplace; taking into consideration that cultural differences are not amplified.

5. Providing With Cross Cultural Training Programmes

HR department need to take initiatives to organize cross cultural training workshops, seminars, conferences to make the people familiar and sensitive to the cultural aspects of the fellow employees and working upon their contextual intelligence which improves the ability of the people to understand the limits of their knowledge and help them to adapt the knowledge of an environment, different from the one in which it was developed. This will help the employees to be sensitive to wards culture of each other without being getting judgmental and pointing out flaws which indirectly spoils the harmony of the entire organisation leading to bad work culture and demotivation.

6. Appointment of Cultural Mentors

The cultural mentors can help a lot in resolving the cross cultural conflicts by making the people aware of the various cultural aspects, norms and behaviour which should be adopted and followed without compromising on their owns and provides a smooth transition for multicultural workforce from cultural shock. It will also help the people to be more sensitive and acceptable to each other culturally which will reduce the cultural barriers between them leading to healthy work relationships which impacts the overall productivity and performance of the organisation.

7.   Reworking on Organisation Culture

Organisations need to rework on their organisation climate by laying down its foundation on the basis of trust, tolerance and mutual respect which binds the people at work together and make them feel as one. It helps in overcoming the cross cultural conflicts by avoiding any kind of stereotyping and biasedness. This can be done by making use of cultural bump theory which addresses the structural need for a change mechanism in cultural programming by incorporating both the strengths of diversity and cross cultural communication training by recognizing and delineating cultural differences. The culture bump (cultural difference) is a phenomenon which arises when an individual has expectations of a particular behaviour within a specific situation and encounters a unlike behaviour when interacting with an individual from a different culture.

FUTURE RESEARCH DIRECTIONS

The authors have tried to explain the concepts and have identified the related causes giving rise to cross cultural conflicts. An attempt has been made to analyze the implications cross cultural conflicts cast on overall organisation performance and productivity. The suggestions or remedial action that can be initiated to resolve the conflicts are also proposed. In future, the researchers can try to propose and initiate work on how conflict can affect the business sustainability and find out appropriate preventive strategies by conducting longitudinal studies on real time data sourced from the corporations employing multicultural workforce. This will provide better understanding of cross cultural diversity issues in real world.

CONCLUSION

The cross cultural diversity has become hardcore reality of today's world and its impact varies from the type of organizational climate and overall strategy of a companies. As more and more firms are moving globally and entering international business arena from their domestic periphery, the impact of cross cultural diversity has increased manifold times. It's very important to manage the cultural differences efficiently for generating gains and getting overall competitive edge. Resolution of cross cultural conflicts is important for the sustainability of the business firms in the long run. It is imperative for organisations to rework and put the heads together to chalk out the roadmap to make the best use of the talent pool available.

The organizations have to ensure that cross cultural diversity is not impacting their organizational culture and affecting their overall productivity and performance. On one hand, where the diversity brings in the strengths of the various culture altogether under one roof and give boost to overall organizational performance and leads it way to success. The journey of success can be put on hold, if conflicts are not addressed at the right point of time. It is essential to channelize the energy of conflicts positively for the overall betterment and welfare of the organization by resolving the conflicts in an agreeable manner.

So, it's imperative for the business firms to capitalize the gains they can achieve by embracing cultural differences at workplace for the betterment and bright future prospects of the business entities by converting bane into boon. As rightly said in the given quote:

Where cross-cultural engagement is concerned, token adjustments are no longer an option. To advance a credible message of God's love for all people in an increasingly diverse society, we must move ourselves entirely as well as the churches we lead. We must adjust to a new reality. (DeYmaz, 2017)

REFERENCES

Afzalur, R. M. (2010). *Managing conflict in organizations.* Transaction Publishers.

Alas, R. (2006). Ethics in countries with different cultural dimensions. *Journal of Business Ethics, 69*(3), 237–247. doi:10.1007/s10551-006-9088-3

Alas, R., & Vadi, M. (2006). The impact of organisational culture on organisational learning and attitudes concerning change from an institutional perspective. *International Journal of Strategic Change Management, 1*(1-2), 155–170. doi:10.1504/IJSCM.2006.011109

Avruch, K. (1998). *Culture & conflict resolution* (Vol. 31). US Institute of Peace Press.

Avruch, K., Black, P., & Scimecca, J. (Eds.). (1998). *Conflict Resolution: Cross-Cultural Perspectives.* New York: Praeger.

Blanding, M. (2013). *How Cultural Conflict undermines workplace creativity.* Retrieved from https://www.forbes.com/sites/hbsworkingknowledge/2013/12/09/how-cultural-conflict-undermines-workplace-creativity/#367bbfb6214f

Chan, D. K. S., & Goto, S. G. (2003). Conflict resolution in the culturally diverse workplace: Some data from Hong Kong employees. *Applied Psychology, 52*(3), 441–460. doi:10.1111/1464-0597.00143

Chaudhary, N. S. (2017). *Cross Cultural Diversity Boon or Bane?* Retrieved August, 23, 2017 from https://www.peoplematters.in/article/culture/cross-cultural-diversity-boon-or-bane-16070

Chen, Y., Tjosvold, D., & Fang, S. S. (2005). Working with foreign managers: Conflict management for effective leader relationships in China. *International Journal of Conflict Management, 16*(3), 265–286. doi:10.1108/eb022932

Chua, R. Y. (2013). The costs of ambient cultural disharmony: Indirect intercultural conflicts in social environment undermine creativity. *Academy of Management Journal, 56*(6), 1545–1577. doi:10.5465/amj.2011.0971

DeYmaz, M., (2017). *Disruption: Repurposing the Church to Redeem the Community.* Nashville, TN: Thomas Nelson; HarperCollins Christian Publishing, Inc.

DuPraw, M. E., & Axner, M. (1997). Working on common cross-cultural communication challenges. In *Toward a More Perfect Union in an Age of Diversity: A Guide to Building Stronger Communities through Public Dialogue.* Academic Press.

Frank, R., & Burton, T. M. (1997, February 4). Pharmacia & Upjohn Faces Culture Clash; Europeans Chafe Under US Rules. *Wall Street Journal.*

Grewe, A. (2005). *"I'm sick to death with you..." or External Character Conflicts in Fawlty Towers.* Munich: GRIN Verlag.

Hofstede, G. (2001). *Culture's consequences: Comparing values, behaviors, institutions, and organizations across nations.* Thousand Oaks, CA: Sage.

Hurn, B., & Tomalin, B. (2013). *Cross-cultural communication: Theory and practice.* Springer. doi:10.1057/9780230391147

Hurn, B. J., & Tomalin, B. (2013). What is Cross-Cultural Communication? In Cross-Cultural Communication (pp. 1-19). Palgrave Macmillan UK.

International Culture. (2008). *The Environment of International Business.* Retrieved from http://www.unice.fr/crookall-cours/iup_cult/_docs/_RUGM_Chapter-05.pdf

Leung, K., & Chan, D. K. S. (1999). Conflict management across cultures. In J. Adamopoulos & Y. Kashima (Eds.), *Social psychology and cultural context: Essays in honor of Harry C. Triandis* (pp. 177–188). Thousand Oaks, CA: Sage. doi:10.4135/9781452220550.n13

Markus, H. R., & Kitayama, S. (1991). Culture and the self: Implications for cognition, emotion, and motivation. *Psychological Review, 98*(2), 224–253. doi:10.1037/0033-295X.98.2.224

Marquis, B. K., & Huston, C. J. (1996). *Leadership Roles and Managers Function in Nursing* (2nd ed.). Philadelphia, PA: Lippincott.

Morris, M. W., Williams, K. Y., Leung, K., Larrick, R., Mendoza, M. T., Bhahtnagar, D., & Hu, J. C. et al. (1998). Conflict management style: Accounting for cross-national differences. *Journal of International Business Studies, 29*(4), 729–747. doi:10.1057/palgrave.jibs.8490050

Pachucki, M. A., & Breiger, R. L. (2010). Cultural holes: Beyond relationality in social networks and culture. *Annual Review of Sociology, 36*(1), 205–224. doi:10.1146/annurev.soc.012809.102615

Sauceda, J. M. (2003). Managing intercultural conflict effectively. In L. A. Samovar & R. E. Porter (Eds.), *Intercultural communication: A reader* (pp. 385–405). Belmont, CA: Wadsworth.

Song, J. H., Kim, H. M., & Kolb, J. A. (2009). The effect of learning organization culture on the relationship between interpersonal trust and organizational commitment. *Human Resource Development Quarterly, 20*(2), 147–167. doi:10.1002/hrdq.20013

Thomas, K. W., & Kilmann, R. H. (1974). *Conflict Mode Instrument*. Sterling Forest, NY: Xicom Inc.

Thonas, R.J. (2000). Irreconcilable Differences. *Accenture Outlook, 1*.

Ting-Toomey, S. (2006). Managing intercultural conflict effectively. In L. A. Samovar, R. E. Porter, & E. R. McDaniel (Eds.), *Intercultural communication: A reader* (pp. 366–377). Belmont, CA: Wadsworth.

Ting-Toomey, S., & Kurogi, A. (1998). Facework competence in intercultural conflict: An updated face-negotiation theory. *International Journal of Intercultural Relations, 22*(2), 187–225. doi:10.1016/S0147-1767(98)00004-2

Toegel, G., & Barsoux, J. L. (2016). *3 Situations where cross-cultural communication creaks down*. Retrieved from https://hbr.org/2016/06/3-situations-where-cross-cultural-communication-breaks-down

Weaver, G. R. (2001). Ethics programs in global businesses: Culture's role in managing ethics. *Journal of Business Ethics*, *30*(1), 3–15. doi:10.1023/A:1006475223493

Section 3
Management Techniques for Cultural Issues and Diversity

Chapter 6
Thinking Globally, Leading Locally:
Defining Leadership in Diverse Workforce

Gursimranjit Singh
I. K. Gujral Punjab Technical University, India

Priyanka Singh
I. K. Gujral Punjab Technical University, India

Maninder Singh
Amritsar College of Engineering and Technology, India

ABSTRACT

Global leadership effectiveness has become one of the major issues in human resource management. It is very important for cross-cultural managers to take into consideration the paradigm shift in the business world, keeping in mind the opportunity for organizational growth and individual development. The key issue that the present corporate leaders have to face is to formulate action plans to tackle diversity in the workforce covering the broader spectrum of dimensions, vis-à-vis, ethnicity, age, gender, educational background, economic status, marital status, and skill sets. Since the corporate environment is greatly accelerated by the globalization and advancements in technology, global leaders need to attain a set of competencies that would facilitate them to realize their vision and thus enhance their performance efficiency and competitiveness. The chapter deals with the specific paradigms of the leadership styles and the management of workforce diversity so as to establish the linkages between leadership style and diversity management.

DOI: 10.4018/978-1-5225-4933-8.ch006

INTRODUCTION

There were never in the world two opinions alike; any more than two hairs or two grains. The most universal quality is diversity. (Michel de Montaigne)

In the recent times, a critical success factor of globalization depends on the potential of a leader who can manage diverse workforce along with solving complex business strategies. One of the mantras for global business success is how effectively a leader manages the diverse workforce. Leadership has become the principal component for all the organizations.

The increase in global market has generated need for international corporations. Global leadership effectiveness has become one of the major issues in human resource management. The discipline of human resource management is looking for an answer that how global leadership should be performed in an effective way in such a competitive tough global market in international business and workforce management.

Leadership is the heart and soul of all organizations but its role and capacity is getting more complex with the enhanced involvement with the technology and global environment. Technological advances have changed the way how organizations do business. It is very important for cross cultural managers to take into consideration the paradigm shift in business world keeping in mind opportunity for organizational growth and individual development. Moreover, international business should focus on the impact of demographics, work ethics, technological advancements, specific job skills to cope with the global changes.

For understanding how organizations are structured and how they are operating, the eco-system model has been applied to the human system. There are many challenges which organizations are facing like demographic changes in workforce combined with international competition both within and outside the organization. Many top brains of the world argue that for surviving in global environment necessitates the development of competitive advantage out of the diverse workplace (Soutar, 2004; Yang, 2005; Kreitz, 2007). But to do so, human resource managers and leaders should redefine management (Jones, 1989). There are many instances that single handed diversity solutions such as concentrating on recruitment or single approach management techniques vis-à-vis providing diversity training to the employees do not create lasting changes (Kossek and Lobel, 1996; McMohan, 2006; Thomas, 1990). Leadership requires commitment, strategy, concrete changes in organizational structure for handling diverse workforce for their growth and holistic development.

Now the question arises as to how HR managers and leaders can take optimum advantage of the diversity? What roles and responsibilities are to be fulfilled by the global leaders in creating and managing diverse organizations? Since diversity is a challenging phenomenon to govern in any organization, it has been extensively researched upon now-a-days. It deals with the issues like being alike and different, religion and culture, justice and tolerance etc. all the nations across the globe are impacted by the opportunities and challenges in the diversity. The present chapter deals with the specific paradigms of the leadership styles and the management of workforce diversity so as to establish the linkages between the leadership style and diversity management.

The proposed chapter envisages addressing comprehensively issues related to leadership in diverse workforce. The chapter would address on the one hand current and urgent issues such as leadership style, cross cultural workforce, workforce conflicts, talent generation and leadership competitiveness such that the quality of leadership in global markets can be enhanced. On the other hand, it also envisages that the effectiveness of global leader would pursue long term goal of building a strong professional global leadership by setting performance standards and creating top class work environment.

The present chapter will highlight leadership in diverse workforce across the globe. It is proposed that leadership style across diverse cultural workforce should have an international mentoring leader such that it benefits from the global best practices and act as a think tank for the global leaders.

Cultural context is becoming one of the significant variables in leadership as employer employee relationship, work ethics, communication styles differ from nation to nation. Leadership abilities are seen differently in different countries. In countries like China, Japan etc., employees rely on non-verbal codes. However, in countries like Great Britain, Germany etc., employees tend to communicate directly. In contrast, employees of Asian countries feel individual praising will influence group harmony and manager should praise entire group. There should be no personal bias in cultural differences as by doing so leaders can better fulfill their responsibility of creating multi-cultural workplace.

Concept of Diversity

The term diversity is defined to include all the characteristics and the experiences that define each one of us as an individual. The Diversity Task Force explains this term by including Race, Ethnicity, Gender, Age, Religion, Disability and Sexual orientation, referred to as "REGARDS". This is based on the simple notion that we all are individuals and possesses different qualities along each of these dimensions.

The term diversity as a concept can be powerful as well as emotional for the people who are dealing with it, either implicitly or explicitly. Diversity has been a dynamic concept, diversity as a concept is both specific as well as it focuses on individual, and contextual, defined through constructs of the society (Moore, 1999). Generally speaking, diversity can be explained as a concept that distinguishes one individual from another that embraces hidden qualities of an individual.

A plethora of research (Digh, 1998a; How, 2007; Johnson, 2003; Simmons-Welburn, 1993) has identified four broader areas of diversity, namely,

1. Personality (traits, skills, abilities)
2. External (culture, religion, nationality, marital or parental status)
3. Internal (IQ, ethnicity, race, gender)
4. Organizational (department, union / non-union, position)

What Is Diversity?

Though the concept of diversified workforce is in existence for a pretty long time, but it gained much popularity in the recent times. Due to the volatile situation sin businesses and the urge to beat the cut throat competition, the need to have a diversified human base was felt. US, UK and many European countries had observed the effects of increase in diversity on production capacity of business and economies of these countries.

It was found that immigration of large number of people from other countries have changed not only the demographic conditions but also the ethnicity, regional, cultural and socio-economic situations. Hence, diversity management got the attraction of various academicians and for the first time, the term "Diversity Management" was coined in the Hudson Institute's Publication Workforce in the year 2000.

The plethora of research on this theme has witnessed that the countries having more diversified population in terms of ethnicity and other characteristics have greater pace of development in various fields. For instance, look at the case of scientists working in NASA. It has been documented that these scientists have given break-through discoveries and resulted in the prosperity of US and increased its dominance in the global scenario.

The term diversity is defined to include all the characteristics and the experiences that define each one of us as an individual. The Diversity Task Force explains this term by including Race, Ethnicity, Gender, Age, Religion, Disability and Sexual orientation, referred to as "REGARDS". This is based on the simple notion that we all are individuals and possess different qualities along each of these dimensions.

Diversity management is not about how we differ; it is about embracing one another's uniqueness. As the globalization is approaching to a next level, and the concept of equality is getting promoted by each and every organization in the world, we are embracing a practice of a wide domain of differences in life styles and personal characteristics within a defined group. In today's world, a diverse workforce is to be incorporated into every organization to make it a key to growth in the fiercely competitive global marketplace. It is not only restricted to demographic, cultural, regional or socio-economic differences, but also includes various dissimilarities on gender, education, skills and color. To minimize the workplace conflicts and misunderstandings in the chain of communication, we need to accept that our world is more diverse than ever.

It is not only about acquiring the necessary knowledge and dynamic skills to manage, but also an essential element of stakeholder management. Diversity management is one of the most challenging and bottom line issue for the managers and leaders as it encompasses different perspectives of different people and also helps in enhancing the work skills and productivity.

Three Postulates for Managing Diversity

1. Embracing diversity in an organization means to recruit and retain employees with a systematic and planned commitment.
2. Understanding different opinions, beliefs, values and skills to make the organizations believe in practicing equality.
3. For reaping the benefits of communication and to overcome the issue of racial and gender biasness, the organization should adopt inclusion of diversified workforce, which is non-vulnerable to group think.

Relationship Between Diversity, Imaginativeness, Innovation and Competitiveness

Creativity is a pre-requisite for successful innovation. Companies having more diversified workforce tend to have a huge potential of innovative ideas that further provide them a competitive edge over the others in market. Diversity promotes application of unique personal skills of employees towards achieving the goals of the organization.

In the present dynamic world, the businesses have to remain sustainable and retain their competitiveness and to survive in such conditions there is a need for providing more value to their products and this could be done through innovation and product development. The process of making enhanced or new product requires a large pool of ideas and skills. Such requirements can be fulfilled by employing a uniform workforce. Hence, adding people having diversity will provide more talent and acknowledging their specialty set of skills.

BACKGROUND

In light of the leadership effectiveness in today's globalized world, the concept of cultural quotient (Rockstuhl et al. 2011) is very much relevant since cultural quotient is mainly related to international experience an individual possesses (Lovuorn and Chen, 2011). Global leader should be proactive and appreciate the diversity they face in leadership to overcome conflicts at workplace.

Cultural context is becoming one of the significant variables in leadership as employer employee relationship, work ethics, and communication styles differ from nation to nation. Leadership abilities are seen differently in different countries. In countries like China, Japan etc., employees rely on non-verbal codes. However, in countries like Great Britain, Germany etc., employees tend to communicate directly. In contrast, employees of Asian countries feel individual praising will influence group harmony and manager should praise entire group. There should be no personal bias in cultural differences as by doing so leaders can better fulfill their responsibility of creating multi-cultural workplace.

It has been widely accepted notion that a diverse workforce is fundamental to corporate success. The key issue that the present corporate leaders have to face is to formulate the action plans so as to tackle the diversity in workforce covering the broader spectrum of dimensions vis-à-vis ethnicity, age, gender, educational background, economic status, marital status and skill sets. It has been seen that over the past two decades, workforce has undergone tremendous changes and this has unveiled the various challenges in front of these corporate managers. In essence, it can be said that in order to manage a diverse workforce, a successful leadership requires excellence across a broader range of skills. It is firmly apprehended that diversity is not self-managing as in most of the instances, whenever diversity is introduced in the workplace; it is the baseline requirement on the part of the leaders to take a proactive role in taking effective steps for incorporating that diversity in the work culture of the organization.

Since the corporate environment is greatly accelerated by the globalization and advancements in technology, the global leaders in the present times need to attain a set of competencies that would facilitate them to realize their vision and thus, enhance their performance efficiency and competitiveness.

Our success as a global company is a direct result of our diverse and talented workforce. Our ability to develop new consumer insights and ideas and to execute in a superior way across the world is the best possible testimony to the power of diversity any organization could ever have. (John Pepper, CEO, Procter & Gamble, 1998)

DIVERSITY AFFECTS THE WORLD

It has been widely accepted notion that a diverse workforce is fundamental to corporate success. The key issue that the present corporate leaders have to face is to formulate the action plans so as to tackle the diversity in workforce covering the broader spectrum of dimensions vis-à-vis ethnicity, age, gender, educational background, economic status, marital status and skill sets. It has been seen that over the past two decades, workforce has undergone tremendous changes and this has unveiled the various challenges in front of these corporate managers. In essence, it can be said that in order to manage a diverse workforce, a successful leadership requires excellence across a broader range of skills. It is firmly apprehended that diversity is not self-managing as in most of the instances, whenever diversity is introduced in the workplace; it is the baseline requirement on the part of the leaders to take a proactive role in taking effective steps for incorporating that diversity in the work culture of the organization.

Since the corporate environment is greatly accelerated by the globalization and advancements in technology, the global leaders in the present times need to attain a set of competencies that would facilitate them to realize their vision and thus, enhance their performance efficiency and competitiveness.

Leadership Styles and Workforce Diversity

The workforce diversity has emerged as one of the biggest challenges for present employers due to its social, economic and moral implications (Lappetito, 1994). Leadership is one of the fundamental components of any organization. With the enhanced involvement in globalization and technological advancements, the global leadership has undergone a tremendous change in terms of its function and capacity. In 21st century, only those leaders can survive who can manage diversity and implement complex business strategies in light of this cross cultural leaders need to manage the diverse workforce with efficiency and effectiveness, known as cultural quotient. It is also known as cultural intelligence (Rockstuhl et al., 2011). As cultural intelligence is related with global experience of leaders, an attempt should be made to evaluate the cultural differences that exist in leadership practices so that they can be on the front foot to solve the complex and dynamic concerns of the diverse workforce.

Challenges for Global Leaders

A workplace to be successful needs a healthy relationship between global leaders and their followers. With the change in global business environment, such as sophisticated technology, innovation, change in demographics has bought a transformation into human life and work. In order to remain competitive, it is essential to build loyalty and trust and establish a close independent link between global HR leaders and followers. Lussier (2005) advocated that there is a significant impact of manager-employer relationship on the behaviour of the employees and hence enhances the degree of their commitment to the leader as well as organization. This reinforces the need to enhance the relationship by spending time together and fulfilling the needs and expectations of the followers, thereby generating value for the organization by guiding and influencing the employees to strive towards the organizational goals. In order to remain competitive and successful, a strong consensus of effective leadership skills is required to overcome global transformation chaos and contribute to sustainable advantage (Amagoh, 2009; Caligiuri and Tarique, 2012; Ulrich and Smallwood, 2012).

Single Work Culture

One of the biggest challenges in front of global leaders is to have people from different cultures and ethnic backgrounds. Along with this challenge, leaders also need to address the issues of demographic differences such as gender, age, race, religion, disability etc. (Anderson and Bostian, 2001; Bock and Greco, 2002).

Workplace Agreement

The other main challenge which lies in front of global leader is to get professional consent and developing a proper understanding of the diverse workforce. Due to varied opinions, thoughts and mindsets of followers these value based differences have to be resolved timely with the help of innovativeness and creative and logical thinking (Johnson, 2002).

Diverse Workforce

With organizational workforce comprising of people from all the generations, it becomes extremely important to manage such a diverse workforce in terms of varying lifestyles, goals, demands etc (Bear and Bostian, 2002; Kelly, 2001).

Uniting Virtual World

The other challenge ahead of a global leader is of uniting virtual teams and strategic e-business partners. Multiple teams working in a virtual world where members communicate electronically and may never meet face to face also is the biggest challenge for global leaders (McCuiston, Wooldridge and Pierce, 2004).

Work Life Balance

The increased number of roles and responsibilities for the employees has posed a threat to balancing the work life by generating various role conflicts. With the increasing number of single parents working in organizations throughout the globe, they develop practices that encourage culture in which they can work without any conflicts between their personal and professional life (Taylor, 2002; Drago, 2000).

Attracting and Retaining Best Talent

The top candidates will work for the organizations that adopt aggressive recruitment policies which focus on recruiting multi ethnic students and active campaigns on job sides using social media as a platform. By promoting diversity in workforce talented personnel can be recruited which result in reducing turnover, promoting creativity in the organization (Silverstein, 1995; Diversity Inc., 2002).

Technological Advancement

Advancement in technology has played a pioneer role in global policies and shaping the structure of global system (Fritsch, 2011). The technological dynamics have changed the way the businesses were carried out by shrinking the world into a global village and improved the quality of life and organizational performance (Aggarwal, 2011). Another significant change in the corporate working is the emergence of virtual workforce, e-leadership and virtual organizations. Wang (2011) propounded the need for diverse leading approaches to manage the virtual working environments.

Leadership Skills for Successful Global Leaders

There is a great demand for the cross cultural leader using appropriate leadership style to influence and inspire diverse employees who can fully assist followers to work at different places and nations breaking the shackles and stereotyping primitive leadership practices. Further, it benefits the organizations having presence at global level.

Leaders around the globe face complex and multi-cultural practices, which require appreciation of individual's uniqueness (Holt and Seki, 2012; Chuang, 2013). Every individual is unique in his /her characteristics, behavior that are shaped by cultural background, values and life experiences.

1. For a better and proper understanding of cross-cultural leadership issues, global leaders should learn about demographics and recognize valuable inputs given by the diverse workforce (Parvis, 2003).
2. To perform more efficiently and effectively in cross cultural environment, global leaders need to conduct a self-awareness test to identify self-strengths and weaknesses. They should also recognize their individual reactions to situations and approaches (Dubrin, 2004; Frost and Walker, 2007).
3. To solve interpersonal problems global leaders should focus on differences between one and others by analyzing leadership competencies when followers have similar geographical background (Kowske and Anthony, 2007). Looking at similarities rather than dissimilarities can be a good approach for global leaders to lead and motivate their followers (Cranford and Glover, 2007). By this, global leaders can bridge the cultural gap within a group.
4. An effective global leader should focus on establishing motivational techniques to develop team spirit among its subordinates by designing various rewards and recognition measures with the help of values and promoting multiple cultural backgrounds (Frost and Walker, 2007). Motivating the employees can be one of the best tools for retaining best of the best talent in the organization.
5. Leading by example and treating the employees with respect is believed to be one of the best practices for the global corporate leaders (Choan, 2003; Roy, 2012) through cultural awareness and enhanced sensitivity to get the desired return on investment (Okoro, 2012).
6. A true leader must appreciate the capabilities and potential of its employees to stimulate them to build confidence and enthusiasm to face the competition (Weiss, 2004). It is important for the leaders to gain an insight into the international businesses and build an edge over the technical skills in practicing management and leadership.
7. The global leaders have to be inclined towards results and forward thinking. They must be capable of identifying the problems and concerns and resolve them from the diverse aspects. Besides, they must also be able to exploit the opportunities to fuel innovation, integrity, trustworthiness and enthusiasm (Gutierrez, Spencer and Zhu, 2012; Rausch, Halfhill, Sherman and Washbush, 2001; Flaum, 2002).
8. Another effective quality of a global leader is that he/she is a cross-cultural thinker who 'thinks globally and leads locally' (Gutierrez, Spencer and Zhu, 2012). A global leader analyzes the current situations to identify the problems and identify the future challenges so as to search for opportunities for the individual and organizational growth. Thinking out of the box is the other quality of global leader to be successful to overcome traditional thinking by

using multiple senses when finding solution to problems and searching for opportunities (Dubrin, 2004).
9. A successful global leader must have a realistic vision which should coincide with environmental challenges in the coming future and also provide value to the various stakeholders of the organization as a whole (Cranford and Glover, 2007).
10. Cultural intelligence is also given the utmost priority for a global leader to be successful (Lovvorn and Chen, 2011). By doing so, the international experience which they have gained will be helpful in transforming their global mindset, which is a fundamental trait of international global leadership and is associated with organizational commitment, trust and healthy manager-employer relationship (Story and Barbuto, 2011). Leader should not only be open-minded but should also think globally to maintain their competitiveness in multi-cultural organizations acting upon the environment (Johnson, 2008).
11. A global leader should be open to innovative and new ideas from amongst the subordinates. He should not be rigid to the creative ideas of the subordinates but should encourage them to discuss their thoughts with him/her so that they can strive towards the achievement of organizational goals more effectively and efficiently (Dubrin, 2004; Roy, 2012).
12. To maintain international competitiveness, global leaders also need negotiation skills. One of the essential skills that every effective leader must possess is the ability to communicate effectively in order to deliver the message accurately while maintaining a good relationship. (Okoro, 2012). A global leader should view the communication as an opportunity to sell a vision and make every endeavor in this regard to meet the expectations of the receiver effectively and efficiently. Honest and open communication can prove to be a solid connection between the leader and its followers (Mendez-Russel, 2001). It also increases the credibility and commitment towards the leader and its organization (Choan, 2003).

Managing Workforce Diversity: The Case of HP

HP is a perfect example of diversity management in the workplace. HP is well known for its diverse and multicultural workforce as it is operating in more than 120 countries (Seltzer, 1997) and having employees over 172,000 worldwide with a Revenue of $104.3billion (HP, 2008), stands as one of the world's largest seller of personal computers and the 5th largest software company in the world. There is no doubt that the diverse workforce which it has is maintained by the great management; great product lines and great market share (19% of the world's volume in desktop computers, for example) (Fisher, 2008). Keeping in mind the diversity in its workforce HP initiates its diversity management policy from the very beginning, as Bill Hewlett and David Packard developed a new management style called 'Management by Walking Around'. Groeger (2008) propounded that right from the beginning; a new type of corporate culture was adopted by the founders which were to be called 'the HP way.

The management style which HP adopted is known as 'Management by Walking Around' and the simple reason behind it is that 'everyone in the organization wants to do a good job' (Menke et al., 2006). This style of leadership has created an atmosphere of trust and mutual understanding among the employees and employer which resulted in profitable and flourishing enterprise.

With the expansion and growth of HP throughout the globe, its work force has become more diverse recognizing and mounting the talents of each individual brings innovative and creativity to HP. This is the one of the main reasons for the high performance at HP. The multicultural, diverse and high-achieving workforce has given HP a strategic advantage over the competitors in the marketplaces. HP motivates its diverse workforce to contribute their best. HP works on the lines to better serve customers, attract, develop and retain a diverse talented workforce. The leaders of HP give prime importance to Trust, mutual respect and dignity in their behavior and actions towards employees. Accordingly, HP can be lead the way in diversity management in place of work, their shared aims, cultural diversity, competent diversity management helps the organization to be more flourishing.

Managerial Implications

As Jamrog (2002) has acclaimed "Understanding that valuing diversity is a contact sport" is crucial before any modification can happen. For enhancing leadership effectiveness with a diverse workforce: premises, strategy, and performance are core competencies which are required by a global leader. The approach that leaders and managers need to accept for successful achievement of the tasks is based on principal of three basic premises which includes:

1. Universal applicability. As situation varies in various aspects there can't be a universal applicability of managing the diverse workforce as it may not work for others. Once global leaders recognize to value diversity in themselves they can adopt this approaches to problem solving, decision making, and supporting and developing workers.
2. Followers are as important as leaders. No leader can lead without followers. Organizations should also focus on the followers and should not assume that everyone can be or wants to be developed into an effective leader.

3. Leaders can be at any level of management. Leadership is one who knows shows and goes the way by influencing and guiding the followers. A leader can be anyone an employee, a manager or an executive.

The following are the five guidelines for global leaders, executives, HR managers and followers to recognize and value diversity:

1. Communication should be given utmost priority. Thoughts sharing, ideas, suggestions; request others to share their thoughts should be welcomed by the leaders. The more the communication, the effective, efficient and speedy the message will be. Lack of proper communication will result to misunderstanding and confusion.
2. Keeping you up to date. Keep in mind your duties and actions throughout the day in such a way that it maximizes contact with multiple people in the organization.
3. Be dynamic in your approach. Be open to suggestions and thoughts of others by adopting the concept of 'Manage and lead by walking around' enthusiasm and desire to interact informally with others of different levels, functions, backgrounds, and experience give you edge to manage a diverse workforce, by doing so personnel are encouraged to share information, and opinions which they may not if they had to make an appointment.
4. Multiple roles for diversity. Become a mentor, a well-wisher, a coach or a guide for inclusion. Believe on your decisions regarding individual, group, and organizational growth; to rule out fearlessness and promote creativity to increased commitment.
5. Support diversity. Rules and regulations should be made in such a way that has a glimpse in your conversations, your actions, and your interaction with colleagues, superiors, and subordinates. Your support will persuade others to follow your lead.

The below mentioned are the five actions for managers and leaders to recognize, consider, expand, and recompense other leaders' and workers' inclusion efforts:

1. Consider leadership prospective of all work forces in your organization.
2. Provide sufficient training and tools.
3. Take the accountability for inclusion.
4. Determine the rewards and appreciate inclusion efforts.
5. Be proactive and encourage your organization to be proactive.

Change is inevitable and it is quite common that it takes time to change. For managing diverse workforce, a leader should follow the approach of rewarding the effort and also provides space for mistakes.

By accepting the above mentioned points a global leader can effectively manage the diverse workforce as he/ she will greatly enhance his/her capabilities and recognise others' ability to value diversity.

CONCLUSION

In order to realize the benefits of successfully leading a diverse workforce, both leaders and employees must accept their responsibility in understanding one another's diversity. Leaders need to be proactive about learning from diversity and committed to establishing a climate of openness, equity, tolerance, and the most important, inclusion. Leaders need to demonstrate excellent communication, facilitation, and team building skills. Leaders need to possess understanding, humor, honesty, and integrity. Organizations need to recognize the need for providing training and socialization opportunities that employees are not exposed to in other areas of their lives. Organizations need to demonstrate their commitment to inclusion in every policy, procedure, initiative, business practice, and decision. Commitment alone will not guarantee results. With execution of a systemic, goal oriented, business-based, measurable, implementation plan for achieving inclusion at all levels of the workforce, especially at the senior levels, and effectively aligning business strategies with current demographic and market realities, an organization can achieve growth, profitability, and sustainability.

REFERENCES

Amagoh, F. (2009). Leadership development and leadership effectiveness. *Management Decision*, *47*(6), 989–999. doi:10.1108/00251740910966695

Anderson, W., & Bostian, B. (2001). *Minority Employment Trends*. St. Petersburg, FL: Human Resource Institute.

Bear, D., & Bostian, B. (2002). *The Generations at Work*. St Petersburg, FL: Human Resource Institute.

Bock, H., & Greco, C. (2002). *Implementing a Beneficially Diverse Organization*. Academic Press.

Caligiuri, P., & Tarique, I. (2012). Dynamic cross-cultural competencies and global leadership effectiveness. *Journal of World Business, 47*(4), 612–622. doi:10.1016/j.jwb.2012.01.014

Choan, P. S. (2003). *Value leadership: The seven principles that drive corporate value in any economic.* Academic Press.

Chuang, S. F. (2013). *Essential skills for leadership effectiveness in diverse workplace development.* Academic Press.

Cranford, S., & Glover, S. (2007). Challenge match: The stakes grow higher for global leaders. *Leadership in Action, 27*(3), 9–14. doi:10.1002/lia.1207

Daniel, S., Agarwal, R., & Stewart, K. J. (2013). The effects of diversity in global, distributed collectives: A study of open source project success. *Information Systems Research, 24*(2), 312–333. doi:10.1287/isre.1120.0435

Digh, P. (1998). Coming to terms with diversity. *HRMagazine, 43*(12), 117.

Drago, R. (2000). Work/family issues in flux: Watch for these upcoming trends. Positive Leadership.

Flaum, S. (2002). Six Ps of great leadership. *Executive Excellence, 19*(8), 3–4.

Frost, J., & Walker, M. (2007). Cross cultural leadership. *Engineering Management, 17*(3), 27–29. doi:10.1049/em:20070303

Gutierrez, B., Spencer, S. M., & Zhu, G. (2012). Thinking globally, leading locally: Chinese, Indian, and Western leadership. *Cross Cultural Management, 19*(1), 67–89. doi:10.1108/13527601211195637

Holt, K., & Seki, K. (2012). Global leadership: A developmental shift for everyone. *Industrial and Organizational Psychology: Perspectives on Science and Practice, 5*(2), 196–215. doi:10.1111/j.1754-9434.2012.01431.x

Johnson, H. H. (2008). Mental models and transformative learning: The key to leadership development. *Human Resource Development Quarterly, 19*(1), 85–89. doi:10.1002/hrdq.1227

Joplin, J. R., & Daus, C. S. (1997). Challenges of leading a diverse workforce. *The Academy of Management Executive, 11*(3), 32–47.

Kelly, D. (2001). *Ranstad Ranks Employee Wants by Age.* Available at: www.hr-esource.com

Kossek, E. E., & Lobel, A. (1996). *Managing diversity*. Blackwell Publishers.

Kowske, B. J., & Anthony, K. (2007). Towards defining leadership competence around the world: What mid-level managers need to know in twelve countries. *Human Resource Development International*, *10*(1), 21–41. doi:10.1080/13678860601170260

Kreitz, P. A. (2008). Best practices for managing organizational diversity. *Journal of Academic Librarianship*, *34*(2), 101–120. doi:10.1016/j.acalib.2007.12.001

Lappetito, J. (1994). Workplace diversity: A leadership challenge. Managing diversity is a social, financial, and moral imperative. *Health Progress (Saint Louis, Mo.)*, *75*(2), 22–27. PMID:10132109

LineF.III. (Ed.). (n.d.). Available at: www.diversityinc.com

Lovvorn, A. S., & Chen, J. S. (2011). Developing a global mindset: The relationship between an international assignment and cultural intelligence. *International Journal of Business and Social Science*, *2*(9).

Lussier, R. (2012). *Human relations in organizations: Applications and skill building*. McGraw-Hill Higher Education.

McCuiston, V. E., Ross Wooldridge, B., & Pierce, C. K. (2004). Leading the diverse workforce: Profit, prospects and progress. *Leadership and Organization Development Journal*, *25*(1), 73–92. doi:10.1108/01437730410512787

McMahon, A. M. (2010). Does workplace diversity matter? A survey of empirical studies on diversity and firm performance, 2000-09. *Journal of Diversity Management*, *5*(2), 37.

Mendez-Russell, A. (2001). Diversity leadership. *Executive Excellence*, *18*(12), 16.

Moore, S. (1999). Understanding and managing diversity among groups at work: Key issues for organizational training and development. *Journal of European Industrial Training*, *23*(4/5), 208–218. doi:10.1108/03090599910272086

Okoro, E. (2012). Cross-cultural etiquette and communication in global business: Toward a strategic framework for managing corporate expansion. *International Journal of Business and Management*, *7*(16), 130. doi:10.5539/ijbm.v7n16p130

Parvis, L. (2003). Diversity and effective leadership in multicultural workplaces. *Journal of Environmental Health*, *65*(7), 37.

Procter & Gamble. (1998). *Diversity*. Retrieved from http://www.pg.com/content/pdf/01_about_pg/01_about_pg_homepage/about_pg_toolbar/download_report/diversity.pdf

Rausch, E., Halfhill, S. M., Sherman, H., & Washbush, J. B. (2001). Practical leadership-in-management education for effective strategies in a rapidly changing world. *Journal of Management Development, 20*(3), 245–258. doi:10.1108/02621710110386381

Rockstuhl, T., Seiler, S., Ang, S., Van Dyne, L., & Annen, H. (2011). Beyond general intelligence (IQ) and emotional intelligence (EQ): The role of cultural intelligence (CQ) on cross-border leadership effectiveness in a globalized world. *The Journal of Social Issues, 67*(4), 825–840. doi:10.1111/j.1540-4560.2011.01730.x

Roy, S. R. (2012). Digital mastery: The skills needed for effective virtual leadership. *International Journal of e-Collaboration, 8*(3), 56–66. doi:10.4018/jec.2012070104

Silverstein, S. (1995, May 5). Workplace diversity efforts thrive despite backlash. *Los Angeles Times*, p. A1.

Simmons-Welburn, J. (1999). Diversity dialogue groups: A model for enhancing work place diversity. *Journal of Library Administration, 27*(1-2), 111–121. doi:10.1300/J111v27n01_08

Soutar, S. (2004). Beyond the Rainbow Diversity extends beyond ethnicity, age, and gender. *Association Management-Washington, 56*(4), 26–33.

Story, J. S., & Barbuto, J. E. Jr. (2011). Global mindset: A construct clarification and framework. *Journal of Leadership & Organizational Studies, 18*(3), 377–384. doi:10.1177/1548051811404421

Taylor, J. (2002, May). For workers, it's all about the balancing act. *Omaha World-Herald*, p. 1d.

Thomas, R. R. (1990). From affirmative action to affirming diversity. *Harvard Business Review, 68*(2), 107–117. PMID:10106515

Ulrich, D., & Smallwood, N. (2012). What is leadership? In *Advances in global leadership* (pp. 9–36). Emerald Group Publishing Limited. doi:10.1108/S1535-1203(2012)0000007005

Wang, M. (2011). Integrating organizational, social, and individual perspectives in Web 2.0-based workplace e-learning. *Information Systems Frontiers, 13*(2), 191–205. doi:10.1007/s10796-009-9191-y

Weiss, W. H. (2004). Effective Leadership: What are the requisites? *Super Vision*, *65*(1), 14–17.

Yang, Y. (2005, August). Developing cultural diversity advantage: The impact of diversity management structures. In *Academy of Management Best Conference Paper* (pp. H1-H6). GDO.

Chapter 7

An Overview of Employer Branding With Special Reference to Indian Organizations

Shikha Rana
IMS Unison University, India

Ravindra Sharma
Swami Rama Himalayan University, India

ABSTRACT

Talent acquisition is the most crucial activity an organization goes through. The reasons for its criticality are not just confined to the cost and time involved in recruiting talent but also matching the right incumbents at the right place and at the right time along with the organizational fit are the most essential factors to deal with. Nowadays, organizations are working in VUCA (volatile, uncertainty, complexity, and ambiguity) environment that seeks a lot in terms of employee performance. Employer branding was initiated by Ambler and Barrow (1990) with an aim to attract and retain the best talent through various activities, and the contemporary research has proven that if branding of the organization is done in an effective manner then it retains the best talent; further, it enhances job engagement and motivation. The present chapter elaborates the concept of employer branding, benefits, and importance of employer branding. Recent surveys and trends of employer branding in Indian organizations have also been discussed.

DOI: 10.4018/978-1-5225-4933-8.ch007

INTRODUCTION

Employer brand was first coined in early 1990 by Ambler and Barrow and through this the concept of brand, was introduced to the field of human resource management. It is the identity of the organization as an employer of choice. An organization becomes attractive place for its employees when it is able to get a tag of good brand. According to a research study percentage of job offers accepted, no. of job applicant per role, average length of tenure and staff engagement if is high in an organization as compared to its counterpart in a particular industry then that organization would emerged as an attractive employer brand (Moroco & Uncles, 2008). Further, employer brand is also ascertained attractiveness of the sector, company's reputation, quality of products and service, location, work environment, salary structure, employee benefits, people and culture, work/life balance and corporate social responsibility (Figurska & Matuska, 2013). Chartered Institute of Personnel and Development (CIPD) has accentuated the concept of employer brand in the following manner:

Employer brand a set of attributes that make an organization distinctive and attractive to those people who will feel an affinity with it and deliver their best performance within it. (CIPD, 2016)

Another prominent organization of human resource management, Society for Human Resource Management (SHRM, 2008) has stressed on employer brand in the following way:

The image of the organization as a great place to work in the minds of current employees and key stakeholders in the external market (active and passive candidates, clients, customers and other key stakeholders)

Employer Branding on the other hand is a process which includes:

The package of functional, economic and psychological benefits provided by employment, and identified with the employing company (Ambler & Barrow, 1996).

Employer branding and its relationship with retention and job engagement can easily be understood by the following definition:

An agreement under which the offer of the employer (manifested in organizational goals, values and initiatives that build trust in the employees) and counteroffer from employees (in the form of a high level of engagement and low retention) are matched (Martin et al., 2005)

Employer branding cast an image of the organization presenting it as a good place to work (Sullivan, 2004). The main function of employer branding is to make company attractive for the potential employees to get the maximum benefit of the market. Now it is considered as an integral part of business strategies (Jackie Orme, 2008). Employer branding has been highly extended to both research and practice (Barrow & Mosley, 2011). Employer branding has emerged as a new concept to meet the challenges of globalization, cut throat competition and changing market scenario. The need for attracting the best talent from the labour market and sustain the top performers is gaining due importance nowadays for the long term success of an organization. The major difference in definition between employer brand and employer branding seems to be that employer brand stresses on the content (employers offerings and values) while employer branding focuses on the aspects of establishing, communicating, and finally delivering the content (employers offerings and values).

Ambler and Barrow (1996) identified the three dimensions of employer branding such as psychological, functional and economic aspect and employer branding can be examined on the basis of these three aspects. Economic aspects deals with the remuneration and rewards, functional aspects includes factors like g. training and development, skills and job related activities for future development of an employee and the psychological aspects includes identity, belongingness and recognition by the organization.

Employer attractiveness is an important aspect associated with employer branding. Berthon et al (2005) defined it as "the envisioned benefits that a potential employee see in working for an specific organization". Berthon et al has proclaimed employer attractiveness to be the antecedent of employer brand equity. In another study conducted by Broek (2015) it has been revealed that employer attractiveness is the first step in employer branding and can be considered as pre phase of employer branding and an important part of the employer brand equity Further the more attractive the employer is perceived by the potential employees more high would be the employer brand equity of the organization. Interest value, Social value, Economic value, Developmental Value and Application value are the important aspects to measure the employer attractiveness which in addition would help the organization in increasing its employer brand equity (Berthon et al,2005). The interest value indicates the degree to which the characteristics like exciting and challenging work environment, novel work practices, use of its employees' creativity to produce high-quality, innovative products and services attracts an employee towards the employer. Further, work environment full of fun, happiness and supportive team atmosphere comes under Social value which determines the degree of employer attractiveness. Economic Value deals with salary, attractive overall compensation package, job security and promotion opportunities. Developmental Value examines the factors like recognition, self-worth, confidence aided with career-enhancing experiences and future employability lastly the application value determines the degree to which an employee is attracted to an employer that provides an opportunity to learn and teach in a customer and human centric environment. All these values enhance the employer attractiveness. Srivastava and Bhatnagar (2008) found out that in order to attract the talent an organization should have characteristics such as caring, enabling, career growth oriented, credible and fair, product and service brand image, positive image, global exposure

As the organizations strive hard to sustain and develop their product brand to attract the customers which is also called as "External Branding" in the same parlance nowadays efforts too are put on developing "brand of employer" on "Internal Branding" to recruit and retain the employees. Various researchers have proclaimed that employees are the internal customers while jobs are the internal products therefore these job products must attract and motivate the employees by satisfying their needs and meeting the objectives of the organization (Berry & Parasuraman,1991). Kotler (1994) too has emphasized the internal marketing as he argued that if the employees are effectively hired, trained and motivated then they would effectively deal with the customers. King and Grace (2007) stressed that employer branding is not just confined to attracting the potential employees but it is equally important to brand for the existing employees.

Employer branding conveys the "value proposition" the totality of the organization's culture, systems, attitudes, and employee relationship along with encouraging people to embrace and share goals for success, productivity, and satisfaction both on personal and professional levels. Employer branding is a distinguishing and relevant opportunity for a company to differentiate itself from the competition creating its branded factors as its USP for employee satisfaction and happiness resulting in retention, productivity and efficiency. Branding was originally used to differentiate tangible products, but over the years it has been applied to differentiating people, places and firms (Peters, 1999). According to a report effective Employer Value Proposition (EVP) management which is a unique set of offerings, associations and values an employer gives to its potential and present employees which further gives employees a reason to work for an employer and reflects the company's competitive advantage. As per a report EVP can bring tangible benefits, including a 20% increase in the pool of potential workers, a four-fold increase in commitment among employees and a 10% decrease in payroll costs. It is the total package of an employer offers including compensation, resources, culture, community, values to employees in exchange for their valuable contribution. As reported by Vivek Rao, HR Business Partner, Ashok Leyland Employee value proposition is an important key to create a great workforce. EVP not only helps in attracting and retaining the talent but also assist in appealing the people from different culture, age groups and functions. Additionally it is beneficial for the existing workforce as process of creating EVP involves a huge level of interaction and conversation with the current employees which in turn increases their trust for the organization and results in enhanced motivation. By creating the EVP an organization understands the HR priorities as it identifies the factors which are important for the existing and potential employees. Further EVP notifies the organization about the specific areas which needs to be focused in order to attract, engage and retain the employees. EVP creates a strong people brand.

Further, employer branding identify and create the company brand message, apply traditional marketing principles to achieve the status of employer of choice (Sutherland et al., 2002). Employer branding is used not only to transfer the message of the personality of a company as an employer of choice, but it also has been used to adapt the tools and techniques usually used to motivate and engage employees. Like a consumer brand, it is an emotional relationship between an employer and employee (Barrow and Mosley, 2011).

Contemporary research has shown that effective internal branding is an important tool for the success of external brand (Susan Hunt). Further, Christopher Van Mossevelde (2010) highlighted that growth and profitability of an organization, dealing with the economic downturns, scarcity of skilled labor, changing perception of new generation and gaining popularity as the best employer all these factors are responsible for the emergence of employer branding.

NEED OF EMPLOYER BRANDING

A research conducted Dr Shirley Jenner and Stephen Taylor, of the Chartered Institute of Personnel and Development (CIPD), has highlighted the factors stressing on the need of employer branding:

- **Brand Power:** From past twenty years the concept of 'Brand' has gained due importance both in organizational and social aspects. It has put a huge positive impact on reputation management, PR, recruitment and consultancy industry. Further it has become a centralized concept due to the unexpected growth and development in Corporate Social Responsibility towards all the stakeholders of the organization.
- **HR Search for Credibility and Strategic Influence:** HR professionals are continuously seeking for credibility and using brand as a powerful tool to increase and enhance the credibility in its operations further putting stress on strategy development in HR operations.
- **Labour Market Conditions:** The third reason for the rise of employer branding is due to labour market conditions. For quite some years labour

market conditions are becoming tough along with stringent business environment therefore these two factors are posing a challenge in front of companies to recruit and retain the best talent. Employer branding is a technique used for winning a 'war for talent' in such a crucial environment.
- **Employee Engagement and Commitment:** Employee engagement is one of the trending issue. Every organization wants an engaged and committed workforce. Recruitment forms the basis of initial satisfaction with workplace and matches the individual goals with that of organizational goals. At this point of time HR policy makers utilizes employer branding to influence who is to be recruited, how they look, behave, speak, think and feel about their employer brand.

BENEFITS OF EMPLOYER BRANDING

Tengle (2011) have listed out the following benefits of employer branding:

- A Long-Term positive impact of the image of organization in the mind of stakeholders
- An increased applications from Unsolicited Candidates
- It helps in attracting good quality of candidates
- Offer-Acceptance increases at a higher rate
- Employee Referrals increases which further results in improved credibility of the incumbents
- Raises the employee Retention percentage.
- Enhances employee motivation;
- Strengthen the commitment and engagement of employees with the organization
- Helps in creating a strong corporate culture
- Gives an organization a competitive edge over its counterparts

DEVELOPING AN EMPLOYER BRANDING STRATEGY

SHRM (2014) stressed on the following aspects to develop employer branding strategy:

- The very important aspect is to be aware of the organization's vision, mission, culture and value system. As after knowing all these thing the required talent would be identified to fulfill the objectives. It is also very indispensable to determine the unique characteristic of organization.

- Another important aspect is to carry out internal research to know the perception of its current employees, as well as of prospective employees, further it is important to understand the expectations of present and prospective employees. An organization must ask the top talent to list out the best characteristics of the employee for which they have chosen to work with organization. After this an organization must determine the attributes of these star employees that the organization would want to attract.
- Other most important aspect is to identify how the organization stands in respect to its competitors. For this a research should be conducted by surveying the applicants either by using Internet searches, social media or reviewing the reports of those organizations which monitors the employer branding activities across various organizations.
- Determining the employee value proposition is of the great importance as it clearly communicates the value of the brand an organization is developing. The employee brand should truly reflect the speciality of the organization and must be well linked with its customer brand.
- Further, employee marketing strategy must be designed. It should be designed focusing on two very important aspects firstly, the recruitment strategy must stresses on getting the targeted applicant base. The career page, recruiting sites, social media and other external recruitment sources must be attractive and revamped according to the time. Secondly regular and consistent communication of employee value proposition to current employees should be dome to ensure retention and engagement.
- Another important aspect of aligning the employer brand with the overall company brand is an important and crucial aspect for the successful implementation of employer branding. In order to ensure holistic branding it is really important to coordinate effectively with the marketing and communications teams.
- Further HR practices like training and development, compensation, coaching and other HR related activities should be well and effectively aligned with employer brand.
- Metrics like hiring quality, brand awareness, satisfaction of employees, employee referrals should be measured and continuously monitored to trace the success of employer brand.

RECENT SURVEYS ON EMPLOYER BRANDING

According to the report of Randstad Employer Brand Research, Google India, the search engine giant has won the title of the most attractive employer in the year

2017 followed by Mercedes–Benz India. Sector wise Amazon India, ITC ltd and Philips India has been awarded as the most attractive employers in E-Commerce, FMCG and Consumer and Healthcare respectively. Among the Indian workforce salary and employee benefits continue to be at the top priority, followed by good work-life balance and job security. However, for the IT professionals, good work-life balance emerged as the top driver while choosing an employer. Further it was also revealed in the report that the Indian employees preferred to work in the IT sector (65%), BFSI (63%) and Retail and FMCG (62%). Furthermore, employees prioritize job content (56%) in contrast to employer brand (44%) while selecting a job. The top media to verify the reputation of a particular brand was verified by company websites and LinkedIn Additionally, most of the employees across all the profiles preferred large multinationals to work with however, employees in IT preferred working for the start-up ecosystem over SME.

Google India got the Randstad Award 2015 for the 'Most Attractive Employer' in India, followed by Sony India which stood second in the competition. While Tata Steel for Manufacturing, P&G for FMCG and Honda India for Automobile verticals has been awarded with special recognition award. Salary and employee benefits (54%), job security (49%), work-life balancing (39%), pleasant working atmosphere (39%), and financial health of the company (38%) have been emerged as the most influential factors in employer branding across the industries. While Indian employees preferred to work with IT and Communication (72%) followed by FMCG and retail (68%) and Automobiles (67%).

A survey conducted by Randstad (2014) salary remained the most important factor in India followed by job security, employer's financial strength. While men in India prefer companies which offer competitive salaries, job security and are financially healthy, women seeked for a good work atmosphere, accessibility and flexible working hours. The survey also identified globally, honesty, security, intelligence and reliability are key characteristics that potential employees look for in an employer. Another survey which was carried out by Business Today (2014) identified Google, Accenture and TCS as top three employer brands. The participants rank the top three companies on six specific attributes like financial compensation, career growth prospects, work-life balance, performance appraisal, stability and other HR practices.

Randstad (2016) in its world wide report highlighted that survey of 25 countries across the world covering almost 75% of the global economy including over more than 2,00,000 prospective and present employees aged between 18-65 years has identified the following top ten attributes of employer branding:

Top ten factors which has emerged as the most attractive attributes for both prospective and present employees and employers across the globe are same to the great extent though rankings may vary. However the employers list too include almost

Table 1. Top ten attributes of employer branding

S.NO	Employer Branding Attributes Stressed by Potential Employees	Employer Branding Attributes Stressed by Employers	Employers Branding Attributes Stressed by Current Employees
1	Salary and Employee Benefits	Financial Health	Salary and employee benefits
2	Long Term Job Security	Strong Management	Long-term job security
3	Pleasant Work atmosphere	Good training	Pleasant working atmosphere
4	Work Life Balance	Salary and Employee Benefits	Good work-life balance
5	Financial Health	Career Prospects	Financially Health
6	Career Prospects	Long term Job Security	Career progression opportunities
7	Job Content	Job Content	interesting job content
8	Good Training	Pleasant Work Atmosphere	conveniently located
9	Strong Commitment	Corporate Social Responsibility	flexible working arrangements
10	Corporate Social Responsibility	Work Life Balance	Good Training

(Randstad, 2016)

all those attributes equally liked by the prospective and present employees with certain exceptions. Work life balance although have been given due importance by the prospective and the current employees but it has been ranked last by the employers.

EMPLOYER BRANDING ACROSS VARIOUS INDIAN ORGANIZATIONS

Hindustan Unilever (HUL)

Hindustan Unilever (HUL) one of the biggest FMCG company serving 2 out of 3 Indians for last eighty years has to revamp their employer branding every year, due to disruptive environment, people getting attracted towards other sectors. HUL has to sustain its brand to retain and attract the best talent. In Nielsen Employer of Choice survey (2010), HUL ranked second across sectors however prior to this from 2003-2010 the condition was not very good as it was not considered as the attractive employer by the campus students hence it lost a huge amount of talent, which further resulted in poor employee attraction and retention. All these factors additionally put a negative impact on overall performance of organization. After being in to this situation HUL started to rethink over their employer branding strategies. HUL became really ambitious to become the top most attractive organization across sectors and functions. HUL put it best to attract the competent people in all functions across sectors, and the consistent revamping of employer branding strategies along with its effective alignment with needs of talent did wonders. HUL stressed only two factors brand and people and treated them as assets. HUL asked its line leaders to allocate maximum time and resources and resources to institute the HUL employer brand to attract the best talent as it emerged as crucial aspect in sustaining and developing the business. The important initiatives taken up by these line managers were organizing Management Training programs, Unilever Future Leaders' Program which were focused mainly on building employer branding. HUL leaders put trainees straightaway into leadership roles directly at the end of training, developed a buddy or mentor program. Further, they initiated a system of reverse feedback for trainee employees and arranged for global stints to understand the foreign culture and markets and rural stints to make them aware of the social responsibility. E-learning domestic developmental plans were also designed international and domestic e-learning developmental plans along with thorough trainee interaction with HUL board members. Another very good initiative taken by HUL was conducting a special Executive General Management for the graduates of IIT at Indian Institute of Management, Bangalore, to entrench a forbearing of business fundamentals before joining as a full time employee. Further, the employer branding strategy developed a pipeline of best talent to take on big roles which in addition helped in taking up huge goals to get the competitive edge in the market. Constructive steps were also taken by HUL to groom the top talent for future responsibilities and duties. All these initiatives helped HUL becoming the first company in India to develop the young talent in their initial years by applying a very regularized, systematic and orderly manner. The management training programme, Unilever Future Leaders' Programme were actually initiated for the overall development of young talent. After this HUL grabbed the Dream Employer award, Employer of Choice award for four consistent years as per the Nielsen Employer Brand Survey (Peoplematters, 2016)

Infosys

Infosys one of the pioneer in IT sector in India which has been awarded as the most attractive employer by several research agencies too follow a very robust employer branding strategies. Infosys has build its brand by branding internally and externally. Employer branding in Infosys is a two way approach which consists of Internal branding and External Branding (Makwana & Dave, 2014). All the HR practices including recruitment, training and development, leadership, performance appraisal and compensation are the part of internal branding whereas road shows, campus connect, career fairs and websites and CSR activities are related to external branding (Makwana & Dave, 2014). Following a very strict criteria of recruiting the employees Infosys put a lot of emphasis on the 'Learning Skills' of prospective employees. Training and development of employees is very consistent further the new recruits are supposed to be trained at Global Education Centre (GEC, Mysore) a world class training centre of Infosys which maps the competency of employees in respect to various criteria related to individual performance and organizational priorities further feedback from the clients is also taken as inputs for the upgradation of these training programs (Chitramani & Deepa, 2013). Chitramani and Deepa (2013) revealed that in order to attract the employees, Infosys has established ILI (Infosys Leadership Institute) where the potential talent is groomed and developed. Infosys is the first organization to start ESOPs (Employee Stock Option Programs) further the compensation system is structured in such a manner where it matches with employee performance, business growth and increased operations. The organization too have a variable pay structure with an effective performance management system. Work Life balance issue is very much dealt with in Infosys as it has instituted a satellite system to enable the employees specifically the new and would be mothers to reduce the commutation time additionally one year break is also given to employees for the issues like childcare, elderly care or higher studies. Infosys also stresses a lot on the career development of employees by providing lot of opportunities and organizing various career growth programs. A lot of autonomy and freedom in operations and decision making is given to its employees for their development. Infosys put noticeable efforts in social development also commonly known as Corporate Social Responsibility which highlights its image among the prospective and present employees. Various initiatives have taken by Infosys for the rural development, women empowerment and other underprivileged people and communities in the society. It has also focused on rural development by constructing hospital wards, conducting regular health check-ups in camps, distributing medicines, donating books etc. further, Infosys too have trained the students of various schools and colleges to assist in community development programs.

May it be recruitment, training and development, performance appraisal, compensation system, career management or corporate social responsibility, employer branding is embedded heavily in all these aspects of Infosys. All the factors make a positive image of Infosys in the mind of current and prospective employees which helps in attracting and retaining the best talent.

Whirlpool

Whirlpool is a 102 year old company, a leading marketer and manufacturer of home appliances in India. Sarthak Raychaudhuri, Vice President-HR, Asia South (2013) explained that Whirlpool has a very strong reason to invest in employer branding. The vision of Whirlpool is to 'create happy homes' by excelling in three aspects namely product innovation, class quality of the product and cost leadership in the market. All these aspects can be achieved through 'happy employees' further, by being an 'employer of choice'. Employer branding is the most strategic mechanism to become employer of choice. The most important initiative taken by Whirlpool to get a competitive edge in employer branding was to opt for CC-Opex Methodology i.e., Customer Centered Operational Excellence. CC-Opex Methodology is based on six sigma approach. This methodology consists of three important phases. The very first phase is associated with extensive research for nine months where the organization tries to find out current talent preferences, what the organization stands for, how an organization differ from others, what are the strategic objectives and what an organization wants to be known for. After knowing and aligning all these aspects the organization moves into the second phase which lasts for three months. In this phase, lot of efforts are put in to formulate the employer branding strategies. Whatever has been discussed in phase one is validated by external experts and internal leadership team. Additionally, revalidation is done by internal employees through survey method after that the employer branding slogan is developed and identity of the organization is created. The third and the final phase which is an ongoing process includes the deployment of the employer branding strategies where promise is made and delivered to the prospective and current employees further communication of the promise to the employees is done on regular basis. Sharma and Das (2016) HR department of Whirlpool stresses on engaging, retaining and building the competencies of the work force. The Whirlpool Service Academy has rigorously trained more than 1200 engineers in order to structure their career path and up gradation of the technical skills. I-grow has also been instituted by the Whirlpool for the engagement and motivation of sales force of the organization. All these initiatives have increased the job engagement up to 85 percent. Further, the organization extensively conduct surveys to know the preference of the prospective candidates about what they look in a company before joining it.

CONCLUSION

Of late employer branding has gained due importance and has emerged as an strategic organizational activity to attract, sustain and retain the best talent in the organization. Nowadays every sector fighting for the competent talent and finding, fitting the right talent in the organization is a huge challenge for the HR managers. Everything in the corporate world is so commercialized that even an organization identity is not untouched with this change, they have to increase their visibility and has to create its brand in the eyes of prospective and current talent. Hence, a great emphasis on employer branding is must. Employee commitment and job engagement too has been focused a lot by the researchers, academicians and organizations as these factors are really vital for the talent retention and contemporary studies has shown a positive linkage of employer branding with these aspects as Levinson (2007) stated that employees who are happy in their work are more likely to stay in that organization, and found that work engagement is significantly related to organizational commitment furthermore, Dawn and Biswas (2010) stressed that a successful employer branding strategy can have a far reaching impact in increasing the number and quality of applicants. Figurska and Matuska(2013) opined that companies with good employer brand are able to gain financial benefits from socio-psychological determinants of employees' engagement and work performance. They build a trust to employer and the sense of pride in belonging to the organization.

Employer branding is an evolving HRM concept in respect to the various product and talent market situations that an organization come across. In order to foresee, identify, and satisfy the future and current employees it is essential to treat them as internal. Nowadays, organizations are no more unaware of the fact that talented employees are conscious of their rights and prerogatives to join, engage, commit, stay, or move on. A very well designed recruitment approach is required to attract and retain the right talent who stays longer and feel committed with the organization. Finally, the foremost reason for employer branding is to sustain the most loyal committed well engaged employees who in return are responsible for the long term growth of an organization (Randstad, 2017).

REFERENCES

Ambler, T., & Barrow, S. (1996). The Employer Brand. *Journal of Brand Management*, 4(3), 185–206. doi:10.1057/bm.1996.42

Barrow, S., & Mosley, R. (2011). *The employer brand: Bringing the best of brand management to people at work*. John Wiley & Sons.

Berry, L. L., & Parasuraman, A. (2004). Marketing services: Competing through quality. Simon and Schuster.

Berthon, P., Ewing, M., & Hah, L. L. (2005). Captivating company: Dimensions of attractiveness in employer branding. *International Journal of Advertising*, 24(2), 151–172. doi:10.1080/02650487.2005.11072912

Broek, M. (2015). *From employer attractiveness to employer branding: Results of a mixed methods research*. Retrieved on August 15, 2017 from http://essay.utwente.nl/66622/7/Broek_BA_MB.pdf

Businesstoday. (2014a). *Microsoft is the most attractive employer in India, finds Randstad survey*. Retrieved on June 28, 2017, from http://www.businesstoday.in/current/corporate/microsoft-is-most-attractive-employer-in-india-randstad-survey/story/205253.html

Businesstoday. (2014b). *The best companies to work for*. Retrieved on May 25, 2017, from http://www.businesstoday.in/magazine/cover-story/business-today-peoplestrong-best-companies-to-work-for-2013/story/208130.html

Chitramani, P., & Deepa, S. (2013). Employer Branding: A Case on Selected Indian IT companies. *Asia Pacific Journal of Marketing & Management Review*, 2(5), 133–141.

CIPD. (2016). *Chartered Institute of Personnel and Development*. Retrieved from http://www.cipd.co.uk

Dawn, S.K., & Biswas, S. (2010). Employer Branding: A New Strategic Dimension of Indian Corporations. *Asian Journal of Management Research*, 21-33.

Figurska, I., & Matuska, E. (2013). Employer branding as a human resources management strategy. *Human Resources Management & Ergonomics*, 7(2).

Hunt, S. (n.d.). *The Importance of Employer Branding*. Retrieved on May 28, 2013 from www.sunlife.ca/static/canada/Customer%20Solutions/.../chapter7.pdf

Kotler, P. (1994). *Analysis, planning, implementation, and control*. Prentice Hall International.

Levinson, E. (2007). *Developing High Employee Engagement Makes Good Business Sense*. Retrieved on April 28, 2015, from www.interactionassociates.com/ideas/2007/05/developing_high_ employee_engagement_makes_good_business_sense.php

Makwana, K., & Dave, G. (2014). Employer Branding: A Case of Infosys. *International Journal of Humanities and Social Science Invention*, 3(6), 42–49.

Martin, G., Beaumont, P., Doig, R., & Pate, J. (2005). Branding: A new performance discourse for HR? *European Management Journal*, 23(1).

Moroko, L., & Uncles, M. D. (2008). Characteristics of successful employer brands. *Journal of Brand Management*, 16(3), 160–175. doi:10.1057/bm.2008.4

Mossevelde, C. V. (2010). *Employer branding five reasons why it matters five step to action*. Retrieved on May 20, 2017, from http://www.employerbrandingtoday.com/uk/2010/03/25/employer-branding-five-reasons-why-it-matters-five-steps-to-action/

Orme, J. (2008). *CIPD Annual conference & exhibition.* Retrieved on January 29, 2013 from http://www.cipd.co.uk/pm/peoplemanagement/b/weblog/archive/2013/01/29/jackie-ormes-speech-to-the-cipds-annual-conference-and-exhibition-2008-09.aspx

Peoplematters. (2015). *Best People Practices – Part 4: Employer Branding Initiatives.* Retrieved on August 14, 2017 from https://www.peoplematters.in/article/employer-branding/best-people-practices-part-4-employer-branding-initiatives-11731

Peoplematters. (2016). *Best Practices: Employer Branding by Hindustan Unilever.* Retrieved on June 27, 2017, from https://www.peoplematters.in/article/employer-branding/best-practices-employer-branding-hindustan-unilever-12782

Peters, T. (1999). *The brand you 50: Fifty ways to transform yourself from an employee into a brand that shouts distinction.* New York, NY: Knopf Publishers.

Randstad. (2015). *Google India wins the Randstad Award 2015 for the 'Most Attractive Employer' in India.* Retrieved on June 25, 2015, from https://www.randstad.in/about-us/press-releases/press-releases/google-india-wins-the-randstad-award-2015-for-the-most-attractive-employer-in-india/

Randstad. (2016). *International Report Randstad Award Results.* Retrieved on June 28, 2017, from file:///C:/Users/acer/Downloads/Employer%20Branding%20-%20international%20insights%20Randstad%20Award%20research%202016%20(2).pdf

Randstad. (2017). *Employer branding for organizational change.* Retrieved on June 30, 2017, from https://www.randstad.in/workforce360/archives/employer-branding-as-an-instrument-of-organisational-change_82/

Randstad. (2017). *Google India emerges as India's most 'attractive employer' Randstad Employer Brand Research 2017.* Retrieved on June 25, 2017, from https://www.randstad.in/about-us/press-releases/press-releases/google-india-emerges-as-indias-most-attractive-employer-randstad-employer-brand-research-2017/

Rao, V. (2016). *Employee Value Proposition: A key to creating a Great Workforce.* Retrieved on August 15, 2017 from https://www.linkedin.com/pulse/employee-value-proposition-key-creating-great-workforce-vivek-rao

Raychoudhri, S. (2013). *India's best employer: Branding initiative.* Retrieved on June 26, 2017, from http://www.greatplacetowork.in/storage/documents/Publications_Documents/Conference_presentations/Whirlpool-_Sarthak_Raychouduri.pdf

Sharma, A., & Das, G. (2016). *Sustaining Employer Branding at Whirlpool of India Ltd.* Retrieved on June 30, 2017 from http://www.etcases.com/media/clnews/14732403033336336502.pdf

SHRM. (2008). *The Employer Brand: A Strategic Tool to Attract, Recruit and Retain Talent*. Retrieved on May, 2013, from www.shrm.org/Research/Articles/Articles/Pages/TheEmployerBrandAStrategicTooltoAttract,RecruitandRetainTalent.aspx

SHRM. (2014). *Branding: What is an employer brand, and how can we develop an employment branding strategy?* Retrieved on June 29, 2017 from https://www.shrm.org/resourcesandtools/tools-and-samples/hr-qa/pages/cms_023007.aspx

Srivastava, P., & Bhatnagar, J. (2010). Employer brand for talent acquisition: An exploration towards its measurement. *Vision*, *14*(1-2), 25–34. doi:10.1177/097226291001400103

Sullivan, J. (2004). *Eight elements of a successful employment brand*. Retrieved on June 21, 2017, from https://www.eremedia.com/ere/the-8-elements-of-a-successful-employment-brand/

Sutherland, M. M., Torricelli, D. G., & Karg, R. F. (2002). Employer-of-choice branding for knowledge workers. *South African Journal of Business Management*, *33*(4), 13–20.

KEY TERMS AND DEFINITIONS

Customer-Centred Operational Excellence (CCOpex): A six sigma-based methodology used by Whirlpool India to design its employer branding strategies.

Employer Branding: Employer branding is the process of promoting the company's image and reputation for attracting and retaining the talent.

Employer Value Proposition (EVP): The employer value proposition (EVP) is a unique set of offerings, associations, and values to positively influence potential and current employees.

Randstad: Randstad is a multinational human resource consulting firm headquartered in Diemen, The Netherlands. Randstad is the world's second-largest HR service provider and also conducts surveys on employer branding in India and across the world.

Chapter 8
Antecedents and Consequences of Employee Engagement for a Diverse Workforce

Shampy Kamboj
Amity University, India

Bijoylaxmi Sarmah
North-Eastern Regional Institute of Science and Technology, India

ABSTRACT

In the recent years, employee engagement has become a hot topic of discussion among popular business press and consulting firms. This topic has created interest in various stakeholder groups ranging from scholarly human resource practitioners to policy makers or government agencies. The interest in employee engagement has progressively increased, however, in academic literature: the concept of employee engagement has been studied rarely and comparatively less is known regarding its antecedents and consequences. Recently, a number of researchers have argued that the challenge of engaging the employees is mounting. Although it seems to conceptually overlap with existing constructs, for instance, job involvement, organizational commitment, still some empirical research confirms that engagement is a separate construct. Therefore, this chapter aims (a) to shed some light in this respect by assessing the association between workforce diversity, specifically in terms of their age and employee engagement, and (b) to provide a variety of precursors and outcomes of employee engagement.

DOI: 10.4018/978-1-5225-4933-8.ch008

Antecedents and Consequences of Employee Engagement for a Diverse Workforce

INTRODUCTION

The notion of employee engagement is a relatively new one, one that has been heavily marketed by human resource (HR) consulting firms that offer advice on how it can be created and leveraged. (Macey & Schneider, 2008, p. 3)

In the recent years, employee engagement has become a hot topic of discussion among popular business press and consulting firms (Anaza *et al.*, 2016). This topic has created interest in various stakeholder groups ranging from scholarly (*e.g.* Kahn, 1990; Schaufeli *et al.*, 2006, 2002), Human resource practitioners (e.g. Harter *et al.*, 2002; Masson *et al.*, 2008), to policy-makers or government agencies (*e.g.* MacLeod & Clarke 2009). On the one hand, the interest in employee engagement has progressively increased (Anaza *et al.*, 2016), however in academic literature, the concept of employee engagement has been studied rarely and comparatively less is known regarding its antecedents and consequences. Recently, a number of researchers' have argued that the challenge of engaging the employees is mounting (Fleming et al., 2005; May et al., 2004; Pech & Slade, 2006). Although it seeming conceptually overlap with existing constructs for instance job involvement, organizational commitment, still some empirical research confirms that engagement is a separate construct (Hallberg & Schaufeli, 2006).

As per a survey of 656 CEOs hailing from the countries across the globe, employee engagement is fourth significant management challenge, following reducing costs, creating loyal customers (Wah, 1999). Indeed, the Gallup Organization found recently that approximately twenty percent of US employees were disengaged and fifty four percent were successfully impartial regarding their work (Fleming et al., 2005). In addition, study conduct by Gallup and Towers Perrin (Seijts & Crim, 2006) advocates that disengage employee is equally challenging in other countries also. Thus, collectively the influence of these two trends - diversity in workforce and the rising challenge of employee engagement could prove problematical for various employers (Avery *et al.*, 2007).The work force diversity will increase the chances of different diversity present in most of the work settings.

Although researcher has connected work force dissimilarity to various outcomes for instance organizational commitment and intention to stay (Riordan, 2000), still the effect of this divergence on employee engagement is uncertain. Understanding regarding this association is important as (a) meta-analytic evidence and the other findings have revealed employee engagement to predict the key outcomes, for instance customer satisfaction, customer loyalty, employee turnover, productivity, safety, and profitability (Harter *et al.*, 2002; Salanova *et al.*, 2005), and (b) because employee engagement has a direct influence on performance, while the influence of job attitudes for example organizational commitment are indirect in nature (Harrison *et al.*, 2006).

Employee engagement has become a broadly used and famous term (Robinson *et al.*, 2004). However, majority of writings about employee engagement can be found in the practitioner journals, where this concept has its base in practice instead of theory and empirical studies. Robinson *et al.* (2004) noted there has been shockingly little empirical and academic research on a subject that has become so famous. Consequently, employee engagement has the emergence of being something called as, "old wine in a new bottle".

Several definitions have been provided for this concept in the academic literature. Initially, Kahn (1990, p. 694) firstly conceptualized work engagement or personal engagement or employee engagement as "the harnessing of organization members' selves to their work roles; in engagement, people employ and express themselves physically, cognitively, and emotionally during role performances." Rothbard (2001, p. 656) defines engagement as "psychological presence but goes further to state that it involves two critical components: attention and absorption. Attention refers to "cognitive availability and the amount of time one spends thinking about a role" while absorption "means being engrossed in a role and refers to the intensity of one's focus on a role."

Schaufeli *et al.* (2002, p. 74) define engagement "as a positive, fulfilling, work-related state of mind that is characterized by vigor, dedication, and absorption." They further state that engagement is not a momentary and specific state, but rather, it is "a more persistent and pervasive affective-cognitive state that is not focused on any particular object, event, individual, or behavior" (p. 74). *Vigor* refers to "high levels of energy and mental resilience while working, willingness to invest effort in work, and persistence in the face of difficulties"; *dedication* represents "a strong psychological involvement in employees' work combined with a strong identification with their work and encompasses feelings of significance, enthusiasm, inspiration, pride, and challenge"; and *absorption* refers to "being happily engrossed in work, whereby time passes quickly and one has difficulties detaching" (Schaufeli *et al.*, 2002, p. 74).

In the literature in academic, engagement is shown as related to but different from the other constructs of organizational behavior. Such as, Robinson *et al.* (2004, p. 8) state that, "engagement contains many of the elements of both commitment and OCB, but is by no means a perfect match with either. In addition, neither commitment nor OCB reflect sufficiently two aspects of engagement – its two-way nature, and the extent to which engaged employees are expected to have an element of business awareness". To sum up, although the meaning and definition of engagement in the practitioner literature repeatedly overlaps with the other constructs, but in academic literature engagement has been defined as a different and distinctive construct, which include cognitive, behavioral and emotional elements that are related with a persons' role performance.

The main appeal of organization management is based on the fact that employee engagement drives the bottom line outcomes. One of the HR consulting firm (Hewitt Associates LLC, 2005, p. 1) point out that "they have established a conclusive, compelling relationship between engagement and profitability through higher productivity, sales, customer satisfaction, and employee retention." According to Macey and Schneider (2008, p. 4), "employee engagement is a desirable condition, has an organizational purpose, and connotes involvement, commitment, passion, enthusiasm, focused effort, and energy, so it has both attitudinal and behavioral components". The antecedents of such behaviors and attitudes are placed in settings under which individual work, and the consequences are reflection to be of value to organization effectiveness (Erickson, 2005).

Therefore, this chapter aims (a) to shed some light in this respect by assessing the association between workforce diversity specifically in terms of their age and employee engagement and (b) to provide a variety of precursors and outcomes of employee engagement.

JOB DEMANDS-RESOURCES MODEL AND EMPLOYEE WORK ENGAGEMENT

Job demands-resources model (JD-R model) is a main theoretical model, which describes the development of employee work engagement. As per Crawford et al. (2010) JD-R model, in a work environment there are two specific working conditions for an employee one is job demands and another is job resources. These two working conditions contribute to either employees' well-being or their stress level, and lead to affect their level of work engagement.

According to Demerouti *et al.* (2001, p. 501), "*Job demands* refers to, "the physical, psychological, social, or organizational aspects of the job that require individuals to exert sustained physical and/or psychological effort and, hence, have certain physiological and/or psychological costs (e.g., exhaustion)". Whereas, according to Schaufeli and Bakker (2004, p. 296) *Job resources* refers to, "those physical, psychological, social, or organizational aspects of the job that either/or (1) reduce job demands and the associated physiological and psychological costs; (2) are functional in achieving work goals; (3) stimulate personal growth, learning and development".

Therefore, job resources can reduce down the job demands and are equally important in their own right. While job demands can hamper employees' work engagement by rising their stress levels during a health-injury process, and job resources can enhance employees' work engagement by rising their intelligence of well-being via a motivational process (Bakker *et al.*, 2003 and Crawford *et al.*, 2010).

The JD-R model is a conceptual framework, which is used to describe employee engagement in the workplace (Bakker & Demerouti, 2007). This model states that resources are what an organization gives to its employees; these resources may include supervisory support, supervisory feedback and autonomy. These resources are expected to (a) "lessen the strain of the

job's demands and the psychological and physiological costs that a company these arduous demands", (b) "be instrumental in the achievement of employee work objectives", and (c) "motivate and stimulate personal growth, development, and learning" (Demerouti et al., 2001). The model attempts to discuss how resources can be utilized to improve engagement and how the interplay among various resources influences engagement. The model also asserts that organizations' engaged employees will provide customer-oriented behaviors and such behaviors will be reflected in their assessment of service employee performance (Yoon & Suh, 2003; Young et al., 2009).

DISCUSSION OF ANTECEDENTS TO EMPLOYEE ENGAGEMENT

Although there is dearth of empirical research in the literature regarding the factors that can predict the employee engagement, from Kahn's (1990) and Maslach *et al.*'s (2001) model it is possible to identify several possible antecedents. The antecedents might vary for both job and organization engagement as a part of employee engagement. These antecedents consist of job characteristics, rewards and recognition, perceived organizational, procedural justice and supervisor support.

The literature has identified conceptual and empirical linkages towards the development of employee engagement although often in disconnected and disparate conversations. Mainly, engagement is mentioned as a behavioral outcome (Shuck & Wollard, 2010) and small attention is given towards the antecedents, which potentially drive the *emotional and cognitive* states of engagement that are believed to facilitate the behavioral manifestation of what can be seen as employee engagement. The subsequent sections discuss the extant literature on employee engagement antecedents starting with the individual antecedents to the organizational antecedents.

Individual Antecedents

Employee engagement is mainly an individual-level variable but it is measured at the organizational level (Shuck & Wollard, 2010). Considering the significant role of employee's individual factors and personality, little is known regarding employee engagement's individual antecedents and other variables that may contribute towards the overall development of employee engagement. In the literature, there are some associations reported; but this issue is not without critique and debate. Such as, the workplace environment and involvement of an employee's in contextually meaningful work is considered to be linked to employee engagement (Rich et al., 2010). Similarly, the perception of culturally, physically safe environments, emotionally, and individual factors, are also related to the employee engagement development as antecedents (May et al., 2004). Work–life balance (Singh, 2010), corporate citizenship behaviors with personal involvement (Glavis & Piderit, 2009), and the linkage in an employee's work to organizational goals (Harter et al., 2002) are well addressed in the existing literature.

Research by European researchers' Schaufeli and Maslach depict that a number of variables for instance dedication, absorption and vigor in work are considered as individual antecedents to the employee engagement development. All of these variables are operationalized in the "Maslach Burnout Inventory" (MBI-GS; Maslach & Leiter, 1997) as the burnout opposite state, other individual variable with its individual antecedents set (e.g., cynicism, ineffectiveness; exhaustion, Maslach & Leiter, 1997) and "Utrecht Engagement Scale" (Schaufeli et al., 2006). Another work by Shirom (2007) and Shagra (2007) depicted a linkage between vigor (i.e., engagement; Maslach et al., 2001) and the extroversion and openness factors of the "Big Five personality variables" (Extroversion, Conscientiousness, Openness, Neuroticism, and Agreeableness). Their work also reported that "*Openness*" predicted engagement and that "*Extroversion*" predicted engagement levels at different points of time.

Other research work regarding individual antecedents is conceptual, and also adding important thought to the current conversation, but a little in contexts of evidence related antecedents. Such as, in a study by Macey and Schneider (2008) revealed that an auto-telic personality, conscientiousness and proactive personality traits positively influence employee engagement development as individual-level antecedents. Their work, based in Maslach et al.'s (2001) and considered that work environment perception of an employee's would lead to organizational outcomes (Maslach & Leiter,1997; Maslach et al., 2001), stated salient cues of an individuals' personality could be a influencing factor in employee engagement development.

Others have suggested that family and work status, a readiness to direct personal energies, emotional connection and stress are connected to the employee engagement development, although these associations are ripe for research and not yet empirically driven. Additionally, various workplace antecedent models have revealed the several individual antecedent variables for instance curiosity (Reio et al., 2006), self-efficacy (Macey & Schneider, 2008), self-esteem, self-perceptions (Xanthopoulou et al., 2007), all contribute an important role in the work-oriented variables development at an individual level. Although any research has not explored these associations and engagement (Maslach & Leiter, 2008), a number of researchers' has demonstrated a relationship between all personality traits like those discussed above and widely researched organizational variables such as involvement, job satisfaction, and commitment (Judge et al., 2004).

Organizational Antecedents

Organizations are always complex and complicated mazes for the employees to navigate. However, when discussed regarding employee engagement, antecedents that drive the engagement development at organizational level take place around basic human needs. Thus, the identification and meeting of basic human needs depicts complexity lack, yet outlines the difficulty of creating organizational situations for engagement to take place. This may resonate for anybody who has tried to internal motivation work teams, which involved different personalities and perceptions at organizational level.

Empirically, the managers' role has been investigated in extant, most considerably from research using the "satisfaction-engagement approach" (Shuck, 2011). Such as, research has suggested the manager self-efficacy role (Arakawa & Greenberg, 2007), managers' role in establishing a supportive climate (Kroth & Keeler, 2009;Plakhotnik et al., 2011), mission and vision implementations on a local level (Fleming & Asplund, 2007), and perception of manager expectations (Bezuijen et al., 2009) research has also stated that managers using non defensive approach (Shuck et al., 2011) positively influence employee engagement. Additional, the culture role (organizational and local micro cultures) have been investigated as an important antecedent variable (Brown &Leigh, 1996; Shuck et al., 2011).

In addition, research has revealed that supportive workplace climates, positive and authentic all work to increment conditions positively affect engagement. Similarly, positive workplace climates (Dollard &Bakker, 2010) have been mentioned to involve the supportive management perception, recognition, in-role tasks role clarity, organizational success, self-express ability, and job challenge and control at appropriate levels (Brown & Leigh, 1996). In addition, as an organizational variable, Culture, is mainly a force which is outside the employee's direct control but always within manager's or a leader sphere of influence, stating a conceptual relationship between engagement and leader behavior(Shuck &Herd, 2011). Moreover, manager conscious choice for team to emphasize on increasing engagement is consider to be a positive antecedent to engagement development; a type of self-fulfilling prophecy effect in workplace. Lastly, organizational initiatives for instance CSR programs that include service work and employee volunteerism have been investigated as an empirically driven antecedent (Lindorff & Peck, 2010).

Cross-cultural literature, which emerging conceptually has depicted that hygiene factors external to the employee contribute potential conditions for their engagement at the organizational level (Schaufeli et al., 2008; Shucket al., 2011). Thus, hygiene factors are operationalized as reasonable working conditions, a reasonable degree of security, including fair pay and trust at low level with the leader (Herzberg, 1959,1968). When these hygiene factors are not fulfilled, employee engagement is not likely to develop. Research regarding providing resources, job control, setting clear expectations support this idea(Harter et al., 2002).

Additionally, a number of authors suggest that learning opportunities (Czarnowsky, 2008)and talent management (Hughes & Rog, 2008) that consist of organizational development and employee initiatives are antecedents to employee engagement. Unfortunately, no empirical work could be identified that emphasized mainly on human resource development role, human resource management and organizational development practices as antecedents to employee engagement, although it is a highly recommended antecedent.

Finally, rewards for instance monetary incentives and pay-for-performance have been examined in the extant literature and connected somewhat to the hygiene discussions and Justice, fair pay issues. Moreover, internal motivations that take place from extrinsic feedback sources in term of job encouragement and sincere recognition have been conceptually associated as antecedents to employee engagement, but no empirical support exists on the association. A number of evidence does state that poorly appropriated monetary structures may underestimate organizational engagement efforts (Demerouti & Cropanzano, 2010; Sparrow & Balain, 2010).

Summary of Antecedents

Varying types and levels of antecedents have been explored and examined with the concept of employee engagement, some empirical and others conceptual. What is clear from this review is that antecedents are not process dependent, but rather functions in the conditions for the state of engagement to develop. Different organizations will come to create an employee engagement culture in different ways, using different strategies and methods that are unique to their organization. In no literature did a one process model fit across all antecedents or strategies. Furthermore, it is also clear that antecedents related to each organization must be in place, but processes to facilitate the development of an engagement culture are also in play. A detailed discussion of the processes for the development of employee engagement is however outside the primary research question used to guide this review and is suggested for further research and scholarly inquiry.

CONSEQUENCES OF EMPLOYEE ENGAGEMENT

The motivation behind the attractiveness of employee engagement is that it has a number of positive outcomes for organizations. As specified earlier, there is a common belief that there is a association between employee engagement and organization results (Harter *et al.*, 2002). However, engagement is an individual level constructs and therefore, if it does cause organization results, it should first have an effect on individual level outcomes. Thus, there is reason to suppose employee engagement to be associated with individuals' intentions, behaviors and attitudes.

Kahn (1992) suggested that engagement resulted into both individual outcomes (i.e. work quality and work experiences), and organizational outcomes (i.e. organizational productivity and growth). In addition, the Maslach *et al.* (2001) model considers engagement as a mediator for the association between work conditions and different outcomes of work (such as burnout, increased withdrawal, job satisfaction, lower performance, organizational citizenship behaviour and organizational commitment (Maslach *et al.*, 2001).

Once employees become more engaged, they usually find their own work more meaningful, inspirational and self-fulfilling, accordingly they become more concentrated, engrossed and dedicated in their works. This motivated and positive mind stay should continue to how they serve and treat customers. As such, a number of research has depicted that engagement affects not only "in-role behavior" but also "proactive behavior" (Sonnentag, 2003) and employee extra-role behavior for instance organizational citizenship behavior (Rich et al., 2010). It seems that an engaged employees have an elaborated view regarding their work role and have a wider set of activities in their jobs. This states that, employee engagement will have a positive effect on how they handle their duties, involving providing superior customer services.

Harter et al. (2002) suggested that engagement is positively associated to significant business performance metrics for instance profitability, customer satisfaction, productivity and loyalty. The similar results in engaged employees will work out of excitement and sheer joy of rendering superior service to customers. Some researchers believed that engaged employees to be friendly, prompt in service delivery, motivated to recommend appropriate products as per customer needs and attentive to customer problems(Young et al., 2009). There are a number of consequences of employee engagement including, first, *Intent to quit*, i.e. workers who have lower levels of dedication revealed greater intentions to quit. Second, *Job satisfaction*, i.e. employees working in larger properties has higher levels of Dedication, Absorption, and Vigor with more job satisfaction. Third, *Employee voice*, i.e. employees who supervised others and usually worked in larger properties depicted high levels of Vigor revealed engaging in more voice behaviors among employee. Fourth, *Work-family conflict*, i.e. employees who supervised others and occupied top levels in organization they usually displayed high levels of Vigor depicted less work-family conflict; employees depicting high levels of Absorption depicted enhanced levels of work-family conflict. Fifth, *Family-work conflict*, i.e. employees who supervised others, occupied top organizational levels, and worked in larger properties, depicted high levels of Vigor and low levels of family-work conflict; workers showing high levels of Absorption also depicted more family-work conflict.

Some other observations are also worth to be noting. First, personal demographic factors were particularly unrelated to employee work outcomes. Second, work situation characteristics responsible for a significant increase in explained variance on their work outcomes. Thus, surprisingly, employees at top organizational levels and supervising others, depicted high favorable outcomes at work in some cases. Third, work engagement also responsible for a significant increase in explained variance on their work outcomes. Interestingly, Absorption and Vigor had an important but different linkage with the two family-work and work-family conflict measures.

REFERENCES

Anaza, N. A., Anaza, N. A., Nowlin, E. L., Nowlin, E. L., Wu, G. J., & Wu, G. J. (2016). Staying engaged on the job: The role of emotional labor, job resources, and customer orientation. *European Journal of Marketing*, *50*(7/8), 1470–1492. doi:10.1108/EJM-11-2014-0682

Arakawa, D., & Greenberg, M. (2007). Optimistic managers and the influence on productivity and employee engagement in a technology organization: Implications for coaching psychologists. *International Coaching Psychology Review*, *2*(1), 78–89.

Avery, D. R., McKay, P. F., & Wilson, D. C. (2007). Engaging the aging workforce: The relationship between perceived age similarity, satisfaction with coworkers, and employee engagement. *The Journal of Applied Psychology*, *92*(6), 25–42. doi:10.1037/0021-9010.92.6.1542 PMID:18020795

Bakker, A., & Demerouti, E. (2008). Towards a model of work engagement. *Career Development International*, *13*(3), 209–223. doi:10.1108/13620430810870476

Bakker, A. B., Demerouti, E., Taris, T. W., Schaufeli, W. B., & Schreurs, P. J. (2003). A multigroup analysis of the job demands-resources model in four home care organizations. *International Journal of Stress Management, 10*(1), 16–38. doi:10.1037/1072-5245.10.1.16

Berry, M. L., & Morris, M. L. (2008). The impact of employee engagement factors and job satisfaction on turnover intent. In T. J. Chermack (Ed.), *Academy of Human Resource Development International Research Conference in the Americas* (pp. 1-3). Panama City, FL: AHRD.

Brown, S. P., & Leigh, T. W. (1996). A new look at psychological climate and its relationship to job involvement, effort, and performance. *The Journal of Applied Psychology, 81*(4), 359–368. doi:10.1037/0021-9010.81.4.358 PMID:8751453

Chalofsky, N., & Krishna, V. (2009). Meaningfulness, commitment, and engagement: The intersection of a deeper level of intrinsic motivation. *Advances in Developing Human Resources, 11*(2), 189–203. doi:10.1177/1523422309333147

Christian, M. S., Garza, A. S., & Slaughter, J. E. (2011). Work engagement: A quantitative review and test of its relations with and contextual performance. *Personnel Psychology, 64*(1), 89–136. doi:10.1111/j.1744-6570.2010.01203.x

Crawford, E. R., LePine, J. A., & Rich, B. L. (2010). *Linking job demands and resources to employee engagement and burnout: a theoretical extension and meta-analytic test*. Academic Press.

Czarnowsky, M. (2008). *Learning's role in employee engagement: An ASTD research Study*. Alexandria, VA: American Society for Training & Development.

Davies, I. A., & Crane, A. (2010). Corporate social responsibility in small- and medium-size enterprises: Investigating employee engagement in fair trade companies. *Business Ethics (Oxford, England), 19*(2), 126–139. doi:10.1111/j.1467-8608.2010.01586.x

Demerouti, E., Bakker, A. B., Nachreiner, F., & Schaufeli, W. B. (2001). The job demands-resources model of burnout. *The Journal of Applied Psychology, 86*(3), 499–512. doi:10.1037/0021-9010.86.3.499 PMID:11419809

Dollard, M. F., & Bakker, A. B. (2010). Psychosocial safety climate as a precursor to conducive work environments, psychological health problems, and employee engagement. *Journal of Occupational and Organizational Psychology, 83*(3), 579–599. doi:10.1348/096317909X470690

Erickson, T. J. (2005, May). Testimony submitted before the US Senate Committee on Health. *Education, Labor and Pensions, 26*.

Evans, C., & Redfern, D. (2010). How can employee engagement be improved at RRG Group? *Industrial and Commercial Training, 42*(5), 265–269. doi:10.1108/00197851011057564

Fleming, J. H., & Asplund, J. (2007). *Human sigma*. New York, NY: Gallup Press.

Fleming, J. H., Coffman, C., & Harter, J. K. (2005). Manage your human sigma. *Harvard Business Review, 83*(7), 106. PMID:16028821

Fornes, S. L., Rocco, T. R., & Wollard, K. K. (2008). Workplace commitment: A conceptual model developed from integrative review of the research. *Human Resource Development Review, 7*(3), 339–357. doi:10.1177/1534484308318760

Glavis, A., & Piderit, S. (2009). How does doing good matter? Effects of corporate citizenship on employees. *Journal of Corporate Citizenship, 36*(36), 51–70. doi:10.9774/GLEAF.4700.2009.wi.00007

Hallberg, U. E., & Schaufeli, W. B. (2006). "Same same" but different? Can work engagement be discriminated from job involvement and organizational commitment? *European Psychologist, 11*(2), 119–127. doi:10.1027/1016-9040.11.2.119

Harrison, D. A., Newman, D. A., & Roth, P. L. (2006). How important are job attitudes? Meta-analytic comparisons of integrative behavioral outcomes and time sequences. *Academy of Management Journal, 49*(2), 305–325. doi:10.5465/AMJ.2006.20786077

Hart, R. K., Conklin, T. A., & Allen, S. J. (2008). Individual leader development: An appreciative inquiry approach. *Advances in Developing Human Resources, 10*(5), 632–650. doi:10.1177/1523422308321950

Harter, J. K., Schmidt, F. L., & Hayes, T. L. (2002). Business-unit-level relationship between employee satisfaction, employee engagement, and business outcomes: A meta-analysis. *The Journal of Applied Psychology, 87*(2), 268–279. doi:10.1037/0021-9010.87.2.268 PMID:12002955

Harter, J. K., Schmidt, F. L., & Hayes, T. L. (2002). Business-unit-level relationship between employee satisfaction, employee engagement, and business outcomes: A meta-analysis. *The Journal of Applied Psychology, 87*(2), 268–279. doi:10.1037/0021-9010.87.2.268 PMID:12002955

Harter, J. K., Schmidt, F. L., & Hayes, T. L. (2002). Business-unit-level relationship between employee satisfaction, employee engagement, and business outcomes: A meta-analysis. *The Journal of Applied Psychology, 87*(2), 268–279. doi:10.1037/0021-9010.87.2.268 PMID:12002955

Herzberg, F. (1959). *The motivation to work*. New York, NY: Wiley.

Herzberg, F. (1968). One more time: How do you motivate employees? *Harvard Business Review, 46*(1), 53–62. PMID:12545925

Hewitt Associates LLC. (2005). *Employee engagement*. Retrieved May 17, 2016, from http://was4.hewitt.com/hewitt/services/talent/subtalent/ee_engagement.htm

Hughes, J., & Rog, E. (2008). Talent management: A strategy for improving employee recruitment, retention and engagement within hospitality organizations. *Human Resource Management International Digest, 16*(7), 12.

Judge, T. A., Van Vianen, A. E. M., & De Pater, I. (2004). Emotional stability, core self-evaluations, and job outcomes: A review of the evidence and an agenda for future research. *Human Performance, 17*(3), 325–346. doi:10.1207/s15327043hup1703_4

Kahn, W. (1990). Psychological conditions of personal engagement and disengagement at work. *Academy of Management Journal, 33*(4), 692–724. doi:10.2307/256287

Kahn, W. A. (1990). Psychological conditions of personal engagement and disengagement at work. *Academy of Management Journal, 33*(4), 692–724. doi:10.2307/256287

Kahn, W. A. (1992). To be fully there: Psychological presence at work. *Human Relations, 45*(4), 321–349. doi:10.1177/001872679204500402

Ketter, P. (2008). What's the big deal about employee engagement? *T+D, 62*(2), 44-49.

Kroth, M., & Keeler, C. (2009). Caring as a managerial strategy. *Human Resource Development Review, 8*(4), 506–531. doi:10.1177/1534484309341558

Lindorff, M., & Peck, J. (2010). Exploring Australian financial leaders' views of corporate social responsibility. *Journal of Management & Organization, 16*(01), 48–65. doi:10.1017/S1833367200002261

Luthans, F., & Jensen, S. M. (2002). Hope: A new positive strength for human resource development. *Human Resource Development Review, 1*(3), 304–322. doi:10.1177/1534484302013003

Macey, W. H., & Schneider, B. (2008). The meaning of employee engagement. *Industrial and Organizational Psychology: Perspectives on Science and Practice*, *1*(1), 3–30. doi:10.1111/j.1754-9434.2007.0002.x

Macey, W. H., & Schneider, B. (2008). The meaning of employee engagement. *Industrial and Organizational Psychology: Perspectives on Science and Practice*, *1*(01), 3–30. doi:10.1111/j.1754-9434.2007.0002.x

MacLeod, D., & Clarke, N. (2009). *Engaging for Success: enhancing performance through employee engagement*. London: Department of Business, Innovation and Skills.

Maslach, C., & Leiter, M. P. (1997). *The truth about burnout: How organizations cause personal stress and what to do about it*. San Francisco, CA: Jossey-Bass.

Maslach, C., & Leiter, M. P. (2008). Early predictors of job burnout and engagement. *The Journal of Applied Psychology*, *93*(3), 498–512. doi:10.1037/0021-9010.93.3.498 PMID:18457483

Maslach, C., Schaufeli, W. B., & Leiter, M. P. (2001). Job burnout. *Annual Review of Psychology*, *52*(1), 397–422. doi:10.1146/annurev.psych.52.1.397 PMID:11148311

Maslach, C., Schaufeli, W. B., & Leiter, M. P. (2001). Job burnout. *Annual Review of Psychology*, *52*(1), 397–422. doi:10.1146/annurev.psych.52.1.397 PMID:11148311

Masson, R. C., Royal, M. A., Agnew, T. G., & Fine, S. (2008). Leveraging employee engagement: The practical implications. *Industrial and Organizational Psychology: Perspectives on Science and Practice*, *1*(1), 56–59. doi:10.1111/j.1754-9434.2007.00009.x

May, D. R., Gilson, R. L., & Harter, L. M. (2004). The psychological conditions of meaningfulness, safety and availability and the engagement of the human spirit at work. *Journal of Occupational and Organizational Psychology*, *77*(1), 11–37. doi:10.1348/096317904322915892

May, D. R., Gilson, R. L., & Harter, L. M. (2004). The psychological conditions of meaningfulness, safety, and availability and the engagement of the human spirit at work. *Journal of Occupational Psychology*, *77*(1), 11–37. doi:10.1348/096317904322915892

Nimon, K., Zigarmi, D., Houson, D., Witt, D., & Diehl, J. (2011). The Work Cognition Inventory: Initial evidence of construct validity. *Human Resource Development Quarterly*, *22*(1), 7–35. doi:10.1002/hrdq.20064

Palmquist, M. (2003). *Relational analysis*. Retrieved from http://writing.colostate.edu/guides/ research/content/com2b2.cfm

Pech, R., & Slade, B. (2006). Employee disengagement: is there evidence of a growing problem? Handbook of Business Strategy, 7(1), 21-25.

Plakhotnik, M., Rocco, T. S., & Roberts, N. (2011). Increasing retention and success of f first time managers: A model of three integral processes for the transition to management. *Human Resource Development Review*, *10*(1), 26–45. doi:10.1177/1534484310386752

Reio, T. G. Jr, & Callahan, J. (2004). Affect, curiosity, and socialization-related learning: A pathanalysis of antecedents to job performance. *Journal of Business and Psychology*, *18*, 35–50.

Reio, T. G. Jr, Petrosko, J. M., Wiswell, A. K., & Thongsukmag, J. (2006). The measurement and conceptualization of curiosity. *The Journal of Genetic Psychology*, *167*(2), 117–135. doi:10.3200/GNTP.167.2.117-135 PMID:16910206

Rich, B. L., Lepine, J. A., & Crawford, E. R. (2010). Job engagement: Antecedents and effects on job performance. *Academy of Management Journal*, *53*(3), 617–635. doi:10.5465/AMJ.2010.51468988

Richman, A. (2006). Everyone wants an engaged workforce how can you create it? *Workspan*, *49*, 36–39.

Riordan, C. M. (2000). Relational demography within groups: Past developments, contradictions, and new directions. In *Research in personnel and human resources management* (pp. 131–173). Emerald Group Publishing Limited. doi:10.1016/S0742-7301(00)19005-X

Robinson, D., Perryman, S., & Hayday, S. (2004). *The drivers of employee engagement*. Report-Institute for Employment Studies.

Rocco, T., Stein, D., & Lee, C. (2003). An exploratory examination of the literature on age and HRD policy development. *Human Resource Development Review*, *2*(2), 155–180. doi:10.1177/1534484303002002004

Rothbard, N. P. (2001). Enriching or depleting? The dynamics of engagement in work and family roles. *Administrative Science Quarterly*, *46*(4), 655–684. doi:10.2307/3094827

Rothmann, S., & Storm, K. (2003, May). *Work engagement in the South African police service*. Paper presented at the 11th European Congress of Work and Organizational Psychology, Lisbon, Portugal.

Saks, A. M. (2006). Antecedents and consequences of employee engagement. *Journal of Managerial Psychology*, *21*(7), 600–619. doi:10.1108/02683940610690169

Salanova, M., Agut, S., & Peiró, J. M. (2005). Linking organizational resources and work engagement to employee performance and customer loyalty: The mediation of service climate. *The Journal of Applied Psychology*, *90*(6), 1217–1227. doi:10.1037/0021-9010.90.6.1217 PMID:16316275

Schaufeli, W. B., & Bakker, A. B. (2004). Job demands, job resources, and their relationship with burnout and engagement: A multi-sample study. *Journal of Organizational Behavior*, *25*(3), 293–315. doi:10.1002/job.248

Schaufeli, W. B., Bakker, A. B., & Salanova, M. (2006). The measurement of work engagement with a short questionnaire: A cross-national study. *Educational and Psychological Measurement*, *66*(4), 701–716. doi:10.1177/0013164405282471

Schaufeli, W. B., Bakker, A. B., & Salanova, M. (2006). The measurement of work engagement with a short questionnaire: A cross-national study. *Educational and Psychological Measurement*, *66*(4), 701–716. doi:10.1177/0013164405282471

Schaufeli, W. B., & Salanova, M. (2010). Work engagement: On how to better catch a slippery concept. *European Journal of Work and Organizational Psychology*, *20*(1), 39–46. doi:10.1080/1359432X.2010.515981

Schaufeli, W. B., Salanova, M., González-Romá, V., & Bakker, A. B. (2002). The measurement of engagement and burnout: A two sample confirmatory factor analytic approach. *Journal of Happiness Studies*, *3*(1), 71–92. doi:10.1023/A:1015630930326

Schaufeli, W. B., Taris, T. W., & Van Rhenen, W. (2008). Workaholism, burnout, and work engagement: Three of a kind or three different kinds of employee well-being? *Applied Psychology*, *57*(2), 173–203. doi:10.1111/j.1464-0597.2007.00285.x

Seijts, G. H., & Crim, D. (2006). What engages employees the most or, the ten C's of employee engagement. *Ivey Business Journal*, *70*(4), 1–5.

Shirom, A. (2007). Explaining vigor: On the antecedents and consequences of vigor as a positive affect at work. In C. L. Cooper & D. Nelson (Eds.), *Positive organizational behavior* (pp. 86–100). London, UK: SAGE. doi:10.4135/9781446212752.n7

Shraga, O. (2007). *Vigor at work: Its construct validity, and its relations with job satisfaction and job characteristics: Triangulating qualitative and quantitative methodologies* (Unpublished doctoral dissertation). Tel Aviv University, Israel.

Shuck, B. (2011). Four emerging perspectives of employee engagement: An integrative literature review. *Human Resource Development Review, 10*(3), 304–328. doi:10.1177/1534484311410840

Shuck, B., & Herd, A. (2011). Employee engagement and leadership: Exploring the conceptual convergence of two paradigms and implications for leadership development in HRD. In K. M. Dirani (Ed.), *Proceedings of the Academy of Human Resource Development, 2011 Annual Conference*. Chicago, IL: AHRD.

Shuck, B., Reio, T., & Rocco, T. (2011). Employee engagement: An antecedent and outcome approach to model development. *Human Resource Development International, 14*, 427–445. doi:10.1080/13678868.2011.601587

Shuck, B., Rocco, T., & Albornoz, C. (2011). Exploring employee engagement from the employee perspective: Implications for HRD. *Journal of European Industrial Training, 35*(4), 300–325. doi:10.1108/03090591111128306

Shuck, B., & Wollard, K. (2010). Employee engagement & HRD: A seminal review of the foundations. *Human Resource Development Review, 9*(1), 89–110. doi:10.1177/1534484309353560

Singh, A. (2010). A study on the perception of work-life balance policies among software professionals. *Journal of Management Research, 9*(2), 51.

Sparrow, P. R., & Balain, S. (2010). Engaging HR strategists: Do the logics match the realities? In S. Albrecht (Ed.), *The handbook of employee engagement: Models, measures and practice* (pp. 263–296). London, UK: Edward-Elgar. doi:10.4337/9781849806374.00033

Torraco, R. (2005). Writing integrative literature reviews: Guidelines and examples. *Human Resource Development Review, 4*(3), 356–367. doi:10.1177/1534484305278283

Wah, L. (1999). Engaging employees a big challenge. *Management Review, 88*(9), 10.

Watt, J., & Piotrowski, C. (2008). Organizational change cynicism: A review of the literature and intervention strategies. *Organization Development Journal, 26*(3), 23.

Xanthopoulou, D., Bakker, A. B., Demerouti, E., & Schaufeli, W. B. (2007). The role of personal resources in the job demands-resources model. *International Journal of Stress Management, 14*(2), 121–141. doi:10.1037/1072-5245.14.2.121

Xanthopoulou, D., Bakker, A. B., Demerouti, E., & Schaufeli, W. B. (2009). Reciprocal relationships between job resources, personal resources, and work engagement. *Journal of Vocational Behavior, 74*(3), 235–244. doi:10.1016/j.jvb.2008.11.003

Chapter 9
Diversity and Inclusion Management:
A Focus on Employee Engagement

Urmila Itam
REVA University, India

Bagali M. M.
REVA University, India

ABSTRACT

Diversity and inclusion have been increasingly recognized and are the most utilized organizational resources over the last three decades. However, research has demonstrated that many organizations may not have the requisite diversity in their midst. Research further highlights that employees might feel that few of their components of their social identities may be valued and included, leaving them feeling excluded. These attitudes may influence employee behaviors, leading to low morale, high absenteeism, low job satisfaction, negative word of mouth, and so on, which will eventually make the estranged employee leave the job/organization. Understanding the impact of diversity and inclusion on individual, group, and organizations performance is analyzed through employee engagement by developing a framework. To develop a framework that provides rigorous theoretical evidence for its ability to determine whether an organization has indeed engendered an inclusive and engaging environment for its employees is the goal of the chapter.

DOI: 10.4018/978-1-5225-4933-8.ch009

Copyright © 2018, IGI Global. Copying or distributing in print or electronic forms without written permission of IGI Global is prohibited.

INTRODUCTION

Excellence through diversity-inclusiveness is one of the organization's toughest goals, though the term often raises confusion, tension, and controversy. When people think about diversity, they may begin with ethnicity, race and then gender. However, diversity is a broader term which includes age, gender, ethnicity, physical qualities, ancestry, race, sexual orientation, education, geographical location, income, parental status, marital status and work experience, but not limited to these dimensions (Loden & Rosener, 1991). The term diversity has interpreted in many ways – "any differences in an individual that distinguishes from our internal and external groups or a broad range of overt and hidden qualities in a person from others or combination of personality, internal, external and organizational areas" (How, 2007; Johnson, 2003; Moore, 1999; Simmons-Welburn, 1999; Digh, 1998a). These differences are vital and evaluated as the prospects that help in advancing the innovation and technology at the workplace and also bring business and people closer to each other than ever before. Keeping this in view, organizations, business, educational systems and other bodies are exploring new ways to serve their stakeholders better and be successful in the markets.

Workforce diversity has become a potent tool which promotes new ways to accomplish individual as well as organizational goals. Global companies like Starbucks, Deloitte, HCL Technologies, Verizon and many other Fortune companies emphasized that companies must hire people with different skills, gender, race, ethnicity, and ages. Also suggested that managers need to learn how to distribute the diversified workforce evenly and equitably across the company's divisions (Morais *et al.*, 2014; Lundrigan *et al.*, 2012; SHRM, 2009). Studies stated that productivity, financial performance, and predictions for growth and survival of the organization is mostly influenced by the diversified workgroups (April & Shockley, 2007; Kossek *et al.*, 2004; Fredman & Davidson, 2002). However, a study by Gallup consultancy concluded that diversity might help organizations to accomplish the set goals, but in the long run, inclusiveness matters a lot in the overall corporate growth (Riffkin & Harter, 2016).

The 'inclusion' philosophy focuses beyond the concept of *some* and shifts the group effort towards the term *all* (April & Blass, 2010). Moreover, inclusiveness requires a fundamental change in the organizational structure, human resource policies, operational procedures, style of leadership and altogether the culture of the organization (Miller, 1998). It indicates that diversity and inclusion is a total culture change at individual, group and the organizational levels. Further, this was supported by the Thomas & Ely (1996) in their work and concluded that effective implementation and maintenance of diversity and inclusion practices develop positive attitudes and behaviors towards the job and organization. According to Robinson, Perryman & Hayday (2004), employee engagement is defined as "positive attitudes held by the employee towards the organization and its values" (p. 4). Therefore, this chapter identifies the various strategies required to manage the diversified workforce and analyses its impact on the employee engagement and organizations performance.

DIVERSITY AND INCLUSION MANAGEMENT

The subject of diversity management has gained much attention with globalization and recognized its need to satisfy and serve the stakeholders globally. Many managers have experienced in the early 1990s, the new trend in the form of workforce diversity due to the implementation of liberalization, privatization and globalization policy in the Indian markets (Harish & Anil, 1996). Organizational scholars stated that future organizations workforce composition might reach to 90% of women and minorities; many of them would be migrants who may lead to communication challenges; also many racial groups will become part of the company's businesses (Johnston & Packer, 1987; Caudron, 1990; Griggs, 1995). Organizations that appreciate the need to develop and train all the segments of their workforce to ensure unique and competitive in the markets are responding to a huge variety of approaches to managing their diversified workforce (Jamieson & O' Mara, 1991).

Several studies defined the term diversity in numerous ways. Diversity is not limited to traditional thinking like race, gender, and disabilities (ASTD, 1996a;1996b). It is "all the way in which people differ to each other "(Hayles, 1996). In broader sense, it includes all the characteristics of an individual and groups such as race, gender, ethnicity, national origin, age, religion, affectional orientation, personality, language, education, physical looks, lifestyle, marital status, beliefs, geographical origin, tenure with the job and organization, and economic status (Triandis, 1994; Wheeler, 1994; Carr, 1993; Caudron, 1992; Thomas, 1992). According to Morrison (1992), diversity has been categorized into four levels as - racial, sexual and ethnic balance; understanding other cultures; culturally different values; and broadly inclusive. Further, from the Griggs (1995), diversity is the collective effort of primary and secondary dimensions. Primary dimensions of diversity cannot change; they shape the self-image of an individual on others and the world. Secondary dimensions can be adjusted by the change in their geographical location, education qualification, tenure and level of job, and much more but not limited which shown in Table 1.

There is no one definition of diversity, it is a broad, dynamic and evolutionary nature of the process and it has a far-reaching impact on individuals and organizations (Tomervik, 1995). The term diversity has so broadly defined by many researchers,

Table 1. Dimensions of diversity management

Primary Dimensions	Secondary Dimensions	Other Dimensions
• Race • Ethnicity • Sex • Age • Disability	• Religion • Culture • Sexual orientation • Political orientation • Geographical origin • Family status • Lifestyle • Education • Experience • Nationality • Language • Thinking ability	• Beliefs • Assumptions • Perceptions • Attitudes • Values • Feelings • Norms

Source: (Mazur, 2010)

that it is all-inclusive and recognizes everyone as part and valued in the process (Griggs, 1995; Jonhson, 1995). The broadness in the concept shifted from *some* to *all* to focus on maximizing diversity to accomplish organizational and individual goals. According to Hayes & Major (2003), inclusiveness means "a collective judgment or perception of belongingness or valued and welcome member" at workgroups, and organizations units. Further, inclusion as the degree to which individuals believes that their role is critical in the organizational process (Mor-Barak & Cherin, 1998). Studies predicted that adopting diversity and inclusion at the workplace would benefit from enhanced employee commitment and effectiveness (Ferdman *et al.*, 2006; Davidson & Ferdman, 2002). Regardless of whether one looks the concept of diversity and inclusion as an individual, societal, or organizational issues, these demographic changes cannot be disregarded, and these will expect to change significantly in future (Jackson & Associates, 1992). These changes have shown the path to many organizations to investigate the business implications and have provided a solid basis for managing and valuing diversity at the workplace.

Organizational researchers explain that managing diversity-inclusiveness is more of empowering or enabling employees (Thomas, 1992). It prescribes philosophically broad approaches to encompass all the dimensions; emphasizes the managerial policies and skills in the accomplishment of the individual and organizational goals (Henderson, 1994a); changing the standard operating procedure to discover the best work culture for each group (Triandis *et al.*, 1994). Valuing diversity-inclusiveness is wise for individual, social, legal and profitability reasons (Hayles, 1992). The importance of managing and valuing diversity has remained in the field of *International Business*, where many multinational corporations force to adopt the strategies that could lead them to recruit, engage and retain a diverse workforce that mirrors its markets (Simons, 1992; Fernandez, 1993). Diplomacy, religious, voluntary associations are the fields that have shaped and pioneer in dealing diversity inclusiveness and also documented managing diversified cultures at the workplace (Simons, 1992).

Business Cases on Diversity-Inclusion Management

Diversity and inclusion strategy at Walmart is "think globally and serve locally". Across the world, this giant retailer continuous to attract, seek and hire diverse talents and fosters a diverse and inclusive culture. According to Walmart - Diversity & Inclusion report (2015), women's representation in total workforce was 57% and 41% in management roles; people of color representation in the total labor force was 40%, 30% in managerial positions and 22% in corporate affairs. Veterans' welcome home commitment, career link mentoring program, and global women's development series are some successful programs by Walmart efforts to embed diversity & inclusion across the company to drive exceptional business results. Continuous commitment to foster a trust-based inclusive environment for the workforce that they feel connected and supported to each other.

Apple believes that 'most innovative company must also be the most diversified company'. The success story of any company is based on the new ideas they developed and implemented and this can be experienced by seeing things in diverse ways. According to Inclusion and Diversity Report of Apple (2017), it strives to represent the communities which are not involved before and also break the historical barriers in technology. This experience a steady growth in the hiring scores of global females from 31% to 37%, 54% of new hires in the United States who are minorities, and also initiated close the pay gaps for similar roles and performance. Although creating inclusive work-culture is more challenging and requires both commitment and action of both employees and management, Apple strives to help and address unconscious racial and gender bias in the workplace. Cultivating diverse leadership and tech talent, supporting in the promotion of LGBTQ equality, investing in providing resources for Veterans and their families, and exploring various new approaches to support employees with disabilities.

Starbucks is well-known and globally accepted brand in the markets by the people. According to Starbucks (2011), business ethics and compliance,

(..) actively develops an environment that is inclusive of all cultures and their unique abilities, strengths, and differences and promotes diversity as a strategic and competitive business advantage for the company (Morais et al., 2014, p. 41).

Starbucks perceives that cultural competence is essential and it should be enacted principally by top management which in turn influences the behavior of managers and its workforce throughout the organization (Elder *et al.*, 2014; Hinkin & Tracey, 2010). At Starbucks, top management has given the option to their employees to work more hours during weekdays to compress their working days (Hinkin & Tracey, 2010). Similarly, provided flex work schedules to meet their partner's schedules and encourages potential talents with disabilities at the workplace (Marques, 2008, p. 253). Also, employees of Starbucks must consider ethical practices and values when managing customers and staff. Top management takes necessary steps in training their managers as well as employees in handling stakeholders with different cultures (Marques, 2008; Hinkin & Tracey, 2010).

Starbucks adopted open communication system, flexible environment, a broad range of training programs, bias-free interviewing systems, analysis of workforce demographics, gender diversity as best practices for their success (Pohlman & Gardiner, 2000; Kochan *et al.,* 2003; Starbucks, 2003; Bunny, 2007; Lundrigan *et al.*, 2012; Jones & George, 2014; Starbucks, 2014). Starbucks wise business practices have its impact on company's performance and image over time. It always evaluates the difference base in the workforce and spends an enormous amount in doing business with women and minorities (Forsythe, 2005). As a result, Starbucks has become one of the best employers of choice to potential employees; socially responsible and respectable company for the partners, as well as most admired and inspired management for the competitors.

Best Practices to Value Diversity and Inclusion Management

During the last two decades, many organizations have realized that the traditional assumptions made about workforce diversity were critical to appreciating in the current business context (Beilinson, 1991; Loden & Rosener, 1991; Walker 1991). The Conference Board conducted research on 166 leading companies and listed few important diversity initiatives such as – 1) career planning and development activities, 2) culture change, performance, and accountability, 3) employee involvement, 4) communication, 5) learning and development initiatives (Winterle, 1992). Further, Gottfredson (1992) categorized three diversity issues related to gender and ethnicity such as – procedure to reduce sex and ethnicity issues during changes in organizational climate, in accommodating immigrants, and in building career outcomes. Two diversity issues related to individual differences such as – procedure to accommodate local conditions and individual differences among employees. Another study conducted by The Conference Board on 69 diversity managers, researchers and consultants found that developing diversity action plans, incorporation of diversity into mission statement, accountability, employee involvement in all functions, career development, community outreach activities, and long-term culture change initiatives were seven innovative diversity inclusion initiatives (Wheeler, 1995).

Similarly, studies also identified various approaches and strategies for managing diversity and inclusion at the workplace. According to Louw (1995), managing diversity consisting of five phases: (1) identifying the needs and analysing them in detail; (2) designing the diversity strategy; (3) framing unique diversity interventions and initiatives; (4) implementing the above three stages; (5) continuous evaluation and monitoring of diversity strategy process. Further Griggs (1995), stressed that acknowledging the differences, educating the employees about the differences, figuring out the differences among the workgroups and valuing and appreciating those differences at work are the essential diversity strategies to be adopted to manage the challenging workplace. Moreover Loden & Rosener (1991), identified various unique diversity strategies from numerous leading-edge organizations. Few important common practices among them are – strategic goals; continuous monitoring of all HR systems; climate setting; training and retraining as an organizational priority; rewards and enhancing benefits based on results; reinforcing the hiring and promotion systems as per the organization's goals (pp. 166-167).

In summary, most successful organizations have undertaken and implemented numerous unique diversity interventions at each level. However, implementing strategy is not a single and isolated approach; it varies accordingly with the organization's vision, mission, and goals (Arrendondo, 1996). Managing diversity and inclusion requires careful selection of innovative interventions and initiatives tied to business requirements. Further, diversity issues need to work down using the strategic planning procedure of the organization. Evidently, researchers acknowledged that organization's need to assess and reassess its diversity and inclusion strategies and consider it as an ongoing process (Carnevale & Stone, 1994; 1995).

EMPLOYEE ENGAGEMENT

Employee Engagement (EE) is termed to be a new paradigm in the academic research. However, much of the practitioners and consultants' works explained how EE could be created and leveraged (Macey & Schneider, 2008). In general, from the literature, it is observed that EE measures the employees' emotional commitment towards the job and organization (Waldman, 2016). The pioneering work on EE associated with Kahn (1990), also called the father of EE. The idea of "personal engagement and personal disengagement" developed on the premise of the intrinsic motivation theory (Kahn, 1990, p.692). While personal engagement is defined as "the employees differ in levels of connecting selves physically, emotionally and cognitively with the work roles, in contrast, personal disengagement as disconnecting once own presence with the work functions" (p. 693). Further, Kahn (1990) adopted qualitative research approach to study the applicability of engagement to work with a sample of sixteen summer camp counselors and sixteen architectures from different firms. Two qualitative studies have conducted while the first survey was carried using open-ended questionnaire methods and the second study adopted in-depth interview method. The findings of the work identified three psychological attributes as *psychological meaningfulness, psychological safety, and psychological availability.*

May et al., (2004), conducted an empirical research to retest the Kahn's (1990) concept of personal engagement and personal disengagement (Shuck, 2010). The replication research study further confirms that all the three psychological attributes had significant positive relationships with personal engagement, and in particular psychological meaningfulness has the highest positive correlation. Finally, May et al., (2004) concluded that the other work related attributes like working conditions, training, and development activities might mediate the effect of personal engagement.

The burnout family of engagement literature is rooted in positive psychology which states that burnout is a destruction of job engagement (Maslach & Leiter, 1997). Later, it was redefined "Job engagement as the opposite of burnout" (Maslach et. al., 2001; Schaufeli et al., 2002; Seppala et al., 2009). According to Maslach et al., (2001), "job quantity, socialization, degrees of fairness, values, rewards, and control" were the six major burnout dimensions identified from the literature. Excessive workloads, lack of monitoring and authority on work, de-motivated reward system, poor relationships with employees and managers, and inadequate supervision leads to burnout.

A meta-analysis conducted on samples of seven thousand nine hundred thirty-nine (7,939) business units from thirty-six (36) firms using Gallup Workplace Audit (GWA) as a measurement tool. GWA was used to measure the perceptions of employees about their job characteristics, associations at the workplace, and the role of leadership and management. Later categorized employees into three categories – a) Engaged employees – exhibit high degrees of performance and works for the growth of the organization, b) Not-engaged – task completed and not associated with team growth and success, c) Actively-disengaged- express their disregards with the job and the organization at every possible situation (Gallup, 2006).

Saks (2006) was the pioneer in differentiating employee engagement as job and organization engagement. The multi-dimensional approach included individual as well as organization focus and stated that employee engagement is a degree of intellectual and passionate commitment towards the once own job and organization (Baumruk, 2004; Shaw, 2005; Richman, 2006; Saks, 2006). Therefore, Saks (2006) defined EE as a "combination of emotional, cognitive and behavior elements linked with individual role performances". Further, an empirical investigation has been carried out by Saks (2006) with a sample of 102 employees of distinct job positions from various organizations and concluded that "job engagement and organization engagement are distinct with each other". The findings of the study stated that perceived organizational support envisages both job engagement and organization engagement while job characteristics contemplate job engagement and procedural justice envisages organization engagement. Also identified that job and organization engagement mediates the relationship between the antecedents (procedural justice, job characteristics, perceived organizational support, perceived supervisor support, rewards and recognition, distributive justice) and consequences (job satisfaction, organizational commitment, intention to quit, organizational citizenship behaviour) (Saks, 2006 p. 604).

Another set of research work divided the idea of employee engagement into three states as "trait engagement – personality characteristics of an individual; psychological state engagement – refer to once own involvement to the job and work engagement; behavioural engagement – refer to encouragement towards innovation and organizational effectiveness" (Macey & Schneider, 2008). The idea of Macey & Schneider (2008) was criticized further that the concept of work engagement was discussed in the early engagement literature and it could not be a new design of distinct meaning (Saks 2008). Further, the idea of state engagement seems to be more than individual job attributes and study fails to provide the supporting arguments (Newman & Harrison, 2008).

In summary, engagement researchers acknowledge that the concept of employee engagement lacks a final consensus; however, researchers are trying to seek clarifications by linking employee engagement with organizational attributes. Dell et al., (2001) suggested that each scholarly work seems to focus on different factors of the construct rather than all at once nevertheless contributing to the nomological space. Hence, EE is viewed as a psychological state and holds several related organizational attributes; each, in turn, showed some form of enthusiasm, absorption, and association. Engagement is all about employees' commitment and passion, as well as, inclination to invest one's discretionary effort to perform beyond the expectation and to help the employer succeed.

HOW DIVERSITY AND INCLUSION BOOST EMPLOYEE ENGAGEMENT

There is no doubt that many studies have proven that there is a significant positive relationship between highly engaged workforce and organizational performance (Deloitte 2015; Fernando, Pedro, & Gonzalo 2013; Avigdor *et al.*, 2007). According to a survey result, 96 percent of top executives' stress that having diversity and inclusive talents at workplace increase the engagement scores as well as organizational performance (Ferry, 2013). In contrast, companies who disrespect the idea of diversity and inclusion in their business strategy have seen highly disengaged workforces

(Riffkin & Harter, 2016). The study conducted by Jones & Harter (2005) stated that intentions of an employee leaving the organization would likely to be high when the employee and the manager were of different race, which in turn leads to disengagement at the workplace. However, if top management able to handle these differences strategically and provide them the best organizational climate may influence the employee intentions to stay with the organization, which in turn leads to high engagement (Jones & Harter 2005). Similarly, Badal & Harter (2013) investigated and confirmed that organizations having diversified workforce and high employee engagement scores record high financial gains.

According to Gallup's study, employee engagement and inclusiveness are believed to be closely related to each other because highly engaged employees are most likely to express that their company values distinct ideas; and responds to discrimination concerns. In contrast, only 3% of the disengaged or actively disengaged workforce agrees with the above statements (Riffkin & Harter, 2016). Based on an EE survey conducted by Sodexo confirms that diversity and inclusion initiatives increased the engagement scores and ranked them as top two drivers of employee engagement (Anand, 2013). Despite having many advantages identified and given by the researchers and consultants, many organizations and the senior management do not have a clear understanding of the effective implementation of diversity and inclusion management at the workplace. Also, they fail to realize the benefits it gives to the individual, group and at the organizational level (Skalsky & McCarthy, 2009).

Diversity-Inclusion and Engagement Framework (DIEF)

According to Fernando, Pedro, & Gonzalo (2013), the objective of any framework related to workforce management must consider two important criteria's – a) generalizability, and b) ultimate goal must lead to the development of individual, group and organizational performance. Drawing from the above assumptions, the author identifies some suitable diversity and inclusion tools from the systematic literature review which can utilize under any organizational circumstances to increase the engagement scores. Intercultural training (McCain, 1996; Koonce, 2001), open communication system (Morais *et al.*. 2014; Starbucks, 2014), Strong senior leadership teams (Daft, 2011; Morais *et al.*. 2014), flexibility at workplace (Mujtaba & Cavico, 2013), balanced work-life (Kossek & Lobel, 1996; Fernando, Pedro, & Gonzalo 2013), equal rewards and recognition policy (Barber & Daly, 1996; Hicks-Clarke & Iles, 2000) or participative performance assessment (Nowack, 1993) are considered as critical diversity and inclusion tools for the framework.

Moreover, interference of contingency variables between workforce policies and performance may disturb the stability of these relationships. Because of the inconsistency, the above-identified diversity-inclusion tools that could lead to superior performance under any settings may contradict (Delery & Doty, 1996). The new idea of theorizing the complex understandings of diversity management was given by Kossek & Lobel (1996) and considered to be the first researcher who studied the benefit of associating internal factors of organizations with diversity-inclusion practices. Further few studies stated that involvement of certain moderating factors such as organization's strategy (Richard & Johnson 1999, 2001; Richard *et al.* 2006), organizational climate (Richard *et al.* 2006) and workforce characteristics (Benschop 2001, p.1167) are vital. These internal factors were grouped and named as diversity climate which defined as a "collection of organizational strategies, structure, and values" (Gonzalez & DeNisi, 2009). Similarly, few European scholars stressed the adoption of external factors like environmental uncertainty (Richard *et al.* 2006), culture (Sippola & Smale, 2007) and sector (Fernando, Pedro, & Gonzalo 2013). Studies also proposed different ideas how diversity-inclusion management models change across countries, and how they are affected by sectors, political, institutional and cultural influences (Goodstein, 1994; Greene *et al.* 2005; Fiona, 2011).

Several psychological studies have proposed that how diversity-inclusiveness impacts on cognitive, emotional and social processes within groups (Kearney *et al.* 2009; Pendry *et al.* 2007; Stockdale & Crosby, 2004; Hobman *et al.* 2003). According to social identity theory, identifying and managing the differences conveniently at individual and groups leads to performance (McKay *et al.* 2009; Pendry *et al.* 2007). The theoretical foundation of EE based on social exchange theory when an employee receives cognitive, emotional and social processes from their workplace; they feel obliged and tend to reciprocate with a high degree of engagement with the job and organization. On the other hand, when an organization fails to provide such conditions for employees, they disconnect themselves with the job and the organization (Kahn, 1990; Maslach *et al.,* 2001). Figure 1 demonstrates the associations developed between diversity-inclusive practices, employee engagement and performance measures. Here, study depicted the construct employee engagement as a mediating variable and internal/external factors as moderating variables.

FUTURE RESEARCH DIRECTIONS

Diversity-inclusion practices are must to excel and sustain financial growth at the country level or the institutional level or company level or the individual level. Keeping update with the change in the global trends in managing the workforce, organizations need to balance their strategies accordingly. Therefore, this section deals with the various key trends that will drive diversity-inclusion policies in future.

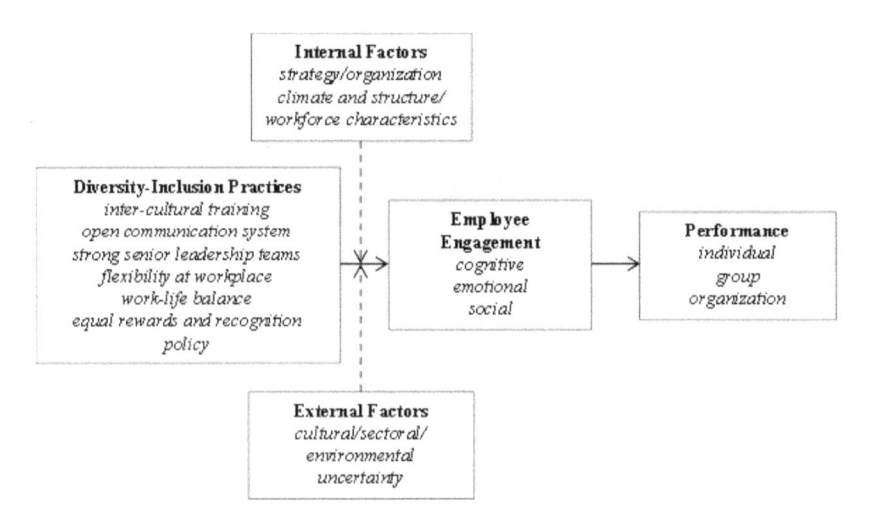

Figure 1. Diversity-inclusion and engagement framework

```
                    ┌─────────────────────────┐
                    │    Internal Factors     │
                    │  strategy/organization  │
                    │   climate and structure/│
                    │ workforce characteristics│
                    └───────────┬─────────────┘
                                │
┌──────────────────────────┐    │    ┌──────────────┐      ┌──────────────┐
│ Diversity-Inclusion      │    │    │   Employee   │      │ Performance  │
│      Practices           │    ▼    │  Engagement  │      │  individual  │
│  inter-cultural training │───▶│───▶│   cognitive  │─────▶│    group     │
│ open communication system│    ▲    │   emotional  │      │ organization │
│ strong senior leadership │    │    │    social    │      │              │
│       teams              │    │    └──────────────┘      └──────────────┘
│ flexibility at workplace │    │
│    work-life balance     │    │
│ equal rewards and        │    │
│   recognition policy     │    │
└──────────────────────────┘    │
                                │
                    ┌───────────┴─────────────┐
                    │    External Factors     │
                    │    cultural/sectoral/   │
                    │      environmental      │
                    │       uncertainty       │
                    └─────────────────────────┘
```

Companies should think beyond the current government legislations like the Equal Employment Opportunities, and other parallel acts that protect the diverse workforce from discrimination.Encouraging more women in boards, avoiding differences when promoting women to leadership positions, and equal pay for any gender are few female economic development activities to be considered. Aging workforce is one of the biggest concern for many global economies that increases not only the pension and healthcare expenses but also slowdowns the economic growth. Hence, the government should raise the retirement age based on health conditions, profession in which individual holding and other similar criteria. To manage the aged and women workforce, companies should encourage flex-work plans like work from anywhere, as well as allowance and health benefits to the parents of young children.

Rebalancing economies is the current buzz word for the countries due to the global recession. Companies want to balance and rebalance their financial position strong globally by spreading their roots into every business, sector, location, and markets. Further, change in migration patterns such as highly skilled, and flexibility in adopting change are some of the essential requirements of many global firms. Companies are very keen in hiring migrants with the above conditions as well as to capture the best talents from the talent pool. With these things in mind, organizations and their workforce must be willing to learn each activity from each other to be productive.

Organizations with wise leadership team will focus more on performance rather than the individual differences such as age, gender, race or sexual orientation, which will, in turn, enhance firms competitiveness. Management must develop diversity strategies, in a way they promote and encourage fair and equal treatment to all the employees and stand as role models for a better workplace where everybody can become part of it.

CONCLUSION

In conclusion, an exhaustive review of available literature on managing diverse workforce demonstrates the importance of various managerial practices in handling the diverse employee base. Ideas like open communication system fosters better work culture; demonstrate how organizations benefited by allowing employees to understand the fellow employees culture using inter-cultural training; involvement at every level irrespective of their differences through equal opportunity practices; the critical senior leadership roles in promoting ethical work culture; tell us how diversity factors challenges and benefits the organizations and its team; and finally, the various internal and external factors that influence the perceptions of an employee towards job and organization.

A brief summation of two business cases helps us to highlight the significance of initiating the implementation of unique and innovative diversity-inclusive practices at workplace. Most important among all the ideas is that the organizational leaders and managers must able to understand the background and differences in the workforce. The practices and methods are given for the management to improve their skills to manage diverse workforce so they can increase the individual, group and organizational performance. An outcome of cultural training not only improves employee communication but also improves the company's visibility at the time of demonstrating the cultural competencies at the corporate level.

Although companies realize the importance of diversity and inclusion practices at their workplace, the challenging effects of internal and external factors like culture, environmental uncertainty, climate, structure, sector and workforce characteristics are not considered much. Therefore, the chapter considered these factors as moderating variables to enhance the diversity climate of an organization further. Moreover, the organizations' culture should be respectful, unique, healthy, flexible, open and active to encourage employee commitment and engagement. On the other hand, improvement in the engagement scores ensures growth at individual, group and organizational performance. At last, the authors, believe that the developed framework can help to overcome the drawbacks outlined and understand how differences in the workforce can be managed and encouraged towards individual, group or organizations growth and development.

REFERENCES

American Society for Training and Development (ASTD). (1996a). *ASTD buyer's guide &consultant directory*. Alexandria, VA: Author.

Anand, R. (2013, February 26). *How Diversity and Inclusion Drive Employee Engagement*. Princeton, NJ: Academic Press.

Apple. (2017). *Inclusion and Diversity*. Retrieved 08 14, 2017, from https://www.apple.com/diversity/: https://www.apple.com/diversity/

April, K., & Blass, E. (2010). Measuring Diversity Practice And Developing Inclusion. *Dimensions*, *1*(1), 59–66.

April, K., & Shockley, M. (2007). *Diversity: New Realities in a Changing World*. Basingstoke, UK: Palgrave Macmillan. doi:10.1057/9780230627529

Arredondo, P. (1996). *Successful diversity management initiatives: A blueprint forplanning and implementation*. Thousand Oaks, CA: Sage.

ASTD. (1996b). *National report on human resources*. Alexandria, VA: Author.

Avigdor, A., Deborah, B., Jennifer, K., Daniel, K., & Bernardo, M. F. (2007). Workgroup inclusion, diversity, and performance. *Gender and Diversity in Organizations Division Academy of Management*, *2007*, 1–24.

Badal, S., & Harter, J. K. (2013). Gender Diversity, Business-Unit Engagement, and Performance. *Journal of Leadership & Organizational Studies*, *21*(4), 354–365. doi:10.1177/1548051813504460

Barber, A. E., & Daly, C. L. (1996). Compensation and diversity: new pay for a new workforce? In E. E. Kossek & S. A. Lobel (Eds.), *Managing Diversity: Human Resource Strategies for Transforming the Workplace*. Cambridge, UK: Blackwell.

Baumruk, R. (2004). The missing link: The role of employee engagement in business success. *Workspan*, *47*, 48–52.

Beilinson, J. (1991). How one company invites workforce 2000 to its door. *Management Review*, *5*(3), 1–3.

Benschop, Y. (2001). Pride, prejudice and performance: Relations between HRM, diversity and performance. *International Journal of Human Resource Management*, *12*(7), 1166–1181. doi:10.1080/09585190110068377

Bunny. (2007, September 13). *Bunny's Story. Starbucks Barista Victimized by Age Discrimination. Industrial Workers of the World*. Retrieved 04 12, 2017, from http://www.iww.org/node/3649

Carnevale, A. P., & Stone. (1994). Diversity beyond the golden rule. *Training & Development, 49*(10), 22–39.

Carnevale, A. P., & Stone, S. C. (1995). *The American mosaic*. New York: McGraw-Hill.

Carr, C. (1993). Diversity and performance: A shotgun marriage? *Performance Improvement Quarterly*, (6): 115–126.

Caudron, S. (1990). Monsanto responds to diversity. *The Personnel Journal, 69*(11), 71–77.

Caudron, S. (1992). U.S. West finds strength in diversity. *The Personnel Journal, 71*(3), 40–44.

Daft, R. L. (2011). The Leadership Experience (5th ed.). Cengage Learning.

Davidson, M. N., & Ferdman, B. M. (2002). The experience of inclusion. In B. Parker, B. M. Ferdman, P. Dass (Orgs.), *Inclusive and effective networks: Linking diversity theory and practice.* Presented at All-Academy symposium presented at the annual conference of the Academy of Management, Denver, CO.

Delery, J. E., & Doty, D. H. (1996). Modes of theorizing in strategic human resource management: Test of universalistic, contingency, and configurational performance predictions. *Academy of Management Journal, 39*(4), 802–835. doi:10.2307/256713

Dell, D., Ainspan, A., Nathan, Bodenberg, A., & Thomas. (2001). Engaging Employees Through Your Brand. The Conference Board.

Deloitte. (2015). *Global Human Capital Trends 2015 Leading in the new world of work*. Deloitte University Press.

Digh, P. (1998a). Coming to terms with diversity. *HRMagazine, 43*(12), 3.

Elder, S. D., Lister, J., & Dauvergne, P. (2014). Big retail and sustainable coffee: A new development studies research agenda. *Progress in Development Studies, 14*(1), 77–90. doi:10.1177/1464993413504354

Ferdman, B. M., Allen, A., Barrera, V., & Vuong, V. (2006). *The experience of inclusion and inclusive behavior.* Unpublished paper. Marshall Goldsmith School of Management, Alliant International University.

Ferdman, B. M., & Davidson, M. N. (2002). Inclusion: What can I and my organization do about it? *The Industrial-Organizational Psychologist, 29*(4), 80–85.

Fernandez, J. P. (1993). *The diversity advantage*. New York: Lexington Books.

Fernando, M. A., Pedro, M. R., & Gonzalo, S. G. (2013). Workforce diversity in strategic human resource management models. *Cross Cultural Management, 20*(1), 39–49. doi:10.1108/13527601311296247

Ferry, K. (2013). *Executive attitudes on diversity positive, but actions lagging, Korn Ferry Institute survey finds*. Los Angeles, CA: Korn Ferry Institute.

Ferry, K. (2013). *Diversity and Inclusion Survey*. Haygroup.

Fiona, C. (2011). Equality, diversity and corporate responsibility. *Equality, Diversity and Inclusion. International Journal (Toronto, Ont.), 30*(8), 719–734.

Forsythe, J. (2005). Starbucks Coffee Company. Leading with diversity. *The New York Times*.

Gallup. (2006). Gallup study: Engaged employees inspire company innovation: national survey finds that passionate workers are most likely to drive organisations forward. *The Gallup Management Journal*.

Gonzalez, J. A., & DeNisi, A. S. (2009). Cross-level effects of demography and diversity climate on organizational attachment and firm effectiveness. *Journal of Organizational Behavior, 30*(1), 21–40. doi:10.1002/job.498

Goodstein, J. D. (1994). Institutional pressures and strategic responsiveness: Employer involvement in work-family issues. *Academy of Management Journal, 37*(2), 350–382. doi:10.2307/256833

Gottfredson, L. S. (1992). Dilemmas in developing diversity programs. In S. E. Jackson (Ed.), *Diversity in the workplace* (pp. 59–83). New York: Guilford Press.

Greene, A. M., Kirton, G., & Wrench, J. (2005). Trade union perspectives on diversity management: A comparison of the UK and Denmark. *European Journal of Industrial Relations, 11*(2), 179–196. doi:10.1177/0959680105053962

Griggs, L. B. (1995). Valuing diversity: Where from ...where to? In L. B. Griggs & L. L. Louw (Eds.), *Valuing diversity: New tools for a new reality* (pp. 1–14). New York: McGraw-Hill.

Harish, C. J., & Anil, V. (1996). Managing workforce diversity for competitiveness The Canadian experience. *International Journal of Manpower, 17*(4/5), 14–29. doi:10.1108/01437729610127677

Hayes, B. C., & Major, D. A. (2003). *Creating inclusive organizations: Its meaning and measurement.* Paper presented at the 18th annual conference of the Society for Industrial and Organizational Psychology, Orlando, FL.

Hayles, V. R. (1996). Diversity training and development. In The ASTD training and development handbook (pp. 104-123). New York: McGraw-Hill.

Hayles, V. R. (1992). Valuing diversity in the food industry. *Food Engineering*, *64*(4), 186.

Henderson, G. (1994a). *Cultural diversity in the workplace: Issues and strategies.* Westport, CT: Quorum Books.

Hicks-Clarke, D., & Iles, P. (2000). Climate for diversity and its effects on career and organisational attitudes and perceptions. *Personnel Review*, *29*(3), 324–345. doi:10.1108/00483480010324689

Hinkin, T. R., & Tracey, J. B. (2010). What makes is so great? An analysis of human resources practices amongst Fortune's best companies to work for. *Cornell Hospitality Quarterly*, *51*(2), 158–170. doi:10.1177/1938965510362487

Hobman, E. V., Bordia, P., & Gallois, C. (2003). Consequences of feeling dissimilar from others in a work teams. *Journal of Business and Psychology*, *17*(3), 301–304. doi:10.1023/A:1022837207241

How should my organization define diversity? (2007). Retrieved 05 11, 2017, from http://www.shrm.org/diversity/library_published/nonIC/CMS_011970.asp#TopOfPag

Jackson, S. E., & Associates. (1992). Diversity in the workplace. In Society for Industrial and Organizational Psychology. New York: Guilford Press.

Jamieson, D., & O'Mara, J. (1991). *Managing workforce 2000: Gaining the diversity advantage.* San Francisco, CA: Jossey-Bass.

Johnson, J. P., III. (2003). *Creating a diverse workforce.* Retrieved 06 11, 2017, from http://www.shrm.org/hrresources/whitepapers_published/CMS_005379.asp#P-

Johnson, S. J. (1995). The status of valuing and managing diversity in Fortune 500 service organizations: Perceptions of top human resource professionals. *Academy of Human Resource Development (AHRD) Conference Proceedings.*

Johnston, W. B., & Packer, A. E. (1987). *Workforce 2000: Work and workers for the 21st century.* Indianapolis, IN: Hudson Institute.

Jones, G. R., & George, J. M. (2014). *Contemporary Management* (8th ed.). New York: McGraw-Hill.

Jones, J. R., & Harter, J. K. (2005). Race effects on the employee engagement-turnover intention relationship. *Journal of Leadership & Organizational Studies, 11*(2), 78–88. doi:10.1177/107179190501100208

Kahn, W. A. (1990). Psychological conditions of personal engagement and disengagement at work. *Academy of Management Journal, 33*(4), 692–724. doi:10.2307/256287

Kearney, E., Gebert, D., & Voelpel, S. C. (2009). When and how diversity benefits teams: The importance of team members' need for cognition. *Academy of Management Journal, 52*(3), 581–598. doi:10.5465/AMJ.2009.41331431

Kochan, T., Bezrukova, K., Ely, R., Jackson, S., Joshi, A., Jehn, K., & Thomas, D. et al. (2003). The effects of diversity on business performance: Report of the diversity research network. *Human Resource Management, 42*(1), 3–21. doi:10.1002/hrm.10061

Koonce, R. (2001). Redefining diversity: It's not just the right to do; it also makes good business sense. *Training & Development, 12*(12), 22–32.

Kossek, E. E., & Lobel, S. A. (1996). *Managing Diversity: Human Resource Strategies for Transforming the Workplace*. Cambridge, UK: Blackwell.

Kossek, E. E., Lobel, S. A., & Brown, J. (2004). 'Human Resource Strategies to Management Workforce Diversity:Examining "The Business Case". In A. M. Konrad, P. Prasad, & J. K. Pringle (Eds.), *Handbook of Workplace Diversity*. Thousand Oaks, CA: Sage Publications.

Lee, Y.-K., Kim, S., & Kim, S. Y. (2013). *The Impact of Internal Branding on Employee Engagement and outcome variables in the Hotel Industry*. Asian Pacific Journal of Tourism Research.

Loden, M., & Rosener, J. B. (1991). *Workforce America! Managing Employee Diversity as a Vital Resource*. Business One Irwin.

Louw, L. L. (1995). No potential lost: The valuing diversity journeyan integrated approach to systemic change. In L. B. Griggs & L. L. Louw (Eds.), *Valuing diversity: New tools for a new reality* (pp. 15–58). New York: McGraw-Hill.

Lundrigan, M., Tangsuvanich, V. L., Wu, S., & Mujtaba, B. (2012). Coaching a diverse workforce: The impact of changing demographics for modern leaders. *International Journal of Humanities and Social Science, 2*(3), 40–48.

Lundrigan, M., Tangsuvanich, V. L., Wu, S., & Mujtaba, B. G. (2012). Coaching a diverseworkforce: The impact of changing demographics for modern leaders. *International Journal of Humanities and Social Science*, *2*(3), 40–48.

Macey, W., & Schneider, B. (2008). The meaning of employee engagement. *Industrial and Organizational Psychology: Perspectives on Science and Practice*, *1*(1), 3–30. doi:10.1111/j.1754-9434.2007.0002.x

Marques, J. F. (2008). Spiritual performance from an organizational perspective: The Starbucks way. *Corporate Governance*, *8*(3), 248–257. doi:10.1108/14720700810879141

Maslach, C., & Leiter, M. P. (1997). *The truth about Burnout*. New York: Jossey-Bass.

Maslach, C., Schaufelli, W. B., & Leiter, M. P. (2001). Job burnout. *Annual Review of Psychology*, *52*(1), 397–422. doi:10.1146/annurev.psych.52.1.397 PMID:11148311

May, D. R., Gilson, R. L., & Harter, L. M. (2004). The psychological conditions of meaningfulness, safety and availability and the engagement of human spirit at work. *Journal of Occupational and Organizational Psychology*, *77*(1), 11–37. doi:10.1348/096317904322915892

Mazur, B. (2010). Cultural Diversity in Organisational Theory and Practice. *Journal of Intercultural Management*, *2*(2), 5–15.

McCain, B. (1996). Multicultural team learning: An approach towards communication competency. *Management Decision*, *34*(6), 65–68. doi:10.1108/00251749610121498

McKay, P., Avery, D. R., & Morris, M. (2009). A tale of two climates: Diversity climate from subordinates' and managers' perspectives and their role in store unit sales. *Personnel Psychology*, *62*(4), 767–791. doi:10.1111/j.1744-6570.2009.01157.x

Miller, F. A. (1998). 'Strategic culture change: The door to achieving high performance and inclusion'. *Public Personnel Management*, *27*(2), 151–160. doi:10.1177/009102609802700203

Moore, S. (1999). Understanding and managing diversity among groups at work: Key issues for organizational training and development. *Journal of European Industrial Training*, *23*(4/5), 208–217. doi:10.1108/03090599910272086

Mor-Barak, M. E., & Cherin, D. A. (1998). A tool to expand organizational understanding of workforce diversity: Exploring a measure of inclusion-exclusion. *Administration in Social Work*, *22*(1), 47–64. doi:10.1300/J147v22n01_04

Morais, U. P., Jacqueline, P., Kevin, S., Lucien, S., Roiner, R., & Yesenia Rivera, M. B. (2014). Managing Diverse Employees at Starbucks: Focusing on Ethics and Inclusion. *International Journal of Learning & Development, 4*(3), 35–50. doi:10.5296/ijld.v4i3.5994

Morrison, A. M. (1992). *The new leaders: Guidelines on leadership diversity in America.* San Francisco, CA: Jossey-Bass.

Mujtaba, B. G., & Cavico, F. J. (2013). Corporate Social Responsibility and Sustainability Model for Global Firms. *Journal of Leadership, Accountability and Ethics, 10*(1), 58–75.

Newman, D. A., & Harrison, D. A. (2008). Been there bottle that: Are state and behavior work engagement and useful construct "wines"? *Industrial and Organizational Psychology: Perspectives on Science and Practice, 1*(1), 31–35. doi:10.1111/j.1754-9434.2007.00003.x

Nowack, K. M. (1993). 360-degree feedback: The whole story. *Training & Development, 47,* 69–72.

Pendry, L., Driscoll, D., & Field, S. (2007). Diversity training: Putting theory into practice. *Journal of Occupational and Organizational Psychology, 80*(1), 27–50. doi:10.1348/096317906X118397

Pohlman, R. A., & Gardiner, G. S. (2000). *Value Driven Management, How to Create and Maximize Value Over Time for Organizational Success.* New York: Amacom.

Ravichandran, K. K., Arasu, R. R., & Arun Kumar, S. S. (2011). The Impact of Emotional Intelligence on Employee Work Engagement Behavior: An Empirical Study. *International Journal of Business and Management, 6*(11), 157–169. doi:10.5539/ijbm.v6n11p157

Richard, O., & Johnson, N. B. (1991). Making the connection between formal human resource diversity practices and organizational effectiveness: Beyond management fashion. *Performance Improvement Quarterly, 12*(1), 77–96. doi:10.1111/j.1937-8327.1999.tb00116.x

Richard, O. C., Ford, D., & Ismail, K. (2006). Exploring the performance effects of visible attribute diversity: The moderating role of span of control and organizational life cycle. *International Journal of Human Resource Management, 17*(12), 2091–2109. doi:10.1080/09585190601000246

Richard, O. C., & Johnson, N. B. (2001). Understanding the impact of human resource diversity practices on firm performance. *Journal of Managerial Issues, 2,* 177–195.

Richman, A. (2006). Everyone wants an engaged workforce how can you create it? *Workspan*, *49*, 36–39.

Riffkin, R., & Harter, J. (2016). *Using Employee Engagement to Build a Diverse Workforce*. Gallup Inc.

Robinson, D., Perryman, S., & Hayday, S. (2004). *The Drivers of Employee Engagement Report 408*. Institute for Employment Studies.

Saks, A. (2008). The Meaning and Bleeding of Employee Engagement: How Muddy Is the Water? *Industrial and Organizational Psychology: Perspectives on Science and Practice*, *1*(1), 40–43. doi:10.1111/j.1754-9434.2007.00005.x

Saks, A. M. (2006). Antecedents and consequences of employee engagement. *Journal of Managerial Psychology*, *21*(7), 600–619. doi:10.1108/02683940610690169

Schaufeli, W. B., Salanova, M., González-romá, V., & Bakker, A. B. (2002). The measurement of engagement and burnout: A two sample confirmatory factor analytic approach. *Journal of Happiness Studies*, *3*(1), 71–92. doi:10.1023/A:1015630930326

Seppälä, P., Mauno, S., Feldt, T., Hakanen, J., Kinnunen, U., & Schaufeli, W. et al.. (2009). The Construct Validity of the Utrecht Work Engagement Scale: Multisample and Longitudinal Evidence. *Journal of Happiness Studies*, *10*(4), 459–481. doi:10.1007/s10902-008-9100-y

Shaw, K. (2005). An engagement strategy process for communicators. *Strategic Communication Management*, *9*(3), 26–29.

SHRM. (2009). *Global Diversity and Inclusion- Perceptions, Practices and Attitudes*. Society for Human Resource.

Shuck, M. B. (2010). *Employee Engagement: An examination of antecedent and outcome varaibles* (Doctoral Thesis). Florida International University.

Simmons-Welburn, J. (1999). Diversity dialogue groups: A model for enhancing work place diversity. *Journal of Library Administration*, *27*(1-2), 111–121. doi:10.1300/J111v27n01_08

Simons, G. F. (1992). *The questions of diversity: Assessment tools for organizations and individuals* (4th ed.). Amherst, MA: ODT Incorporated.

Sippola, A., & Smale, A. (2007). The global integration of diversity management: A longitudinal case study. *International Journal of Human Resource Management*, *18*(11), 1895–1916. doi:10.1080/09585190701638101

Skalsky, P., & McCarthy, G. (2009). *Diversity Management in Australia and its Impact on Employee Engagement*. World at Work.

Starbucks. (2003). *Living our values. Corporate Social Responsibility. Fiscal 2003*. Annual Report. Author.

Starbucks. (2011). *Business ethics and compliance*. Author.

Starbucks. (2014). *Diversity and inclusion*. Author.

Stockdale, M. S., & Crosby, F. (2004). *The Psychology and Management of Workplace Diversity*. Boston, MA: Blackwell.

Thomas, D. A., & Ely, R. (1996, September/October). Making differences matter: A new paradigm for managing diversity. *Harvard Business Review*, 79–90.

Thomas, R. R. (1992). Managing diversity: A conceptual framework. In *Diversity in the workplace* (pp. 306–317). New York: Guilford Press.

Tomervik, K. (1995). Workforce diversity in Fortune 500, corporations headquartered in Minnesota: Concepts and practices. *Academy of Human Resource Development (AHRD) Conference Proceedings*.

Triandis, H. C. (1994). *Culture and social behavior*. New York: McGraw-Hill.

Triandis, H. C., Kurowski, L. L., & Gelfand, M. J. (1994). Workplace diversity. In H. C. Triandis, M. Dunnette, & L. M. Hough (Eds.), *Handbook of industrial and organizational psychology* (pp. 770–827). Palo Alto, CA: Consulting PsychologistsPress.

Waldman. (2016). *The Importance of Diversity and inclusion on Employee Engagement*. The Employee Engagement Blog.

Walker, B. A. (1991). Valuing differences: The concept and a model. In M. A. Smith & S. J. Johnson (Eds.), *Valuing differences in the workplace* (pp. 23–44). Alexandria, VA: ASTD Press.

Walmart. (2015). *Diversity & Inclusion*. Global Office of Diversity and Inclusion.

Wheeler, M. L. (1994). *Diversity training*. New York: The Conference Board.

Wheeler, M. L. (1995). *Diversity: Business rationale and strategies*. New York: The Conference Board.

Winter, M. (1992). *Workforce diversity: Corporate challenges*. New York: The Conference Board.

KEY TERMS AND DEFINITIONS

Cognitive: It is a psychological process of acquisition and understanding of knowledge, experience, and the senses.

Culture: It is a complex set of shared values, beliefs, and behaviors that are taught, learned, and shared by a group of people.

EE: Abbreviation of employee engagement.

Emotional: It is a complex state of feeling that results in physical and psychological changes that influence thought and behavior.

Equal Employment Opportunity: These terms are used to ensure that barriers to inclusion and historical sources of exclusion are eliminated.

Leaders: All the employees who are responsible for showing their leadership skills to accomplish the organization's vision, mission, and goals.

Performance: It comprises the actual output or results of an entity as measured against its intended outputs.

Workforce Management: It is an integrated set of processes that an organization utilizes to enhance the performance of its employees on the individual, departmental, and unit-wide level.

Chapter 10
Relationship Between Empowerment and Organizational Commitment:
An Empirical Study of IT Industry

Bhanu Priya
Gurukul Kangri University, India

Vandana Singh
Gurukul Kangri University, India

ABSTRACT

This study was done to examine the relationship between empowerment and organizational commitment in the employees of IT sector. Data were collected from 70 employees of IT sector. The study used questionnaire method for the purpose of data collection. Two questionnaires, namely empowerment and organizational commitment, were used to collect the data for the study. SPSS software was used for data operation. The results of correlation showed a significant positive relationship between employees' empowerment and their commitment to organizations. Analyses also revealed a significant positive relationship between the employees' empowerment dimensions (i.e., meaning, competence, self-determination, and impact) and their organization commitment.

DOI: 10.4018/978-1-5225-4933-8.ch010

INTRODUCTION

In recent years the issue of employee empowerment has received increasing attention (Zani and Pietrantoni, 2001). Despite its popularity though relatively little rigorous empirical research has been conducted on its antecedents and consequences (Menon, 2001). Today's organizations are continuously developing technologies and operational processes for excellence in the field of competition. In today's competitive world, one of the important tools for change, to survive organization and to achieve the goals and the concerned missions is human element.Dramatic changes are taking place within the world of work, as organizations seek to keep pace with an ever-growing rate of change driven by technological advances and changes in patterns of consumer demand (Howard, 1995).

Empowerment is the new fuel for the growing and booming workplace (Scott & Jaffe, 1993). Moreover, according to Lawler, Mohrman and Benson, (2001, cited in Spreitzer, 2007) today, more than 70 percent of organizations have adopted some kind of empowerment initiative for at least part of their workforce. Other than that, to be successful in today's business environment, companies need the knowledge, ideas, energy, and creativity of every employee, from front line workers to the top level managers in the executive suite.

For the purpose of global or even stay at some level, training and placement of new forces to continue the growth and development is required and the future belongs to those who have plan and goal for it (Robbins el al., 2002). Therefore, nowadays the most important source of competitive advantage in organizations is committed, motivated and conscientious employees. Unfortunately, its potential talent often does not use in the organization. Therefore, empowerment is remembered the main challenge of managers in the current era. As a result of these challenges, managers must prepare organizations condition so that each person can be stronger, as a committed and competent workforce is one of the conditions necessary for the effective functioning in the modern organization.

Aspirations, goal and ambitions of today's workforce are high as it consists of young and comprehend people. So, it can be said that, there is a need of paradigm shift for today's HR. So, that its primary role, people management should be shift to aspirations management. Employees must be understood firstly as an individuals and then as professional.

As we know that IT sector is a highly service-oriented sector and the employees have direct contact with the customers. To provide better and prompt services to its customers it is essential for the employees to be empowered. The aim of the current study is to identify the extent of usage of empowerment tools in an organization and also to study how empowerment contributes to the working in organizations by measuring the role efficacy level of the employees working in the IT sector.

Organization are continuously upgrading their technology, process & systems to cope with competition & challenging environment. Organizational commitment is defined as an individual identification with and involvement in the organization characterized by strong beliefs & acceptance of the organization.

"While there is agreement among scholars that the concept of organizational commitment indicates the link of an employee to an organization, there has been a controversy over the nature of organizational commitment" (Kumari & Priya, 2017). Organizational commitment focuses on employees' commitment to the organization. Meyer and Allen (1997) refer to Morrow & McElroy's (1993) statement that organizational commitment is the most maturely developed of all the work commitment constructs.

Meyer and Allen (2007) divide organizational commitment into three dimensions: affective, continuance, and normative commitment. Affective commitment refers to employees' emotional attachment, identification with, and involvement in the organization. Employees with a strong affective commitment stay with the organization because they want to. Continuance commitment refers to employees' assessment of whether the costs of leaving the organization are greater than the costs of staying. Employees who perceive that the costs of leaving the organization are greater than the costs of staying remain because they need to. Normative commitment refers to employees' feelings of obligation to the organization. Employees with high levels of normative commitment stay with the organization because they feel they ought to. Organizational Commitment can be defined as strength of feeling of responsibility that an employee has towards the mission of the organizations. Affective commitment results in better performance and more meaningful contributions, followed by normative commitment, followed by continuance commitment (Meyer & Allen, 1997).

LITERATURE REVIEW

Nazdro, Rusuli, Nagarubini and Hakim *(2017)* findings of the study indicated that when the nurses feel empowered by giving them autonomy, freedom and opportunity in determining how they do their job, they will be more committed to their their job. There is a positive significant relationship between empowerment and organizational commitment of employees.

Rana and Singh *(2016)* investigated the relationship between organizational commitment, empowerment and demographic variables. Analyses revealed that age and income significantly correlated with organizational commitment, while empowerment was positively significantly correlated with age, marital status, education and experience of the employees. The study found that affective and normative commitment was the significant predictor of empowerment.

Ali and Yangaiya *(2015)* examined the teachers' empowerment (TE) mediated the relationship between distributed leadership and teachers' organizational commitment. The findings of the study indicated that school distributed leadership had considerable effect on teachers' organizational commitment (standardized coefficient .39). The study also proved that teacher empowerment considerably mediates the relationship between distributed leadership and teachers' commitment (standardized coefficient 0.26).

Bani, Yasoureini, and Mesgarpour *(2014)* empirically investigated the relationship between employees' psychological empowerment and organizational commitment in revenue agency of city of Semnan, Iran. The results indicated that there were positive and meaningful relationships between psychological empowerment and organizational commitment components.

Hashmi and Naqvi *(2012)* Findings of their study would not only helpful for banks in Pakistan but these can be instrumental for other organizations for arousing the feelings of commitment with organization in employees. Organizational commitment is strength of any organization. Psychological empowerment plays a significant role in committing employees with organization. Perception of meaningful tasks, autonomy in work, feeling of skillfulness in performing tasks and perception of impacting work outcomes in employees lead to high level of commitment of employees with organization. It is a common phenomenon from the ages back that if you have to get something, you have to invest something. Therefore, organizations must provide such working environment in which employees not only feel psychologically empowered but also become satisfied with their job which will ultimately lead to high level of organizational commitment.

Jha *(2011)* study confirms that the psychological empowerment influences affective and normative commitment positively. However no relationship was found between psychological empowerment and continuance commitment.

Ahmad and Oranye *(2010)* examined the relationships between nurses' empowerment, job satisfaction and organizational commitment. The results of the study revealed that although the Malaysian nurses felt more empowered and committed to their organization, the English nurses were more satisfied with their job. So it was concluded that empowerment do not generate the same results in all countries, and reflects empirical evidence from most cross cultural studies.

Crook *(2010)* states that the key problems of African Public Services are understaffing and lack of organizational commitment. It is argued that the best way foreword is to identify and work with the competent managers to be found in islands of effectiveness encouraging and spreading more effective kinds of incentives and developing more positive organizational cultures.

Nicholson *(2009)* indicated that supervisory leadership practice usage and agent's affective and normative commitment are positively related and agents affective, normative and continuance commitment are negatively related to turnover intention. Job and organizational tenure are not significantly related to organizational commitment.

Allen and Robert *(2008)* investigated proximal institutional predictors or organizational commitment in college students. The study examined the relationship of student-organ fit, satisfaction with faculty, student self-evaluation of academic performance, class level, class attendance time, gender and age upon affective, normative and continuance commitment. The intent of the study was to look at student commitment variables in light of potential business strategy implication for recruitment and retention of students.

Bordin and Casinir *(2007)* findings of the study have shown that several factors are antecedents of psychological empowerment and that empowerment can increase organizational commitment and job satisfaction. More importantly, the findings reveal that supervisory support is an important determinant of the effects of empowerment on job satisfaction.

Kazlauskaite, Buciuniene, and Turauskas *(2006)* stated that the levels of both organizational commitment and organizational empowerments in Lithuanian upscale hotels are rather low, while the correlation between them is rather strong. This implies that improvement of conditions that foster empowerment would lead to a higher level of employee organizational commitment, especially the level of affective commitment that is of greater importance for the organization, as in this case commitment rests on common values and stimulates emotional attachment to the organization.

Lok, Westwood, and Crawford *(2005)* investigated the relationship between perception of organizational subculture and their significance for organizational commitment. Results indicated that perceived subculture has a strong relationship with commitment. They further identified the relative strength of specific types of leadership style and specific types of subculture with commitment.

Jyothi *(2004)* quoted a study on the relation between human resource practices and employee commitment in hotels in United Kingdom and stated that objective recruitment and selection strategies, structural training and development are strongly associated with highly committed employees.

Berg, Kalleberg, and Appelbaum *(2003)* examined whether a high commitment environment would positively impact work family balance in part through its affect on organizational commitment. In their study, a high commitment environment was defined as one that provides intrinsically rewarding jobs, has supportive supervisors and high performance work practices. They found affective commitment did partially mediate the relationship between high commitment organizational practices and work family balance.

RESEARCH OBJECTIVES

- To assess the relationship between empowerment and organizational commitment of IT employee.
- To examine the relationship between empowerment dimension and organizational commitment of IT employees.

RESEARCH HYPOTHESES

- **Hypothesis 1:** There is significant positive relationship between empowerment and organizational commitment.
- **Hypothesis 2:** There is significant positive relationship between empowerment dimension and organizational commitment.
- **Hypothesis 2(a):** There is significant positive relationship between meaning and organizational commitment.
- **Hypothesis 2(b):** There is significant positive relationship between competence and organizational commitment.
- **Hypothesis 2(c):** There is significant positive relationship between self-determination and organizational commitment.
- **Hypothesis 2(d):** There is significant positive relationship between impact and organizational commitment.

RESEARCH METHODOLOGY

The Sample

The sample represented varied range of respondents representing the diversity of the total population. The demographic variables like gender, age, marital status and experience of the employees were included for data collection. Table 1 represents the frequency distribution of the respondents on each of the demographic variables.

Table 1 shows that, from 70 respondents, 50 (71.4%) are male and 20 (28.6%) are female respondents. Out of study participants 46 (65.7%) are married and 24 (34.3%) are unmarried. The sample is representative of all age groups. Majority of the respondents (35.7%) are of the age group between 21 – 25 years. When experience of the respondents is considered it is understood from the table above that nearly half of the sample (42.9%) of the respondents have between 5 – 15 years of experience.

Table 1. Demographic characteristics of the study participants

Demographic Variables		Frequency	Percentage
Gender	Male	50	71.4
	Female	20	28.6
Age	21 - 25 years	25	35.7
	26-35 years	17	24.3
	36-45 years	13	18.6
	45-55 years	10	14.3
	Above the age of 56	5	7.1
Marital Status	Married	46	65.7
	Unmarried	24	34.3
Experience	Above 5 years	25	35.7
	5 – 15 years	30	42.9
	Above 15 years	15	21.4

Sampling Method

Primary data was collected from the respondents by using a questionnaire. A sample of 70 respondents from IT Sector constituted the sample for the study. Convenient sampling technique was adopted to collect the data.

Variables

For this study, empowerment was considered as an independent variable and the organizational commitment as dependent variable.

Tools Used for Data Collection

Empowerment questionnaire developed by Spreitzer's was used to measure the empowerment and its four dimensions. To attain the responses related to the Organizational Commitment, a scale developed by & Mayer (2011) was used.

The reliability of all the two scales has been estimated with the help of Cronbach's alpha and values of reliability are presented in Table 2.

The Cronbach's values for the scales empowerment, and organizational commitment were 0.723 and 0.809 respectively.

Table 2. Reliability analysis

Variables	Cronbach's Alpha
Empowerment	0.723
Organizational Commitment	0.809

DATA ANALYSIS AND INTERPRETATION

Table 3 shows that, the correlation coefficient between empowerment and organizational commitment is 0.967, which indicates that a positive relationship exists between empowerment and organizational commitment at 0.01 level of significance.

On the basis of above result it can be inferred that the first hypothesis is accepted (i.e. There is significant relationship between empowerment and organizational commitment of the IT employees).

Table 4 depicts that, the correlation coefficient between meaning (i.e. dimension of empowerment) and organizational commitment is 0.792, which indicates that a positive relationship exists between meaning and organizational commitment at 0.01 level of significance.

On the basis of above result it can be inferred that the second hypothesis 2(a) is accepted (i.e. There is significant relationship between meaning and organizational commitment of the IT employees).

Table 5 depicts that, the correlation coefficient between competence (i.e. dimension of empowerment) and organizational commitment is 0.703, which indicates that a positive relationship exists between competence and organizational commitment at 0.01 level of significance.

Table 3. Correlation between empowerment and organizational commitment

		Empowerment	Organizational Commitment
Empowerment	Pearson Correlation	1	0.967**
	Sig. (2-tailed)	-	.000
	N	70	70
Organizational Commitment	Pearson Correlation	0.967**	1
	Sig. (2-tailed)	.000	-
	N	70	70

**. Correlation is significant at the 0.01 level (2-tailed).

Table 4. Correlation between meaning and organizational commitment

		Meaning	Organizational Commitment
Meaning	Pearson Correlation	1	0.792**
	Sig. (2-tailed)	-	.000
	N	70	70
Organizational Commitment	Pearson Correlation	0.792**	1
	Sig. (2-tailed)	.000	-
	N	70	70

**. Correlation is significant at the 0.01 level (2-tailed).

Table 5. Correlation between competence and organizational commitment

		Competence	Organizational Commitment
Competence	Pearson Correlation	1	0.703**
	Sig. (2-tailed)	-	.000
	N	70	70
Organizational Commitment	Pearson Correlation	0.703**	1
	Sig. (2-tailed)	.000	-
	N	70	70

**. Correlation is significant at the 0.01 level (2-tailed).

On the basis of above result it can be inferred that the second hypothesis 2(b) is accepted (i.e. There is significant relationship between competence and organizational commitment of the IT employees).

Table 6 shows that, the correlation between self-determination (i.e. dimension of empowerment) and organizational commitment is 0.771, which indicates that a positive relationship exists between self- determination and organizational commitment at 0.01 level of significance.

On the basis of above result it can be inferred that the second 2(c) hypothesis is accepted (i.e. There is significant relationship between self-determination and organizational commitment of the IT employees).

Table 7 depicts that, the correlation between impact (i.e. dimension of empowerment) and organizational commitment is 0.761, which indicates that a positive relationship exists between impact and organizational commitment at 0.01 level of significance.

Table 6. Correlation between self- determination and organizational commitment

		Self- Determination	Organizational Commitment
Self- Determination	Pearson Correlation	1	0.771**
	Sig. (2-tailed)	-	.000
	N	70	70
Organizational Commitment	Pearson Correlation	0.771**	1
	Sig. (2-tailed)	.000	-
	N	70	70

**. Correlation is significant at the 0.01 level (2-tailed).

Table 7. Correlation between impact and organizational commitment

		Impact	Organizational Commitment
Impact	Pearson Correlation	1	0.761**
	Sig. (2-tailed)	-	.000
	N	70	70
Organizational Commitment	Pearson Correlation	0.761**	1
	Sig. (2-tailed)	.000	-
	N	70	70

**. Correlation is significant at the 0.01 level (2-tailed).

On the basis of above result it can be inferred that the second hypothesis 2(d) is accepted (i.e. There is significant relationship between impact and organizational commitment of the IT employees).

CONCLUSION

The overall aim of this study was to investigate the relationship between empowerment and organizational commitment. The results suggest that empowerment is a factor that should not be neglected in theorizing on how motivation takes shape (Dewettinck & Ameijde, 2011). Empowerment has significant and positive effects on organizational commitment (Cho et al., 2006; Smith, Andrusyszyn & Laschinger, 2010). Having the opportunity to build strong relationships with peers, access information and resources, increase the staff's commitment.

Demographic profile of respondents shows the percentage out of sample of N = 70 for each demographic variables separately. The percentage of males is more than females in this study. In age group criteria, the age between 21 -25 shows more percentage than all other age groups. The results depicts that percentage of married employees is more than unmarried employees in banks. In job tenure criteria, 5-15 years experiences have more percentage than all other tenure periods.

The Pearson correlation coefficient test was used to test the research hypotheses. The results associated with the research hypothesis are as follows: The correlation matrix indicates that employee's empowerment has a significant correlation with organizational commitment. Thus, our first hypothesis has been accepted, the empowerment showed a positive relationship with employees' commitment to organization with a correlation coefficient of 0.967, which is significant at 0.01 level (2-tailed). The results of the study are supported by the study of Cho et al., 2006; Smith, Andrusyszyn & Laschinger, 2010. This illustrates that, with increasing employee empowerment, it would be expected to increase the employees' organizational commitment.

The relationship between empowerment dimensions (i.e. meaning, competence, self-determination & impact) and organizational commitment of the employees are positive and significant with the correlation coefficient of 0.792, 0.703, 0.771 and 0.761 respectively, at 0.01 level (2-tailed) of significance. Thus, our second hypothesis and sub-hypotheses (2a, 2b, 2c, 2d) have been accepted. So, with increasing employee meaning, competence, self-determination and impact, it would be expected to increase the employees' organizational commitment.

It could be concluded that higher the empowered employees, higher their commitment towards their organization of the IT sector.

SOLUTIONS AND RECOMMENDATIONS

With the results of the hypothesis testing, the following suggestion is offered: In relation to the first hypothesis and according to the results of the Pearson correlation test positive correlation indicates that higher the organizational commitment higher the empowerment. It is suggested that to increase organizational commitment, employee empowerment variables should be considered. Create a sense of competence in staff, job meaningful by employees, sense of impact in staff and choice in employees are factors that should be considered by the directors to increase employee empowerment. In relation to the second hypothesis, significant relationship between empowerment dimension i.e. (impact, competence, self-determination & impact) and organizational commitment of the employees of bank sector, it is observed that staff mastery and skill can be improved with training periods and this sense may inspire the employees that they are valued. Using methods such as giving more authority to employees caused directly engaging of them in work and understanding its more importance. It is suggested that organization space be so that employees have the opportunity to learn skills to others. Managers provide a space where employees can make use of their skills. It is suggested to both systems that consider empowerment variables as variables affecting the organizational commitment to benefit from the results to improve organizational commitment.

REFERENCES

Ahadi, S., & Suandi, T. (2014). Structural Empowerment and Organizational Commitment: The Mediating Role of Psychological Empowerment in Malaysian Research Universities. *Journal of Asian Development Studies*, *3*(1), 44–65.

Ahmad, N., & Oranye, N. O. (2010). Empowerment, Job Satisfaction and Organizational Commitment: A Comparative Analysis of Nurses Working In Malaysia and England. *Journal of Nursing Management*, *18*(5), 582–591. doi:10.1111/j.1365-2834.2010.01093.x PMID:20636507

Ali, H.M., &Yangaiya, S.A. (2015). Distributed Leadership and Empowerment Influence on Teachers Organizational Commitment. *Academic Journal of Interdisciplinary Studies, 4*(1).

Allen, R. E. (2008). Predictors of Organizational Commitment in College Students. *Dissertation Abstracts International*, *68*(7).

Bani, M., Yasoureini, M., & Mesgarpour, A. (2014). A Study on Relationship between Employees' Psychological Empowerment and Organizational Commitment. *Management Science Letters*, *4*(6), 1197–1200. doi:10.5267/j.msl.2014.5.007

Berg, P., Kalleberg, A. L., & Appellbaum, E. (2003). Balancing Work and Family: The Role of High Commitment Environments. *Industrial Relations*, *42*(2), 168–188. doi:10.1111/1468-232X.00286

Bordin, C., & Casinir, T. B. G. (2007). The Antecedents and Consequences of Psychological Empowerment among Singaporean IT Employees. *Management Research News, 30*.

Cho, J., Laschinger, H. K. S., & Wong, C. (2006). Workplace Empowerment, Work Engagement and Organizational Commitment of New Graduate Nurses. *Canadian Journal of Nursing Leadership*, *19*(3), 43–60. doi:10.12927/cjnl.2006.18368 PMID:17039996

Crook, C. R. (2010). Rethinking Civil Service Reform in African Islands of Effectiveness and Organizational Commitment. *Commonwealth and Comparative Politics*, *48*(4), 479–504. doi:10.1080/14662043.2010.522037

Dewettinck, K., & Ameijde, M. (2011). Linking Leadership Empowerment Behavior to Employee Attitudes and Behavioral Intentions: Testing the Mediating Role of Psychological Empowerment. *Personnel Review*, *40*(3), 284–305. doi:10.1108/00483481111118621

Hashmi, M.S., & Naqvi, I.H. (2012). Psychological Empowerment: A Key to Boost organizational Commitment, Evidence from Banking Sector of Pakistan. *International Journal of Human Resource Studies, 2*.

Jafari, V., Moradi, M., & Ahanchi, M. (2013). An Examination of the Relationship between Empowerment and Organizational Commitment (Case Study Kurdistan Province Electric Staff). *Interdisciplinary Journal of Contemporary Research in Business*, *4*(12).

Jha, S. (2011). Influence of Psychological Empowerment on Affective, Normative and Continuance Commitment: A Study in the Indian IT Industry. *Journal of Indian Business Research, 3*.

Jyothi, P. (2004). Practice of HR Functions in a Small Scale Organization. *Sedme*, *31*(4), 19–26.

Kazlauskaite, R., Buciuniene, I., & Turauskas, L. (2006). Building Employee Commitment in the Hospitality Industry. *Baltic Journal of Management*, 1.

Kumari, P., & Priya, B. (2017, January). Organizational Commitment: A Comparative Study of Public and Private Sector Bank Managers. *International Journal of Business and Management Invention*, *6*(1), 38–47. Retrieved from http://www.ijbmi.org/papers/Vol(6)1/Version-3/G0601033847.pdf

Lawler, E. E., Mohrman, S. A., & Benson, G. (2001). *Organizing for high performance: Employee Involvement, TQM, Reengineering, and Knowledge Management in the Fortune 1000*. San Francisco, CA: Jossey-Bass.

Lok, P., Westwood, R., & Crawford, J. (2005). Perceptions of Organizational Subculture and Their Significance for Organizational Commitment. *The Journal of Applied Psychology*, *54*(4), 490–514. doi:10.1111/j.1464-0597.2005.00222.x

Mogheli, A., Hasanpour, A., & Hasanpour, M. (2009). The Relationship between Employee Empowerment and Organizational Commitment. *Public Administration Publication*, *1*(2), 119–132.

Nicholson, M. W. (2009). *Leadership practices, organizational commitment and turnover intentions: A correlational study in a call centre* (Ph.D Thesis). University of Phoenix.

Poorkyani, M., Abayi, N.H., & Zareie, F. (2015). An Investigation on the Relationship between Psychological Empowerment and Organizational commitment (A Case Study of the Employees of Public Organizations in Kerman). *International Journal of Scientific Management and Development, 3*(1), 757-766.

Robbins, T. L., Crino, M. D., & Fredendall, L. D. (2002). An Integrative Model of the Empowerment Process. *Human Resource Management*, *12*(1), 419–443. doi:10.1016/S1053-4822(02)00068-2

Smith, L. M., Andrusyszyn, M. A., & Laschinger, H. K. S. (2010). Effects of Workplace Incivility and Empowerment on Newly-Graduated Nurses' Organizational Commitment. *Journal of Nursing Management*, *18*(8), 1004–1015. doi:10.1111/j.1365-2834.2010.01165.x PMID:21073572

Spreitzer, G. M. (2007). *A Review of More Than Twenty Years of Research on Empowerment at Work. In The Handbook of Organizational Behavior.* Sage Publications.

Chapter 11
Role of Team Climate in Improving Team Functioning and Team Empowerment

Alpa D. Parmar
The Maharaja Sayajirao University of Baroda, India

Chhaya Patel
The Maharaja Sayajirao University of Baroda, India

ABSTRACT

The changing work force dynamics have great impact on organisation effectiveness as it requires proper and deep understanding of organisation structure and working patterns. The organisations are changing their workgroups into teams and that requires deep understanding of how teams are functioning and how they work within the organisation. The social climate plays a significant role in the improvement of the team climate, which provides shared belief amongst the team member of organisations and leads to the development of positive team climate. This chapter refers to the theory of team climate and provides a different perspective that reflects the difference between team climate and organisational climate. The changing work force diversity and pattern of organisation structure really needs understanding of team climate and how it can contribute to developing conducive team climate for learning within the organisation. Further, the chapter emphasises role of team climate in terms of team functioning and team empowerment.

DOI: 10.4018/978-1-5225-4933-8.ch011

INTRODUCTION

Concept of Social Climate

The climate represents a team's "Shared perceptions of organisational policies, procedures and practices, both formal and informal" (Schneider, 1990:22). The Encyclopaedia of Psychology and behavioural science states that Social climate (represents both psychological climate and social context) is typically defined as the perception of a social environment that tends to be shared by a group of people. (pp.1551). Therefore, Climate refers to "the set of norms, attitudes, and expectations that individuals perceive to operate in a specific social context" (Pirola-Merlo, Hartel, Mann, &Hirst, 2002: 564)

Concept of Organisational Climate

During 1930's an attempt was made by Lewin, Lippitt and White to study how climate had impact on behaviour through induced atmospheres created by the leaders. They found significant relevance in studying the influence of change in behaviour pattern of group members. This lead a stepping stone in understanding climate and its power in influencing the group behaviour. According to Bowen and Ostroff (2004) reflected the understanding of organisational climate is referred as shared perception of what the organization is in terms of practices, policies, procedures, routines and rewards (e.g., Schneider, 2000; James & Jones, 1974; James & Jones, 1979).With the" human relations movement pioneered by Hawthorne, researchers turned their attention from the "hard" physical environment to the "soft" psychological environment; thus the concept of organizational climate was born." Through the analyses of various contributions of several researches carried out on Understanding behaviour in organisations, yet few of the questions are still unanswered. They are: Why internal climates matter for organisations to be concerned about? What dimensions that focuses on psychological climate are important for understanding behaviour? Thus let us understand the concept of Team climate how it evolved from social climate.

Concept of Team Climate

The Team climate emerges from the "social interactions" among team members (Schneider & Reichers, 1983). Numerous studies observed that "social interactions", team member's communication and discuss several characteristics of their environment, and they helped to understand and develop a shared interpretation about "team environment". This interpretation can be designed according to climate facets

(Anderson and West, 1990, 1994, 1998). The climate refers to the social interaction and relationship amongst the team a member that helps the team members to share their views in terms of innovation and help them to develop in achieving their objectives through shared vision and proper task orientation.

How Team Climate Differs From Organisational Climate

The difference in understanding organisational climate and team climate is matter of focus for organisation which need to achieve their goals without any hindrance. As several researchers have viewed climate from different perspectives they have used the same term organizational climate which some researchers have objected as it has different meaning at different levels. According to Howe, James and Jones (1979) organizational climate is only the description of what actually exists in the workplace, independent of distortion due to different perspectives. Schneider (1972) in the study further reveals in search of understanding the climate construct at insurance agency employees at different hierarchical levels observed that most members at different levels perceived climate at different levels, Schneider in the study concluded that probably there is no thing as organizational climate rather at different levels climate may exists as group climate. According to Howe (1977)* the study on two groups in the same organization. It was observed group climate depicting descriptive psychological climate which is perceived as group climate behaviour majorly group members are reflecting within the objective environment. In other words the group climate reflects descriptive psychological climate of individual group members with reference to the situation wherein they work together. The perception of climate is usually related to organizations perspectives and relation with work groups or teams. However, organizations as social systems comprising of many subunits and groups of employees, so "aggregating individual perception about the shared climate" as per organization is difficult to obtain (Danserau and Alluto, 1990; Jackofsky and Slocum, 1988). The various subunits within organizations differ in the characteristics of work environments provided for members of an organization. In addition to this, the various groups of employees differ in their perspectives and their focus on organizational characteristics. Thus, an organization comprises not just one climate, but a variety of different climate sectors and concepts, depending on the subunits (e.g. work groups) and viewpoints (e.g. by job category) of the organizational members. Likewise, work teams can fail because they are not able to build a "positive work climate…consistent supportive team environment and "participative safety climate", which breaks down as conflicts based on personal relations, values or norms develop (Jehn 1997, p.25).

Industry-related safety studies have identified several organizational attributes that contribute to safe employee behaviours. Among these attributes are frequency of non-routine work processes, level of work hazards, level of cooperativeness between employees and supervisors, level of work group cohesiveness, extent of supervisory management of safety actions, and supervisor experience (Simard and Marchand, 1995). Safety studies also suggest that the organization's climate of safety is measureable at the work group level and that the team members place on safety is influenced significantly by supervisor behavior rather than policies and procedures (Simard and Marchand, 1995; Zohar, 2000). In addition, when climates are apparent as less safe, work groups cause a greater number of safety errors.

According to Curral et al. (2001) stated different teams, including teams belonging to organizations, "carrying different tasks requiring a great deal of innovativeness and development quality are associated with higher participation amongst team members, which helped them to do the tasks more innovatively" (p.201).

Kopelman et al. (1990) discuss climate as "Climate is formed from the practices, policies, and procedures of the organization". Thus, a change in practices should effect a change in the impact of climate (Kopelman et al., 1990). Team climate differs from organizational climate, as it focuses on the proximate work environment of individuals which is related to each other as a part of socially significant subsystems within an organization.

Accordingly, Basaglia et al. (2010, p. 544) suggest the following definition: "At the team level, the climate is defined as shared perceptions of the kinds of behaviors, practices, and processes that are supported by a team.

The researcher from several literature reviewed tried to agree to the point that certain characteristics reflects the construct and differentiate Organisational Climate from team climate those characteristics are as follows:

1. Organisational Climate is generally considered to be the construct that can change over time with company's policies, procedures and practices. The climate is defined as shared perceptions of the kinds of behaviours, practices, and processes that are supported by a team.
2. It is observed by and mutual between organisational members, which can be outcome of consensus among employees. The work team that permits team members to allocate shared meaning to events that are important for the team, and determine the actions that will lead to desired outcomes
3. It contains of international imitations of the organisation that employees form through interaction within the departments and through the organisational policies, structures and processes. Team climate denotes the manner of synergy
4. Organisational Climate perceptions are descriptions of work environments, organisational environment events and conditions. Team climate is characterized by "interaction between individuals and units".

Thus the group climate function majorly effects these psychological processes which sort out from a number of stimuli present in the work environment, the relevant ones for the individual, resulting in a meaningful perception to describe the work environment. Thus both parameters are interconnected and interdependent on Individual aspects pertaining to the situation and environment they are observing at workplace.

DIVERSITY AND PATTERN OF ORGANISATION STRUCTURE

A research conducted by Kinnie et al (1996) firms select from a menu the methods their business needs, delayering or the negative approach of downsizing, positive steps. Team-based work organizations, cross-functional management and development teams, emphasis on horizontal business processes rather than vertical structures. HRM policies aimed at high performance and commitment and including communication programmes and participation in decision making. Organization structures are strongly influenced by personal and human considerations – such as the inclinations of top management, the strengths and weaknesses of management generally, the availability of people to work in the new organization and the need to take account of the feelings of those who will be exposed to change.

Tata Communications Limited (TCL) is a global telecommunications company. As the sixth largest mobile service provider in India, TCL is renowned for its cutting-edge, one-of-a-kind innovation - including the world's only, wholly-owned fibre ring around the world and Ethernet ring serving the Middle East.

TCL's focuses on commitment and belief towards creating a workplace that reaps the benefits of diversity.

At TCL's they actively support diversity, work together to socialise, ideate, frame, and implement initiatives in the Diversity & Inclusion. They follow unitary approach emphasising on the organisation and its employees to focus on common goal and employees benefit from the successes achieved by the organisation. Therefore, there is a stress on harmonious relationships and team working. (AON, 2017)

The diversity is becoming a new trend for creating high performance organisation. Companies like Google, IBM and other Global firms. Managing diversity at workplace is a comprehensive process for forming a work environment that comprises everyone. Every manager now has to consider an organisation with diverse workforce for creative and innovative organisation. When creating an effective diverse workforce, an effective manager should focus on individual awareness. Diverse work teams bring high value with more intangible assets to organizations. Formalization of organizational processes improves team empowerment by decreasing uncertainty within the Organisation, whereas formalization of jobs and roles moderates the effect of decentralization and reduces team empowerment by reducing team's flexibility in taking benefit of decentralization. These results show the significance of organization structure as an antecedent of empowerment.

THE ROLE OF TEAM CLIMATE IN TEAM EFFECTIVENESS: IMPROVEMENT OF TEAM FUNCTIONING AND TEAM EMPOWERMENT

Nowadays every organisations wants to be high performance driven organisation. The high performance organisation can be develop through involving performance driven teams. These was mention by Burton et al. (2004) as high performance firms requires a good fit between organizational climate and organizational strategy. Hence, organizations that emphasize interdependence and interpersonal interaction foster collaboration and are more likely to produce an effective team.

At Microsoft Business Solutions (MBS), Darci Kleindl as general manager of sales excellence and sales enablement for the Microsoft Business Solutions (MBS) group inherited a global team of customer support managers, all of whom work with diverse clientele customer's organization, consultants, and external customers. Intially "Darci understands that to have great products and phenomenal software, they need to have the smartest people need to work as team. As they have diverse workforce they preferred the Five Behaviors; it's the operating system for teamwork. They established a framework to build six-month program establishes a common language for the team to communicate, standardize expectations to improve accountability, strengthen leadership abilities, and create an emotionally intelligent culture for effective team functioning and empowerment. The Five Behaviors of a Cohesive Team is a comprehensive team development program at Google based on the work of Patrick Lencioni. It helps both team members and leaders understand how their unique group dynamic can work together to build a more effective team and achieve sustainable results. (Becker, 2015)

The collaboration is an important criterion found in most of the study to understand team effectiveness. "The capacity to plan and coordinate tasks and information has been identified as an important determinant of team effectiveness" (Stevens & Campion, 1994, p. 516). The focus of the service differentiation strategy lies on providing high quality customer services. In order to deliver this high quality, the employees must work together. High trust, high morale and low conflict within the company are necessary to ensure good communication between the employees. Leader credibility and moderate resistance to change support the stability of services. Therefore, to understand the role of team climate in team functioning the following identified five climate factors as being central in determining effective team functioning.

These five factors are:

1. **Participative Safety:** Developing trust participation among team members and their opinions and ideas (Level of empowerment and trust).

At Google's team effectiveness research as well as tools to help team's foster psychological safety. The Psychological Safety is a natural strategy in the workplace for self-protection. At Google, the team members feel with one another, they are to admit mistakes, to partner, and to take on new roles. And it affects pretty much every important dimension we look at for employees. Individuals on teams with higher psychological safety are never thinking of exit from Google, they're more likely to harness the power of diverse ideas from their teammates, they bring in more revenue, and they're rated as effective twice as often by executives. *(Rozovsky, 2015)*

2. **Support for Innovation:** Level of support and encouragement provided by the team for innovative ideas and creativity.

At Ford Motor Company, the organisation emphasizes excellence in its organizational culture of support for innovation at work place as their core values. (Lombardo, 2017)

3. **Team Vision:** Team defines clear goals and objectives.

At General Electric (GE) they want to create environment in there are no boundaries. At GE they want to create an internal teams that is able to work as a cohesive unit and focus their objectives on addressing common goals.(Hegar & Hodgetts, 2007).

4. **Task Orientation:** The team efforts in achieving excellence in what it does.

At General Electric (GE) began developing boundary less organisation establishing work out sessions, each group, led by outside facilitator, then they would focus on ways in which task orientation could be streamlined. As a result of task orientation sessions, GE was able to increase their productivity. (Hegar & Hodgetts, 2007).

5. **Social Desirability:** A Social impression management by team members. (Social Character and Image).

At GE has empowered its bosses and given them more opportunities for motivating the workers. (*Hegar & Hodgetts, 2007)*

Thus, the five factors focus the team climate for improvement of team functioning. West (1990, p.309) and West and Anderson (1996, p.239).According to Anderson and West (1994, p. 3) team climate denotes the manner of synergy that the team has evolved and it can include several different aspects like communication patterns, participation, safety, norms, cohesiveness, task style, vision, and innovativeness. A team that is empowered has the authority, information and skills to make decisions that intensify the drive and performance results. Also, how well a team functions depends largely on how well it is structured (its architecture), how well team members behave toward one another (their interpersonal relation- ships) and the quality of team leadership.

The Team Effectiveness Depends on Team Functioning and Team Empowerment

Team Functioning

The Team functioning is to foster the aspects of inducing team work that are essential to the team for team effectiveness at workplace. If an individuals in team view themselves align with team goals, their feeling develop cohesiveness towards each other developing an environment that helps an organisation to increase their efficiency. (Turner & Reynolds, 2010). This is to say that team functioning direct effect on team effectiveness, like cohesion, collaboration, Purpose, conflict and customer satisfaction (Eisenbeiss & Otten, 2008; Kozlowski & Ilgen, 2006; Polzer, Milton, & Swann, 2002),

There are 6 main factors that influence the *Team Functioning*:

1. Team Spirit
2. Cohesion / Team Relationship,
3. Collaboration and Problem Solving & Decision Making,
4. Purpose and Objectives,
5. Conflict,
6. Customer Focus.

1. Team Spirit

Team spirit is the key agents to performance and success. The most essential aspect of sharing a common goal is constructing a team spirit. Team spirit is a feeling of collaboration. Team spirit is the aspect that can take any business to dominance, expansion, and success. For a group of people in which each team member wants the team to get succeeded, they can expect a high degree of motivation, commitment, and cooperation that lead to higher "team performance", the exceptional results and high efficiency. As J. Richard Hackman discussed in the design of work teams. If "team spirit and performance" of a particular team differ from those of their co-workers, this team might develop discriminatory behavior by focusing on what distinguishes them from the rest of the crowd. Thus, this study considered "team spirit" as a medium of team effectiveness and can become productive for the organization as a whole. Team spirit often produces a healthy dose of friendly competition; not in the sense that each individual is trying to outdo their colleagues, rather, as the group contribute to the overall success of the company, team members will work assiduously to avoid being seen as the weak link in the chain. Conversely, innate trust in a co-worker's abilities enables one to concentrate fully on one's own tasks and responsibilities, without fear of interruption.

2. Cohesiveness /Team Relationships

Cohesiveness is largely influenced by the "interpersonal relationships" of group members (Pelled et al., 1999, p.1). Cohesiveness implies a feeling of togetherness with other group members. Healthy "interpersonal relations" help to maintain effective relationships with team members which contribute to better information exchanges and decision-making" in teams (Pelled et al., 1999, p.2). Jones (1993) also includes a measure of "team cohesiveness" in his research on team effectiveness. For the purposes of this study, "the feeling of unity or togetherness that exists among team members and the degree to which a group exists or operates as a unified within the organization" will be used as the definition of team relationships. Stevens and Campion (1994) also support the importance of interpersonal skills for effective team performance. They state that "team effectiveness depends mostly on the ability of individual members to effectively manage interpersonal relations with one another" (p. 506). Team members can feel cohesion with their teammates but it depends on organizational values and belief. Successful business strategies are usually carried out by an effective team with a high level of team cohesiveness. Highly cohesive teams are more committed to the goals and activities, are happy when the team succeeds and feel part of something significant, all of which increases self-esteem which in turn increases performance.

For Example at Corning Inc.'s Glass and Glass ceramic research and development Laboratory, Innovation is generated by people in the particular area through cohesion created at workplace to develop new kinds of glass.

3. Collaborative, Problem-Solving and Decision-Making

The collaboration is an important criterion found in most of the study to understand team effectiveness. "The capacity to plan and coordinate tasks and information has been identified as an important determinant of team effectiveness" (Stevens and Campion, 1994, p. 516).Problem-solving is an important skill for work teams (Guzzo and Shea, 1992; West et al, 1998). Work teams face what can sometimes be a challenge in problem-solving efforts—collaboration with others on their team Effective problem-solving is an important skill for individual contributors as well as work teams. For example, a nuclear power plant failure could result in horrific consequences for its surrounding community, although such failures are extremely rare (Kohn et al., 1999). As discussed earlier, team members work together on interdependent tasks. This is what separates teams from groups or individuals working in isolation. According to Kirkman and Rosen (1999) "the ability to recognize circumstances in which group members need to work together to solve problems, identify the specialized people to be involved in the problem-solving, and determine an appropriate solution to the problem" will be used as the definition to represent the collaborative problem-solving dimension. According to Tannenbaum et al. (1996) state that "decision-making is centrally important for effective team functioning. We need to design and develop team interventions that will allow team members to practice how to use task-relevant information for effective team functioning and decision making" (p. 519).

For Examples, At Toyota Facet5 programme was launch to develop cooperation among employees for continuous improvement. Facet5 accreditation and the profile analysis gave Toyota's HR Department and the teams which participated a great insight into each other, improving effectiveness and co-operation. (Facet5 Case Studies, n.d.)

4. Purpose and Objectives

According to (Salas et.al. 2005, p. 570) in a complex environment where many variables remain unknown, "objectives" can be difficult to specify and many factors change rapidly. When the team has clear states of objectives to which all members feel committed towards goal. Higher level motivation, fewer demands, higher production, problem-solving and more initiatives are the desirable outcomes of clear objectives and goals which are thepurpose of the team as such.

For example, At DELL, In 1993, John Medica was put in charge of the Notebook division of DELL. During that time the division had several projects undergoing and several projects got canceled which lead to morale down of employees. This was disheartening to the employees who had worked hard on those projects. This lead to productivity reduction and lack of motivation among teams. Thus, company decided to focus the division's efforts on the new Latitude XP. By aligning the team's goals on a single project and encouraging them to work together, DELL saw an improvement in productivity and morale. "Dell realized that aligning teams toward a common objective and creating the same incentive system across the entire company would help direct everyone's talent toward creating value for customers and shareholders." (Terrapin Adventures, 2016),

5. Conflict

Numerous researchershave found evidence that "effective conflict management improves team performance and functioning". (Montoya-Weiss et al., 2001; Jehn and Chatman, 2000; Evans and Dion, 1991; Sundstrom et al., 1990). According to Varney (1989) reports that conflict continued to be a problem in the teams functioning within a large energy company, even after training meetings on how to handle conflict it exhibited the negative impact on team members. Mohrman et al. (1995) expand on the importance of conflict resolution for team effectiveness:

Conflict resolution skills may be at the center of what is required to work collaboratively in the lateral organization. Conflicts resolving is the ability to surpass the differences, to develop a shared understanding, and to work for mutual solutions (p. 251)

6. Customer Focus

Team effectiveness used for this research states, effective work teams seek to meet the expectations of key complements, including customers (Sundstrom, 1999, pg.20). If teams are empowered to work with each of their customers, having straight contact with the customer, team members can control and improve their operations and take corrective actions to resolve problems. Graham and Englund (1997:10) emphasize the impact of the increased focus on customer service, observing that "…to provide today's customers with better solutions, team members need to focus on customer needs. The new organization uses multi-disciplinary teams that move across the organization on the customer's behalf to provide a better solution." For example at AT&T, Apple, IBM, McDonalds, Toyota and other MNCs have given their teams the latest technological advancement and trained them to deal with diverse customers. This world class organisation maintain continuous improvement through benchmarking, re-engineering, innovation based reward system, empowering and restructuring their teams for customers satisfaction.

Team Empowerment

Empowerment has been defined as, "employees having autonomous decision-making capabilities and acting as partners in the business" (Ettorre, 1997). He elaborated that sharing with junior employees comprise four organizational ingredients; a.) Information about organization's performance. b) Knowledge that enables employees to understand and contribute to organizational performance c) Rewards based on the organization's performance and d) Power to make decisions that influence organizational direction and performance.

Organizational formalization (Khandawalla, 1974) may have a beneficial influence on team empowerment by decreasing within-company environmental ambiguity faced by the team, whereas the formalization of work roles (Delery& Doty, 1996) may interrupt empowerment by coercing teams' flexibility.

The key benefit of empowering a work team is the increased ability to achieve the team objectives and goals. Work teams include the people who best recognise the processes they work with daily. Team members recognise the obstacles to achieve the team goals and they are aware of potential opportunities. By empowering the team, decisions can be made on the faster and improvements to the process can be made as and when necessary.Impact allows teams to enhance learning by improving team members' collective understanding of a situation. Determination and motivation are likely to transform into higher levels of learning and process improvement (Edmondson, 2002).

According to Kirkman & Rosen,(1997) they stated that when empowered team members experience impact, or knowledge of how their work affects others, they are more likely to have the information necessary to make accurate adjustments in their work. Empowerment has been empirically linked to innovation at both the team (Burpitt&Bigoness, 1997) and individual levels of analysis (Spreitzer, 1995). Thus team climate innovativeness has impact on team empowerment for team effectiveness.

For example, The Panama canal project in the early 1900's is example of empowerment leadership and team work where in the second chief engineer John F. Stevens knew how to organize work environments and team climate that can energized and motivated team members, which allowed to complete project on schedule. (Hegar & Hodgetts, 2007, p. 280)

The 5 main factors that influence the *Team Empowerment* are: Communication, Team Leadership, Role Clarity, Development / Continuous Improvement and Reward & Recognition.

1. Communication

Campion et al. (1996) found that process features of the team, including communication, most strongly associated to team effectiveness measures in their study. "Effective communication had always a great influence on team processes and outcomes. It is a solid factor of many current models of work team performance" (Stevens and Campion, 1994, p. 511). Stout, Salas, and Fowlkes (1997) "Research in the area of team communication has been showed mixed results, Furthermore, Ahmed (1998, p. 36) points out that face to face communication promotes innovation. Some studies showing generally positive relationships between communication and team performance and some studies showing generally showed negative relationships" (p. 171). The research conducted for this thesis shall provide some clarity regarding the relationship between communication and team effectiveness. For example, Steve Wright, President and Owner of Wright Builders, Central Texas area, 1976 stated that since team concept is working in organisation as structure the flow of communication has been open in all directions throughout the entire firm. He even stated that "communication is the most essential key in providing the best customer service available." He stated that communication play an important role in team effectiveness for building a high level of trust between company and his partners.

2. Team Leadership

When team leaders delegate responsibility, employee act as input and enhance team members' senses of control and monitor, the team members are more likely to experience meaning and impact in their work (Hackman, 1987). The team leader ensures appropriate resources are available to the team, provides training and coaching opportunities, take care of rewards and recognition and influences team empowerment to accomplish team goals. Team Leadership defined as, "the degree to which a leader serves for the team" and obtain result and outcome as required. Guion(1998), defines leadership as the ability to influence others, including "protecting a group from an unproductive route, suggesting alternative solutions, asking critical questions, planning, coordinating, monitoring progress, and providing feedback to others" (p. 154).

At General Electric, CEO Jack Welch emphasize the power of team leadership in action. As Welch himself said, "We've developed an incredibly talented team of people running our major businesses, and, perhaps more important, there's a healthy sense of collegiality, mutual trust, and respect for performance that pervades this organization." (Daum, 2002).

Team leadership can also play a major role in improving interpersonal and group processes within the team. According to Leenders, van Engelen and Kratzer, (2003 p.85), team leaders play a role of 'communication integrators' are very crucial for the success of the team. Team Leaders also create positive team processes by developing understanding of team member relationships existing, creating team-based reward systems, and selecting only those team members who are capable to do the work. (Lurey and Raisinghani, 2001, p.532).It is important to recognize that the functional view of team leadership is deliberately inclusive when it comes to who satisfies these team needs (Hackman, 2005; Hackman & Walton, 1986; McGrath, 1962). Because multiple individuals are often capable of satisfying team needs, it has been suggested that we "devote attention to the study of leadership rather than leaders," in part because of the "observation that many every-day groups have different leaders in different situations" (McGrath, 1962: 3). Team leadership is thus conceptualized as the process of team need satisfaction in the service of enhancing team effectiveness. This team leadership function involves two key tasks. The first task involves "supporting the structure of the team with the task environment" and safeguarding that this alignment is conserved over time as the task environment changes. The second task involves ensuring that the team not only has the requisite knowledge and skills for task performance, but also that the team is composed in such a way that team members form trusting and cooperative relationships. Team leadership research provides compelling evidence that setting challenging goals and clear performance expectations is one of the most important leadership functions for facilitating effective team performance. Team effectiveness and the impact of team leader consideration and responsiveness was tested in a study of intact teams of middle-and upper-level managers of a Fortune 500 company (Korsgaard et al., 1995). In this article, decisions made in teams with high levels of consideration behavior by leaders were perceived by team members as much fair as decisions in low-consideration. Members of high-consideration groups also were significantly more committed to the decisions made, especially when their level of influence was low.

At Equilibria introduced the team to the concepts of E-Colors and Personal Intervention through the 8 Essentials framework. The 8 Essentials is a team leadership coaching tool and gave this team a framework to understand some of the breakdowns they were experiencing and have conversations to clear the elephants in the room and start understanding one another and communicating better. (Equilibria, 2017)

3. Role Clarity

Role clarity is an important element of overall team effectiveness (Feistritzer and Jones, 2014). Research on roles in establishments has mainly focused on three role perceptions: role clarity, role conflict, and role ambiguity (Esper et al., 2008). Role clarity has been denotedas a lack of role ambiguity and conflict.(Rizzo, House, and Lirtzman, 1970). According to several studies, it was clear that role clarity is important "… an individual team member has a clear understanding of his or her task and has "clear information" associated with a particular role in the team." (Bray and Brawley, 2002). The understanding of each other's roles will affect the attitudes of team members which increases cohesiveness and collective orientation, promotes autonomy, … job satisfaction, self-accountability, and commitment towards the project, organization and team success (Braun and Avital, 2007).

4. Continuous Improvement

The essence of continuous improvement involves production improvisation and improvements in all aspects of customer value, including quality, design, and timely delivery, while lowering cost. Although the concepts of continuous improvement were covered in some of the individual researchers on team assessments, the only assessment that measured it under its own heading was the Team Effectiveness Assessment (TEA) ("Team Effectiveness," n.d.). An incorporation of the concepts led to the following definition of continuous improvement: "the constant effort by the team to eliminate reduce wastage and response time, design simplification of both products and processes, and improve quality and customer service."

For example:

Ford motors they plan, teamwork is among the most important priorities in the company's organizational culture. This characteristic of the firm's organizational culture entails employee participation. The company also emphasizes personal development through team involvement and support. Ford's organizational culture facilitates teamwork combined with individual knowledge and skills development. (Lombaro, 2017)

Even at FedEx, they apply continuous improvement as strategy to ensure that teams maintain their focus on increasing of quality delivery of product on time through Service Quality Indicators. (FedEx Express, 2007)

5. Reward and Recognition

There is a definite link between the purpose of the individual within the teams to stay at their workplace and the recognition/rewards they are awarded for their team performance. Some studies have shown "a positive correlation between recognition given for work that is well done performance, team tenure and loyalty with their current employer." (Tesluk, Vance, and Mathieu, 1999,p.416; Kopelman, 1979;

Rubin, Munz, and Bommer, 2005). A logical link is that such individual needs and expectations carry over to expectations of a collective group of individuals in a work team. Rewarding employees' attempts at being creative and innovative, as well as actual innovation outcomes, is likely to facilitate innovation. Abbey and Dickson (1983) found rewards for recognition of performance and the willingness to experiment with ideas were important facets of the climate of innovative R & D units. Eisenberg and Cameron (1996) found support for the innovation that extrinsic rewards positively affect the implementation phase of the innovation process at the individual level. Team members' perceptions of team desirability, organizational support, and organizational outcomes also have been assessed in industry (Bishop et al., 2000). The expectation of the investigators was that favourable employee perceptions would produce improved levels of organizational commitment and better production outcomes. In these studies, favourable perception of the work group was consistently found to be related to level of employee performance and intention to remain employed at the study institution.

At General Motors, For example, a special committees are determines how and when bonuses are awarded to the team showing better performance.

IMPLICATIONS

This article will help HR professionals and Practitioners to understand the team climate and its role in dealing with team climate and team functioning for achieving organisation effectiveness. It also helps to understand how to deal with team climate improvement.

1. Firstly, to understand the team climate because various researches have studied on organizational climate and culture but not specific to the team climate.
2. Secondly, it emphasis on the areas of team climate and team effectiveness which is the need of industries. They are gradually undergoing changes from group towards team, many organisations are modifying their organizational structures and converting them to effective work team for organizational effectiveness.
3. Thirdly, the article contributed to the academic as well as professional development of the organisation through the ways of improving team climate and team effectiveness by analysing various factor influencing it. Better outcomes will be achieved when team members perceive a supportive team climate and an empowering team context with clear and jointly developed goals, an appropriate mix of skills and expertise, and rewards linked to team performance.

CONCLUSION

The climate of the organisation - how it is perceived and experienced by those who work within it - will also influence the effectiveness of teams (Allen, 1996). It suggested from the article that it's the role of line managers lies at the heart of the leadership and relationship since it is mainly line managers' behavior that serves as a core basis on which employees develop shared understandings of a social climate where teamwork and cooperation are desired and valued by the organisation. The article suggests that the effective management of social relations may require a process-based HR leadership for the development of positive team climate for improvement in team effectiveness. The organisation that are more successful in adopting innovation and new challenges are looking forward to new Human resource strategies that can help them to deal with complex and diverse work force. Successful implementation of Teamwork as a best practice means the team climate needs to be conducive to fostering growing team autonomy. The organisation with successful teams are providing mentorship programmes and senior management commitment to meet diversity challenges. This means that the potential impact of the factors mentioned needs to be taken into consideration when drawing up a vision for teams. Team members must monitor each other and provide each other feedback to maximize team functioning. However, feedback here focuses on team process and its improvement rather than solely on team outcomes. To ensure that feedback occurs, team members must be trained to deliver timely, behavioural, and specific feedback to one another.

REFERENCES

Abramson, J. S. (1990). Making teams works. *Social Work with Groups*, *12*(4), 45–63. doi:10.1300/J009v12n04_04

Abramson, J. S., & Bronstein, L. R. (2004). Group Process Dynamics & Skills in Interdisciplinary Teamwork. In C. Garvin, M. Galinsky, & L. Gutierrez (Eds.), *Group Work Handbook*. Guilford Press.

Alderfer, C. P. (1977). *"Groups and Intergroup Relations," Improving Life at Work* (J. R. Hackman & J. L. Suttle, Eds.). Santa Monica, CA: Goodyear.

AON. (2017). *Insights from Best Employers 2016*. Retrieved from http://aonhewitt.co.in/Home/Aon-Best-Employers-India/insights/Insights-from-2016/Case-studies

Becker, E. (2015, April 8). *Team Building and Group Dynamics.* Retrieved from https://www.td.org/Publications/Magazines/TD/TD-Archive/2015/04/Team-Building-and-Group-Dynamics

Burpitt, W. J., & Bigoness, W. J. (1997). Leadership and innovation among teams: The impact of empowerment. *Small Group Research, 28*(3), 414–423. doi:10.1177/1046496497283005

Danserau, F., & Alluto, J. A. (1990). Level-of-analysis issues in climate and culture research. In B. Schneider (Ed.), *Organizational Climate and Culture* (pp. 193–236). San Francisco, CA: Jossey Bass.

Dansereau, F., Alluto, I. A., & Yammarino, F. J. (1984). *Theory testing in organizational behavior: The varient approach.* Englewood Cliffs, NJ: Prentice Hall.

Daum, J. (2002, December 28). *The New Economy Analyst Report.* Retrieved from http://www.juergendaum.com/news/12_28_2002.htm

Delery, J. E., & Doty, D. H. (1996). Modes of theorizing in strategic human resource management: Tests of universalistic, contingency, and configurational performance predictions. *Academy of Management Journal, 39*(4), 802–835. doi:10.2307/256713

Edmondson, A. (2002). The local and variegated nature of learning in organizations: A group-level perspective. *Organization Science, 13*(2), 128–146. doi:10.1287/orsc.13.2.128.530

Equilibria. (2017). *How a Monthly Meeting Changed From 'A Waste Of Time' to a Positive Collaboration.* Retrieved from http://www.equilibria.com/case-studies/communication-teamwork/case-study-2/

Ettorre, B. (1997). The Empowerment Gap: Hype vs. Reality. *BRFocus, 62*, 4–6.

Facet5 Case Studies. (n.d.). *Facet5: The most versatile asset in your organisational toolbox.* Retrieved from http://www.facet5global.com/facet5-solutions-case-studies/facet5-the-most-versatile-asset-in-your-organisational-toolbox

FedEx Express. (2007, March 5). *FedEx Express Names Beth Galetti, Vice President of Information Technology.* Retrieved from http://www.fedex.com/cgi-bin/content.cgi?tcmplatc=gb_pr&content=about%2Fpressreleases%2Femea%2Fpr030507&cc=gb

General Electric. (2017). *Welcome to GE.COM.* Retrieved from https://www.ge.com

Guttmann, H. M. (2007, June 1). *Teamwork and Empowerment.* Retrieved from http://guttmandev.com/news-detail/teamwork-and-empowermen

Hegar, K., & Hodgetts, R. M. (2007). *Modern Human Relation at Work* (9th ed.). Thomson South-Western.

Ingersoll, G., & Schmitt, M. (2004). *Home - PubMed - NCBI*. Retrieved from https://www.ncbi.nlm.nih.gov/pubmed

Khandawalla, P. N. (1974). Mass output orientation of operations technology and organization structure. *Administrative Science Quarterly*, *19*(1), 74–97. doi:10.2307/2391789

Kinnie, N., Hutchinson, S., Purcell, J., Rayton, B., & Swart, J. (2005). Satisfaction with HR practices and commitment to the organisation: Why one size does not fit all. *Human Resource Management Journal*, *15*(4), 9–29. doi:10.1111/j.1748-8583.2005.tb00293.x

Kirkman, B. L., & Rosen, B. (1997). A model of work team empowerment. In R. W. Woodman & W. A. Pasmore (Eds.), *Research in organizational change and development* (Vol. 10, pp. 131–167). Greenwich, CT: JAI Press.

Korsgaard, M. A., Schweiger, D. M., & Sapienza, H. J. (1995). Building commitment, attachment, and trust in strategic decision-making teams: The role of procedural justice. *Academy of Management Journal*, *38*(1), 60–84. doi:10.2307/256728

Lombardo, J. (2017, February 5). *Ford Motor Company's Organizational Culture Analysis*. Retrieved from http://panmore.com/ford-motor-company-organizational-culture-analysis

OMRON Global. (2017). Retrieved September 28, 2017, from https://www.omron.com/

Parmar, A. (2017). *A study on team climate its relationship with team effectiveness for organisational development in manufacturing sectors of central Gujarat* (Unpublished Ph.D. thesis). The Maharaja Sayajirao University of Baroda, Vadodara.

Reddin, B. (1988). The output oriented organization. Gower Publishing Company Limited.

Rees, F. (1997). *Teamwork from start to finish*. San Francisco, CA: Jossey-Bass.

Roosevelt, T. R. Jr. (2001). *Elements of a successful diversity process*. The American Institute for Managing Diversity.

Rozovsky, J. (2015, November 17). *The five keys to a successful Google team*. Retrieved from https://rework.withgoogle.com/blog/five-keys-to-a-successful-google-team/

Schein, E. (1992). *Organizational Culture and Leadership* (2nd ed.). San Francisco, CA: Jossey-Bass.

Schneider, B., Bowen, D. E., Ehrhart, M. G., & Holcombe, K. M. (2000). The climate for service: Evolution of a construct. In N. M. Ashkanasy, C. P. Wilderom, & M. F. Peterson (Eds.), *Handbook of organizational culture and climate* (pp. 21–36). Thousand Oaks, CA: Sage.

Shaw, M. E. (1976). *Group dynamics*. New York: McGraw-Hill.

Simard, M., & Marchand, A. (1995). A multilevel analysis of organisational factors related to the taking of safety initiatives by work groups. *Safety Science*, *21*(2), 113–129. doi:10.1016/0925-7535(95)00050-X

Spreitzer, G. M. (1995). Psychological empowerment in the workplace: Dimensions, measurement, and validation. *Academy of Management Journal*, *38*(5), 1442–1465. doi:10.2307/256865

Stevens, M. J., & Campion, M. A. (1994). The knowledge, skills, and ability requirements for teamwork: Implications for human resource management. *Journal of Management*, *20*(2), 503–530. doi:10.1177/014920639402000210

Terrapin Adventures. (2016, February 29). *Case Study: How Teamwork, Competition Motivate Employees*. Retrieved from https://www.terrapinadventures.com/blog/case-study-how-teamwork-competition-motivate-employees/

Zohar, D. (2000). A group-level model of safety climate: Testing the effect of group climate on microaccidents in manufacturing jobs. *The Journal of Applied Psychology*, *85*(4), 587–596. doi:10.1037/0021-9010.85.4.587 PMID:10948803

Chapter 12
Workplace Discrimination:
The Most Critical Issue in Managing Diversity

Shikha Sharma
Punjabi University, India

Nimarta Mann
Punjabi University, India

ABSTRACT

Diverse workforce is now a global phenomenon. The quality of interaction between people of diversified cultures in the organization has significant association with the marketing, managing, as well as human resource functions. The majority organizations are indulging in diversity management programmes so that they can benefit from the varied skills. But discriminatory behaviour against people of different backgrounds than majorities in the workplace act as a hindrance in taking full advantage of workplace diversity. This chapter reveals different forms in which discrimination can arise in a discrimination-free environment. The organizational as well as individual factors that cause discrimination at the workplace are discussed. The aftereffects that are related to discriminatory behavior at work, which render both employees as well as organization at disadvantage, are also highlighted. The chapter will help by highlighting the issue faced by thousands of employees every year and suggesting steps that need to be undertaken to remove discrimination from the workplace settings.

INTRODUCTION

With rise in globalization, organizations are becoming more multifarious. Interaction between organizations as well as individuals of different cultural backgrounds is also increasing at a fast pace, which has led to opening of broad employment opportunities throughout the globe. Employers are interested in hiring employees of diverse backgrounds to take advantage of different kind of skills, technical knowledge and experiences. Having diverse workforce is advantageous for both employees as well as organizations as it augments opportunities for new markets, employment, innovation, and organization's image (Esty et al. 1995). A variety of intelligence, expertise and characteristics are required by organizations in order to achieve success. Diverse employee pool assures that an organization has extensive mixture of knowledge and expertise at workplace which takes them on verge over others.

With the various benefits involved there also arise some negative aspects that are related to the effective management of diverse workforce. Organizations dedicated to diversified manpower wish to build an atmosphere where everyone, irrespective of their demographic, social, cultural, economic or any other differences in their background, does their best for the organization. Workplace diversity actually means building an environment where all members of organization can work collectively and with harmony regardless of their disparities. Effective management of diverse workforce involves making most out of the different and unique talents but certain barriers act as hindrance in this.

One of the most critical issues which are prevalent in this respect is of Workplace Discrimination. Workplace discrimination denotes to differential treatment while recruiting, assigning job positions, evaluations and payments. Several types of harassments also come under workplace discrimination (Devah, 2009). It involves treating persons differently mostly because of their gender, age, race or physical appearance. For example if there is a situation where a female candidate is offered a lower salary package than a male candidate for the same job responsibilities, or a candidate is denied employment due to age, then in both cases female candidate as well as aged candidate are victims of workplace discrimination.

Merely having the knowledge of what workplace discrimination means cannot help any organization in getting rid of it until and unless the reason for its origination in the work settings is identified. By having knowledge of the major reasons that lead to creation of a work environment that is not supportive of diversity helps organizations to take preventive measures.

Workplace discrimination can be anticipated at different levels of employment decisions, such as, hiring, compensation, Promotions, Fringe benefits, authority allocation, trainings, etc. On the whole, it precipitates and intensifies in equal treatment at workplace.

Workplace discrimination leads to various negative effects on employee as well as organization as a whole. Victims of discrimination may reduce their efforts at workplace which may further lead to reduction in productivity of organization, it can also cause various psychological and health related problems in employees.

To effectively manage a diverse workforce one should be aware of the challenges involved. Knowledge of the concept of workplace discrimination, its various types, factors that give rise to such discrimination and its consequences proves to be of great support for those who are involved in managing diverse workforce.

CHALLENGES TO WORKPLACE DIVERSITY

Workplace diversity involves people of multifarious characteristics working collectively in an organization. In current scenario, organizations are hiring people of diverse backgrounds to take advantage of different skills to become more and more successful. It seems very easy to employ diverse workforce at same organization and put them at work in same departments but it includes people of different gender, age, qualifications, nationality, religious beliefs, etc. Diversity implicates one's believes about themselves as well as others in the organization that in turn influences their day to day behaviour with each other.

To make most of the skills of such a diverse workforce every organization is required to take efficient human resource management functions. The competent Human resource functions need to tackle various issues that confront with diverse workforce such as communication problems and compliancy.

The advancements and of an organization is to a very extent related to its competency in managing its diverse workforce effectively and deriving full benefits from it. Effective Management of diverse workforce involves organizations ability to promptly address the challenges of workforce diversity and successful development and implementation of plans and policies to tackle the issues.

Successful implementation of diversity programs leads to various benefits for the organization but there exist many threats that act as hindrance. One of these challenges is of Workplace Discrimination which adversely affects well being of employees as well as organizations.

Discrimination at Workplace

Invalidating or restricting the right of equal opportunity or employment by differentiating or excluding any person on the basis of gender, race, religion or nationality is termed as workplace discrimination. (ILO Convention No.111,1958)

Workplace Discrimination

Discrimination means any unfavourable conduct or intention to treat any person unfavourably due to any particular characteristic. Discrimination at workplace is the most intricate and complicated issue in present time. It is very tough to recognize and differentiate the root cause of this obstacle in managing diverse workforce.

Workplace discrimination includes sheer misconduct on the job mixed up with various hidden forms of behaviours having more powerful impact. The most contiguous forms of workplace discrimination include disparate treatment at pre- and post-employment stages.

- **Pre-Employment Discrimination:** Discrimination at the stage of pre-employment means differential treatment with members of minority groups during process of recruitment and selection.
- **Post-Employment Discrimination:** Discrimination at the post-employment stage refers to discrimination while placing members of minority groups on job, allocating responsibilities, setting of wages and compensation, providing career advancement opportunities as well as daily interactions during work.

Discrimination also exists in the form of biased policies, structure, practices and systems of organizations that render minorities to disadvantage.

When various factors interact in a complicated diverse organizational system, discrimination arises as an issue which is faced by the minorities by not even noticing its existence. These hidden biases lead to major problems of race, sex, age, etc. based discrimination at the workplace. It has detrimental effects on the well being of the victims of discrimination.

Targets of workplace discrimination mostly are females, disabled people, aged people and homosexuals who are treated less favourably in comparison to males, heterosexuals, physically and mentally fit and younger people. When an employee is treated unfavorably on the basis of a social group, gender or race to which that employee belongs ignoring his/her individual talent then that employee is said to be victim of workplace discrimination. Perceiving an employee as less capable of performing tasks due to certain disability, gender or age is considered illegal on the part of employer. Furthermore an organization cannot deny employment to a person because of their association with a person of particular ethnicity, race or religion. Harassment of an employee also comes under workplace discrimination.

The most evident form of workplace discrimination is racial and ethnicity based, but recently other forms of discrimination have also gained strong attention. Various bases on which employees are discriminated before and after employment include:-

- **Disability:** Disability discrimination implies discriminating physically challenged people by not recruiting them, not providing suitable support

mechanisms at work or paying them less as compared to others. Disable people are put to face financial deprivation due to such disparate treatment.
- **Age:** With the heightened trend of retrenchment and reconstitution of workforce as well as more stress on younger generation in current recession period the workers of older age are facing more discrimination at the workplace.
- **Gender:** Despite the extensive growth made by women in their financial status, there still exist situations that render female employees at disadvantage in the workplace. Jobs are segregated on the basis of gender, women are underpaid as compared to male counterparts and they are given less opportunities for advancement and rarely promoted to the top positions.
- **Sexual Orientation:** Discriminating on the basis of sexual orientation of a person may probably be the least cited area among all other categories that form basis for workplace discrimination still it is evident from various studies that homosexuals face disparate treatment in getting job as well as income.

While framing company policies and practices it is the responsibility of employers to maintain uniformity despite of the differences in gender, religion, age or ethnicity of employees. For example:- A policy of short hair of all employees in an organization may not be considered discriminatory if it is requirement of job in spite of being unacceptable by people of certain religion.

The wider universal meaning of discrimination is to make distinction. Still, it is considered by majority people as derogatory or negative word as it usually involves associating unfair perceptions to disparities among people that give rise to differential actions against them. These kinds of discriminatory behaviour in an organization cause heartbreak and distress. Workplace discrimination is therefore a communal integrity concern where one solution is advised to be juridical control. Discrimination takes place when a person faces differential treatment because of a personal attribute, whether it is not visibly unfavourable treatment.

Discrimination is dealing with someone in a different manner as compared to others.It takes place in situations where an employer behaves less favourably with one worker as compared to others at work without considering their worth. For example: - If a female employee gets lesser amount for similar work done by her male counterpart, then she is victim of workplace discrimination due to her gender. In another example if an older worker is left out for new technology trainings then he is victim of workplace discrimination due to his age.

Following studies show the prevalence of workplace discrimination in organizations in different countries despite of increase in need for diverse workforce on a global pace.

Upadhyay et al. (2005) studied the issues related to gender discrimination in Indian IT industry and found significant differences between male and female with regard to career advancement opportunities. Women were provided jobs at low positions with lower pay and limited growth opportunities.

Bendick et al. (2010) empirically examined the role of employer in employment discrimination on the basis of race/ethnicity in prosperous restaurants of New York City. Matched Pair Testing was used to test employers' unbiased acknowledgements to demographic features of employees. For conducting test, 37 employees and college students were recruited as testers. The testers performed 138 tests in Manhattan during the period of January 2006 and June 2007 out of which 43 tests were completed. Various forms of biasness in hiring practices of employer were found as coloured applicants were more rejected while recruiting as compared to white applicants despite of similar education and experience. In many cases coloured applicants were not allowed to apply, were not offered job interview and were asked suspecting questions. Even post hiring discrimination was found as coloured employees were offered lower pay and positions as compared to their white counterparts at work which leads to lower quality of work for them. It was found that 39% of tested restaurants were biased in their hiring practices. Post hiring discrimination was not tested and even biasness on the basis of gender and age were not tested as pairs were different only in terms of race or ethnicity.

Brauer et al. (2011) analysed the role of changing persons' perceptions about their dissimilarity with members of other ethnicity on level of discrimination. Experimental study was made on undergraduate students of psychology from Clermonte University, France. It was concluded that if perceptions about similarity with other groups is increased then it further reduces the level of prejudice and discrimination.

Cavico et al. (2013) inquired the issue of inequality faced by employees who perceive themselves as less attractive. They investigated the legal, ethical and practical aspects of the problem of existence of discrimination based on physical appearance at the time of hiring and at workplace. With a view to understand the legal aspects all the federal, state and civil laws related to employment and found that it was not illegal to discriminate on the basis of looks at workplace and it was also not safeguarded by any law. For studying whether it is justified to discriminate against someone on the basis of his/her physical appearance four approaches to ethics related to egoism, relativism, utilitarianism and Kantian were studied and was found that it was not unethical to discriminate on the basis of physicality. Practicality was studied from the point of view of stakeholders, customers, workers and managers. After doing all scrutiny outcome of the study was that discrimination on the basis of how a person looks is legal and moral but it turns illegal if it is related to any other form of discrimination which is secured by employment law.

Parrey et al. (2013) critically investigated secondary data from Census 2001 about ratio of working male versus working female in major districts of Jammu & Kashmir. It was found that ratio of working women was lower than working men and major factor contributing to this difference was discrimination at workplaces on the basis of gender of employee. Women willingly worked more than required by their job specifications yet their contributions were given less consideration than their male colleagues. Such unindemnified work lead to lower female to male ratio which ultimately reduce productivity of organisations.

Musilova et al. (2014) observed the presence of age related discrimination in the constitution of Czech Republic in relation to Corporate Social Responsibility of organisations. Secondary sources such as investigation reports of adjudicator and verdicts of Czech courts were analysed for the study. Maximum numbers of cases of age discrimination were found in the advertisement of vacancy by the organisations. Older people were treated unequally while hiring and while at the job. There was also lack of proper policies to gain knowledge from ageing workforce. Main reason of presence of such kind of biasness was social perceptions about low competency level and learning skills of aged workforce. Equal and justified treatment with employees of all age comes under corporate social responsibility of every organisation failing which leads to lower performance of the company.

Discrimination can arise at any point in the work setting. Some of the areas in which employees face disparate treatment at workplace are as follows:

- Denial of employment opportunity.
- Discharging or Reducing shifts at work.
- Withholding training and career advancement opportunities.
- Getting less amount paid compared to others with equal qualifications and experience for the same work done.
- Deliberate withholding of required knowledge for performing job.
- Given unrealistic goals to achieve.
- Getting jokes or slurs directed due to personal characteristic.

Employers are liable to protect employees at all levels of employment, such as:

- **Recruitment:** While job advertisements and conducting interviews it must be taken care of that someone is not put to disadvantage and everyone gets equal opportunity to apply Terms and conditions of employment should not be biased. Everyone should get equal chance of getting trained for up gradation of their skills. Promotions should not be biased due to prejudiced behaviour. While transferring employees on other job or area disparate treatment should not be done. Performance appraisals should be based on performance and not

on personal characteristic. Nobody should be restrained from employment benefits. No one should be demoted or dismissed unfairly. When someone is being subjected to improper jokes, slurs or taunts on the basis of their personal characteristics or because of their association with particular social group.
- **Salary & Wages:** Salary & Wages should be assigned on the basis of job responsibilities carried out by individuals and there should not be any discrimination. For example, paying less wages to women for same work done by male employee.
- **Interview:** Asking questions related to personal life, children, health conditions, age,religion and rejecting a person on the basis of their answers on above mentioned questions neglecting their qualifications and experience is also considered as discriminatory behavior prior to recruitment.
- **Dismissal:** When a female is dismissed from the job on getting pregnant she is victim of workplace discrimination even if someone is dismissed because of their religious beliefs or any other personal characteristic they are victims of workplace discrimination.

ANTECEDENTS OF WORKPLACE DISCRIMINATION

Nowadays, organizations recruit from diverse areas due to increase in globalization. We can easily see a mixture of employees of different ages, ethnicity, nationalities and gender. In such a diversified workforce when people of different backgrounds come together its bit natural for them to have different point of views different interest areas and different standards of living. There exist various factors that give rise to discriminatory behaviours at the workplace. Some of these causes are due to difference in individual characteristics. For example: - A male manager may favour male subordinates which lead to discrimination against females. Factors that lead to occurrence of workplace discrimination are not limited to individual factors but also include various causes present at the Organizational level. Discriminatory policies and procedures inherited in the organization structure also leads to discrimination against certain individuals Following are some Individual and Organizational level antecedents that lead to Workplace Discrimination.

Individual Level

- **Stereotypes:** Stereotypes are denoted to "a set of attributes ascribed to a group and imputed to its individual members simply because they belong to that group" (Heilman 1983). It generally includes improper and unfavourable inferences about any group and its members. Stereotypes impose negative effects on career advancement opportunities of members of group. Many scholars have conducted research on misleading perceptions, stereotypes and assumptions of managers. (Kanter 1977) studied behaviours of managers and found that they are unwilling to allocate the responsibility of performing highly critical activities to those employees who they perceive to have lower capability to perform efficiently. In spite of the fact that this kind of highlighted critical activities lead to development in career. (Morrison & Von Glinow 1990).

- **Stigmatization:** Stigma is a symbol of disrespect, disrepute, dishonour or admonishment, assigned to a person's character. Various studies conducted in this perspective have proved that those persons who have such stigma attached to their reputation due to their age, race or gender came across varied forms of discrimination at work
- **Self-Restricting Behaviors:** Scholars have identified the fact that females and members of minority groups at times intentionally back out from various opportunities that can lead to development in their career graph, this kind of behaviour is termed as Self Restricting or Limiting Behaviour. This kind of behaviour includes both impulsive as well as competent element. Self limiting behaviour is inherited as an impulsive element in a person's mind when a person faces disparate and negative treatment for many years. On the other hand, the competence element comes when a person is not provided opportunity to work on challenging tasks which causes reduced competence level as compared to members of majority groups in the workplace.

Organizational Determinants

Various organizational factors determine whether discriminatory behaviour is supported, overlooked, or strongly confronted in an organization. These factors include organizational culture, structure, strategies, climate, personnel management practices as well as type of leadership which play a crucial role in determining the magnitude of workplace discrimination.

- **Leadership:** Top leadership plays very important role in strengthening of diversity management programmes in any organization. Discriminatory behaviour of top management reduces the strength of diversity drive in an organization. If the top leaders of an organization are not strongly committed

to effective management of diversity programmes all others in organization get an indication that discriminatory behaviour is tolerable and is not a big issue.
- **Strategies and Policies:** It is always stated in clear and precise terms in formal strategies and policy manuals of organization that discriminatory behaviour will not be accepted in any situation and organization strongly commits to the diversity management programme. But in some cases unintentionally the organizational policies render some people at disadvantage.
- **Organization Culture:** Weak organizational culture in which members of the organization do not have consensus fail to promote diversity and discourage discriminatory behaviours.
- **Organization Structure:** Greater workforce composition of homogeneous characteristics in an organization leads to favourable treatment for those of similar characteristics in employment related decisions. Apart from employment related decisions people of diverse characteristics are also excluded from social gatherings and networks due to various communication barriers
- **Human Resource Management Function:** If Human Resource Management function is strong in an organization it possesses great influential power on the behaviours of employees. Organizational policies that promote diversity are strongly followed and discriminatory treatment is strongly opposed.

TYPES OF WORKPLACE DISCRIMINATION

Discrimination exists before and after employment in different form. In spite of being accepted as a dire necessity to encourage equal opportunity in employment at a global level, the issue of workplace discrimination still persist as a major problem in managing global diverse workforce. Two types of discrimination exist in an organization-direct and indirect.

Direct Discrimination

When an employee is treated unfavourably due to any personal characteristic like age, gender, race or disability, it is termed as direct. For example, if a teaching job was open only for female applicants it would be called direct discrimination. The main reason that leads to direct discrimination is false assumptions or perceptions about capability of people with particular characteristics. Some people also become victims of direct discrimination due to their association with certain groups or people.

Indirect Discrimination

When employment conditions in an organization render employees of particular characteristic at disadvantage as compared to others working in same status, it is called Indirect Discrimination. For example: - if a job advertisement invites only clean shaven candidates it is unjustified for members of particular religion. Whether intentionally done or not this kind of treatment is considered illegal. It arises in the form of illogical conditions and policies that lead to unfavourable treatment of some particular persons.

Harassment

Everyone is entitled to protection from unjust treatment or harassment at workplace. Harassment is defined as behaviour which is disrespectful and threatening for any employee in the organization. Employees harass other employees having distinct characteristic by making racial or sexist comments or directing slurs or jokes in order to degrade, weaken or torture the victim. For example, making fun of someone at work by uploading photoshopped picture of that person on company's wall portraying him/her as a joker. It also includes sexually harassing someone at work.

Victimisation

Victimisation is a situation that arises as a result of discriminatory treatment reported by the victim. Victims of workplace discrimination who raised voice against the system are sometimes treated unfairly due to the complaints made by them in the form of withholding their promotions, false allegations etc.

CONSEQUENCES OF WORKPLACE DISCRIMINATION

Facing discrimination at work has many detrimental effects on the well being of individual. Effects of being discriminated last much longer in the mind of victims than just a single day bad experience. Many victims get distressed and serious health issues because of facing workplace discrimination. Some individuals indulge in unhealthy behaviours with intention to harm organization or some other individual to compensate the discriminatory behaviour faced by them. A work environment where discrimination exists not only negatively affects the victims but also renders the diversity management programmes of the organization as void. It spoils the reputation of the organization in the market place and is considered not a good place to work at. Along with the reputation organization also loses to utilize diverse skills as its diversity image no longer remains prevalent. Last but not the least financial losses as a result of penalties from discrimination claims cannot be overlooked.

Discriminatory behaviour done by even one individual in an organization can have its effect on the organization as a whole. Even one instance that creates an impression that particular organization is unfair to females, minorities, disabled persons or homosexuals leads to long term difficulties in getting people from these groups at work. The crippling consequences of discrimination at workplace are hostile work environment, weakened workforce and reduced profitability of the organization.

Detailed description of various after effects of Workplace discrimination are as follows:

Reduced Productivity

Employees who face discriminatory treatment at workplace get demotivated and their productivity is reduced. The absenteeism and turnover rate is also increased which leads to increased efforts in recruiting and training new employees which further reduces productivity of the organization.

- **Legal Consequences:** Discrimination charges in the court often impose fines and penalties on the employer. If the employer loses the case filed against them they need to pay high amount as compensation as well as legal fees of the victim. Court can also order the employer to give the job back to an employee who is terminated unfairly.
- **Reduced Income and Revenue:** If an organization is publicized as being engaged in discriminatory behaviours it also loses its customers and consequently sales and revenue fall down.
- **Reduced Employee Morale:** Facing discrimination at workplace effect mental as well as physical health of the victim employees. According to the reports of Equal Employment Opportunity Commission being victim of unjust treatment at workplace leads to stress, anxiety and depression in employees. They are least interested in doing work enthusiastically when they are aware of the fact that advancement procedure in the organization is unjust and biased and not related to actual performance.
- **Hostile Work Environment:** The most substantial effect of workplace discrimination is the creation of hostile work environment. It becomes very difficult for the diverse workforce to work in such a negative work environment due to lack of trust and communication gaps. Satisfaction level of employees working in such environment is also very low.
- **Increase in Unemployment:** Discrimination in hiring and recruitment in the form of biased selection procedures lead to increase in unemployment

rate by not recruiting suitable candidates of certain characteristics even if the position remains unfilled.

Therefore, a single act of discrimination has its effects on individual, organization as well as society.

SOLUTIONS AND RECOMMENDATIONS

Some steps if undertaken properly can help in reducing workplace discrimination and improving the work environment by making it a better place to work at for diverse workforce.

- **Unbiased Job Allocation:** Allocating job responsibilities on the basis of ability of the employee and not under the influence of any stereotypes associated. This will remove the biasness in the process of allocation of authorities and responsibilities and everyone will be provided equal opportunity despite of differences in personal characteristics.
- **Formalization:** Following more formal and disciplined methods for performance evaluations which assess the efforts of all employees on an equal measure. Formalization of performance evaluations removes the biased performance evaluations by properly defining the standards of performance.
- **Reward Based Promotion:** Linking rewards with promoting diversity friendly environment for top leaders. Rewards act as motivation for leaders to take actions to promote and instil more diversity friendly environment.
- **Interactive Environment:** Promoting more interactions among members of organization by creating formal networks. This kind of initiative by organizations helps members of diverse communities and background to communicate with each other which further leads to a friendly environment.
- **Diversity Trainings:** Time to time organizing diversity trainings in an organization educates employees about Equal Employment Opportunity rights as well as creates cultural awareness among them.
- **Anti-Discrimination Laws:** Proper laws should be formulated by Government to protect rights of employees at workplace.

CONCLUSION

Majority corporate in the 21st Century are strong supporters of inclusion of diverse workforce at their places. Yet maximum organizations having diverse work culture face many challenges while managing its day to day interactions. Workplace discrimination is the biggest and most critical issue that acts as hindrance in the successful implementation of diversity management programmes. Lack of commitment and disinterest towards diversity management programmes by the top management as well as governing authorities further increases the problem of disparate treatment at workplace. Problem of discrimination is constantly becoming worse to worst despite of various steps taken by organizations to eliminate it from its work settings.

It is the primary responsibility of organizations to frame transparent and unbiased policies and strategies related to the employment. Top leaders who are responsible for making various employment related decisions should act fairly and not show prejudice or biasness in their decisions.

Healthy work environments that promote and respect diverse cultures are subject to attraction by most skilled persons. Discrimination free environment leads to increase in morale of employees as it inculcates feeling of mutual trust and cooperation among them and others at work. Happy employees further lead to increase in profitability and productivity of organization. The organization also have verge over other competitors in the market as more reputable organization.

Hence, for effective management of diverse workforce with distinct characteristics like different age group, gender, nationalities, race, appearance, physical attributes, languages every organization first needs to check that policies, top leaders or any other aspect is not discriminatory that renders any particular group at disadvantage. Any complain or hint related to discriminatory behaviour should be taken seriously and strong corrective action to rectify it should be taken so that it is not repeated in future. It should be stated in clear and precise terms to the employees of the organization that any kind of discriminatory behaviour is not acceptable in the workplace. An organization that is able to build an image of discrimination free workplace becomes more competent and also builds a good reputation in society. More customers as well as more skilled and qualified people get linked to the organization.

To conclude the chapter, we must say that workplace discrimination still persist as a major challenge in front of organizations in management of diverse workforce but having true knowledge of its various forms and factors that give rise to discrimination at workplace, one can prevent such actions to take place in future.

REFERENCES

Bilkis, A., Habib, S. B., & Sharmin, T. (2010). A review of discrimination in employment and workplace. *ASA University Review*, 137-150.

Brondolo, E., Rahim, R., Grimaldi, S. J., Ashraf, A., Bui, N., & Schwartz, J. C. (2015). Place of birth effects on self reported discrimination: Variations by type of discrimination. *International Journal of Intercultural Relations, 49*, 212–222. doi:10.1016/j.ijintrel.2015.10.001 PMID:27647943

Butt, J., & Neil, A. O. (2004). *'Let's Move On' Black and Minority Ethnic older people's views on research findings*. Layerthorpe: Joseph Rowntree Foundation.

Chaput, A. (2012). *The impact of the use of favoritism on work groups*. Schmidt Labor Research Center Seminar Series.

De Boer, E. M., Bakker, A. B., Syroitt, J. E., & Schaufeli, W. B. (2002). Unfairness at work as a predictor of absenteeism. *Journal of Organizational Behavior, 23*(2), 181–197. doi:10.1002/job.135

Esty, K. C., Griffin, R., & Hirsch, M. S. (1995). *Workplace diversity*. Adams Media.

Goldsmith, A. H., Sedo, S. Jr, Darity, W. Jr, & Hamilton, D. (2004). The labor supply consequences of perceptions of employment discrimination during search and on the job: Integrating neoclassical theory and cognitive dissconance. *Journal of Economic Psychology, 25*(1), 15–39. doi:10.1016/S0167-4870(02)00210-6

Haberfeld, Y. (1992). Employment Discrimination: An Organizational Model. *Academy of Management Journal, 35*(1), 161–180. doi:10.2307/256476

Hemphill, H., & Haines, R. (1997). *Discrimination, Harassment, and the Failure of Diversity Training*. Santa Barbara, CA: ABC-CLIO.

International Labour Organization Convention 111. (1958). *Discrimination (Employment and Occupation)*. Retrieved from http://www.ilo.org/global/standards/subjects-covered-by-international-labour-standards/equality-of-opportunity-and-treatment/lang--en/index.htm

Ishaq, H. M., & Zuilfqar, A. (2014). To investigate the moderating role of favoritism on employees motivation. Sci. Int.(Lahore), 347-351.

Jeong, M. y., & Won, S. y. (2013). Factors affecting female worker's perceived discrimination in the workplace: An analysis using the Korean longitudinal survey of women and family. *GSPR*, 71-103.

Jones, G. E. (1997). Advancement opportunity issues for persons with disabilities. *Human Resource Management Review, 7*(1), 55–76. doi:10.1016/S1053-4822(97)90005-X

Jr, M. B., Rodriguez, R. E., & Jayaraman, S. (2010). Employment Discrimination in upscale restaurants: Evidence from matched pair testing. *The Social Science Journal*, 802–818.

Lawrence, T. B., & Robinson, S. L. (2007). Ain't Misbehavin:Workplace Deviance as Organizational Resistance. *Journal of Management*, *33*(3), 378–394. doi:10.1177/0149206307300816

Malone, M. (2017, July 5). *Consequences of Discrimination in the Workplace*. Retrieved from http://oureverydaylife.com/consequences-discrimination-workplace-3934.html

Maurer, T. J., & Rafuse, N. E. (2001). Learning, not litigating:Managing employee development and avoiding claims of age discrimination. *The Academy of Management Executive*, *15*(4), 110–121. doi:10.5465/AME.2001.5898395

Mirage, L. (1994). Development of an instrument measuring valence of ethnicity and perception of discrimination. *Journal of Multicultural Counseling and Development*, 49–59.

Muafi. (2011). Causes and Consequence Deviant Workplace Behavior. *International Journal of Innovation, Management and Technology*, 123-126.

Nyab, N. (2010, September 21). *What are the Effects of Workplace Discrimination?* Retrieved from http://www.brighthub.com/office/human-resources/articles/87966.aspx

Pager, D., Bonikowski, B., & Western, B. (2009). Race at Work: Results from a Field Experiment of Discrimination in a Low Wage Labor Market. *American Sociological Review*, *74*(5), 777–799. doi:10.1177/000312240907400505 PMID:20689685

Parrey, A. H., & Bhasin, J. (2013). Gender Discrimination in workforce and discretionary work effort-A prospective approach. *International Monthly Refereed Journal of Research in Management & Technology*, 114-121.

Perry, E. L., & Finkelstein, L. M. (1999). Toward a broader view of age discrimination in employment related decisions: A joint consideration of organizational factors and cognitive processes. *Human Resource Management Review*, *9*(1), 21–49. doi:10.1016/S1053-4822(99)00010-8

Prasad, L. M. (2006). *Organisational Behaviour* (4th ed.). New Delhi: Sultan Chand & Sons.

Prendergast, C., & Topel, R. H. (1996). Favoritism in Organizations. *Journal of Political Economy*, *104*(5), 958–978. doi:10.1086/262048

Reskin, B. F. (2000). The Proximate Causes of Employment Discrimination. *Contemporary Sociology*, *29*(2), 319–328. doi:10.2307/2654387

Robbins, S. P. (2003). *Organizational Behaviour*. Prentice Hall.

Robbins, S. P., & Judge, T. A. (2007). *Organizational Behavior* (12th ed.). Pearson Education, Inc.

Robinson, S. L., & Benett, R. J. (1995). A typology of Deviant workplace behaviors: A multidimensional scaling study. *Academy of Management Journal*, *38*(2), 555–572. doi:10.2307/256693

Rose, A. (2016). *Consequences of Discrimination in the Workplace*. Retrieved from http://woman.thenest.com/consequences-discrimination-workplace-15256.html

Sanchez, J. I., & Brock, P. (1996). Outcomes of Perceived Discrimination among Hispanic Employees: Is Diversity Management A Luxury or A Necessity. *Academy of Management Journal*, *39*(3), 704–719. doi:10.2307/256660

Stainback, K., Ratliff, T. N., & Roscigno, V. J. (2011). The context of workplace sex discrimination:Sex composition,Workplace Culture and Relative Power. *Social Forces*, *89*(4), 1165–1188. doi:10.1093/sf/89.4.1165

Upadhya, C., Gurumurthy, A., Singh, P. J., Mundkur, A., & Swamy, M. (2005). *Gender Issues in the Indian Software Outsourcing Industry*. Elsevier.

WaldmanP. (n.d.). Retrieved from Linkedin: https://www.linkedin.com/pulse/promoting-equality-workplace-phillip-waldman

ADDITIONAL READING

Adams, J. S. (1965). Inequity in Social Exchange. *Advances in Experimental Social Psychology*, *2*, 267–299. doi:10.1016/S0065-2601(08)60108-2

Afshar, A. F., & Alishahi, A. G. (2015). The role of conscientiousness on job stress and deviant work behavior:The variable share of perceived organizationa support. *Indian Journal of Fundamental and Applied Life Sciences*, 226-231.

Appelbaum, S. H., Iaconi, G. D., & Matousek, A. (2007). Positive and Negative deviant workplace behaviors: causes,impacts and solutions. *Corporate Governance*, *7*(5), 586–598. doi:10.1108/14720700710827176

Baah, K. D. (2014). Organizational antecedents and perceptions of fairness in policy implementation among employees in the banking sector of Ghana. *African Journal of Business Management*, 816–831.

Bamberger, P., Dvir, M. A., & Harel, G. (1995). Gender based wage and promotion discrimination in Israeli high technology firms: Do unions make a difference? *Academy of Management Journal, 38*(6), 1744–1761. doi:10.2307/256853

Barnes, D. C. (1992, July). *Disability and employment.* Retrieved from University of Leeds: disability-studies.leeds.ac.uk/files/library/Barnes-dis-and-emp.pdf

Blau, G. (1994). Testing a two-dimensional measure of job research behavior. *Organizational Behavior and Human Decision Processes, 59*(2), 288–312. doi:10.1006/obhd.1994.1061

Jiang, J. (2015). Agency workers identification: The moderating effect of perceived employment discrimination. *Social and Bahavioral Sciences*, 306-314.

Triana, M., Jayasinghe, M., & Pieper, J. R. (2015). Perceived workplace racial discrimination and its correlates: A meta-analysis. *Journal of Organizational Behavior, 36*(4), 491–513. doi:10.1002/job.1988

Chapter 13
Developing Strategic Leadership in the Indian Context:
Leadership

Minisha Gupta
IMS Unison University, India

ABSTRACT

With intense competition, it has become quite challenging for organizations to continuously create and innovate. Since leadership has been identified as an effective key factor in attaining sustainable competitive edge, there remains a lack of research to assess the role of leadership most likely to cause creativity and innovation. This chapter tries to conceptualize the impact of developing strategic leadership in Indian organizations. This has a significant impact on organizational creativity and innovation. Firms facing recession need to develop their leaders as strategic leaders who can generate a positive wave in the organization, provide direction to employees, generate genuine interest among employees to learn and grow. Strategic leaders develop commitment among employees by providing a vision and goal to them. They think strategically and frame policies as per employees' needs and expectations. This study demonstrates the impact of strategic leadership style to generate creativity and innovation among their subordinates.

DOI: 10.4018/978-1-5225-4933-8.ch013

INTRODUCTION

In today's dynamic and disrupting global business setting, continuous change in organizational systems, processes, and structures is crucial for sustaining business success and competitive advantage. As continuous change becomes necessary, organizations learn to leverage their core competence and develop survival strategies, in order to face the challenges of rapidly increasing competitive scenario, dwindling product life cycles, and changing customer norms. The key to attain effective management of these rapid and disruptive changes is initiating effective leadership.

In a survey conducted by JobBuzz, a Timesjob rating platform, 900 employees have participated. Their responses to the questions were as under (Table 1).

From Table 1, it can be easily identified that how much Indian organizations are in need of infusing an effective leadership. Leaders not only motivate their followers but also enhance organizational culture, policies, and work environment. Indian organizations have collectivistic culture, which means work places are like families for the employees. People develop certain feelings and bonds which encourages them to work with dedication and loyalty. In Indian scenario leadership development is gradually gaining attraction, as the concept of leadership is important to any aspect of ensuring effectiveness and managing change in organizations. There are certain challenges related with developing leadership due to the continuously changing business contexts and the pressures to respond to the demands of company and expectations of consumers.

Table 1. Reasons for infusing leadership in Indian organizations

Questions Asked From Respondents	Excellent	Satisfactory	Very Poor
Management Leadership skills	25	35	40
Necessary resources	40	0	60
Use of available resources	20	0	80
Employees interaction with top management	5	0	95
Problem handling by top management	10	0	90
Public Relation	35	0	65
Work culture	25	45	30
Scope of improvement like Workplace flexibility	0	35	65
Scope of improvement like Compensation scheme	0	25	75
Scope of improvement like Work environment	0	20	80
Amendment in leadership style	0	15	85

Source: Katha, 2017

Developing leadership is necessary for organizational success and researchers have suggested that there is an urgent need to develop effective leadership skills and invest in it as per changing dynamic environment. Though the question is very old that whether leaders are born or can be developed. Early theories of leadership proposed that leaders were born and not made. However, various theories argued that leadership skills and behavior can be learnt or acquired over a period of time.

Recruiting leaders is equally important to developing leaders. There is a large pool of capable people in India for every industry. Thus, organizations should initiate hiring people who are visionary and attain diversified skills to put their maximum efforts in attaining organizational sustainability. Employees should also have the ability to be nurtured as becoming leaders. However, there is a big challenge lying in the same.

CHALLENGES IN DEVELOPING STRATEGIC LEADERSHIP

Strategic leadership is passing through its development stage. Therefore, there are several challenges which are to be faced while developing this concept in Indian context. Few of these challenges are as under:

1. **Economic Cycle:** Indian economic cycle is highly dynamic and is full of turbulent situations. Indian companies need to develop such a leader who can sense the uncertainty of market and maintain sustainability of the organization.
2. **Increased Attrition Rate:** Continuous attrition of employees raises the question of survival for organizations. For growth and expansion retention of talented employees is required and can be attained if strategic leadership is initiated in organizations. Such leaders share organization's vision and strategies to imbibe a sense of belongingness among employees and become able to retain talent.
3. **Developing Role Models:** Indian companies are facing the scarcity of role models. Leaders like Ratan Tata, Rahul Bajaj, Azim Premji, Lakshmi Narayan Mittal, Anand Mahindra, are few. They have inspired not only their followers but also people around the world. However, they are few in number which highlights the issue of missing a role model from Indian firms who can share working context and culture. Moreover, a leader should also be able to handle the challenges and communicate the vision to their subordinates for attaining continuous growth and sustainability.
4. **Exposure to R&D:** Most of the leaders are not exposed to the R&D centers of the organization. This hampers their ability to communicate and solve critical

customer issues. This also hinders creative and innovative outcomes of a leader. Therefore, organizations should encourage research oriented approach among leaders.

5. **Gaining Followers' Trust:** Indian organizations are facing this critical issue of winning their follower's trust. Companies need to initiate such leadership skills where they will be able to effectively address turmoil and connect directly to their followers. A leader's positivity and transparency impact followers' perceived trust, defined in terms of willingness to be vulnerable, and effectiveness of their leader.

6. **Diversified Workforce:** In Indian organizations, workforce belongs to diversified work groups. They share similarities and differences in terms of age, cultural background, physical abilities, race, religion, gender, and sexual orientation. Their social and psychological characteristics also vary from each other. Such workforce is difficult to manage but is necessary for organizations to generate core competence. Heterogeneous employees share their knowledge and ideas to sort out challenging problems and generate prolific results. However, this can only be possible if a leader shares organizational vision and strategies with them, which can only be done through strategic leadership.

Unless leaders put their versatile experiences through filters of analysis and link it to the macro economic and social changes, they would not be able to update themselves with their organizations and help it to design a strategy to survive in competitive markets. Thus, raises a need to develop strategic leadership in organizations.

STRATEGIC LEADERSHIP

The Greek word "Strategos" means a general in command of an army. Strategy means plan or a roadmap of certain activities. It is an ability to defeat opponents for developing a unified system of global governance. Sun Tzu's *Art of War* (ca.400 B.C.) is widely cited as a source of strategic principles for leaders. Thus, strategic leadership is defined as the ability to influence others to voluntarily take routine decisions for long term organizational stability (Finkelstein & Hambrick, 1996). Strategic leaders foresee advance in time to set goals for the organization (Arnott, 1995). They transform critical situations into meaningful opportunities. They can protect organizations' profit from market risk with their strategic thinking and activities. Such a leader understands the emergent strategy process that requires planning and executing tasks for organizational success. S/he controls and monitor employees' performance and, thus, comes up as a blend mix or a final outcome of all leadership styles. 98 senior executives of different Indian companies were interviewed to discover the measures by which Indian leaders drive their organization to high performance (Cappelli, Singh, Singh, & Useem, 2010). Most of them neither specified their ability nor team effort. The key to their success was focusing on human resource, the people with whom they are working with.

155 Pakistani employees working in profit-oriented service sector were surveyed to analyze the impact of leadership on organizational performance (Choudhary, Akhtar, & Zaheer, 2012). Transformational leaders use their energies to engage followers toward goal attainment. They influence their followers and involve them in learning and development. Transactional leaders follow transactions that are the ways followers perform. They react according to the performance of followers and believe in reward and punishment transactions. It creates stress and fear among the followers and their focus shifted from performing quality work to completing their tasks.

Indian organizations are crowded with managerial (Sameer Dhanrajani, Cognizant), visionary (Dhirubhai Ambani, Reliance), bureaucratic (Mahatma Gandhi), or autocratic leaders (Indira Gandhi), but faced a great scarcity of strategic leader. Other leadership styles lead to average returns, but achieve less and that too with a risk of losing wealth. In comparison to them, strategic leadership continuously engages in the wealth creation process in established as well as entrepreneurial firms (Boal & Hooijberg, 2001). Leaders such as Mark Zuckerburgh, Hillary Clinton, Bill Gates, Richard Branson, Donald Trumph, Steve Jobs are few of the strategic leaders who attain success not on their own but with their visionary approach and strategic leadership skills. They have the ability to influence others to willingly take routine decisions to enhance sustainability and growth of the organizations (Ireland & Hitt, 1999). They take leadership as an opportunity for the valuable service to employees by focusing on their development and well-being. Strategic leaders have following characteristics:

- A collusive mixture of different leadership styles.
- Emphasize more on ethics and value oriented decisions.
- Handles both daily routine activities as well as long term opportunities.
- Create and execute strategies for immediate effect and long-term viability.
- Expect for positivity and strength from their superiors, peers, subordinates, and themselves.
- Exercise strategic and financial controls.
- Share both tacit and explicit knowledge in organization.

- Inject both linear and nonlinear thinking.
- Make a difference in the organization with their strategic thinking.

Thus, it has been clear now that, strategic leader fulfill all the requirements of a dynamic and a visionary leader to face challenges and solve business complexities. They identify risk and measure to come up with that also. They influence others and get the work done by them which helps in wealth creation and organizations' long term existence in turbulent business situations.

Research on strategic leadership focuses on executives who have overall responsibility for an organization, based on the principle that "ultimately, they account forwhat happens to the organization" (Hambrick & Mason, 1984).Strategic leadership is defined as "the leader's ability to anticipate, envision, and maintain flexibility and to empower others to create strategic change as necessary" (Hitt, Ireland, & Rowe, 2005). It is multifunctional, involves managing through others, and helps organizations cope with change that seems to be increasing exponentially in today's globalized business environment. Strategic leader possess the ability to accommodate and integrateorganizations' business environment and to manage complex information processing (Jansen, Vera, & Crossan, 2009). It focuses on strategic productivity by developing an environment in which employees forecast the organization's needs in context of their own job. Strategic leaders encourage employees in an organization to follow their own ideas. They initiate learning in organizations and make use of reward and incentive system for encouraging creativity and innovation among employees (Vera & Crossan, 2004). It is important to attain satisfactory performance when confronting to the challenges of the global economy.

Strategic leadership is composed of two different words: strategy and leadership. Strategy is considered as a perspective to view the future and a measure of evaluating current activities of the organization (Porter, 1980). However, leadership is a process of influencing others to achieve the desired output from them (Bush & Glover, 2003). Joining these two words results in the form of such leadership style where influence is created to achieve desired output for minimizing risk and expanding business opportunities for the future. They share vision, motivate, guide, offer hope, and provide a caring experience by establishing a quality relationship with the followers and subordinates. A strategic leader should have the following abilities segregated as organizational and personal.

ORGANIZATIONAL ABILITIES

1. **Strategic Orientation:** When the mission and vision statement of the organization along with long term goals are synchronized, then it can attain

sustainable competitive advantage. A strategic leader synchronizes routine activities with the desired goals or pre-established targets of the organization. He shares organizational goals and vision with the followers in order to achieve the targets.

2. **Task Reflexivity:** One important role played by strategic leader is in developing action plan for transforming strategies into desired actions so that predefined motives can be attained. Reflection, planning, and action are the three major steps of this process taken by strategic leader. To identify the ground realities or past performance of the organization for evaluating its strengths and weaknesses, plan according to organization's working abilities and act as per the defined framework.

3. **Coordinate People and Organizational Goals:** Strategic leader holds the responsibility for accumulating the resources at a single platform in order to exploit and explore all the resource for achieving core competence. Such leader motivates people to align their goals with organization'sto work with dedication and deliver satisfactory results.

4. **Bring Change in the Organization:** Strategic leader senses the urge to bring change for leveraging resources and attaining competitive edge over others. They put their efforts on changing traditional and updated structure, policies, technology, to inject new ways of enhancing creativity and innovation.

5. **Develop Strategic Capabilities:** Strategic leader should emphasize on developing core competencies in the organization. Change is necessary to initiate inworking methodology, existing procedures, communicating and sharing knowledge to boost organizational learning, and commoditizing. It is equally important to focus on developing decision making and problem solving skills as core competencies of the employees.

PERSONAL ABILITIES

1. **Passionate About Change:** A strategic leader should constantly involve in infusing new technologies to the organization. The ultimate aim should be to improve organizational excellence through creativity and innovation and sustain in the competitive world. They should also concentrate on leveraging organizational resources and company's core competence to attain long term sustainability.

2. **Absorptive Capacity:** It is must for leader to acquire knowledge and disseminate among its members so that a culture of learning can be imbibed in the organization. A leader can gather the information, analyze it and dispense

it so that members discuss the information and learn new skills and generate core competence for the organization.
3. **Adaptive Capacity:** Any change cannot be done at random in organizations, thus, it is important for a leader to identify the requirements of initiating change. It is also important to consider the method for implementing change in organization to reduce resistance among employees.
4. **Leadership Wisdom:** For accomplishing desired targets a leader must be provided wisdom. It helps them in responding quickly to the uncertain situations, balancing relationships, settling down disputes, and inculcating values in the organization.

FEATURES OF STRATEGIC LEADERSHIP

A strategic leader is one equipped with the following features/ characteristics:

1. To have a vision
2. To be compassionate
3. To leverage organize resources
4. To handle task passionately
5. To be emotionally intelligent
6. To have spiritual quotient

RESPONSIBILITIES OF STRATEGIC LEADER

Being strategic a leader must perform the following responsibilities in the organization:

1. To develop organizational framework
2. To formulate strategies
3. To share their strategic vision with subordinates
4. To motivate team members
5. To maintain locus of control
6. To initiate a culture of learning
7. To collect and share knowledge
8. To resolve conflict (if any)

IMPORTANCE OF STRATEGIC LEADERSHIP IN FIRM'S PERFORMANCE

Strategic leadership is a person's ability to anticipate, envision, maintain flexibility, think strategically, and work with others to initiate changes that will create a viable future for the organization (Ireland & Hitt, 1999). Since, strategic leadership is complex, therefore, it has been described that strategic leadership is effective only if applied on the available resources. Human resource is a critical part of any organization, therefore, strategic leadership focuses on managing and developing this most valuable asset of the organization. Strategic leader tries to develop and mobilize human capital along with focus on making teams. They also try to build and utilize groups as a means of developing effective, collaborative relationship. Such relationships enable members to collaborate in ways that contribute to creating and using competitive advantages. Collaborative relationships are fruitful for organizations. Teams with diverse and rich talent combine together to solve problems in a complex and dynamic business environment. This provides competitive advantage to organizations and they will be able to develop a vision for future.

Strategic leaders also develop a culture of trust among members of the organization. For example Ratan Tata has developed a sense of belongingness and trust among his subordinates. Members share their knowledge and shortcoming and try to develop themselves with mutual cooperation. These efforts induce learning within organizational members. Trust and learning facilitates effective teamwork which results in creative and innovative outcomes. Strategic leaders need to function as both transformational and transactional to manage organizational learning (Vera & Crossan, 2004). However, organizational learning and performance can only be possible if there is appropriate exploration and exploitation of resources (He & Wong, 2004; Gibson & Birkinshaw, 2004). With effective coordination, organizational learning and leveraging of resources, a strategic leader adopts sustainable competitive advantage. They will be able to transform organizational structures, initiate technological advancements and bring in creativity and innovation as major sources of attaining sustainability.

CONCLUSION

This study tries to highlight the role and importance of strategic leadership in Indian organizations. Time has gone when success depends upon achieving high profits. With the changing business models and dynamic scenario, there is a pressure on

Figure 1. Conceptual framework of strategic leadership

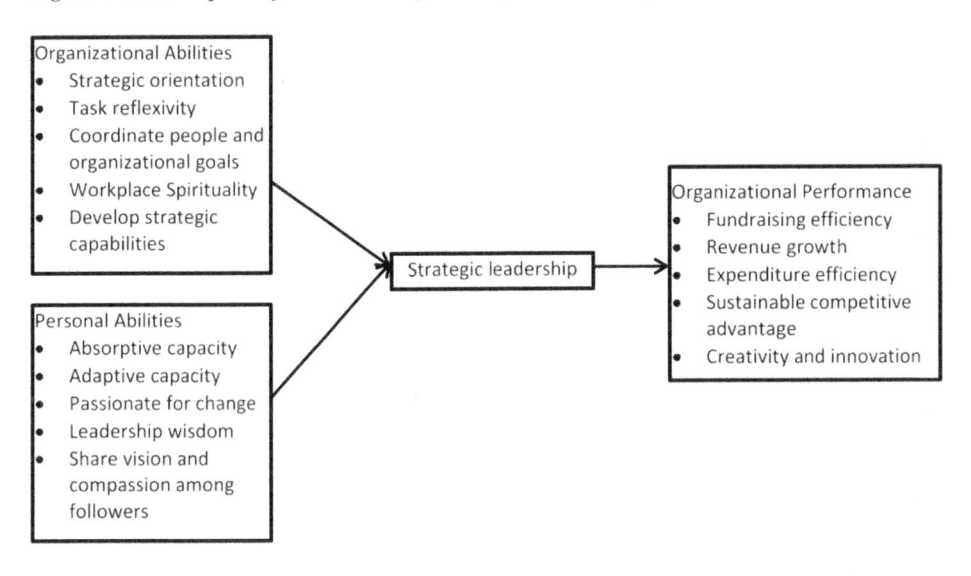

Organizational Abilities
- Strategic orientation
- Task reflexivity
- Coordinate people and organizational goals
- Workplace Spirituality
- Develop strategic capabilities

Personal Abilities
- Absorptive capacity
- Adaptive capacity
- Passionate for change
- Leadership wisdom
- Share vision and compassion among followers

→ **Strategic leadership** →

Organizational Performance
- Fundraising efficiency
- Revenue growth
- Expenditure efficiency
- Sustainable competitive advantage
- Creativity and innovation

companies to prioritize on attaining sustainability. Achieving sustainability is not an easy task. It is a joint effort of shop floor workers, blue collar employees and top management. All this can be coordinated if the vision and goals are combined and properly communicated at all the levels of management. For carrying out this tedious task and managing resistance among all, there is a need for a visionary leader who can transform into any role fit for attaining organizational sustainability. There comes the importance of infusing strategic leadership in organizations. A leader, who shares vision, manages emotions, infuse learning, change traditions, and coordinate at all the levels of management. Thus, strategic leader is important for Indian organizations, where people from different cultures, religion, background, and educationwork together under single roof. They need to work together and manage their conflicts. They have to focus on learning and enhancing their core competence. They have to emphasize on leveraging organizational resources in order to properly exploit and explore them for activities like problem solving and decision making. To attain all these things and organizational objectives, it becomes necessary to initiate the concept of strategic leadership. Organizations need to hire and develop young and talented individuals who can focus on prioritizing organizational objectives with their skills and abilities.

Organizations have to initiate leadership development practices. They can start with setting up a center to hire people with right talent who can enhance organizational growth. At all the levels of management, leadership skills are essential, irrespective of the complexity. Organizations can develop leadership skills in order to make them learn to work effectively with technical teams and motivate them to create innovative outcomes. Team members have a tendency to follow those working with core team and having exceptional technical knowledge.

Success of an organization depends on the skills of the leaders which can be considered as the ability to manage in a dynamic environment, increase in organizational productivity, mentoring and coaching followers, motivating team members, coordinating and directing people. A leader is aware of getting things done by fostering creativity and innovation within organization.

It is imperative for Indian companies to initiate strategic leadership development programs. They can initiate classroom based programs or coaching and mentoring activities, or talent management tools, or other formal development programs. Since, initiation is easier then implementation, therefore, organizations should focus on combining strategic leadership development programs along with implementation programs. Organizations can deploy a culture of recognizing and rewarding talent of employees. Such initiative encourages employee engagement as well as substantial growth of strategic leaders in the organization. Moreover, employees can also be promoted and supported by senior management through leadership development initiatives. On the basis of industry, career model including career path and plan can be developed by top management to encourage employees. They can identify the niche for promoting them towards leadership development programs. To provide global exposure, groom and lead them, manage and handle situations in different context and identifying a larger picture of company can also be considered as a major ways of promoting strategic leadership in organizations.

Strategic leadership needs to be supported and developed among aspiring Indian leaders so that leaders of outside country can be replaced. Therefore, there is a need to develop systems for initiating and implementing programs to hire and develop talent. Focus on developing talented individuals is important in order to create and innovate continuously and achieve sustainable competitive advantage.

REFERENCES

Arnott, D. H. (1995). The five lenses of leadership. *The Journal of Leadership Studies*, *2*(1), 137–141. doi:10.1177/107179199500200112

Boal, K. B., & Hooijberg, R. (2001). Strategic leadership research: Moving on. *The Leadership Quarterly*, *11*(4), 515–549. doi:10.1016/S1048-9843(00)00057-6

Bush, T., & Glover, D. (2003). *Leadership development: A literature review*. Nottingham, UK: National College for School Leadership.

Cappelli, P., Singh, H., Singh, J. V., & Useem, M. (2010). Leadership lessons from India. *Harvard Business Review*, *88*(3), 90–97. PMID:20402052

Choudhary, A. I., Akhtar, S. A., & Zaheer, A. (2012). Impact of Transformational and Servant Leadership on Organizational Performance: A Comparative Analysis. *Journal of Business Ethics*, *116*(2), 433–440. doi:10.1007/s10551-012-1470-8

Finkelstein, S., & Hambrick, D. C. (1996). *Strategic leadership: Top executives and their effects on organizations*. West Publishing Company.

Gibson, C. B., & Birkinshaw, J. (2004). The antecedents, consequences, and mediating role of organizational ambidexterity. *Academy of Management Journal*, *47*(2), 209–226. doi:10.2307/20159573

Hambrick, D. C., & Mason, P. A. (1984). Upper echelons: The organization as a reflection of its top managers. *Academy of Management Review*, *9*(2), 193–206.

He, Z. L., & Wong, P. K. (2004). Exploration vs. exploitation: An empirical test of the ambidexterity hypothesis. *Organization Science*, *15*(4), 481–494. doi:10.1287/orsc.1040.0078

Hitt, M. A., Ireland, R. D., & Rowe, G. W. (2005). Strategic leadership: Strategy, resources, ethics and succession. *Handbook on responsible leadership and governance in global business*, 19-41.

Ireland, R. D., & Hitt, M. A. (1999). Achieving and maintaining strategic competitiveness in the 21st century: The role of strategic leadership. *The Academy of Management Executive*, *13*(1), 43–57.

Jansen, J. J., Vera, D., & Crossan, M. (2009). Strategic leadership for exploration and exploitation: The moderating role of environmental dynamism. *The Leadership Quarterly*, *20*(1), 5–18. doi:10.1016/j.leaqua.2008.11.008

Porter, M. E. (1980). Competitive strategy: Techniques for analyzing industries and competition. Academic Press.

Vera, D., & Crossan, M. (2004). Strategic leadership and organizational learning. *Academy of Management Review*, *29*(2), 222–240.

Yukl, G. A. (1981). *Leadership in organizations*. Pearson Education India.

Chapter 14
Relativity Applies to Physics, Not Ethics

Purna Prabhakar Nandamuri
IFHE University, India

Mukesh Kumar Mishra
IFHE University, India

Gowthami Ch
ITM Business School, India

ABSTRACT

Ethical relativism is the most prevalent philosophical sub discipline. Ethical relativism represents that there is no moral right or wrong, asserting that morals evolve and change with social norms over a period of time. As the businesses have been growing transnational, this has become a burden rather than advantage, leading to confusion about whether to follow the host country or the home country cultural standards. Adopting the host country cultural values might end up with contradictory and inconsistent practices in the same organization whereas strictly believing in the home country culture might lead to rigidity and chaos in respective markets, forfeiting the opportunities. Thus, overcoming the mindset of ethical relativism has become a big burden on multinational businesses. Eventually, there lies a great hope for ethical universalism rather than relativism in the context of cross-cultural and diverse businesses.

DOI: 10.4018/978-1-5225-4933-8.ch014

INTRODUCTION

An American politician and the 54th Speaker of the United States House of Representatives, Paul Ryan once said "If you ask me what the biggest problem in America is, I'm not going to tell you debt, deficits, statistics, economics—I'll tell you its moral relativism" (Mccormack, 2011), signifying the vitality of the issue in 21st Century. Relativism has been emerging to be the most prevalent and reviled doctrines of our time, permeating the entire gamut of philosophical sub disciplines. Relativism illustrates that the view point of each individual is equally valid as "each thing appears to me, so it is for me, and as it appears to you, so it is for you - you and I each being a man" (Plato, 1926). The philosophized conception that right and wrong are not absolute values, but are personalized according to the individual and his or her circumstances or cultural orientation. Relativism theorizes that truth is different for different people. This is established on the notion that there is no ultimate standard of good or evil, and every decision about right and wrong is a produce of pertinent society. For instance, the same wind could be cold to one person and hot to another. Even though relativism is of recent coinage, it roots back to the ancient Greece, as a philosophical doctrine, with some of the traces to the very beginnings of Western philosophy. In the 20th Century, the popularity of relativism owes to Einstein's Special Theory of Relativity[1], used by Gilbert Harman[2] as a model for philosophical versions of relativism. Harman (1975) says that:

Even an object's mass, according to Einstein's Theory of Relativity, is relative to a choice of spatio-temporal framework. An object can have one mass in relation to one such framework and a different mass in relation to another. .... I am going to argue for a similar claim about moral right and wrong. ... I am going to argue that moral right and wrong .... are always relative to a choice of moral framework.

Further, many social scientists, under the influence of Karl Marx[3] and Max Weber[4], assigned credibility to the idea that human beliefs and actions could be understood and assessed only relative to their socio-economic circumstances as they are highly correlated to the background of cultural presuppositions, interests and values. "*I have traveled in 201 countries and the strangest thing I saw was man*", says Robert L. Ripley[5] (Stanton, 2011), the Modern Marco Polo, who published in *Believe It or Not*[6] that "one man sat and stared at the sun for fifteen years, which ultimately blinded him and made him incapable of moving his legs from inactivity. Another was buried alive for 40 days in suspended animation and survived.... Some foreign practices amuse us, such as that of Japanese men who tattoo their entire bodies. Others make us squeamish, such as a Latin American culinary practice of eating handfuls of live bugs in tortillas. But other foreign cultural practices spark a moral reaction, such as countries that impose harsh penalties on women who have premarital sex, even execution. In the U.S., by contrast, premarital sex is normal behavior and, according to one study, since the 1950s, about 95 percent of Americans have had premarital sex. According to another study, 60 to 70 percent of Americans under age 55 believe that such behavior is morally acceptable. Attitudes about many sexual behaviors are especially diverse from culture to culture with issues such as homosexuality, public nudity, polygamy, polyandry, adultery, pornography, and prostitution. Reactions can radically differ not only from country to country, but also within the same country from one subculture to another, or at differing points in time". These culturally-conflicting standards of behavior make every one wonder whether morality is condensed to mere social convention, challenging the impression that there is a fixed standard of morality for everyone and leaving a key question whether moral standards exist independently of human social creations. The philosophy that moral standards exist independent of human social creations is known as *moral objectivism* whereas *moral relativism* believes that they are just human inventions. Relativists strongly hold that moral standards are purely human inventions that are created either by individual people or human societies; change through time and society; and do not necessarily apply universally to all people or social groups, and their application depends on human preference.

Moral or ethical relativism has been one of the widely debated topics in Western philosophical fora, and the views of early relativists remain largely unchanged even today. Ethical relativism is the opinion that moral judgments and beliefs about right and wrong, good and bad, varies greatly across time and context and the correctness is subjective of relativity of individual or cultural perceptions. The world is inhabited by different societies with distinct idiosyncrasies and cultural sensibilities, which serve as the foundations of moral value judgments. Ethical relativism represents the position that there are no moral absolutes, no moral right or wrong. This position would assert that morals evolve and change with social norms over a period of time. This philosophy allows people to mutate ethically as the culture, knowledge, and technology change in society. As different societies have different legal systems, different people speak different languages, different groups of people play different versions of football, and different people may hold different moral standards. Moralities acknowledged at one time may fail to be accepted at another time. Individuals within any given group may believe in different moralities. Further, a person may acknowledge different mutually incompatible moralities at different times and even at the same time. Thus, it is hardly possible either to establish that a particular morality as the correct one or to believe in a single standard.

The Greek historian Herodotus[7] provides one of the ancient expressions of cultural relativism by concluding that "everyone without exception believes his own native customs, and the religion he was brought up in, to be the best" (Herodotus, 2003).

Drawing on anthropological data compiled by earlier Greek historians, Sextus[8] furnishes multiple examples of divergent moral standards such as variable attitudes about theft, food habits, infanticide, homosexuality, incest, cannibalism, human sacrifice, killing of the elderly, and consumption of animal flesh etc, to establish the sweeping claim that the moral behavior of different societies conflict with each other, and the moral standards that they espouse also conflict since every moral belief is stranded in the attitude of particular culture. After Sextus, Thomas Aquinas[9] contends that "reason is perverted by passion, or evil habit, or an evil disposition of nature," because people habitually let their passions overpower their reason (Weinreb, 1990). Later, the French philosopher Michel Montaigne[10] defends cultural relativism in his *Of Custom*[11] by declaring that custom has the power to shape every possible kind of cultural practice and peer pressure is so strong that people automatically approve of their society's customs. He further writes in *Of Cannibals*[12] that 'each man calls barbarism whatever is not his own practice'. Friedrich Nietzsche[13] states that "there is no such thing as moral phenomena, but only a moral interpretation of phenomena." He goes a step ahead to reject the naive faith that human beliefs just reflect reality and hypothesizes that each of human beliefs is grounded in a standpoint that is neither correct nor incorrect, and accordingly there are no moral facts but only moral interpretations of phenomena giving rise to different moral codes. He tags the desire for moral absolutes is nothing but a misguided quest for the impossible. In this process, the culture or society emerges to be the chief authority to decide what is right for each individual within that society. Consequently the individual's will is subordinated to the will of the cultural majority. Therefore, conventional relativism believes that no moral standards can universally be applied to all people and at all times and it would not be sensible to resolve that a specific set of cultural practices to be veracious as all cultural practices, at the generic level, are equally valid. Thus, the operational definition of ethical relativism could be proposed that w*henever two people or two societies disagree about the morality of an act, both sides are equally correct.* The correctness of moral judgments and beliefs is relative to specific cultural perspectives. In the Indian context also, the *Jaina Anekantavada*[14] principle of Mahavira[15] believes that 'truth and reality are perceived differently from diverse points of view' and hence no single point of view is the complete truth. Multiple factors contribute for this phenomenon.

Cultural Diversity

Centuries ago, when information was rarely accessible about the distant lands, corresponding cultures were relatively isolated. So, the cultural practices and traditions of one's own society might reasonably have been thought to be the only right way of doing things. But, in the present age of universal information exchange, it is obvious that each specific cultural system represents only one of an endless number and, hence, it is no longer sensible to consider the practices of one specific culture as authentic. However, the genuine fact to be accepted is that individuals and societies embrace and continuously disagree on moral issues. For instance, most of the societies around the world believe that the Eskimos allowing their elderly to die by starvation, is morally wrong. It would be unbelievable to observe the Spartans of ancient Greece and the Dobu of New Guinea believe that stealing is morally right. Many cultures around the world have been practicing infanticide and a tribe in East Africa throws deformed infants to the hippopotamus, which is highly condemned by many other societies. Sexual practices such as homosexuality, polygamy, permitted in some societies, are believed to be immoral by many other cultures. Ruth Benedict, a popular anthropologist, pronounces a tribe in Melanesia which views cooperation and kindness as vices. Colin Turnbull has documented that the Ik in northern Uganda have no sense of duty toward their children or parents. There are some societies that make it a duty for children to kill their aging parents (Pojman, 1955). Thus, in view of such a tremendous cultural diversity prevailing across various societies around the world, it is not reasonable to believe that a specific set of cultural practices can be the one and only right practice. Hence, it must be concluded that all cultural practices are equally valid.

Ethnocentric Approach

Ethnocentrism, in general, means adjudicating another culture through the eyes of one's own culture rather than attempting to see things from their perspective, which, inevitably leads to rank own culture as superior to others. Most people, in the modern environment, agree that ethnocentrism, ethically, is a pernicious form of discrimination, as racism and sexism. Conventional relativism avoids such approach and maintains that all cultures are equally valid.

Cultural Conditioning

It is true that most of the opinions about right and wrong are acquired. The values of one's own society are instilled, since infancy, by parents, friends, books, television, movies, and priests or preachers. For example, an American child, today, opines that women and minorities deserve equal opportunities like other white men, contrary to the same a hundred years ago. Thus, people are conditioned by their respective cultures to believe and maintain the ethical values in vogue. To articulate a neutral and objective assessment of other cultures, one must throw off all the cultural baggage that have been inherited from own social environment and break free from cultural conditioning that has fashioned the minds, emotions and personalities. However, conventional relativists assert that it would not be a realistic human possibility as people can never get beyond their cultural conditioning. Since people are incapable of freeing themselves from the cultural conditioning, it is obvious that what kinds of judgments would be made about other cultures. According to conventional relativism, judging other cultures should, altogether be avoided.

Lack of Knowledge

If some fact or practice is believed to be the right one, where to access the relevant information about what that fact was? Some people suggest that certain sacred texts contain the answers for such dilemmas. But, conventional relativism points out that people raised to believe in one sacred text opine that theirs is the only one truthful and all others are immoral. If religion is kept out of this discussion, the question is equally challenging. Differences of opinion are resolved through experimental methods and empirical observations in science. But, there do not seem to be any experiments that can be run or empirical observations that can be used to resolve ethical disagreements. Hence, there seems to be no way to prove some answers right and other answers wrong in ethics. As no one has a privileged access to the absolute truth about morality, conventional relativism wishes to avoid treating one's own ethical opinions as infallible and indubitable and treats all to be equally valid or correct.

After all, disagreement exists even about scientific matters. Some people believe that disease is caused by evil spirits, while others believe it is caused by microbes, but we do not on that account, conclude that disease has no *real* cause. The same might be true of ethics—disagreement might only mean that some people are more enlightened than others. For instance, 72 percent of Americans agree that 'there is no such thing as absolute truth; two people could define truth in totally conflicting ways, but both could still be correct' (Barna, 1994). 'A man does not call a line crooked unless he has some idea of a straight line', says C. S. Lewis in *Mere Christianity*[16]. Further, 71 percent of Americans agree that there were no absolute standards that apply to everybody in all situations. In view of the prolonged debate on ethical relativism in intellectual and philosophical circles, it is imperative to look into the way it influences the business sector, as any cultural development leaves a considerable impact on the business sector of the society.

ETHICAL RELATIVISM AND BUSINESS

Culture is a changing phenomenon which exerts a profound impact on organizational performance. Understanding the relevant culture and working within the constraints is mandatory for organizational effectiveness. Hence, constant study of, and adjustment to, its influence on the organizational structures, processes, and behaviors is a matter of priority for every business. The essence of corporate identity reflects 'what a company really is' rather than what a company might advocate. A few examples are categorically illustrated here to elucidate how differently cultures approach the businesses:

A popular American joke says that the signature placed on the dotted line is the first step towards a trial. An American would sue even his mother if he believes that she violated a written agreement. Another wide spread *dirty little secret*[17] in business is bribery. A survey of 3600 companies among 69 countries by the World Bank in late 2010 reveals that many considered corrupt practices such as bribery were inevitable to get things done when facing the possibility of losing contracts to competitors and even 40 percent admitted having done so. This figure jumped to 60 percent in the case of former Soviet Union (Kaikati, Sullivan, Virgo, Carr, & Katherine, 2000). The bribes paid by German companies alone, in 1996, were over $3 billion as estimated by World Business magazine (Tanzi, 1998). The US Commerce Department reported that bribery was an essential factor in 294 commercial contracts worth US$145 billion during the preceding five years to 1999 (Fiddler, 1999). Every year, Western businesses pay an estimated US$80 billion in bribes to influence and win contracts, which is sufficient to eradicate global poverty, as the United Nations Organization believes (Hawley, 2000). Bribery prevails across many societies with versatile names such as success fee, commissions etc. Until recently, bribery was seen as a normal business practice as countries like UK, France, and Germany treated bribes as legitimate business expenses. "Bribery is a common way of doing business

Table 1. Different cultural business approaches

Business contracts: Different Communities Assign Varying Importance to the Written Contracts.		
US and Germany	Japan	USSR (Erstwhile)
• **Americans and Germans insist on detailed contract carefully written into many pages covering relevant legal provisions.** • Dishonoring the formal contract is moral bankruptcy for Americans while Germans respect the contract, once signed, with sanctity and expect their business partners to follow the same.	• For Japanese, contracts are indicative and any issue would be resolved by arbitration rather than approaching legal processes. • Every contract includes *henko jiji* - a complete renegotiation clause allowing for major changes of circumstances (Mitchell, 2003). • For a Japanese business executive, informal and verbal commitment is worth more than a written contract and breach of such commitment would be a moral fault more serious than failing on a written contract.	The Russians hold a totally different conception of contracts than Westerners as any contract signed with a Russian company hasn't any value since they treat a contract as a statement of intent rather than a strict requirement.

in a lot of places", says Steve Veltkamp, president of Biz$hop, an American Exim business and consulting firm (Moira, 2000). Bribery, nepotism, and exploitation of the members of less privileged classes are taken for granted in some locales, but in others these actions cross a moral boundary (Forsyth & O'Boyle, 2011). Around 140 nations have joined the United Nations Convention against Corruption (UNCAC) by 2016, while 16 nations yet to ratify the convention. Despite such a high degree of awareness against bribery and corruption, there still exists many countries rank high on corruption index published annually by Transparency International[18]. India has been ranked 79th out of 176 countries in the Corruption Perception Index[19] (CPI), 2016, while there are some countries with less degree of corruption while some others rank very high on global corruption perception index. For example, the status report of the public sector corruption among different regions of the world, as reported by the CPI, 2016, is tabulated region-wise for clarity.

"In too many countries, people are deprived of their most basic needs and go to bed hungry every night because of corruption, while the powerful and corrupt enjoy lavish lifestyles with impunity," says Ugaz (2016), Chair, Transparency International. Nations such as Canada, Luxembourg, Netherlands, Singapore, Switzerland, Norway, Sweden, Finland, Denmark, and New Zealand etc. are considered to be the least corrupt cultures whereas, countries like Somalia, North Korea, Afghanistan, Sudan, Libya, Iraq, Turkmenistan, Syria, and Uzbekistan are known for highest degrees

Table 2. Public sector corruption as reported in 2016 Corruption Perceptions Index

Corruption: Public Sector Corruption as Reported in 2016 Corruption Perceptions Index		
Region	Average Score	Remarks
Global	43/100	Not even a single country scores close to top marks, while over 120 countries score below 50 on the scale of 0 (highly corrupt) to 100 (very clean). Less than a third of countries score above while 69 percent of countries worldwide score below the midpoint '50'.
The Americas	44/100	^
Asia Pacific	44/100	^
Eastern Europe & Central Asia	34/100	^
European Union & Western Europe	66/100	^
Middle East & North Africa	38/100	^
Sub Saharan Africa	31/100	^
Top 10 Countries (*least corrupt*)		New Zealand and Denmark in joint first place (with a score of 90), followed by Finland (3rd), Sweden (4th), Switzerland (5th), Norway (6th), Singapore (7th), Netherlands (8th), Canada (9th) and Germany (10th).
Counties bottom of the index (*High degree of corruption*)		Somalia was ranked the most corrupt country. Other countries with lower rankings were Syria, South Sudan, North Korea, Afghanistan, and Iraq.

Source: Transparency International, 2017

of corruption. In some countries people meticulously conform to governance procedures and regulations pertaining to business practices, but in some others, either the regulatory framework is nonexistent or intentionally flouted (Ferrell, Gresham & Fraedrich, 1989). In some cultures employees are averse to maximize their personal benefits at the expense of either the company as a whole or other individuals (Forsyth & O'Boyle, 2011). But in some societies, employees dally during work breaks, report sick to enjoy some time off, take undue credit for the work not done by them, and even pilfer company supplies for personal use. While bribes are accepted to be usual business in many countries, United States prohibits payments made with the aim of gaining or maintaining business through Foreign Corrupt Practices Act, 1977, with an exception that some payments are acceptable if they don't violate local laws. Gifts, for instance, to officers working for foreign corporations are legal. But, it is very difficult to distinguish between a gift and a bribe in a given situation. In some cultures, offering gifts is an entrenched part of doing business. But, the question that what to call such acceptable gifts resulting in some sort of business benefits, remains unanswered. In China, offering gifts is considered to be culturally meaningful and logical, as a part of *guanxi*[20] network, rooted in the Confucian canons[21] of righteousness (*yi*), face (*myan dz*), mutual rights and duties (*quanli yu yiwu*), benevolence (*ren*), and correct decorum (*li mao*). On one hand, piles of information of corruption in many aspects of doing business in China is unfolding while China is the most preferred place on earth for multinational companies (MNCs) exploiting cheaper labor, on the other hand. Many a time, the gifting system is mistaken for bribe by those unfamiliar with such cultures. Even the management gurus treat *guanxi* as culturally acceptable (Steidlmeier, 1999).

What is ethical or unethical in society may not be the treated same in business as it operates under different environments and with versatile objectives aligned around either profit or wealth maximization. Public attention has recently turned towards this aspect of the businesses as they grow into transnational operations. The primary question is that whether business has anything to do with the society's moral standards. Even though many people deny the connection, every business activity has certain things in common with morality. But, regional disparities, regarding these things in common with morality, are clearly evident, when observed in a global perspective, as elucidated here:

The Western firms such as McDonald's, Kentucky Fried Chicken, Pizza Hut, Starbucks, and Burger King, etc. operate in Arab markets by segregating eating zones for men and women. The sections for men are usually comfortable and lavish up to Western standards while the areas meant for families or females are frequently neglected and run down, with separate entrance. Furthermore, these American restaurants deny entrance to Western women who show up without their husbands. When questioned about gender - discrimination, these businesses responded that

Table 3. Morality in business in a global perspective

Issue	Region		
	United States	**Europe**	**Asia**
Responsibility for ethical conduct in business	The individual	Social control by the Collective	Top management
Guidelines for *ethical behavior*	Corporate codes of ethics	Negotiated legal Framework of business	Managerial discretion
The key factor in business ethics	The corporation	Government, trade unions, corporate associations	Government and corporations
key issues in *business ethics*	Misconduct and immorality in single decisions situations	Social issues in organizing the framework of business.	Corporate Governance and accountability

Source: *(*Amith, 2016)

they have to respect and observe local customs (King, 2001). In case of South Africa, the basis of discrimination was racial, the black people. The basic rule to follow is the ancient adage of, 'When in Rome, do what the Romans do' (Johnson, 1985).

Another potential area of discussion under the case of ethical relativism is *differential compensation* for the same work in different cultures and contexts. It is obvious that transnational businesses exploit the abundant labor available underdeveloped countries by paying several times less than what they would have paid for the same work in their countries of origin. In this respect, transnational corporations are vehemently accused of adopting selfish policies by underpaying employees of underdeveloped countries. Another facet of the same issue is gender-based exploitation. In some societies, where religion does not prevent women's participation in economic activity, women employees are paid much lower than their counterparts. Forsyth, O'Boyle, and McDaniel (2008) reported that levels of idealism and relativism vary across regions of the world in predictable ways, after a comprehensive examination of 29 countries. Another study contrasting US and Moroccan business managers, significant differences in idealism and relativism were found between the two countries where the Moroccan managers were more idealistic than the US managers (Oumlil & Balloun, 2009). It is, however, imperative that ethical relativism is not mistaken for the adage, *When in Rome, do as the Romans do.* In business, ethical relativity often transforms into conventional morality and unethical actions are often justified as commonly accepted practices (Miesing & Preble, 1985).

The global business environment is turning subtle to the ethical conduct and practices which made imperative for the businesses to resort to ethical practices

Table 4. Fundamental sources of ethical dilemmas in multinational business

Source of Ethical Dilemmas	Fundamental Issues That Vary Across Regions of the World
1. Corruption	Making payments to government bureaucrats, public servants, and politicians.
2. Industrial espionage	The methods of obtaining competitors' information.
3. Relation with the environment	Respecting and following environmental standards imposed by the global as well as local legislations and staying competitive.
4. Relation with the employees	Following different personnel policies regarding employment, promotion and compensation of the employees in different markets.
5. Relation with the consumers	Providing complete information about the features to the target consumers in order to maintain the consumers' health and life, even though the host country legislation allows.

Source: GANGONE, 2010

despite the competitive scenarios. A recent examination of Global 2000 companies reveal that more than 35 percent of them have instated ethics officer position to enforce ethics and promote ethical behavior. Research also advocates that companies committed to ethical conduct outperform those that do not. The question of ethics cannot be disjointed from any aspect of the business. Ethical relativity, in business, often advances into conventional morality, resulting into 'commonly accepted practices' or 'best practices' at the industry or national or cultural level. But, advancing into that state of business is a challenging task since businesses have to cater to conflicting obligations towards divergent stakeholders. If Indonesians are tolerant to the bribery of their bureaucrats, their attitude is no better or worse than that of people in Denmark or Singapore who refuse to offer or accept bribes. This inadequacy of cultural relativism, in business context, however, becomes apparent when the practices in question are more damaging than petty bribery or insider trading. Infosys Technologies serves as one of the best instances of a business validating this hypothesis, by demonstrating that a business can be made phenomenally successful by engaging in ethical business practices. Ethical relativism is concerned not only with the premise that different moral standards and ethical beliefs exist, but also questions whether there is any commonality over-riding those differences. In the mixed chorus of contending moral standards and varied ethical systems, it is essential to look into the possibility of discerning any single principle that unifies them all. Otherwise, the business as well as the civil world would be left with the weak and unsatisfactory conclusion that all ethical systems are equally valid, and that an individual's choice has to be relative to his or her nurturing or education or position or country or culture (Hosmer, 1987). Thus, ethical relativism turns to be a burden, rather than benefit, to the modern businesses.

BUSINESS AND THE BURDEN OF ETHICAL RELATIVISM

Given the modern business situation that more and more corporations are operating in the transnational market place, the implications of cultural relativism for the business community are mounting. During the course of time, cultural relativism has emerged to be the single most issue of concern for global businesses (Freeman & Gilbert, 1988). Cross-cultural comparisons of managers' ethical attitudes has been prompting the multinationals towards earnestly orientating new managers to conflicting cultural values in different countries of operation (Becker & Fritzsche, 1987), to make them understand that ethical relativity is not a simple case of 'our ethics versus their ethics' (Longenecker, McKinney, & Moore, 1988). This leaves the manager with a dichotomous decision as to which ethical standard to be adopted under what circumstances. There appear a plenty of business decisions bearing relevance to the issue of ethical relativism among the contemporary corporate world. The widely prevailing practice of *kickbacks* in transnational business transactions, whilst not a new trend and is as old as the sin itself, poses a greater threat to the ethical conduct of business. General Electric (GE) had worldwide profits of $14.2 billion in 2010, but actually paid no U.S. income tax. The New York Times, in March 2011, reported that the company took advantage of 'innovative accounting practices' to move profits offshore. But, GE receives revenue from numerous U.S. government contracts and has been the beneficiary of the vast U.S. economic infrastructure. The financial management prowess of the enlightened company could reduce the corporate tax obligation to the bottom line results. Hypothetically, the auditors have taken full advantage of the provisions of the Internal Revenue Code. Can anyone argue this is unethical? Another glaring corporate evidence is from the widely pervasive Google Inc. In January of 2006, Google launched its China-focused 'google.cn' search engine, subject to censorship by the Chinese government, which was perceived to be dir4ectly in conflict with the corporate ideals and specifically with their motto *Don't be evil,* which, in turn, created a wide spread perception that Google had sold out on their business morals. However, owing to numerous run-ins with the Chinese government, Google proclaimed that they were no longer willing to provide censored search results on google.cn and redirected users to a site in Hong Kong. Further, Google has threatened to pull the rest of their business operations out of China in case of the persistence of similar business environment. Understanding the reality that the Chinese government was not ready to change its policy, Google's stand was futile. In this business context, whether Google was right or wrong is a matter of judgment and opinion. But, it is worth mentioning that Google has not gone through with its threat and still is operating in China and the search engine continues to be censored.

In the late 1980s, Some European pharmaceuticals and tanneries were trying to dump highly toxic waste on Africa's west coast, during 1980s, and finally Nigeria came forward to take. The highly toxic polychlorinated biphenyls were dumped near a residential area through unprotected local workers, without their knowledge that the deposited material was toxic waste. Many under developed and poor countries are unable to police the unscrupulous transnational corporations adequately because of ineffective enforcement and inadequate regulations. A cultural relativist would have no problem with that outcome. But the big question is that what moral right a business has to tamper with the legitimate right for health and safety of the people in that country. When Levi Strauss identified, in 1992, that the Tan family, a large supplier, was allegedly forcing around 1,200 Filipino and Chinese women workers to work for as long as 74 hours per week in guarded compounds on the Mariana Islands, they decided to break off business relations with the Tans, after repeated warnings. Levi Strauss relied on Global Sourcing and Operating Guidelines, formerly called the Business Partner Terms of Engagement, a written code of conduct, while dealing with the supplier. Levi Strauss, again discovered, in 1990s, that two of its suppliers in Bangladesh employed children under the age of 14, which was against the company's principles but accepted in Bangladesh. Forcing the suppliers to fire the children would have caused serious hardship for the families of the children. In a creative arrangement, Levi Strauss convinced the suppliers to pay the regular wages while the children attended school, and to offer each child a job at age 14, while Levi Strauss came forward to pay tuition fee and for books and uniforms. Around 90 percent of the Fortune 500 companies maintain the written codes of conduct to deal with partners across different countries. Johnson & Johnson, well known for its Credo Challenge sessions, allows it' managers discuss ethical angle of their current business problems and even encouraged to be critical about the company's credo and make suggestions, which are passed on to the senior managers. Entertaining and respecting differences is an essential ethical practice. Research shows that management ethics and values differ across cultures. Respecting such differences means identifying that every culture has hidden strengths as well as apparent weaknesses. For instance, managers in Hong Kong have a higher tolerance for some forms of bribery than their Western counterparts. But they are not tolerant towards failure to acknowledge a subordinate's work. During 1950, a senior executive of Motorola was negotiating on a $10 million sale with South American government officials, which would contribute nearly 25 percent of the company's annual net profits. But, the officials were demanding $1 million towards *fees* as the negotiations neared completion. However, the Motorola executive had decided to opt out of the deal because Robert Galvin, the then CEO, not only supported the executive's decision but also made explicit that Motorola would neither accept the sale on any terms nor do business with those government officials again. Motorola's values and the code of conduct, states that:

Employees of Motorola will respect the laws, customs, and traditions of each country in which they operate, but will, at the same time, engage in no course of conduct which, even if legal, customary, and accepted in any such country, could be deemed to be in violation of the accepted business ethics of Motorola or the laws of the United States relating to business ethics (Donaldson, 1996).

Texas Instruments has created the Global Business Practices Council accommodating managers from all countries of their operation, to discuss and decide over the issues of international business ethics.

A prominent example form the Indian cultural context is that some successful Indian companies provide their employees the direct opportunity to gain a job with the company, for one of their children once certain level of education is completed. The companies honor this commitment even when they can find other applicants with more qualifications than the employee's child. This perk is most cherished by the employees, but the Western countries brand it as unacceptable nepotism, violating the equal employment opportunities regulation. Given this difference in ethical attitudes, the response of US businesses is critical that whether to proceed partnering with Indian companies or refuse them as partners or suppliers. These are only a glimpse of the untold numerous issues pertaining to the burden of ethical relativism in business.

The practical nature of global business justifies that the ethical universalistic project is notwithstanding. Exponents of ethical relativism raise multiple objections to such effort. First, ethical relativisms insist that morality is about individual culture. To them culture is the pivot upon which moral value-analysis rests. Secondly, the notion of right or wrong in moral value judgment, according to ethical relativists, is based on the relevant social norms which, in turn, are the products of individual cultures. Therefore, there cannot be an absolute moral value judgment suitable for all cultures. Thirdly, studies on practical experiences have also confirmed that there are activities in human affairs that can only be understood in specific cultural contexts e.g. language, arts etc. Finally, the UNESCO's (2001) insistence on universal declaration of cultural diversities is a confirmation of the overwhelming global recognition of the realities ethical relativism. Since there are many businesses across different cultures, there bound to be different business moral values to reflect apparent cultural diversities. The position of ethical relativism may seem plausible in some sense. For instance, while corruption is seen as a fact of life that is permissible in business activities of some African cultures, the same cultural fact is being detested in some

Western countries. The difficulty humans have in acting ethically or, in Aristotle's terms, applying 'right reason and correct desire' is problematic across all societies and has been documented for over two millennia.

It is as simple as that the moral clarity often blurs when one leaves home and crosses the nation's boundaries. Any multinational business should run into a dilemma whether to invest in a foreign country where civil and political rights are violated or discriminatory employment policies are practiced, or strict environmental and health regulations are not adhered to. Hence, ethical conduct certainty is elusive without a backdrop of shared attitudes and defining laws and judicial procedures. On the other hand, if transnational companies decide to fill top-level managerial positions in a host nation with people from the home country, whose standards should prevail? Even the best-informed assumptions about business practice in foreign settings fail since what works for a company in home market shall fail in a country of different cultural and ethical standards. What philosophies that can help to work through the labyrinth of cultural differences and establish uniform codes of conduct for global businesses? How can companies answer the toughest question in global business ethics: What a company should do when they identify that the host country's ethical standards seem mediocre or worse than that of home country? According to cultural relativism, no culture's ethical standards are better than any other's. Therefore, there are no rights and wrongs internationally. If the people of Indonesia endure the bribery of their bureaucrats, their attitude is no better or worse than that of people in Denmark or Singapore who refuse to accept such behavior. In some cultures, loyalty to a community - family, organization, or society, is the basis for all ethical behaviors and standards. The Japanese define business ethics in terms of loyalty to their companies, their business networks, and their nation while Americans place higher value on liberty than on loyalty. Low wages is considered to be unethical in advanced cultures, but developing nations may be acting ethically by accepting lower wages to promote investments and improve living standards. It is very difficult to determine on which side the truth lies. Thus, it would be very difficult for the business managers to operate in another culture without being aware of their attitude toward ethics. Following the ethical standards of either host country or the home country always lead to some sort of risk. In the absence of any sort of international consensus on standards of business conduct, businesses must find an answer for this dilemma, even with great difficulty. As there is *no Esperanto of global ethics*, it would be possible to articulate some *core human values* which define minimum ethical standards for all companies must guide the managerial actions in multinational contexts. The United Nations' Universal Declaration of Human Rights (UDHR)[22], may serve the purpose to some extent. To be broadly relevant, these core values must comprise of the elements found in both Western and non-Western cultural and religious traditions. Despite significant differences between the two opposing cultural and religious traditions, both articulate a set of shared attitudes about fundamental human values such as respect for human dignity, respect for basic rights, and good citizenship. The list of *world's most ethical companies*[23], from various countries, covering a wide spectrum of the industries, published annually by Ethisphere[24], serves a typical evidence in this context. Only 124 businesses from all the industries across the globe are rated as the most ethical companies, during 2016.

It is once again evident that ethical management is truly a burden on businesses across the world and across the industries, as the proportion of the 'most ethical companies' is very much minute when compared to the total population of either the countries or the companies. Most of the countries have either no representation or a meagre representation, through a single company labeled as the most ethical

Table 5. World's most ethical companies, 2016 (country-wise)

Country	Number	Industries / Sectors
USA	98 companies	Manufacturing; Insurance; Oil & Gas; Electronics; Healthcare; Logistics; Telecommunications; Software; Real Estate; Engineering; Consumer Products; Automotive; Financial Services; Business Services; Chemicals; Medical Devices; Pharmaceuticals; Construction; Food & Beverage; Packaging; Machine Tools; Apparel; Outsourcing Services; Hospitality; Payment Services; Security & Protection Services; Energy & Utilities; Banking Trucks & Other Vehicles; Retail; Environmental Services; Aerospace & Defense; Leisure & Recreation; Scientific & Technical Services; Metals, Minerals & Mining; Specialty Eateries; Apparel; Business Services; I T Services, etc..
UK	04 companies	
France	03 companies	
Ireland	02 companies	
India	02 companies	
Hong Kong	01 company	
Sweden	01 company	
Belgium	01 company	
Switzerland	01 company	
Australia	01 company	
Singapore	01 company	
Poland	01 company	
Japan	01 company	
Italy	01 company	
Spain	01 company	
Sweden	01 company	
Mexico	01 company	
Portugal	01 company	
Canada	01 company	
Guatemala	01 company	
Total	124 companies	

Source: (Ethisphere, 2017)

Relativity Applies to Physics, Not Ethics

one, in the list. However, the ethical company has no correlation with the type of industry or sector, since the listed 124 companies represent an array of sectors. Thus, ethical business can be believed to be relevant to the management of that business and the country or region in which it operates or originates, and certainly not relevant to specific industries or sectors. Thus, businesses world-wide consider that doing ethical business is rather a burden than a virtue.

However, this shall positively be treated as the starting point of ethical conduct for all companies at home and abroad. Companies need to translate the core human values into core business values to create a moral compass for business practices. The multinational businesses must strive to establish some moral universals, by achieving a balance among the conflicting cultures, rather than swept away by ethical relativism. Ethical relativism as well as absolutism undisputedly agree that circumstances make a difference. For example, whether it is morally permissible to enter a house depends on whether one is the owner, a guest, or a burglar.

BALANCING THE EXTREMES: MORAL UNIVERSALS

If everyone acts on the basis of his or her self-interest and ignores the wellbeing of others, life would be nasty, brutish, solitary, and short, as Thomas Hobbs[25] writes. If every individual puts up an overwhelming claim to be judged by no standard except his or her own, moral chaos prevails and all effective standards collapse altogether. As

Figure 1.

Countries: Only 20 countries make their names into the list, out of the 195 countries (*recognized by the United Nations Organization*) that exist on earth.

Companies: Only 124 companies are honored to be the most ethical companies, out of an approximate of more than 235 million registered companies across the world (*Based on web sources*) from all nations of the world.

Industries: The 124 companies from 20 countries spread across a wide range of different industries / sectors, proving that the *ethical buainess is not a function of any industry, but a critical function of the management of the business.*

this moral chaos is clearly not the case, one could tacitly assume that an amorphous, yet undefined, moral standard does exist. As Harman (1975) has stated, the question of whether there is a single true morality is an unresolved issue in moral philosophy. Every society is right in its reasoning for its own moral standards. But confusion starts about several correct premises if they are seen from different perspectives. The empirical nature of the moral standards makes it possible for comparison, across cultures, to identify the possibility of tentative universal moral standards. It would also be interesting to consider abandoning national boundaries and, based on empirical research, build up new parameters of moral conduct. Effectively, one would be identifying the universal moral standards appropriate to specific social groupings recognizing that these groups may be cross-cultural. Anthropologists have observed that the basic values of all societies comprise of many of the same elements and the differences might increase as one moves toward the superficial end of the scale. Ethical relativism gives raise to some fundamental questions such as how ethics can serve as guide if change from one group to another where each group justify its actions. If everybody thinks that he or she is correct, what can be the basis of correctness? Hence, there must be some degree of resemblance in ethical stances, especially in the context of multinational businesses. It seems to be impossible, from one aspect, but there always lies a light at the end of the tunnel. It would be difficult to believe that all shall have the same morality at bottom, despite of the religious beliefs. But, one certainty is that, all worship the same god, with different names and versatile incarnations. Even though, the legal systems at bottom are dissimilar, the basic system of law is uniform. In spite of innumerable languages spoken at the group level, there exists a universal grammar system that applies to all languages that children learn without instruction. Since the advent of globalization, many societies, hitherto unfamiliar, are moving culturally closer and turning more homogenous, which might pave the way for some semblance of universal ethical standards someday. The ever greatest heroes of mankind, Mahatma Gandhi from India and Martin Luther King, Jr. from USA, stood up to the system and fought against the tyranny of the majority. Irrespective of the majority psyche or what anyone else in a specific culture thinks, each individual member of a society should decide about what kind of lifestyle and what kind of values should be practiced to live true to oneself. A positive indication towards such development is that some rules are indeed culture free. In the multinational business context also, companies must assist managers to discriminate between practices that are different and wrong. For relativist, nothing is sacred and nothing is wrong while many things that are different are wrong for an absolutist. Neither extreme enlightens the real world of business decision making. The answer lies somewhere in between: developing ethical parameters from the similar ethical beliefs creates the potential for replication through multinational business.

REFERENCES

Barna, G. (1994). Virtual America. *Regal, 83,* 283.

Becker, H., & Fritzsche, D. J. (1987). A comparison of ethical behaviour of American, French and German managers. *The Columbia Journal of World Business, 22*(4), 87–95.

Corruption Perceptions Index. 2016. (n.d.). Retrieved from https://www.transparency.org/news/feature/corruption_perceptions_index_2016

Donaldson, T. (1996). Values in tension: Ethics away from home. *Harvard Business Review, 74*(5), 48–62.

Ferrell, O. C., Gresham, L., & Fraedrich, J. (1989). A synthesis of ethical decision making models for marketing. *Journal of Macromarketing, 9*(2), 55–64. doi:10.1177/027614678900900207

Fiddler, S. (1999, July 7). Defence contracts 'pervaded by graft'. *Financial Times.*

Forsyth, D. R., & O'Boyle, E. H. Jr. (2011). Rules, standards, and ethics: Relativism predicts cross-national differences in the codification of moral standards. *International Business Review, 20*(2), 353–361. doi:10.1016/j.ibusrev.2010.07.008

Forsyth, D. R., O'Boyle, E. H. Jr, & McDaniel, M. (2008). East meets west: A meta-analytic investigation of cultural variations in idealism and relativism. *Journal of Business Ethics, 83*(4), 813–833. doi:10.1007/s10551-008-9667-6

Freeman, R. E., & Gilbert, D. R. (1988). *Corporate strategy and the search for ethics.* Englewood Cliffs, NJ: Prentice- Hall.

Harman, G. (1975). Moral relativism defended. *The Philosophical Review, 84*(1), 3–22. doi:10.2307/2184078

Hawley, S. (2000). *Exporting corruption - privatization, multinationals and bribery.* Retrieved from: http://www.eldis.org/vfile/upload/1/document/0708/DOC8375.pdf

Herodotus, . (2003). *The histories: Reissue edition (J. M. Marincola* (A. De Selincourt Trans. & Ed.). Penguin Classics.

Hosmer, L. T. (1987). *The ethics of management.* Homewood, IL: Irwin Management.

Johnson, L. H. (1985). Bribery in international markets: Diagnosis, clarification and remedy. *Journal of Business Ethics, 4*(6), 447–455. doi:10.1007/BF00382606

Kaikati, J. G., Sullivan, G. M., Virgo, J. M., Carr, T. R., & Katherine, S. V. (2000). The price of international business morality: Twenty years under the Foreign Corrupt Practices Act. *Journal of Business Ethics*, *26*(3), 213–222. doi:10.1023/A:1006015110422

King, C. I. (2001, December 22). Saudi Arabia's apartheid. *The Washington Post*. Retrieved from https://www.washingtonpost.com/archive/opinions/2001/12/22/saudi-arabias-apartheid/6dc54ab8-37bc-4a87-86f4-c0b489fc8b8e/?utm_term=.5417d2f31901

Longenecker, J. G., McKinney, J. A., & Moore, C. W. (1988). The ethical issue of international bribery: A study of attitudes among US business professionals. *Journal of Business Ethics*, *7*(5), 341–346. doi:10.1007/BF00382536

Mccormack, J. (2011, November 18). Paul Ryan: The biggest problem in America isn't debt, it's moral relativism. *The Weekly Standard*, (Nov): 18.

Miesing, P., & Preble, J. F. (1985). A comparison of five business philosophies. *Journal of Business Ethics*, *4*(6), 465–476. doi:10.1007/BF00382609

Moira, A. (2000). Here comes the bribe. *Entrepreneur*, *28*(10), 48.

Oumlil, A. B., & Balloun, J. L. (2009). Ethical decision-making differences between American and Moroccan managers. *Journal of Business Ethics*, *84*(4), 457–478. doi:10.1007/s10551-008-9719-y

Plato. (1926). Laws, Volume II: Books 7-12 (R. G. Bury, Trans.). Loeb Classical Library 192. Cambridge, MA: Harvard University Press.

Pojman, P. L. (1955). *Ethics: Discovering right and wrong (3rd ed.)*. Belmont, CA: Wadsworth Publishing Company.

Stanton, M. (2011). *Killer stuff and tons of money: An insider's look at the world of flea markets, antiques, and collecting*. Penguin Books.

Steidlmeier, P. (1999). Gift giving, bribery and corruption: Ethical management of business relationships in China. *Journal of Business Ethics*, *20*(2), 121–133. doi:10.1023/A:1005960026519

Tanzi, V. (1998). Corruption around the world - Causes, consequences, scope and cures. *IMF Staff Papers*, *45*(4), 559–594. doi:10.2307/3867585

Ugaz, J. (2016). *Corruption perceptions index 2016*. Retrieved from https://www.transparency.org/news/feature/corruption_perceptions_index_2016

UNESCO. (2001). *Universal declaration on cultural diversity*. Retrieved from: http://unesdoc.unesco.org/images/0012/001271/127162e.pdf

Weinreb, L. (1990). *Natural Law and Justice*. Cambridge, MA: Harvard University Press.

ENDNOTES

[1] Einstein's special theory of relativity is all about what's relative and what's absolute about time, space, and motion. It was originally proposed in 1905 by Albert Einstein in the paper "On the Electrodynamics of Moving Bodies".

[2] Gilbert Harman (born 1938) is an American philosopher, teaching at Princeton University since 1963, who has published widely in philosophy.

[3] Karl Marx (1818 – 1883) was a Prussian-born philosopher, economist, sociologist, journalist, and revolutionary socialist. Marx's theories about society, economics, and politics are collectively understood as Marxism

[4] Maximilian Karl Emil 'Max' Weber (1864 – 1920) was a German sociologist, philosopher, jurist, and political economist. His ideas profoundly influenced social theory and social research. Weber is often cited, with Émile Durkheim and Karl Marx, as among the three founders of sociology.

[5] Robert L. Ripley (1890–1949), an American cartoonist, explorer, reporter, adventurer, and collector, nicknamed as the modern Marko Polo, traveled to 201 countries in 35 years seeking the odd, the unusual, and the unexplained and published in 'Believe It or Not!'- The newspaper panel series, radio show, and television show featuring odd facts from around the world.

[6] Ripley's Believe It or Not! is an American franchise, founded by Robert Ripley, which deals in bizarre events and items so strange and unusual that readers might question the claims. The Believe It or Not panel proved popular and was later adapted into a wide variety of formats, including radio, television, comic books, a chain of museums, and a book series. The Ripley collection includes 20,000 photographs, 30,000 artifacts and more than 100,000 cartoon panels. With 80-plus attractions, the Orlando-based Ripley Entertainment, Inc., a division of the Jim Pattison Group, is a global company with an annual attendance of more than 12 million guests. Today there are 33 Ripley's Believe It or Not! Museums in ten countries, dozens of Ripley books, a huge internet web presence, and hundreds of television videos in the company's archive vaults.

7 Herodotus (484–425 BC) was a Greek historian who lived in the fifth century BC and a contemporary of Thucydides, Socrates, and Euripides. He is often referred to as "The Father of History"

8 Sextus Empiricus (160 – 210 CE, n.b., dates uncertain), was a Greek physician and philosopher.

9 Saint Thomas Aquinas (1225 – 1274), was an Italian Dominican friar, Catholic priest, and Doctor of the Church. He was an immensely influential philosopher, theologian, and jurist.

10 Michel de Montaigne (1533-1592BC) is widely appreciated as one of the most important figures in the late French Renaissance, both for his literary innovations as well as for his contributions to philosophy.

11 Michel de Montaigne's literary and philosophical work is contained in his *Essays*, which he began to write in 1572 and first published in 1580 in the form of two books.

12 Of Cannibals, is an essay by Michel de Montaigne, describing the ceremonies of the Tupinambá people in Brazil. In particular, he reported about how the group ceremoniously ate the bodies of their dead enemies as a matter of honor. In his work, he uses cultural relativism and compares the cannibalism to the "barbarianism" of 16th-century Europe

13 Friedrich Wilhelm Nietzsche (1844 – 1900) was a German philosopher, cultural critic, poet, philologist, and Latin and Greek scholar whose work has exerted a profound influence on Western philosophy and modern intellectual history.

14 The principle of the Anekantavada or Syadvada is a very valuable contribution of Jainism to world thought. This doctrine is also known as the theory of Relativity or the Philosophy of Non-absolutism or the philosophy of Relative Pluralism.

15 Lord Mahavira (599-527 BC) was the twenty-fourth and last Jain Tirthankara according to the Jain philosophy.

16 Mere Christianity is a theological book by C. S. Lewis, adapted from a series of BBC radio talks made between 1941 and 1944

17 'Dirty Little Secret' is a song by American rock band The All-American Rejects, from their second studio album Move Along, in 2005.

18 Transparency International is a global movement with the vision of a world free of corruption, operating through its international secretariat in Berlin and chapters in more than 100 countries.

19 Transparency International (TI) has published the Corruption Perceptions Index (CPI) since 1996, annually ranking countries "by their perceived levels of corruption, as determined by expert assessments and opinion surveys. The CPI currently ranks 176 countries on a scale from 100 (very clean) to 0 (highly corrupt).

[20] As one of the major dynamics of Chinese society, guanxi (roughly translated as "relationship") has been a pervasive part of the Chinese business world, binding millions of Chinese enterprises, social groups and individuals into a complex socio-economic web. Guanxi is considered the life-blood of the macro-economy and micro-business conduct in the Chinese society, and researchers are one in saying that the guanxi network is one of the key determinants of business success in this part of the world.

[21] The Five Classics and Four Books were the basis of the civil examination in imperial China and can be considered the Confucian canon. The Five Classics consists of the Book of Odes, Book of Documents, Book of Changes, Book of Rites, and the Spring and Autumn Annals. The Four Books are comprised of the Doctrine of the Mean, the Great Learning, Mencius, and the Analects.

[22] The Universal Declaration of Human Rights (UDHR) was drafted by representatives with different legal and cultural backgrounds from all regions of the world and proclaimed by the United Nations General Assembly in December 1948 as a common standard of achievements for all peoples and all nations. It sets out, for the first time, fundamental human rights to be universally protected.

[23] The World's Most Ethical Companies® program honors companies that excel in three areas – promoting ethical business standards and practices internally, enabling managers and employees to make good choices, and shaping future industry standards by introducing tomorrow's best practices today. Ethisphere's Ethics Quotient® is a proprietary rating system that collects and objectively scores self-reported data in five weighted categories.

[24] The Ethisphere Institute is a US based organization that defines and measures corporate ethical standards, recognizes companies that excel, and promotes best practices in corporate ethics. The company publishes Ethisphere Magazine and announces its World's Most Ethical Companies awards once a year.

[25] Thomas Hobbes (1588-1679), an English philosopher, the founding father of modern political philosophy.

Chapter 15
Performance Appraisal Techniques Across Various Sectors in India

Shikha Rana
IMS Unison University, India

ABSTRACT

In recent times competitive and outperforming employees are of the utmost requirement for the success and sustenance of any organization. Organizations hire employees to achieve long-term and short-term goals so that they can get an edge over competitors and can meet the challenges posed by the continuously changing environment. Therefore, employees strive hard and give their level best to the organization and prove their worth by showing exemplary performance. At this juncture it becomes really important for the employers to know the exact level of employee performance as every employee differs in skills, abilities, and competence. This chapter discusses the concept, development of performance appraisal, and techniques of performance appraisal that are used across various sectors in India.

INTRODUCTION

Of late performance appraisal has gained lot of attention as it has emerged as a critical factor for an organization's long term success as it measures how well employees perform. Further, the information derived from performance appraisal is utilized to ensure that performance meets present standards and improves overtime. Performance appraisal gives clear cut criteria about the performance and other aspects. It is considered as the most important Human Resource Activity which

DOI: 10.4018/978-1-5225-4933-8.ch015

lays foundation for many other functions like promotion, salary increment, training & development, succession planning and many more. Performance appraisal is a very important aspect for the sustainable competitive advantage of an organization (Huselid & Becker, 2011). Nowadays organizations consider their workforce as an asset, therefore responsible to satisfy their internal customers i.e., employees. Today there are a number of organizations that uses performance appraisal strategically to support company goals and values, better focus employee efforts, and align employee performance with the company mission. Companies and researches have increasingly stressed the use of the employee evaluations for motivational and organizational planning purposes (Filiz K. McNamara, 2011). Cascio (1998) has emphasized the importance of performance appraisal in the following manner:

Performance appraisal is a process to improve employee's work performance by helping them realize and use their full potential in carrying out the organization's missions and to provide information to employees for use in making work related decisions.

Fletcher (2001) added rewards in performance appraisal as he stated that performance appraisal is an activity through which organizations seek to assess employees and develop their competence, enhance performance and distribute rewards.

Hence, performance appraisal is a technique utilized in a systematic and factual way to evaluate the actual performance of employees against the standards set by the organization followed by feedback from the senior for examining the relative worth or competency of the employee while performing the task (Dessler, 2011).

Further, performance appraisal is a key for effective assessment and development of Human resources (Ashok Khurana & Kanika Goyal, 2010). Performance appraisal also known as performance evaluation, progress rating, merit rating, merit evaluation, is that part of the formal assessment process in which an output of an employee in the form of performance during a specified period of time is assessed in the organization (Chhabra, 2008).

The most important objective of performance appraisal is to upgrade the performance of the individual employee, which results in the overall improvement of organizational performance (Mullins, 2002). Performance appraisal is one of the human resource techniques that may be used to manage performance effectively as it gives useful information which, further, assists in improving other aspects of the performance management process. Rewards, which are received by employees on their outstanding performance in an organization, are the outcome of Performance appraisal system (Mathis and Jackson, 2008). A properly designed performance appraisal system assists in achieving targets and objectives of the organization which further enhances the performance of employees. As a matter of fact, performance appraisal data is extremely important for almost all the functional areas of the organization.

Robert J. Greene, CEO of Reward Systems Inc., stated that performance appraisal is the single largest factor which is solely responsible for organizational effectiveness. (Tyler, 2005) If ignored then the organization fails. Further, it should be strategically linked with the organization's mission, vision, and values.

EVOLUTION OF PERFORMANCE APPRAISAL TECHNIQUES

Performance appraisal techniques answers the "how" of performance i.e., how a particular performance will be evaluated. In order to answer this question it is of great importance to know the type of techniques, which had been evolved over a period of time. Many techniques of performance appraisal had been unfolded since its inception. "Man to Man" rating system was adopted by the US army in early 1900 during the first world for assessing its personnel (Scott and Clothier, 1923). As this concept of assessment got lot of success therefore, industries and business organizations adopted it (Scott et al, 1941).Graphic Rating scale was developed by Donald Paterson in 1922. Later on Forced choice distribution and Critical Incident Techniques were conceptualized. These two methods were designed to reduce rating error and biases (Sisson, 1948; Richardson, 1949) but these techniques proved to be very difficult to apply (Flanagan, 1954). All these methods were developed during the first half of 19th century and performance appraisal was used mainly for administrative purposes like retention, discharge, promotion, salary administration (DeVries et al, 1981; Murphy & Cleveland, 1995; Patten, 1977). In this phase performance appraisal were not only loosely related to employee development but also they were used mainly for reducing the workforce and removal of employees leading to the dissatisfaction of employees (DeVries et al., 1981). The second half of the 19th century marked the beginning of result oriented performance appraisals (Wiese & Buckley,1998). This phase brought into picture various important techniques of performance appraisal which are currently prevalent in the organizations. Some major techniques were MBO (Peter Drucker, 1954), Behaviourally Anchored Rating Scales (Smith & Kendall, 1963), Self Appraisal, 360 Degree Appraisal. These techniques to the great extent enhanced employee involvement, self assessment, feedback, and result orientation in performance appraisal (Steve Brooks, 2015). Recently, the whole approach of performance appraisal has shifted from control to motivational and developmental one where the main objective is to link organizational goals to employee's goals and career prospects through ongoing auditing, development & improvement of employees' performance and future potential.

TYPES OF PERFORMANCE APPRAISAL TECHNIQUES

Many techniques have been designed to evaluate the performance of employees. These techniques have variations because of several reasons. These methods differ in the sources of psychological traits and qualities to be measured. Firstly, all the traits may differ due to distinct job requirements. Secondly, these methods are not identical because of the dissimilar employees who are being rated like blue-collar & white-collar employees working in an organization. Thirdly, they differ due to the degree of accuracy they show in evaluation of performance. The most widely used categorization of performance appraisal techniques have been done by Strauss & Sayles (1971). They have classified methods into traditional and modern methods:

TRADITIONAL METHODS

1. **Graphic Rating Scales:** This is the most widely used method for appraising the performance. Rating scales are made up of various numerical scales which represents job related performance qualities such as loyalty, output, enthusiasm, initiative, decisiveness attitude etc. Each scales consist of two categories which ranges from excellent to poor giving positive rating at one end of the scale and negative rating at the other end of the scale. The entire score is calculated in numeric terms and final conclusions are drawn-up.
2. **Straight Ranking Method:** This is the oldest and simplest method of measuring the performance. It compare one man as a whole with all other men of a group and place him in a simple rank order. In this way ordering is done from the best to the worst of all the employees working in a group irrespective of the type of work they perform
3. **Checklist:** Under this method, a series of statements of traits are presented related to an employee's behavior. The rater then check the questions, which are the statement of traits of an employee, in yes and no form. In this method the rater is only responsible for reporting or checking as final evaluation is done by the HR department of the organization.
4. **Grading Method:** In this technique, the rater incorporates some characteristic of the employee like leadership, cooperativeness, self-expression, job knowledge and finally marks them according to the scale. Categories are formed and carefully defined like A stands for Outstanding, E stands for Poor. The actual performance is then fitted in to these grades.
5. **Forced Choice Method:** This method was unfolded by Joseph Tiffin to reduce the rater's bias so that all the employees may not be rated either on the

positive side or negative end of the scale. The appraisal form consist of a no. of statements which describes an individual. These statements may be grouped into two, three or even four parts. Form may contain all the favorable statements only, sometimes all the unfavorable statement or may contain a combination of two. The rater make two checks in each group, one for the statement which best describes an individual and one for the statement which least describe the employee. Rater is compelled to check a "most" and a "least" in each group therefore, the terminology used here is forced choice.

6. **Critical Incidents Method:** In this technique, a list of those job requirement is prepared which are extremely important for the success or failure on the job. The importance of this method lies in those episodes or events which either proved to be profitable & fruitful or resulted in a loss for the organization. Managers keeps a written record of those events so that they can be easily recalled at the time of formal appraisal.

7. **Field Review Method:** In this method, an individual person from the HR department conducts the interview with managers of a particular department and seeks information about each employee working under him. The interviewer questions the supervisor about the requirements of the job in his department and about the performance of each subordinate in his/her job. The overall ratings are obtained by classifying the performance in three categories ie., outstanding, satisfactory and unsatisfactory.

MODERN METHODS

1. **Management by Objectives:** This method was introduced by Peter Drucker in 1954. It is the process where the managers and subordinates together sits in order to decide about the common goals further, decisions are made to decide the areas of responsibility of individual employee. Performance is rated against the fulfillment of objectives which are commonly set by both employees and managers.

2. **Behaviorally Anchored Rating Scales:** This behavior centric technique was developed by Smith & Kendall in 1963. It is a combination of the above mentioned techniques of Rating Scales and Critical Incident Method. In this technique the raters rank and validate specific behaviors for each of the components.

3. **Assessment Centres:** An assessment center is a centralized location where managers participate in job related exercises which mainly focuses on their behaviors through in-basket techniques, case studies and role playing. These assessment centres analyse the employees potential for future higher level

jobs and for the purposes of promotion. The managers are assessed by trained psychologists and success of these appraisals largely depends upon the skills of psychologists who do the assessment.

4. **360-Degree Feedback:** Twentieth century marked the beginning of 360 degree appraisal or multi-rater appraisal where the employee is rated by peers, self, superior, customers and subordinates. This technique is highly useful in self-development as feedback is provided by almost all the stakeholders of the organization.

WORKFORCE DIVERSITY AND ITS RELATION WITH PERFORMANCE APPRAISAL

Esty et al. (1995) has defined diversity as "acknowledging, understanding, accepting, and valuing differences among people with respect to age, class, race, ethnicity, gender, disabilities, etc." Workforce diversity means heterogeneous workforce which indeed is a product of globalization, shortage of talent, stiff competition and increasing consumer demands. SHRM (1995) stated that in order to yield higher productivity and gain competitive advantage, organization must embrace diversity. Organizations does not function in isolation as they have become an indispensable part of global economy and people from diverse traditions, language, beliefs, culture, backgrounds are coming together to work for these organizations. Workforce diversity is a complex phenomenon to manage in an organization but if managed effectively then it creates a competitive advantage which further leads to effective decision making, creativity and innovation, greater success in marketing, and results in optimal distribution of economic opportunity (Cox, 1991; Cox and Blake, 1991). In certain research studies it has also been identified that diverse workforce can provide effective services as they are very much capable of understanding the customer needs (Wentling and Palma-Rivas, 2000).

Jackson et al. (1995) opined that diversity consists of all the possible ways people can differ. According to this school of thought, employees do not only differ because of their race, gender, age and other demographic categories, but also because of their values, abilities, organizational function, tenure and personality. Demographic workforce diversity is being stressed a lot in various research studies. Age, Gender, Education and other ethnic aspects of diversity has been researched to gain an insight into diverse work force. It has been revealed in a study that if an organization is able to foster a good environment for workforce diversity then it leads to higher motivation, enhanced knowledge, better skill transfer, increased creativity and good decision making which will stimulate the organizational growth.(Amaram, 2011).

If managed effectively, workforce diversity, enhances productivity as management take several measures to manage diversity by offering them proper compensation, appraising them in a justifiable manner and providing health care facilities. These aspects makes the employee more dedicated and committed towards the organization and they give their level best irrespective of their cultural background and ethnicity which further results in increased productivity and profit. Further, it helps in learning and growth, exchanging ideas, proper communication etc (Dike, 2013).

A study conducted on workforce diversity revealed that several dimensions like gender, ethnicity and educational background has an enormous impact on the performance of employees (Chew et al., 2011). Further Baer et al. (2006) found that teams which are diverse in terms of education and experience performs outstandingly as compared to the less diverse teams. Grobler et al (2006) too stated that employees who continuously enhances their learning & education performs well as these enhancements leads to skill development and more self confidence. In yet another study it was revealed that racial diversity leads to effective firm's performance (Koonce).Hence, the above studies shows that diverse workforce if effectively managed leads to higher performance & productivity.

Available literature has shown that human resource practices plays an eminent role in managing the diversified workforce. In earlier studies it has been reported by Schuler et al.(1993) that in order to manage the diversity the performance of the employees should be evaluated objectively and not subjectively as it increases the fairness of the performance appraisal process. Further Fulkerson & Schuler (1992) opined that the language of performance appraisal must stress on the performance aspects and not the personality of employees and the appraisal should remain neutral in cultural aspects. Several researchers proclaimed that manager's performance should also be assessed on the basis of, steps taken by them to hire and promote the minorities and women, so that their role can be judged in promoting workforce diversity (Morrison, 1992; Sessa, 1992). Performance- related pay itself is an important element to effectively manage the diversity as whole performance would be evaluated strongly on the basis of performance of employees and not diversity. Some researchers have also revealed that similarities on the basis of demographics like age, gender or race between managers and employees leads to higher ratings on performance, organizational citizenship and lower ambiguities in role also women have been given lower ratings on their performance (Tsui & Gutek, 1999; Ohlott et al., 1994).

All the above studies shows that workforce diversity can be managed with effective application of human resource practices which involves performance appraisal too.

MAJOR SECTORS IN INDIA: AN OVERVIEW

Indian economy comprises of various sectors like IT, Pharma, Banking, Retail and Healthcare etc. According to Central Statistics Organization India has appeared as the rapid growing economy globally. As per the Govt. of India the economy of India will grow and shoot up by 7.1 per cent in FY 2016-17. The vigorous and robust govt reforms in the year 2015 & 2016 had an enormous impact on the Indian Economy. Banking, Pharma and IT sector are some of the major sectors of Indian Economy. A brief description of these sectors is as follows:

Banking Sector

The banking sector of India has emerged as the fastest growing sector and an important driver of economic growth. Development of the economy and liberalization policies has transformed the whole banking industry of India in a revolutionized manner. From last few year banking industry has gone through remarkable changes in order to gain competitive edge over international banking organizations. The banks have started focusing on profit banking, cashless banking and electronic banking. As proclaimed by RBI the Indian banking sector is not only capitalized but also regulated.

The banking sector consist of mainly 5 banks namely Reserve banks of India, Indian Scheduled Commercial Banks, Foreign Banks, Non-scheduled banks and Co-operative banks. Indian Scheduled Commercial banks are divided into State Bank of India, twenty nationalized banks, Regional rural banks and other scheduled commercial banks. As Public-sector banks holds nearly 80 percent of the market, hence private banks has a small share in the market. As stated by Standard & Poor's the credit growth in India's banking sector would upgrade to 11-13 percent in Financial Year 2017

IT Sector

India is a global brand name in the IT sector. It accounts for approximately 67 per cent of the US$ 124-130 billion market. The industry employs about 10 million workforces. Moreover, the IT industry in India has cost competitiveness in rendering its IT services as compared to other nations. Nowadays, India is giving due importance to Intellectual capital by tying up with several glabal IT players for establishing their innovation centres. Further, the IT industry has also fostered the demand in the Indian education sector, especially for engineering and computer science. The Indian IT industry is divided into four major segments – IT services, Business Process Management (BPM), software products and engineering services, and hardware.

The Indian IT sector is expected to grow at a rate of 12-14 per cent for Financial year 2016-17 in constant currency terms. Further, the current annual revenue would be tripled by the Financial year 2025. TCS captures 10.4 per cent of India's total IT & ITeS sector revenue in FY16. The top five IT firms contribute over 25 per cent to the total industry revenue, making the market more competitive.

Pharma Sector

As reported by Equity Master the Indian pharmaceuticals market is the third largest in terms of volume and thirteenth largest in terms of value. Additionally, India is the largest provider of generic drugs internationally with the Indian generics accounting for 20 per cent of global exports in terms of volume. India holds an important position in the global pharmaceuticals sector. The Indian pharma industry, which is expected to grow over 15 per cent per annum between 2015 and 2020, will have an edge over global pharma industry, which is set to grow at an annual rate of 5 per cent between the same period. According to the consulting firm McKinsey & Company, India's pharmaceutical sector will touch 55 billion USD by 2020.

India would probably be among the top three pharmaceutical markets by incremental growth and sixth largest market globally in absolute size. India's cost of production is significantly lower than that of the US and almost half of that of Europe and gives competitive edge to India over others.

PERFORMANCE APPRAISAL TECHNIQUES ACROSS VARIOUS SECTORS IN INDIA

Techniques of performance appraisal may vary according to different sectors in India. Turgur & Mert (2014) reported that different performance appraisal techniques have been used by the companies working in the same sectors, system having alike features as they go by their choice rather by the similarities. As discussed earlier performance appraisal techniques are broadly divided into two categories like traditional methods and modern methods but many organizations in India still inclined towards using traditional appraisal techniques as opposed to modern methods (Sing & Vadivelu, 2016). In this section the techniques of performance appraisal which has been used by Banking, IT and Pharma sectors have been elucidated.

Banking sector, since its inception has played a very crucial role in the enhancement, upliftment and improvement of the Indian economy. The Indian economy is now on a verge of major change, by implementing various policies. Optimistic business environment, improved consumer assurance and more regulated inflation will uplift the economic growth. More infrastructure spending, fast implementation of policies will provide further augment the growth. All this will lead to strong growth of the banking sector also as fastest growing business will go to banks for their credit requirements therefore, assisting the banking sector grow in future. As we know lot much is required in terms of performance from the employees of banking sector therefore it is of great importance to be aware of the techniques which are used by banks to appraise their employees. Most of the Public sector banks conduct yearly appraisal of the employees mainly based on past performance (Srivastava & Rai, 2012)

State Bank of India which is one of the largest public sector commercial bank in India in terms of assets, deposits, profits, branches, customers and employees has recently rolled up a new system of performance appraisal and that is "Career Development System" where the KRAs (Key Result Areas) would be identified and employees having same profiles would be rated against each other on the basis of five grades such as AAA, AA,A B and C. Career Development system is originally meant to reward the top performers but loosely linked with identifying low performers (Kurian,2015). Rao (2004) mentioned that Punjab National Bank, used developmental performance appraisal for evaluating its employees where ten distinguished formats had been used for ten varying categories of employees for appraising their performance. Self appraisal is the main technique which is primarily practiced by the Public Sector banks like PNB, Indian Overseas Bank Corporation Bank, UCO Bank, Central Bank of India, Dena Bank, Bank of Baroda and Union Bank of India (Rao, 2004).

Private sector banks another important growth enhancer for Indian economy utilizes various performance appraisal techniques for its employees. Previous studies opined that private sector banks uses 360 Degree appraisal for the evaluation of its employees (Rani et al, 2014). ICICI one of the major private player uses graphic rating scales for examining the performance of its employees. Here the performance, abilities and competencies of employees are rated on a scale against certain well defined parameters. Axis Bank one of the leading private bank have switched from the bell curved appraisal to the new appraisal method "Accelerate". In this new method stress would be on learning and capability development of employees as revealed by Business Standards. According to the Sustainability Report of Yes bank (2015-16) it has adopted Yes-Talent Optimization Program which ensures transparent, timely, unbiased and multi-level performance evaluation of all the executives further the annual appraisal is extremely merit- based. Karnataka bank another private lender to go for open appraisal system where the immediate supervisor assesses the performance of its employee at three distinct levels like subordinate staff, clerks and executives. The bank deploys the graphing rating scale for the subordinate staff and clerks where they are rated against various traits and characteristics. Further, officers on probation are appraised by the branch head by using the self-appraisal technique which is followed by an interview

Another important sector of India which has emerged as the strongest drivers for the growth of economy is the IT sector. It has been reported by Nasscom and Zinnov Management Consulting Private Ltd that India, which is the fourth largest in the world for young IT start-ups and home to 3,000 technology start-ups, would be extended to 11,500 tech start-ups by 2020. (Srivastava, 2015). All these factors are leading to the effective appraisal of employees. Hence IT organizations are using various effective techniques to appraise the performance of employees. Chandhana and Easow (2015) had identified that top ten IT companies of India i.e., TCS, Infosys, Wipro, Tech Mahindra, HCL Technologies, Mphasis, Oracle Financial Services, Mindtree, Polaris Technology and Rolta India are extensively using either 360 Degree method or Balance Score Card. Wipro & HCL uses both Self-Appraisal and 360-degree appraisal for evaluating the performance of employees. Wipro uses self-Appraisal at both lower and higher levels of management while 360 Degree have been used only at middle and higher level in the organization (Neeraj Kumari,2016). She further proclaims that for rating the employees Wipro uses GP Rating Scale where 'G' stands for Process and performance of an employee while 'P' stands for personal effectiveness of an employee. Employees are then rated according to this scale on a bell shaped curve. As reported by Sen (2016) nowadays Wipro has vanished the forced choice distribution method by rolling out a new system of conducting quarterly performance evaluations which is followed by continuous and regular quarterly feedback. Oracle emphasizes personal scorecards, competency- based appraisal and multi participant appraisal techniques to enhance the productivity of employees.

Infosys too has abandoned the old bell-shaped curve appraisal by introducing icount where the individual performance would be focused and managers would be empowered by being flexible in their operations (Rajarshi,2016). Further, icount will give continuous feedback on short term performance to the employees throughout the year and the basic idea behind iCount is that every employee must contribute to the organization by an effective performance (Shankar,2016). As per the report of Economic Times Accenture another big name in IT has also vanished the bell curve appraisal by introducing a real time, progressive appraisal which focuses on setting priorities jointly and rewarding the employees at the same time. The existing appraisal would be inclined towards "Performance Achievement" and opt for holistic approach towards employee's career growth. Additionally the leaders in Accenture would coach the employees on their performance-related issues. As per the Fortune Global Forum IBM another leader in IT has dropped annual appraisal system by launching "CheckPoint" performance appraisal technique which will evaluate the quarterly performance of employees. In checkpoint appraisal the performance would be monitored and evaluated against five dimensions such as business results, client's success, skills, individual responsibilities to others and innovations. The new appraisal systems aims at improving the productivity of employees by being target-oriented (Sen & Alawadhi, 2016; Zillman, 2016)

Lastly, Pharma, a very momentous sector has accelerated its growth nationally and globally, as the branded generics dominates nearly 70-80 percent of the retail market further Indian Pharmaceutical market would grow to USD 55 billion to 2020 with a constant proliferation to the huge market access and it would commensurate with all the developed markets except China, Japan and US. Though in terms of volume it would proximate the US market (Bhadoria et al, 2012). All these aspects notifies the importance of employees in the Pharma sector as it is growing expeditiously therefore an effective performance appraisal would motivate and induces the performance of its employees. Piramal healthcare have a very comprehensive performance management system known as eVolve where scores are calculated on the basis of Key Result Areas and Critical Values like communication skills, initiatives, team work, customer responsiveness etc in which self appraisal and appraisal by superior is done adding the score of KRAs and Critical Values. Ninety percent weightage is given to KRAs while ten percent weightage is given to "Critical Attributes". A research study conducted on ten pharmaceuticals has revealed that performance appraisal is practiced yearly and half yearly which is in tune with career planning and growth. Sun Pharmaceuticals is also practicing technology enabled performance management system known as PRIDE which is six monthly review process equally involves employer and employees while setting the standards and systematic feedback and clearly defines the 'What'& 'How' of performance. (Economic Times, 2017). GlaxoSmithKline pharmaceuticals follows 360 Degree performance appraisal and goals are clearly defined and well linked with the organizational strategies further supported by the six GlaxoSmithKline Expectations which makes the performance appraisal more result-oriented. Additionally the current appraisal system strengthen the reward-based performance (Milne, 2015; GSK, 2017). Cadila Healthcare another big shot in pharma industry administers the modern technique of performance appraisal "Assessment centres". This technique is used for succession planning to fill the higher level positions like DGM & Senior Vice President (People Matters, 2016). Torrent pharmaceutical practices an annual appraisal system applying the Self-Assessment technique where assessment of employee is done by self, immediate supervisor and head of the department and performance- based rewards are also enjoyed by the employees (Torrent Annual Report, 2016). Novartis pharma too has introduced the Assessment Centre technique of appraisal to fill key positions (Novartis Annual Report, 2016). Further Novartis also examines the top executive performance against balance scorecard objectives and Novartis' values and behaviors which are rated on a three point rating scale.

CONCLUSION

Performance appraisal, since its inception in early 1900 till the present time have been practiced and researched conscientiously and rigorously. It has always aroused interest among employers, employees and researchers. Beginning with just a mere tool of performance assessment for the administrative purposes it has now become a domain which not only focuses on performance assessment but also defines, develops, monitors and improves the performance of people in the organization. In order to keep a pace with strict, stringent, tough external environment it is an absolute requirement to keep the employees motivated, engaged and committed towards the organization as employees have always proved to be the stepping stones in the success of every organization. If ignored then it results in the organizations failure in achieving goals and targets. Performance appraisal is a technique if conducted fairly, implemented effectively leads to the huge satisfaction of employees and resolves the issues like underperformance, low productivity, low morale, non-engagement etc.

Performance appraisal nowadays have to be intact with the changing organizational and employees needs further it has to be aligned with the long and short term strategies of the organization. Time has changed a lot in terms of technology, structure, task, culture and people. Therefore it's the need of the hour to change the performance appraisal system accordingly. Globalization has led to the increased workforce diversity, 24*7 work environment, performance-based rewards and all these factors makes it mandatory to perform outstandingly. Every employee performs to the highest level and at this point the importance of performance appraisal increases many fold as it decides for promotion, pay increase, rewards and other increments for outperformers.

As discussed in the chapter the three distinct sectors Banking, IT and Pharma have opted for the mix of traditional and modern methods. Majority of the public sector banks are practicing Self-Appraisal technique to evaluate the performance of employees though SBI is an exception which has implemented a new grading system which would definitely enhance the motivation and productivity of employees however, it does not talk about the consequences, if the employee underperforms. The private sector banks have opted for open, transparent, and feedback oriented performance appraisal methods which are more result-oriented. IT Sector is implementing very robust techniques of performance appraisal which are in tune with the current business scenario and wants a lot of contribution from employees in terms effective performance. IT sector too has shown a very positive and innovative outlook by revamping its performance appraisal system. Majority of the IT companies have discarded the old appraisal method of bell curve evaluation and implemented certain new methods of performance evaluation. Performance appraisal rather called as performance management in IT organizations. These new methods of performance appraisal have been developed with various objectives like performance achievement, employee development & engagement. Infosys's "icount", IBM's "CheckPoint" stresses on continous monitoring of performance throughout the year at the same time giving timely feedback to the employees. Defining proper Key Result Areas (KRAs) on which the performance would be appraised too has become a part of the existing appraisal system in IT sector. Hence, these KRAs clearly defines the tasks which enables the company and employees to know the exact criteria of performance evaluation. Performance appraisal in Pharma sector too has shown a huge improvement as these companies too are concentrating on defining performance by setting KRAs for its employees and developing competencies to achieve those KRAs further providing regular feedback to the employees on their current performance. For top levels executives the performance evaluation is even more rigorous and tough as these pharma companies are using vigorous and powerful tools like Balance Score card and Assessment Centres for appraising the performance and taking important decisions on succession planning.

The above aspects lists out that though both traditional and modern approaches are being implemented but one thing is not uncommon among these sectors that performance appraisal is becoming development, feedback & result-oriented. Annual appraisals are becoming stale with the passage of time. Organizations for the sustenance and growth implementing an open & transparent appraisal system for its employees. Employees nowadays are well aware of 'What' and 'How' of performance. They jointly sets the goals along with the supervisor further agreement to the goals result in high performance of employees. Further the existing appraisal techniques in the organization is extremely backed by a consistent feedback about every aspect of performance.

Performance appraisal is of huge importance as it manages various other HR functions like training & development, promotions, salary increments most importantly it serves as a base for Human resource planning which includes recruitment & selection and succession planning. Performance appraisal nowadays is no more an administrative and bureaucratic work rather it is becoming a regular activity which consistently focuses on performance improvement. Hence it is necessary to make performance appraisal more strategically aligned with the overall objectives of the organization as well as of the diversified employees. However, a lot of restructuring of performance appraisal is required in those organizations where still they are in a habit of using close performance appraisals, low on feedback, zero performance-based rewards and loosely linked with identifying poor performers and training & development. These aspects may affect the financial aspects like profitability and sales, human resource aspects like attrition and retention rate in a negative manner. The prevailing stiff competition, globalization, economic downturn has lead to the usage of those performance appraisal techniques which are not just performance-oriented but also employee friendly because it induces their commitment, performance and productivity in the organization.

Workforce diversity too have been discussed in the present chapter which states that globalization, competition and raising demand of customers have given birth to workforce diversity as talented people with extra ordinary caliber are required in order to meet the challenges posed by the continuous changing environment. Hence, these diversities should be dealt with in an effective manner to improve the performance of employees. Further several studies discussed in the chapter in relation to performance appraisal and workforce diversity have revealed that diversified workforce can be managed by the effective implementation of human resource practices. In context to the performance appraisal, if the evaluation of performance of employees is done in a strict fashion in relation to performance only and objectively and not on the basis of different caste, community, culture and ethnicity then it gives rise to improved productivity, profits and overall performance.

Employees want more objective criteria on which their performance shall be evaluated further employees also want to take detailed feedback so to discuss over performance-related issues. Organizations nowadays overhauling their performance appraisal systems in order to cope up with the changing organizational needs and perceptions and expectations of diversified workforce.

REFERENCES

Accenture too drops bell shaped curve appraisals. (2015). Retrieved on May 20, 2017, from http://economictimes.indiatimes.com/news/international/business/accenture-too-drops-bell-curve-appraisals/articleshow/48230902.cms

Amaram, D. I. (2011). Cultural diversity: Implications for workplace management. *Journal of Diversity Management*, 2(4), 1–6. doi:10.19030/jdm.v2i4.5017

Anand, N. (2016). *Axis bank moves away from bell curve system*. Retrieved on May 21, 2017, from http://www.business-standard.com/article/economy-policy/axis-bank-moves-away-from-bell-curve-system-116021700035

Annual Report of Torrent Pharmaceuticals. (2016) Retrieved on May 14, 2017, from http://www.torrentpharma.com/download/financials/annual_report/AR-2015-16.pdf

Appraisals: Companies across sectors on what they did to make performance appraisal a win-win process. (2017). Retrieved on May 10, 2017, from http://economictimes.indiatimes.com/jobs/appraisals-companies-across-sectors-on-what-they-did-to-make-performance-appraisal-a-win-win-process/articleshow/58056096.cms

Baer, M., Kempf, A., & Ruenzi, S. (2006). *Determinants and consequences of team management in the mutual fund industry*. Working Paper.

Banking sector in India. (2017). Retrieved on May 29, 2017, from https://www.ibef.org/industry/banking-india.aspx

Best practices: Talent assessment methodologies by Cadila healthcare. (2016). Retrieved on April 21, 2017, from https://www.peoplematters.in/article/talent-acquisition/best-practices-talent-assessment-methodologies-cadila-healthcare-12765

Bhadoria, V., Bhajanka, A., Chakraborty, K., & Mitra, P. (2012). *India pharma 2020: Propelling access and acceptance, realizing true potential*. McKinsey & Co.

Brooks, S. (2015). *A Brief History of Performance Management*. Retrieved on May 22, 2017, from https://www.peoplehr.com/blog/index.php/2015/03/25/a-brief-history-of-performance-management/

Cascio, W. F. (1998). *Managing human resources*. Boston: McGraw Hill.

Chandhana, K., & Easow, D. T. (2015). Performance Appraisal Method Used in Top 10 IT Companies-360 Degree Feedback & Balanced Score Card: A Review. *Bonfring International Journal of Industrial Engineering and Management Science, 5*(2), 73.

Chew, E. W., Lee, K. M., Tan, S. C., & Tee, S. F. (2011). *The effects of workforce diversity towards the employee performance in an organization* (Doctoral dissertation). UTAR.

Chhabra, T. N. (2008). *Human resource management: concepts and issues*. Delhi: Dhanpat Rai & Co.

Cox Jr, T. (1991). The multicultural organization. *The Executive*, 34-47.

Cox, T. H., & Blake, S. (1991). Managing cultural diversity: Implications for organizational competitiveness. *The Executive*, 45-56.

Dessler, G. (2011). Fundamentals of human resource management. Pearson Higher Ed.

Dike, P. (2013). *The impact of workplace diversity on organizations*. Academic Press.

Esty, K., Griffin, R., & Schorr-Hirsh, M. (1995). *Workplace diversity. A manager's guide to solving problems and turning diversity into a competitive advantage*. Avon, MA: Adams Media Corporation.

Flanagan, J. C. (1954). The critical incident technique. *Psychological Bulletin, 51*(4), 327–358. doi:10.1037/h0061470 PMID:13177800

Fletcher, C. (2001). Performance appraisal and management: The developing research agenda. *Journal of Occupational and Organizational Psychology, 74*(4), 473–487. doi:10.1348/096317901167488

Fulkerson, J. R., & Schuler, R. S. (1992). *Managing worldwide diversity at Pepsi-Cola International*. Academic Press.

Ganesh, A., & Rao, A. (2012). Performance Appraisal an Integrated Process-A Case Study with Reference to Karnataka Bank LTD. *Abhigyan, 29*(4), 23–37.

Glocalizing responsible banking: Mindshare and outcomes in India. (2016). Retrieved on April 13, 2017, from https://www.yesbank.in/pdf/glocalizing_responsible_banking_mind_share_outcomes_in_india.pdf

Grobler, B. R., Moloi, K. C., Loock, C. F., Bisschoff, T. C., & Mestry, R. J. (2006). Creating a school environment for the effective management of cultural diversity. *Educational Management Administration & Leadership, 34*(4), 449–472. doi:10.1177/1741143206068211

Huselid, M. A., & Becker, B. E. (2011). Bridging micro and macro domains: Workforce differentiation and strategic human resource management. *Journal of Management, 37*(2), 421–428. doi:10.1177/0149206310373400

Indian economy overview, market size, growth, development and statistics. (2017). Retrieved on May 11, 2017, from https://www.ibef.org/economy/indian-economy-overview

Indian Pharmaceutical Industry. (2017). Retrieved on May 27, 2017 fromhttps://www.ibef.org/industry/information-technology-india.aspx

IT industry in India. (2017). Retrieved on April 27, 2017, from https://www.ibef.org/industry/information-technology-india.aspx

Jackson, S. E., May, K. E., & Whitney, K. (1995). Understanding the dynamics of diversity in decision-making teams. *Team Effectiveness and Decision Making in Organizations, 204*, 261.

Khurana, A., & Goyal, K. (2010). *Performance appraisal: A key to HR assessment and Development*. Retrieved on January 21, 2015 from http://papers.ssrn.com/sol3/papers.cfm?abstract_id=1714151

Koonce, R. (n.d.). *Redefining Diversity: It's Not Just the Right Thing to Do. It Also Makes Good Business Sense*. Retrieved on August 29, 2017 from https://www.questia.com/magazine/1G1-83045836/redefining-diversity-it-s-not-just-the-right-thing

Kumari, N. (2016). A study of performance management system in Wipro. *International Journal of Human Resource & Industrial Research*, 3(7), 37–45.

Kurian, V. (2015). *New appraisal system in the works at sbi*. Retrieved on May 21, 2017, from http://www.thehindubusinessline.com/money-and-banking/new-staff-appraisal-system-in-the-works-at-sbi/article6979003.ece

Macnamara, F. K. (2011). *Strategic Role of Performance Appraisal*. Retrieved on June 22, 2014 from https://www.academia.edu/ 707671/ Strategic _Role _of_ Performance_ Appraisals

Mathis, R. L., & Jackson, J. H. (2008). *Human resource management*. Mason, OH: South-Western Cengage Leaning.

Mayhew, R. (n.d.). *How does diversity affect HR functions?* Retrieved on August 28, 2017 from http://smallbusiness.chron.com/diversity-affect-hr-functions-59653.html

Milne, J. (2015). *Behavioural benefits from employee feedback at GlaxoSmithKline*. Retrieved on May 15, 2017, from http://diginomica.com/2015/06/29/behavioral-benefits-from-employee-feedback-at-glaxosmithkline/

Morrison, A. M. (1992). The New Leaders: Guidelines on Leadership Diversity in America. Jossey-Bass, Inc.

Mullins, L. J. (2002). *Management organizational behavior*. Harlow: Pearson Education Limited.

Murphy, K. R., & Cleveland, J. N. (1995). *Understanding performance appraisal: Social, organizational and goal-based perspectives*. Thousand Oaks, CA: Sage Publications.

Novartis annual report. (2016). Retrieved on April 21, 2017, from https://www.novartis.com/sites/www.novartis.com/files/novartis-annual-report-2016-en.pdf

Ohlott, P., Ruderman, M., & McCauley, C. (1994). Gender differences in managers' development job experiences. *Academy of Management Journal*, 37(1), 46–67. doi:10.2307/256769

Patten, T. H. (1977). *Pay: Employee compensation and incentive plans*. Free Press.

Rajarshi. (2016). *How organizations have changed their Performance Reviews*. Retrieved on May 22, 2017, from https://grosum.com/blog/how_organizations_have_changed_their_performance_reviews/

Rani, L., Kumar, N., & Kumar, S. (2012). Performnce appraisals research: A study of performance appraisals practicies in private bank. *ABHINAV National Monthly Refreed Journal of Research in Commerce & Management*, *3*(2), 108–113.

Rao, T. V. (2004). *Performance Management and Appraisal Systems: HR tools for global competitiveness*. SAGE Publications India.

Richardson, M. W. (1949). Forced-choice performance reports: A modern merit-rating method. *Personnel*, *26*, 205–212.

Scott, W. D., & Clothier, R. C. (1923). *Personnel Management: Principles, practices, and points of view*. New York: A.W. Shaw.

Scott, W. D., Clothier, R. C., & Spriegel, W. R. (1941). *Personnel management*. New York: McGraw-Hill.

Sen, A. (2016). *Wipro sets stage for broad overhaul for appraisal system ditches bell curve as part of pilot*. Retrieved on March 5, 2017, from http://economictimes.indiatimes.com/tech/ites/wipro-sets-stage-for-broad-overhaul-of-appraisal-system-ditches-bell-curve-as-part-of pilot/articleshow/51216872.cms

Sen, A., & Alawadhi, N. (2016). *Good bye annual appraisals IBM says hello to checkpoint*. Retrieved on May 22, 2017, from http://tech.economictimes.indiatimes.com/news/corporate/good-bye-annual-appraisals-ibm-says-hello-to-checkpoint/50829448

Sessa, V. I. (1992). *Managing diversity at the Xerox Corporation: Balanced workforce goals and caucus groups*. Academic Press.

Shankar, B. (2016). *Infosys using new system icount assess employee performance*. Retrieved on May 27, 2017, from http://www.ibtimes.co.in/infosys-using-new-system-icount-assess-employee-performance-666114

Shrivastava, P., & Rai, U. K. (2012). Performance appraisal practices in Indian banks. *Integral Review*, *5*(2), 46.

Sisson, E. D. (1948). Forced-choice: The new army rating. *Personnel Psychology*, *1*(3), 365–438. doi:10.1111/j.1744-6570.1948.tb01316.x

Smith, P. C., & Kendall, L. M. (1963). Retranslation of expectations: An approach to the construction of unambiguous anchors for rating scale. *The Journal of Applied Psychology*, *47*(2), 149–155. doi:10.1037/h0047060

Society for Human Resource Management (SHRM). (1998). *SHRM survey explores the best in diversity practices. Fortune 500 firms outpace the competition with greater commitment to diversity.* Retrieved on August 28, 2017 from http://www.shrm.org/

Srivastava, M. (2015, January 4). *India set to increase tech start-ups base to 11,500: report.* Retrieved from http://www.livemint.com/Industry/JvotTawbmJzMVXyrKZ8CPM/India-set-to-increase-tech-startups-base-to-11500-report.html

Strauss, G., & Sayles, L. (1971). *Personnel – The human problems in management.* New Delhi: Prentice Hall of India.

Techniques for Assessment of Performance and the Factors Affecting Assessments. (n.d.). Retrieved on June 02, 2017, from http://www.managementstudyguide.com/performance-assessment-techniques.htm

Tsui, A. S., & Gutek, B. A. (1999). *Demographic differences in organizations: Current research and future directions.* Lexington Books.

Tyler K. (2005). *Performance Art.* Retrieved from https://www.shrm.org/hr-today/news/hr-magazine/pages/0805tyler.aspx

Wentling, R. M., & Palma-Rivas, N. (2000). Current status of diversity initiatives in selected multinational corporations. *Human Resource Development Quarterly, 11*(1), 35–60. doi:10.1002/1532-1096(200021)11:1<35::AID-HRDQ4>3.0.CO;2-#

Wiese, D. L., & Buckley, M. R. (1998). The evolution of the performance appraisal process. *Journal of Management History, 4*(3), 233–249. doi:10.1108/13552529810231003

Working at GSK. (n.d.). Retrieved on May 29, 2017, from http://www.gsk.com/en-gb/responsibility/our-people/working-at-gsk/

Zillman, C. (2016). *IBM is blowing up its Annual Performance Review.* Retrieved on May 25, 2017, from http://fortune.com/2016/02/01/ibm-employee-performance-reviews/

KEY TERMS AND DEFINITIONS

360 Degree Appraisal: It is a performance appraisal technique where an employee is assessed by all the stakeholders associated with the organization.

Assessment Centres: It is a performance assessment tool to obtain information about employees' abilities and future potential.

Balance Scorecard: A balanced scorecard is a performance metric used in strategic management to identify and improve various internal functions of a business and their resulting external outcomes.

Graphic Rating Scale: Graphic rating is a numerical scale where the job-related behaviors and traits are rated in order to assess the performance.

KRAs: Key result areas refers to the general areas of outputs or outcomes for which the department's role is responsible.

Performance Appraisal/Evaluation/Assessment: It refers to the yearly, half yearly, or quarterly assessment of the employee's performance in an organization.

Self-Appraisal: Self-appraisal is a technique of evaluating one's own performance.

Workforce Diversity: It means the differences among the employees of the organization on the basis of gender, age, caste, ethnic background, education, experience, language, and organizational functions.

Chapter 16
Exploring the Relationship Between Organizational Culture and WLB

Smita Singh
University of Lucknow, India

ABSTRACT

The objective of the chapter is to investigate the relationship between organisational culture and work-life balance Questionnaires for organisational culture and work-life balance were developed and tested and the relationship between the two explored. The main findings were 1) organisational culture has a significant impact on work-life balance, and 2) more than rewards, it is support in terms of resources, roles, and empathy that have a significant impact on WLB of an individual. It is the prevailing culture that determines whether an employee does or does not take the benefit of existing family-friendly or work/life policies. While the organization may include policies related to work/life in its human resource manual, it is the culture of the organization that instills confidence in the individual to make use of the offered options. The chapter highlights the issues arising when organisational culture lacks empathy.

INTRODUCTION

Organizational culture has been in the spotlight in the past few years (Schein 1985; Kotter and Heskett, 1992; Deshpande et al., 1993; Hofstede, 2001; Kassem et al., 2017). At the same time the very concept of Organisational Culture is an enigma that few are able to fully decipher. However the ever changing interpersonal equations

DOI: 10.4018/978-1-5225-4933-8.ch016

in organisations, the high attrition rates and decreased organisational commitment necessitates that organisational culture be critically examined. Organisational culture is intangible and hence difficult to replicate. In a world heavily dependent on technology and where almost everything tangible can be easily replicated, this uniqueness of organisational culture is what can give an organisation its competitive edge. The better the understanding an organisation has of its cultural dimensions, the better can it mould and control the behavioural aspects of its workforce. Darden (2004) favours developing a strong organizational culture as it builds strong commitment towards the organization and its objectives (Baker, 1980), helps the new incumbents to socialize, create a sense of belongingness, ensures coordination, facilitates good communication and mutual understanding and guides employee behavior. The importance of organizational culture cannot be denied in understanding organizational behavior, particularly the behavior of employees working within it. How employees perceive their work-life balance is one of these behavioural aspects which often goes on to define the job commitment, satisfaction and the performance of an employee. The hectic nature of today's work schedules has firmly placed the organisational spotlight on encouraging and maintaining the work-life balance of employees. A conflict between work and life, forces one to forgo rewards in one sphere for obtaining rewards in the other. Greenhouse and Beutell (1985) postulate that at times work responsibilities may interfere with family role demands and sometimes family demands may interfere with work responsibilities causing stress in both the cases. The stress could be as much a result of a feeling of guilt about the choices made (Quick et al., 2004) as due to a spillover resulting from worries carried over to work from issues at life or vice-versa. The strain experienced by the individual causes adverse psychological and physical impact and this often spills over to the other areas of an individual's life (Edwards and Rothbard, 2000). Organisational empathy, which is a function of organisational culture, can help reduce spillovers from work to life sphere. However, it is seen that the impact of organizational culture on work-life balance remains largely unexplored, particularly in developing nations.

The current study seeks to explore the relationship between organizational culture and work-life balance of Indian employees working in banks in order to identify those dimensions of the culture which are most significant and to suggest strategies for enhancement of work-life balance. Banking sector was taken as the area of study as there have been sweeping changes in the working culture of banks in the past two decades. A sector, which till 1991 was mostly given to public sector operations, was opened up for the private sector and foreign banks. Of late computerized core banking operations, financial inclusion, BASEL norms, Unique Identification (UID) projects, increased emphasis on rural banking, demonetization, have all had an unprecedented impact on the organizational culture of banks, especially the public sector banks. Linked with these changes, the working pattern and schedule of an average banker has undergone a transformation, which is reflected in the attitudes, morale and work-life balance issues faced by them. The study therefore, tries to understand the factors in the organizational culture of the Indian public and private sector banks and their impact on the work-life issues of the bankers. It also tries to offer suggestions on how these issues may be improved upon and what can be done for facilitating a better job satisfaction and job performance by improving the work-life balance of an individual.

REVIEW OF LITERATURE

Organizational Culture

Organizational culture has been defined in terms of "the pattern of shared values and beliefs that help give the members of an organization meaning, and provide them with the rules for behavior in the organization" (Deshpande and Webster, 1989, p. 2). Schein (1985) postulated that culture comprises assumptions, and values, artefacts. Assumptions pertain to the widely held views on human character and social interrelationships which are unconsciously assumed. Values refer to outcomes that are preferred and the means of realizing them. Artefacts represent the physical aspect of culture and include rituals, norms, and traditions. The aspect of culture related to values finds a reflection in the cultural projections of any organization (Zammuto and Krakower, 1991, p. 85). Martins (1987, 1997) has identified the strategic intent of the organisation, reputation of the company, business processes, employee goals and requirements, interrelationships and governance as the aspects of organizational culture. Culture deals more with emotional aspects, helping an employee relate well or otherwise with the given work. Thus, organizational culture could well be an aggregation of employee values and beliefs (Ouchi, 1987 cited in Erdem and Keklik, 2013, pg 104). What it means is that there may be some convergence among the researchers on the meaning of culture but they tend to emphasize upon different elements of culture. In the present study, *organizational culture is regarded as a set of values well entrenched across the organization such that these impact employees' feelings and attitudes towards their work-life.*

Work-Life Balance

Work-life balance has evolved around the idea of balancing work, life and family responsibilities. The term Work-Life now extends to include other life activities like study, exercise, community work, hobbies, care of elderly as well and not just care of dependent children as was recognised under the term work-family. Clark (2000, p 751) states balance in terms of "Satisfaction and good functioning at work and at home with a minimum of role conflict".

If individuals feel they lack a proper balance and gelling of work and life roles, they are likely to have inconsistent feelings about the outcomes. (Frone et al., 1997). This implies a bi-directional relationship where work can interfere with non-work responsibilities (Work-Life conflict) and vice versa (life/work conflict) or in other words there is interdependence of work and life on each other and the spill-over from one domain to the other can be either positive or negative. The negative spillover is generally regarded as "a form of inter-role conflict in which work and family demands are mutually incompatible so that meeting demands in one domain makes it difficult to meet demands in the other" (Higgins et al., 2007, p 1). Research findings (Duxbury and Higgins, 2001; Quick et al., 1997; Frone et al, 1997; Aryee, 1992) show that work-life conflict or negative spillovers affects individuals in three ways: individual outcome, organizational outcome and performance. Organizational distress is expressed in the form of increased cases of absenteeism, higher attrition rate, failure in handling work-induced stress to a reduction in job satisfaction, lack of commitment and decreased productivity (Duxbury et al., 1991; Higgins et al., 1992). It is not necessary for spillover to be always negative. When the spill-over from either of the domains is positive in nature, it leads to enhancement and enrichment of the experience in the other domain. Family-to-work enhancement or positive spill over thus, can be termed as 'inter-role facilitation' (Grave et al., 2007) or work-family enhancement. Outcomes of positive spill over or family-to-work enhancement are three pronged - life satisfaction, career satisfaction and work performance. For the purpose of current study, *work-life balance means the employees' perception that they are able to manage their responsibilities both at work place and home with very little strain.*

Relationship Between Organizational Culture and Work-Life Balance

Studies have shown relationship between organizational culture and an individual's fit into the organization. The compatibility of an individual's characteristics with those of the organization impacts his behavior. Studies (Holland, 1985; Joyce and Slocum, 1984) have drawn upon psychology to suggest that an individual's values, expectations and beliefs interact with the organizational variables such as traditions, norms, rewards that in turn influence the formation of his attitude and subsequent behavior. O'Reilly et al. (1991) argue that the individual commitment can be increased by ensuring a fit between individual preferences and organizational cultures. Individuals play different roles in their lives. Role overload, role conflict and lack of senior level support can act as major contributors to stress (Kumar, 2006) as well as work-life conflict.

The common perception about the impact of an overlap or a commitment concurrence between the two domains of family and work is interference leading to conflict. The premise rests on the scarcity hypothesis (Goode, 1960), role theory (Katz and Kahn, 1978) and the identity theory (Burke and Reitzes, 1991). The Scarcity hypothesis states that the physical and psychological resources available with an individual are fixed in nature. The greater the amount allocated to one domain, the lesser would be available for the other domain or roles (Goode, 1960). It is this depletion that leads to interference and consequently to compromises in the performance and results (Graves et al., 2007). The Role theory propagated by Kahn et al., (1964) states that any organization is built on an arrangement of roles which hinge on suitable allocation of job duties to roles and the personnel's drive to accomplish the designated role. The organizations orient their employees in the appointed role, provide feedback on their performance, motivate them to cover the gap in the performance and disciplined for failure to achieve the expected goals. While roles generally consist of few recurrent tasks, at times it is the need for balancing multiple, incompatible and ambiguous roles, which makes them complicated (Katz and Kahn, 1978). It is these complexities which produce strains leading to negative or indifferent attitudes towards work (Schaubroeck et al., 1993), thus, adversely impacting the effectiveness of the organization. The Identity theory states that individuals have multiple role identities and with each of these they attach certain expectations. For each of these identities, the individual strives to strike a balance between his expectations and experiences. Roles recognised by an individual as having greater expectations and hence, higher commitment, would have greater time and energy devoted to them, to help translate the expectations into reality (Burke and Reitzes, 1991).

Organizational culture and the nature of support provided by the supervisor can have a significant impact on the work-life balance of an individual. A range of options either provided for by the employer or supported by the organization viz. flexible working options, bouquet of leaves, health promotion programs or employee facilitation policies are all aimed at ensuring a healthy work-life balance for the employees (Kossek and Nichol, 1992). Care of dependents whether children or elderly is often facilitated by the organization by financing crèche/day care center and consultation/referral facilities, thus easing the dependent care concerns for the employees (Kossek, 1990). Other than the stated assistance options, very strong support system in the organization is in the form of colleagues and peers (House and Wells, 1978), superiors (LaRocco et al., 1980; Ganster et al., 1986; Hopkins, 1997), and the organizational culture. All of these help in alleviating the felt complexity and has a positive impact in achieving work-life balance. What the above discussion means in the context of current study is that the organizational culture can affect work-life balance through cultural variables such as role overload, role perception, role conflict, interpersonal relationships, support system, flexible working hours, availability of resources and authority and so on. In the present study, we propose that organizational culture impacts Work-Life balance.

RESEARCH METHODOLOGY

Six banks, three public and three private, were part of the study. Data was collected by administering structured questionnaires to 250 bank staff working in northern India. 226 questionnaires complete in all respects were retained for analysis. The technique used for selecting sample units was multi-stage sampling. The scale on Organizational Culture (OC) was based on focused group discussions and literature review (O'Reilly et al., 1991, Sashkin, 1991, Kilmann and Saxton, 1983). The scale comprised value statements which reflect the cultural setting in the organization. Exploratory Factor Analysis was used to understand the internal underlying structure of the constructs as well as to measure their reliability. Further, varimax, which is an orthogonal rotation technique was used while applying Exploratory Factor Analysis. The reason for using the orthogonal rotation was the underlying assumption that the factors are uncorrelated to each other. Originally a 27 item scale was tested which had a KMO value of 0.703, explaining a total variability of 75.8 per cent with five factors emerged. The reliability of the scale and sub-scales was checked and one sub-scale (of three items) with low reliability and an item which was cross loading on two factors were dropped. Thereafter, factor analysis was run on the remaining 23 items. The refined scale with four factors had an improved KMO of 0.726, explaining 74 percent of the variability with item communalities ranging from 0.612 to 0.869. The scale reported reliability of 0.797 with the sub-scale reliabilities ranging from 0.828 to 0.941. The results of factor analysis and reliability for OC scale are given in Table 1. The factors were named as Rewards and Achievement Orientation; Work Orientation; Resource and Role Orientation; Family Neglect Orientation.

The constructs for forming a scale measuring Work-Life balance were identified by conducting focused group discussions as well as through literature review (Carlson et al., 2000; Wesley et al., 2005). Factor Analysis was done to identify the underlying factors. Communalities derived from the factor analysis were all relatively large (greater than 0.5, falling in the range 0.640 to 0.913). The final version had twenty one items, grouped in four factors and explaining 80.5 percent of variability was used. The factors were named as Work Spillover in Family; Work-Life Enrichment; Family Spillover in Work; Work-Life Depletion. Reliability of the Work-Life

Table 1. Organizational culture scale: Summary of factor analysis, factor items and reliability values

Items	Rewards and Achievement Orientation	Work orientation	Resource and Role Orientation	Family Neglect Orientation
Inspires best performance 6	.923			
Feeling of acceptance	.900			
Feel encouraged to take pride in organization	.870			
Encourages high performance	.850			
Emphasis on high level of quality	.836			
Achievement orientation	.724			
Provides challenging opportunities	.678			
Work is satisfying	.661			
Advancement opportunities present	.655			
Identification with organizational values	.645			
Constructive feedback provided	.644			
Feeling of guilty about taking time off for personal or family reasons		.894		
Unrealistic work expectations		.866		
High work pressures and long working hours		.843		
High work overload		.834		
Poor organizational support		.640		
Role clarity			.869	
Less job complexity			.788	
Authority in position			.750	
Resources available for work			.711	
High work inflexibility				.875
Non-recognition of family needs				.873
Non-family friendly policies				.871
Eigen Value	8.340	3.660	2.863	2.093
Cronbach's α	0.941	0.894	0.828	0.879
Mean	49.08	27.26	12.16	6.25
SD	11.51	4.82	4.86	2.95

Balance scale and the constituent subscales were estimated using Cronbach's alpha coefficient. It was 0.893 for the scale with subscale reliability ranging from 0.748 to 0.965. Reliability estimates and factor analysis results for Work-Life Balance scale are shown in Table 2.

Table 2. Work-Life balance scale: Summary of factor analysis, factor items and reliability values

Items	Work Spillover in Family	Work-Life Enrichment	Family Spillover in Work	Work-Life Depletion
Work encroaches on family time	.919			
Work takes up too much time	.907			
Work related activities affect family	.879			
Work demands interfere in family life	.872			
Work takes up time meant for family	.855			
Work prevents contributing at home	.849			
Job strain makes family activity difficult	.835			
Balancing work and home responsibilities strains me	.793			
Work related duties force changes in familyactivitiesWFC5	.786			
Work responsibilities drain me emotionallySBC4	.745			
Work pressures lead to irritability at home S	.731			
Family relationships suffer due to work strain	.713			
Skills learnt at work are effective at home too		-.944		
Skills effective at home, are effective at work, too		-.885		
Problem solving approach in job works at home as well BBC1		-.712		
Family demands encroach on work time F			.860	
Family responsibilities interfere in work schedules FWC4			.854	
Work duties get postponed due to family responsibilities FWC2			.822	
Family related strain reduces work performance FWC5			.814	
Response to interpersonal problems at home and work is different BBC5				.872
Behaviour at home and work is differentBBC4				.808
Eigen values	9.700	3.147	2.762	1.303
Cronbach's α	0.966	0.881	0.866	0.856
Mean	48.70	14.12	9.74	8.33
SD	17.05	3.12	4.05	2.48
Note: Responses were recorded on a seven point scale. 1=strongly disagree; 7=strongly agree				

DATA ANALYSIS

The majority of the respondents were male (59.7%) with 40.3% female respondents. Over half of those who participated in the study had professional qualifications (57.5%), followed by 21.2% postgraduates and 4.4% undergraduates. A greater part of the sample (66.4%) belonged to the age group of 30-39 years, with almost equal respondents, 30% and 28% in the age groups of 20-29 and 40-49 respectively.

Table 3 and 4 give the result of the regression analysis which was undertaken to establish the relationship links in Organizational Culture and Work-Life Balance. Findings show that Organizational Culture has statistically significant relationship with Work-Life Balance. The sub-dimensions of OC scale: Work Orientation; Resource and Role Orientation; Family Neglect Orientation are significant determinants of Work-Life balance while Rewards and Achievement Orientation does not have a significant impact on determining the Work-Life balance. The adjusted R^2 for the regression is 0.733, implying that Work Orientation; Resource and Role Orientation; Family Neglect Orientation together account for 73.3% of the variance in the Work-Life balance scores. Further, it is seen that Resource and Role Orientation has the maximum contribution to the Work-Life balance scores, followed by the Family Neglect Orientation and Work Orientation respectively.

Table 3. Relationship between organisational culture and work-life balance

	Standardized Coefficients β	t	Sig.
Constant		19.841	.000
Work-Life Balance: Rewards and Achievement Orientation	.037	.958	.339
Work-Life Balance: Work Orientation	-.289	-7.950	.000
Work-Life Balance: Resource and Role Orientation	.545	14.276	.000
Work-Life Balance: Family Support Orientation	-.503	-14.472	.000

Table 4. Model summary[b]

Model	R	R Square	Adjusted R Square	Std. Error of the Estimate	R Square Change	F Change	df1	df2	Sig. F Change	Durbin-Watson
1	.859(a)	.738	.733	9.13646	.738	155.790	4	221	.000	2.130

1. **Predictors:** (Constant), Rewards and Achievement Orientation; Work Orientation; Resource and Role Orientation; Family Support Orientation
2. **Dependent Variable:** WLB_SUMScale

The regression equation for Work-life Balance on organizational culture factors is:

Work-Life Balance = 101.714 + 0.057 (Rewards and Achievement Orientation) - 1.060 (Work Orientation) + 1.985 (Family Neglect Orientation) - 3.0018 (Resource and Role Orientation)

DISCUSSION AND IMPLICATIONS

The current study supports relationship between organizational culture and work-life balance of employees. The regression analysis indicates that Rewards and Achievement Orientation of the organizational culture is not a significant contributor Work-Life balance of an employee. However, it was interesting to observe that Resource and Role orientation showed positive association with Work-Life balance while Work Orientation and Family Neglect Orientation had negative association. It suggests that role clarity, less job complexity coupled with adequate authority in position and availability of resources lead to Work-Life balance. Lack of adequate support in terms of role clarity and resource access as part of the organizational culture leads to lowered Work-Life balance. This is especially relevant in case of managerial staff, where responsibilities if not matched by adequate authority can lead to dissatisfaction and disenchantment from work.

Work Orientation has a negative relationship with the Work-Life balance scores. Unrealistic work expectations, high work load coupled with long hours of working and lack of organizational support, all contribute in reducing the Work-Life balance of the person. Therefore, the Work orientation culture in the organization needs to be conducive to promoting Work-Life balance of the employees. Achieving Work-Life balance in face of pressing family related duties and responsibilities becomes extremely difficult if the family support orientation is lacking in the organization. In India the nuclear family structure is gradually replacing the joint family system and implications for Work-Life balance can be drawn based on this trend. Majority of the respondents are married (84%), with nuclear family structure (68.1%) and belong to the age group of 30-39 years (66.4%). High work

flexibility, greater degree of recognition of family needs and presence of family friendly policies at the work place has a positive influence in enhancing the Work-Life balance of the staff. The predominant age group of 30-39 is the most involved in developing their career and at the same time are at a crucial stage in managing their family as well. Therefore, it is relevant that an organizational culture promoting Family Support should be looked upon favourably by the working staff.

The study has significant implications for managers. It is the prevailing culture which determines whether an employee does or does not take the benefit of existing family-friendly or Work-Life policies. While the organization may include policies related to Work-Life in its Human Resource Manual, it is the culture of the organization that instills confidence in the individual to make use of the offered options. There are studies (Milliken et al., 1998, McDonald et al., 2005) which have highlighted employee unwillingness to avail Work-Life policies due to organisational culture which look down upon employees opting for the family-friendly options. Improving organizational culture and making it family friendly can indirectly help improve the employees' perception of his Work-Life balance, in turn enhancing the efficiency and efficacy of the individual. Hence, managers and supervisors should try and create a Work-Life friendly organizational culture both in letter and spirit.

Role ambiguity has negative implications for Work-Life balance of the employees. Absence of clarity in what to do, how to do and how many people are involved in a team, leads to confusion, duplication of efforts and wasted time, energy and effort. Role ambiguity is quite often the result of incomplete, inaccurate communication which leaves things partially explained. Being unclear on what one'' role is, increases the effort required to accomplish the task. At times, this extra effort made results in disturbing the equation between work and life. Thus, effort should be made to improve role clarity, enabling the individual to understand his work better and feel at ease with his work environment. Gaining a better understanding of one's role facilitates better output and therefore, a greater satisfaction from the work done.

The more complex the job of an individual is, the more challenging it becomes. Job complexity results from the number of factors that are a part of the job (Wood, 1986). As the number of factors in a job increase, the complexity also goes up. This complexity can be both rewarding and unrewarding. How job complexity will affect an individual depends to quite an extent upon the culture of the organization. While job complexity can be rewarding in itself it should be complimented by a supportive organizational culture. When the organizational culture does not facilitate and provide adequate support to deal with complexity, it leads to dissatisfaction, distress and dejection in the employee. In such a situation, the job complexity has a negative impact on Work-Life balance. Hence, it is important that the organizational culture is made conducive when the job complexity increases.

Responsibility and authority go hand-in-hand. Organizations should ensure that managers and employees are given responsibilities with enough authority to help them in discharging their duties with ease. Strategic leadership is required for driving change in organizational culture and for ensuring that the implemented change in culture is sustained. For any individual to perform his job well, resources at his disposal are of vital importance. Scarcity of resources vitiates the organizational climate and also handicaps the performance. Managers and supervisors can facilitate smoother working by looking at a more collaborative use of resources. Organisations need to realize that employees would be happy only if their homes and personal life is in synchronization with the professional life. The need of the hour is to lay greater emphasis on efficient output through realistic expectations. Work design should take into account the technical interdependence and technical complexity as also the social needs and growth needs of the staff member before assigning strenuous tasks. Long hours of work do not ensure best output. Work timings should be regulated to help employees balance their work and life.

CONCLUSION

The current study aimed at looking at the factors influencing work-life balance and its relationship with organisational culture in a developing country context. The study also focuses on the link between family orientation/support and organisational culture. Since, family and work are the two prime areas in most individual's lives, the study the current study has far reaching implications for managers and organizations. A thought which emerges is related to the cultural variations found in the public and private sector workings in India. The public sector working patterns of fixed hours, low accountability and weak linkages between performance and rewards are coming under scrutiny and giving way to the performance oriented, high achievement and high rewards organizational culture of the private sector firms. While this transformation has shaken up the public sector into making its organizational culture more competitive in nature, private sector is also fast realizing the bane of promoting a culture of 'working till you drop dead'. Organizations have to find a middle path, developing and sustaining an organizational culture which will ensure the Work-Life balance of the employee and at same time promote efficient and smart working.

Limitations

In light of the fact that there have been sweeping changes in the banking scenario in the recent past, was the reason for basing the study on the Indian banking sector. However, the banks considered for the same were primarily in the Northern and Western region of India and were selected public and private sector banks. Thus, the scope of the study was restricted to a comparatively small region and the replication of the results for Southern and Eastern parts of the Country might not be feasible.

The banking sector in India has a mix of public, private, foreign and cooperative banks. Only two categories, public and private were considered. Hence, a complete comparative study is missing in this case. Further, this study has not compared the data for public and private sector banks, which could have offered a clearer perspective.

Future Scope of Research

The changes affecting the organizational culture in the banks have been multifarious. Understanding the impact of each of these viz. core banking, BASEL norms, demonetization, on the culture of the banks would offer a more appropriate insight into their individual impact on the work-life issues of employees. A longitudinal study which takes into account such future changes in the banks working pattern and the consequent impact on the work culture and the work-life issues, would offer a crisper insight.

REFERENCES

Allen, T. D. (2001). Family-supportive work environments: The role of organizational perceptions. *Journal of Vocational Behavior*, *58*(3), 414–435. doi:10.1006/jvbe.2000.1774

Aryee, S. (1992). Antecedents and outcomes of work-family conflict among married professional women: Evidence from Singapore. *Human Relations*, *45*(8), 813–837. doi:10.1177/001872679204500804

Baker, E. L. (1980). Managing organizational culture. *Management Review*, *69*(7), 8–13.

Burke, P. J., & Reitzes, D. C. (1991). An identity theory approach to commitment. *Social Psychology Quarterly*, 239–251.

Carlson, D. S., Kacmar, K. M., & Williams, L. J. (2000). Construction and initial validation of a multidimensional measure of work-family conflict. *Journal of Vocational Behavior*, *56*(2), 249–276.

Darden, C. (2004). Legacy leadership. *Executive Excellence*, *21*(5), 11–12.

Deshpandé, R., Farley, J. U., & Webster, F. E. Jr. (1993). Corporate culture, customer orientation, and innovativeness in Japanese firms: A quadrad analysis. *Journal of Marketing*, *57*(1), 23–37. doi:10.2307/1252055

Deshpande, R., & Webster, F. E. Jr. (1989). Organizational culture and marketing: Defining the research agenda. *Journal of Marketing, 53*(1), 3–15. doi:10.2307/1251521

Duxbury, L., & Higgins, C. (2001). *Work-Life Balance in the New Millennium: Where Are We? Where Do We Need to Go?* Work Network, Canadian Policy Research Networks.

Duxbury, L. E., & Higgins, C. A. (1991). Gender differences in work-family conflict. *The Journal of Applied Psychology, 76*(1), 60–74. doi:10.1037/0021-9010.76.1.60

Edwards, J. R., & Rothbard, N. P. (2000). Mechanisms linking work and family: Clarifying the relationship between work and family constructs. *Academy of Management Review, 25*(1), 178–199.

Erdem, A. P. D. R., & Keklik, A. P. D. B. (2013). Beyond Family-Friendly Organizations: Life-Friendly Organizations-Organizational Culture of Life-Friendly Organizations. *International Journal of Humanities and Social Science, 3*(4), 102–113.

Frone, M. R., Russell, M., & Cooper, M. L. (1992). Prevalence of work-family conflict: Are work and family boundaries asymmetrically permeable? *Journal of Organizational Behavior, 13*(7), 723–729. doi:10.1002/job.4030130708

Frone, M. R., Yardley, J. K., & Markel, K. S. (1997). Developing and testing an integrative model of the work-family interface. *Journal of Vocational Behavior, 50*(2), 145–167. doi:10.1006/jvbe.1996.1577

Galinsky, E., Bond, J. T., & Friedman, D. E. (1996). The role of employers in addressing the needs of employed parents. *The Journal of Social Issues, 52*(3), 111–136. doi:10.1111/j.1540-4560.1996.tb01582.x

Ganster, D. C., Fusilier, M. R., & Mayes, B. T. (1986). Role of social support in the experience of stress at work. *The Journal of Applied Psychology, 71*(1), 102–110. doi:10.1037/0021-9010.71.1.102 PMID:3957849

Goode, W. J. (1960). A theory of role strain. *American Sociological Review, 25*(4), 483–496. doi:10.2307/2092933

Graves, L. M., Ohlott, P. J., & Ruderman, M. N. (2007). Commitment to family roles: Effects on managers' attitudes and performance. *The Journal of Applied Psychology, 92*(1), 44–56. doi:10.1037/0021-9010.92.1.44 PMID:17227150

Greenhaus, J. H., & Beutell, N. J. (1985). Organizational and Family Social Support and Work-Family Conflict. *Academy of Management Journal, 10*, 76–88.

Hayman, J. (2005). Psychometric assessment of an instrument designed to measure work life balance. *Research and Practice in Human Resource Management, 13*(1), 85–91.

Higgins, C., Duxbury, L., & Lyons, S. (2007). *Reducing work-life conflict: What works. What doesn't.* Retrieved from travail/balancing-equilibre/sum-res-eng.php

Higgins, C. A., & Duxbury, L. E. (1992, July). Dual-career and traditional-career men. *Journal of Organizational Behavior, 13*(4), 389–411. doi:10.1002/job.4030130407

Hofstede, G. H. (2001). *Culture's consequences: Comparing values, behaviors, institutions and organizations across nations.* Thousand Oaks, CA: Sage.

Holland, J. L. (1985). *Making Vocational Choices* (2nd ed.). Englewood Cliffs, NJ: Prentice-Hall.

Hopkins, K. M. (1997). Supervisor intervention with troubled workers: A social identity perspective. *Human Relations, 50*(10), 1215–1238. doi:10.1177/001872679705001002

House, J. S., & Wells, J. A. (1978, April). Occupational stress, social support and health. In *Reducing occupational stress: Proceedings of a conference* (pp. 78-140). Washington, DC: DHEW (NIOSH).

Joyce, W. F., & Slocum, J. W. (1984). Strategic Context and Organizational Climate. In B. Schneider (Ed.), *Organizational Climate and Culture.* San Francisco, CA: Jossey-Bass.

Kahn, R. L., Wolfe, D. M., Quinn, R. P., Snoek, J. D., & Rosenthal, R. A. (1964). *Organizational Stress: Studies in Role Conflict and Ambiguity.* New York: Wiley.

Kassem, R., Ajmal, M. M., & Khan, M. (2017). The Relationship Between Organizational Culture and Business Excellence: Case Study from United Arab Emirates. In Organizational Culture and Behavior: Concepts, Methodologies, Tools, and Applications (pp. 732-751). IGI Global.

Katz, D., & Kahn, R. L. (1978). *The Social Psychology of Organizations* (Vol. 2). New York: Wiley.

Kilmann, R. H., & Saxton, M. J. (1983). Kilmann-Saxton culture-gap survey. Pittsburgh, PA: Academic Press.

Kossek, E. E. (1990). Diversity in child care assistance needs: Employee problems, preferences, and work-related outcomes. *Personnel Psychology, 43*(4), 769–791. doi:10.1111/j.1744-6570.1990.tb00682.x

Kossek, E. E., & Nichol, V. (1992). The effects of on-site child care on employee attitudes and performance. *Personnel Psychology, 45*(3), 485–509. doi:10.1111/j.1744-6570.1992.tb00857.x

Kotter, J. P., & Heskett, J. L. (1992). *Corporate Culture and Performance.* New York, NY: Free Press.

LaRocco, J. M., House, J. S., & French, J. R. P. (1980). Social support, occupational stress, and health. *Journal of Health and Social Behavior, 21*(3), 202–218. doi:10.2307/2136616 PMID:7410798

Lau, C. M., & Ngo, H. Y. (2004). The HR system, organizational culture, and product innovation. *International Business Review, 13*(6), 685–703. doi:10.1016/j.ibusrev.2004.08.001

Lewis, S. (1997). 'Family friendly' employment policies: A route to changing organizational culture or playing about at the margins? *Gender, Work and Organization, 4*(1), 13–23. doi:10.1111/1468-0432.00020

Lewis, S. (2001). Restructuring workplace cultures: The ultimate work-family challenge? *Women in Management Review, 16*(1), 21–29. doi:10.1108/09649420110380256

Lewis, S., & Cooper, C. L. (1999). The work-family research agenda in change contexts. *Journal of Occupational Health Psychology, 4*(4), 382–393. doi:10.1037/1076-8998.4.4.382 PMID:10526842

Martin, J., & Siehl, C. (1983). Organizational culture and counterculture: An uneasy symbiosis. *Organizational Dynamics, 12*(2), 52–64. doi:10.1016/0090-2616(83)90033-5

Martins, N. (1987). *Elandsrand Gold-mine: Organisational culture survey.* Unpublished report, Johannesburg.

McDonald, P., Brown, K., & Bradley, L. (2005). Explanations for the provision-utilisation gap in work-life policy. *Women in Management Review, 20*(1), 37–55. doi:10.1108/09649420510579568

Milliken, F. J., Martins, L. L., & Morgan, H. (1998). Explaining organizational responsiveness to work-family issues: The role of human resource executives as issue interpreters. *Academy of Management Journal, 41*(5), 580–592. doi:10.2307/256944

O'Reilly, C. A., Chatman, J., & Caldwell, D. F. (1991). People and organizational culture: A profile comparison approach to assessing person-organization fit. *Academy of Management Journal, 34*(3), 487–516. doi:10.2307/256404

Quick, J.C., Piotrkowski, C., Jenkins, L., & Brooks, Y.B. (2004). *Four dimensions of healthy work: Stress, work-family relations, violence prevention, and relationships at work*. Academic Press.

Quick, J. C., Quick, J. D., Nelson, D. L., & Hurrell, J. J. Jr. (1997). *Preventive stress management in organizations*. American Psychological Association. doi:10.1037/10238-000

Quinn, R. E., & Spreitzer, G. M. (1991). The psychometrics of the competing values culture instrument and an analysis of the impact of organizational culture on quality of life. *Emerald.*, 5, 115–142.

Rozensky, R. H., Johnson, N. G., Goodheart, C. D., & Hammond, W. (2004). *Psychology builds a healthy world: Opportunities for research and practice*. American Psychological Association. doi:10.1037/10678-000

Sashkin, M. (1991). *Pillars of excellence: Organizational beliefs questionnaire*. Organization Design and Development.

Schaubroeck, J., Ganster, D. C., Sime, W. E., & Ditman, D. (1993). A field experiment testing supervisory role clarification. *Personnel Psychology*, 46(1), 1–25. doi:10.1111/j.1744-6570.1993.tb00865.x

Schein, E.H. (1985). How culture forms, develops, and changes. *Gaining Control of the Corporate Culture*, 17-43.

Wesley, J. R., & Muthuswamy, P. R. (2005). Work-family conflict in India-An empirical study. *SCMS Journal of Indian Management*, 95-102.

Wood, R. E. (1986). Task complexity: Definition of the construct. *Organizational Behavior and Human Decision Processes*, 37(1), 60–82. doi:10.1016/0749-5978(86)90044-0

Zammuto, R. F., & Krakower, J. Y. (1991). *Quantitative and qualitative studies of organizational culture*. JAI Press Inc.

Chapter 17
Human Resource Management in Indian Microfinance Institutions

Richa Das
IMS Unison University, India

ABSTRACT

Over the years, microfinance has assumed a great importance all over the world. The reason behind the increasing importance of microfinance in poverty alleviation is considered a prime objective in all developing and underdeveloped countries. Traditionally, MFIs did not have a defined HR policy or structure, since the size of the organization was always very small. The last few years have seen an upswing in the size of the organizations and also in the margins generated by MFIs. The purpose of this chapter is to analyze the human resource management issues and challenges faced in microfinance industry in India.

INTRODUCTION

About 238 million people in India live below the poverty line with the per capita income of less than one dollar per day. Since independence, policy makers and practitioners have been trying to improve the lives of these poor and fight against poverty. This got reflected in the successive five-year plans, which had the objectives of "growth with equity" and "social justice". The planners, however, realized that rapid growth did not bring about "trickle down" effect, particularly so in rural areas. This realization led to the restructuring of institutions and schematic lending to facilitate better accessibility of credit for the underprivileged. Thus, initiatives in

DOI: 10.4018/978-1-5225-4933-8.ch017

Copyright © 2018, IGI Global. Copying or distributing in print or electronic forms without written permission of IGI Global is prohibited.

this regard were taken by building an institutional framework through nationalization of banks and creation of regional rural banks. Hence, the tasks of microfinance are the promotion of greater financial inclusion and, in the process, improve the social and economic welfare of the poor

Microfinance is defined as an "attempt to improve access to small deposits and loans for the poor households neglected by banks" (Schreiner and Morduch, 2001). Morduch (1999) explains Microfinance Institutions as specialized financial institutions, consolidated under the banner of microfinance, sharing the responsibility to work for financial inclusion. The main objectives of Microfinance Institutions are financial inclusion, poverty reduction, women empowerment and sustainability.

Over the period of time Indian Microfinance Sector has shown an impressive growth in terms of client coverage. Microfinance sector is a labor intensive sector. Human resource is the backbone of any MFIs. However, finding and retaining skilled manpower, to manage its growth is among the major challenges of the Indian Microfinance sector. There are several reasons for failure to attract competent personnel in microfinances sector by the MFIs. Firstly, different organizations such as banks, welfare organizations, NGOs and financial organizations have entered in this sector and have implemented diverse business models to run the show (Basargekar, 2013). Creating a leading MFI takes more than charging the right price and knowing how to design a financial offering. Secondly, indicators to measure the performance of human resources is varied, and it takes into consideration social performance along with profitability, which does not give clear picture of the industry to the bystander (Basargekar, 2013).

Workforce diversity encompasses race, gender, ethnic group, age, personality, cognitive style, tenure, organizational function and education of the employees in the organization. Understanding how HR responsibilities change during growth, communicating effectively with the expanding workforce, finding best people to join team, providing training opportunities, supporting staff performance and transferring institutional culture to establish work expectations and values are important in supporting a MFI's growth. Supporting diverse workforce in MFIs creates a powerful and sustainable tool for economic growth. According to Ikeayibe (2010) inappropriate Human Resource may serve as major havoc to the sustenance of MFIs and argued that staff of MFIs is fundamentally relevant towards the success or otherwise of MFIs.

This chapter presents a brief overview of the Microfinance Industry its Objectives, and current status of Microfinance Industry in India. The chapter also explores key issues and challenges faced by Microfinance Institutions (MFIs) in India. Finally, this chapter discusses Human Resource Management, and its present scenario in Indian MFIs.

A BRIEF OVERVIEW OF MICROFINANCE

United Nations Millennium Goals state that by 2015 the number of people living in extreme poverty should be half of what it was in 2000 (World Bank, 2000). Over the time researchers have shown that those underprivileged are creditworthy (Ahmed et al., 2006; Coleman, 2006; Hiatt and Woodworth, 2006). Microfinance has established itself as an integral part of financial sector policies of emerging and developing countries in the past decade for underprivileged population. Microfinance spans a range of financial instruments including credit, savings, insurance, mortgages, and retirement plans, all of which are denominated in small amounts, making them accessible to individuals previously shut out from formal means of borrowing and saving. The majority of microfinance is aimed at the estimated 2.8 billion people who live on less than $2 a day in the developing world.

Hubka, and Zaidi (2005) defined Microfinance as a credit methodology, which employs effective collateral substitute for short-term and working capital loans to micro-entrepreneurs. According to Otero (1999) Microfinance is "the provision of financial services to low-income poor and very poor self-employed people". Robinson (2001) defines microfinance as 'small-scale financial services–primarily credit and savings provided to people who farm or fish or herd; who operate small enterprises or microenterprises where goods are produced, recycled, repaired, or sold; who provide services; who work for wages or commissions; who gain income from renting out small amounts of land, vehicles, draft animals, or machinery and tools; and to other individuals and groups at the local levels of developing countries, both rural and urban'.

In India, microfinance gained momentum during the mid-1990s with the emergence of Basix India, SHARE, and SNF as major players in the field of microfinance. Between 2000 and 2003, a number of new players, primarily Spandana and SKS, with innovative business models emerged on the microfinance radar of India. The spectacular returns and scalable business models adopted by these firms attracted the attention of commercial banks like ICICI Bank, HDFC Bank, and ABN AMRO Bank. Most of these banks syndicated an exclusive microfinance lending cells and started looking for microfinance as a business opportunity rather than a section of their priority sector obligation. Microfinance gained further momentum after 2003 and the sector started growing at a pace of more than 100% from every year The commercial banks started aggressively considering national and international equity funds in India and microfinance rose as a business opportunity. Riding on this new wave, a number of new Micro Finance Institutions (MFIs) like Ujjivan, Swadhar, Sonata, Bandhan, Arohan and KAS Foundation came into existence (Alok, 2006).

OBJECTIVE OF MFIS

The main objectives of MFIs are as follows:

1. **Financial Inclusion:** According to United Nation Capital Development Fund (2006) microfinance aims to produce a well-functioning financial system, which is more comprehensive in nature.
2. **Poverty Reduction:** The primary goal of microfinance is to reduce poverty in developing countries by providing poor with basic financial services that will enable them to earn more, accumulate assets, and protect themselves from unexpected setbacks (Orrick et al, 2012). Otero (1999) stressed that MFIs address major constraint of the poor, i.e., shortage of material capital. Many researcher advocates MFIs reduce vulnerability of poor and enhance their quality of life (Gibbons & Meehan 2002; Bakhtiari 2006).
3. **Women Empowerment:** Few studies from Uganda suggest that there is status upliftment of women within the family and gains control in the family business as an impact of microcredit (Wakoko, 2004; Lakwo, 2006). According to United Nations Fund for Women (2001) the objective of women empowerment complements MFIs aim of poverty alleviation.
4. **Sustainability:** MFIs highlight the need for financial sustainability of all the participants in the business. According to Rhyne (1998) sustainability is not an end, but a mean to create improved benefit through financial outreach to poor.

CURRENT STATUS OF MFIS IN INDIA

Inadequacies in access to formal finance have led to the growth of Microfinance in India. In India, Microfinance operates through two main channels: a) banking system through self-help groups and b) lending through Microfinance Institutions.

MFIs have evolved into a vibrant segment of the financial sector exhibiting a variety of business models in recent years. According to Sa-Dhan's "Bharat Microfinance Report 2015" MFIs currently operate in 28 states, 5 union territories and 568 districts of India. The reported MFIs have a client base of 37 million with an outstanding portfolio of Rs.48882 crore. The average loan outstanding per borrower stood at Rs.13162 and 80% loans were used for income generation purposes. Outreach grew by 13% and loan outstanding grew by 33% over the previous years. The southern region of India has the highest share of both outreach and loan outstanding, followed by Eastern region. The proportion of urbane clientele increased from 44% in 2013-14 to 67% in 2014-15. Women borrowers constitute 97% of the total clientele of

MFIs, SC/ST borrowers constitute 28% and minorities constitute 18% of total clients (Bharat Microfinance Report 2015).

As per MFIN Annual Report 2015-16, data lending by MFIs exhibited a growth with 50% jump in loans disbursed consecutively in the last three years from Rs. 23682 Crore during 2013-14 to Rs. 37599 Crore and further to Rs. 61860 Crore during 2015-16 (MFIN Annual Report 2015-16). NABARD Report of 2015-16 states that the total loan to MFIs by banks and financial institutions increased by over 36.90% during 2015-16 as against 47.73 during the previous year. During 2015-16, refinance to the tune of Rs. 2300 Crore have been distributed to 17 MFIs. NABARD expended a sum of Rs. 52.92 Crore from Women Self Help Group Development Fund and Financial Inclusion Fund. During 2015-16 more than 5100 training programmes were conducted and about 1.81 lakh participants were trained by NABARD. Village level Programmes on MFIs were sponsored by NABARD with support of banks in 13 priority states (NABARD Report of 2015-16).

In a short span of 30 years microfinance has transformed itself from a credit-based rural development scheme that has claimed to reduce poverty and empower poor women, to a $70 billion financial industry. In the process, the traditional NGO-led model has given way to the commercialized institutions, resulting in an increased emphasis on profit making. Though MFIs unconventional group-lending model has the potential to mitigate risk and facilitate financial intermediation at the bottom of the pyramid, it has one major challenge associated with it—high intermediation costs. To cover the high intermediation costs by generating a surplus from its operations and remain operationally self-sustainable are a daunting task for MFIs.

According to a report published in Live Mint on 30th January 2017, India's microfinance industry is showing signs of overheating in a possible reminder of the crisis that hit micro lenders in Andhra Pradesh in 2010. Around 1.26 million microfinance borrowers had received top-up loans over and above their existing loan amounts as on December 2016 end. Further, Crif High Mark has defined top-up loans as those with a ticket size of less than Rs10,000 and where customers have at least two active loans. Typically, such a loan is taken for a period up to nine months. It has also been found that 70% of these borrowers have at least three loans running at the same time, while Reserve Bank of India guidelines mandate that not more than two microfinance Institutions (MFIs) can give loan to the same borrower simultaneously.

KEY ISSUES AND CHALLENGES OF MFIS IN INDIA

Access to financial services to all have been recognized as a human right and has been part of millennium goal. Microfinance provides access to various financial services like savings, credit, and insurance to economically poor section of the population. However, the MFIs in India face certain issues and challenges which are discussed in the following sub-sections:

Low Outreach

In India, MFI outreach is only 8% as compared to 65% in Bangladesh (Nasir, 2013). Also, it has been observed that MFIs in India focus more on women clients than men which further decreases the outreach of MFIs.

High Interest Rate

The interest rates charged by MFIs in India range between 18% to 30%, which poor population find it difficult to pay. This again decreases the outreach of MFIs in the country.

Client Retention

Client retention in Indian MFIs is restricted to around 28% (Nasir, 2013) due to lack of awareness, education and information regarding MFI services.

Loan Default

Around 73% of loan default has been identified in Indian MFIs. Loan default derails the growth and expansion of MFIs. Reasons of loan defaults can be attributed to crop failure or fall in commodity prices.

Lack of Information

Due to low level of education among poor and language barrier, it is difficult to pass on information to the clients by MFIs. Also getting credit information from poor clients is difficult to obtain because of their reliance on informal lenders such as sahukars and zamindars.

Weak Regulatory Framework

The Government is yet to develop and pass a legal and regulatory framework conducive to MFIs, which makes the operation of MFIs more difficult.

High Transaction Cost

The volume of transactions in MFIs is very small, whereas the fixed cost involved in those transactions is very high. If the producer's fixed cost in proportion of his total cost is higher, the element of risk in business increases in same proportion. Moreover, if the demand for the product falls or the marginal cost increases, it becomes very difficult for the producer to adjust the cost by cutting output.

Lack of Access to Funding

Requisite financial support is not being provided to MFIs by concerned agencies. 68% MFIs report that government doesn't support them to meet the funds requirement.

HUMAN RESOURCE MANAGEMENT: A BRIEF INTRODUCTION

Human Resource Management (HRM) has been defined as the "mobilization, motivation, development, and deployment of human beings in and through work" (World Health Organization, 2007). HRM handles the design of formal systems in an organization to ensure effective and efficient use of human talent to achieve organizational goals (Ahmadreza et al, 2014). Human Resource Management deals with essentially subjective quantities of human being like "skill" and "promo ability" (Li, Chen, 2010).

Recent studies proved that organizations are identifying that their employees are their most valuable assets (Stambor, 2006). Combs et al (2006) studied the process of regulation of human resource for increasing productivity. Today organization doesn't consider their employee as a cost factor, but as an important asset to the organization (Golding, 2010).

Sar et al. (1972) observed that with the shift of focus from manufacturing industry to service and with increasing technological changes, human resource has become the ingredient to the nation's well-being and in service oriented industry like banks and hospitals especially, it has become more important. The human resources need to be treated with great care and human resource issues require special attention of decision makers at the strategic level (Som, 2007).

HR ISSUES AND CHALLENGES OF MFIS

Over the period of time Indian Microfinance Sector has shown an impressive growth in terms of client coverage and outstanding portfolio. However, finding and retaining skilled manpower to manage its growth is the major challenges to the Indian Microfinance sector.

Issues related to manpower planning were ranked in first five in 2008 survey and fourteenth in 2012 survey conducted by The Centre for the Study of Financial Innovations (CSFI) Survey of Microfinance. The survey conducted by Microfinance Insights (2008) states that more than 51 percent of MFIs in India consider human capital issues as the most pressing issue in comparison to financial issues, technical issues and turnover issues. In managing human capital, recruitment of qualified staff is considered to be the utmost important challenge (32% organizations considered it most important) followed by preventing turnover (28%) and training and capacity building (24%). It is estimated that with this growing rate, the requirement of skilled manpower in this sector is likely to increase to 2.5 lakh in next decade, out of which nearly 20,000 will be required at middle level management and 1,50,000 will be required as loan officers or area/ programme leaders (Sector Report- Microfinance India, 2009). In practice more than 55% of the development of an employee occurs through on-the-job experience followed by 15% through job relationship and regular feedback mechanism (Mbeba, 2007). As per Sa-Dhan, one of the leading MFI in India, there are less than 25 institutes which are involved in imparting training and development activities in the field of microfinance. This number is grossly inadequate as compared to present as well as future needs of the MFIs.

Jha and Singh (2015) examined the human resource (HR) issues faced by the microfinance institutions (MFIs) in India. They identified HR issues faced by MFIs are high attrition rate, over burden of work, low compensation, and informal hiring. Selvaraj (2012) focused his research on the importance and challenges of HR department in MFIs. He found most of the HR functions are being carried out on ad-hoc basis in MFIs and proposed HR department requires strong support from the board as well as senior management. Raghav (2012) found communication gap between top and operational staffs, lack of MFI experience, overload of work are the reasons for high attrition rate in MFIs in India. Batra (2012) recognized high turnover, lack of training as common HR issues faced by MFIs. Ikeanyibe (2009) stated that one of the crucial reasons behind slow growth of microfinance in Nigeria is poor human resource management in this sector. Alok (2006) in his work compared two microfinance institutions in India regarding HR planning, recruitment and deployment policies. Schreiner et al. (2001) put forward MFIs need to train staffs in financial domain and professional information management to improve their efficiency. They also proposed MFIs should focus on formulation of effective incentive plans for their staff members, if they want to explore new markets. Churchill (1997) classified HR challenges in MFIs as sectoral level, organizational level, and individual level.

The important problems faced by MFIs are discussed in the following sub-sections.

Recruitment and Retention of Qualified Staff Members

The requirement of manpower in microfinance has been rising from 4000 in the year 2002 to 45,000 in the year 2009 in India (Alok, 2006). Cook and Jaggers (2005) stated the importance of staff retention policies for MFIs as they account for the direct cost of high turnover in terms of lost productivity, new recruitment cost, training and development cost, etc. Raghav (2012) cited examples of few cases where MFIs in South India have used innovative tools to control high attrition of field workers and branch officers by hiring local people after doing ground verification of the candidates and grooming field officers and loan officers to become branch officers in the long run.

Overburdening of Staff Members

MFIs have large base of borrowers availing very small loans (Hulme and Mosley, 1996). These large numbers of borrowers overburden the staffs working in MFIs by increasing the ratio of borrowers to total staff in MFI and thereby decreasing the productivity of each staffs (Rashid et al., 2013).

Training and Development of Staff Members

Mubarik (2008) discusses the critical role of training and development in microfinance industry and states it acts like a multiplier if implemented properly. It also requires variety of training which is continuously evolving and aligning itself with changing needs and objectives of MFIs (Krumm, 2007). Churchill (1997) states that foundation of any microfinance organization lies at the locus of interaction between the organization and its clients. The role of front line staff or loan offices, area leaders is very significant in building this relation. In such case training can act as a multiplier.

Compensation and Benefits Plans

Studies show that compensation and benefits system in many MFIs is not attractive. The compensation and benefit plans need to be structured scientifically to develop productivity based incentives and structure based on accounts/ clients load per credit officer and loan recoveries (MFIs in India: An analytical study of its financial, Human Resource and Managerial aspects of selected institutions).

Human Resource Planning and Policies

Women's World Banking report on development of competency based human resource management (2007) states that microfinance organizations today cannot wholly rely on leadership qualities and capabilities of their leaders, because as a growing organization it is required that development of capabilities of all the personnel in the organization must take place.

Performance Management System

Performance Management system is not very well defined in the Indian MFIs leading to high attrition rate in the industry. Prevailing performance Management system needs to be relooked at from the point of suitability and relevance to each of the grades rather than the same system for all the grades (Shastry, 2014).

Lack of Female Employees

Female borrowers constitute the major part of total borrowings of any MFIs (Armendariz & Morduch, 2010). But there is severe scarcity of female employees and their participation in the management of MFIs. Analysis shows that the attrition rate is low in organization employing more women.

Staff Grievance Redressal Systems

Very few of the MFIs in India have staff grievance redressal systems in their organization. Lack of awareness among staff of such systems and where aware, unwillingness to invoke the system needs to be tackled (Shastry, 2014).

Challenges of MFIs in Growing Stage

According to Helmuth, Parrot & Cracknell (2004), key challenges faced by growing MFIs is to control the high performance of human resources, because HRM system comes under stress during high growth stage. Pityn & Helmuth (2007) proposed a tool kit to develop HRM system in MFI based on its size and stage of development such as small size having up to 20 staff, medium size having 20 to 49 staff and large MFI having more than 50 staff members.

RESULT

Human Resource challenges that MFIs face are similar to that of mainstream organization like hiring the right people, finding the organization fit and retaining employees. While the host of changes has been seen in the HR policies of MFI sector over the period of time, there are critical areas that need immediate attention like working hours of employees, training and development programs, performance management system and staff redressal mechanism.

CONCLUSION

The topics covered in this chapter were overview of microfinance, current status of MFIs in India, key issues and challenges faced by MFIs in India, overview of Human Resource Management, and HRM issues and challenges of MFIs. Due to high customer - employee ratio in MFIs, human resource management needs to be given priority for proper functioning of the organization. One of the problems of human resource management is manpower planning, which mainly involves hiring, promotion, and exit of employees.

One of the reasons behind the failure of MFIs is the inexperience of management in handling the kind of market. The human resources who are mostly recruited from the banking industry have problems in generating demand, serving clients, meeting performance objectives. Their decisions have not been able to provide the desired result for the industry. Hence, it becomes necessary to on the part of MFIs to have a defined HR policy. The policies generated will ensure better performance for the MFI. The discussion suggests the decision makers to choose appropriate policies for minimizing the current and future shortage of employees in the industry.

REFERENCES

Ahmadreza, I., Ebraza, A., & Afsar, K. M. A. (2014). Analysis of different HRM policies Effect on Organization Knowledge Level. *Research Journal of Recent Sciences*, *3*(3), 12–22.

Ahmed, S. M., Petzold, M., Kabir, Z. N., & Tomson, G. (2006). Targeted intervention for the ultra poor in rural Bangladesh: Does it make any difference in their health-seeking behaviour? *Social Science & Medicine*, *63*(11), 2899–2911. doi:10.1016/j.socscimed.2006.07.024 PMID:16954049

Armendáriz, B., & Morduch, J. (2010). *The economics of microfinance*. MIT Press.

Bakhtiari, S. (2006). Microfinance and poverty reduction: Some international evidence. *International Business & Economics Research Journal, 5*(12).

Basargekar, P. (2013). Can Human Resource challenges halt the growth of Microfinance in India. *Indian Journal of Management Science, 3*(1).

Batra, V. (2012). The State of Microfinance in India: Emergence, Delivery Models and Issues. *Journal of International Economics, 3*(1).

CGAP. (2009). *Microfinance and the Financial Crisis*. Retrieved from http://www.cgap.org/gm/document1.9.7439/CGAP%20Virtual%20Conference%202008%20Summary.pdf

Churchill, C. (1997). Managing growth: The organizational architecture of microfinance institutions. *USAID Microenterprise Best Practices Project Paper, 7*, 26–81.

Coleman, B. E. (2006). Microfinance in Northeast Thailand: Who benefits and how much? *World Development, 34*(9), 1612–1638. doi:10.1016/j.worlddev.2006.01.006

Combs, J., Liu, Y., Hall, A., & Ketchen, D. (2006). How much do high-performance work practices matter? A meta-analysis of their effects on organizational performance. *Personnel Psychology, 59*(3), 501–528. doi:10.1111/j.1744-6570.2006.00045.x

Cook, M., & Jaggers, T. (2005). Strategies for staff retention. *Exchanging Views Series, 3*.

Cooper, K., & Lee, G. (2009). Managing the dynamics of projects and changes at Fluor. *Conference of the System Dynamics Society. In Proceedings from the 27th International Conference of the System Dynamics Society*, 1-27.

Deepak, A. (2006). *HR Planning, recruitment and deployment: challenges related to recruitment policies, HR policies and practices*. Available at http://m2iconsulting.com/wp-content/uploads/2014/12/HR-Issues.pdf

Gibbons, D. S., & Meehan, J. W. (2002). *Financing microfinance for poverty reduction*. Retrieved from http://www.microcreditsummit.org/papers/financing.pdf

Golding, N. (2010). Strategic human resource management. In *Human Resource Management A Contemporary Approach* (6th ed.; pp. 30-82). Person Financial Times/Prentice Hall.

Gu, L., & Chen, S. (2010). A System Dynamics Approach to Human Resource Mangement. In *International conference on Management and Service Science*. IEEE.

Helmuth, J., Parrot, L., & Cracknell, D. (2004). *Human Resource Management for Growing MFIs*. MicroSave Briefing Note – 53. Available at http://www.Microsave.org

Hiatt, S. R., & Woodworth, W. P. (2006). Alleviating poverty through microfinance: Village banking outcomes in Central America. *The Social Science Journal, 43*(3), 471–477. doi:10.1016/j.soscij.2006.04.017

Hubka, A., & Zaidi, R. (2005). Impact of Government Regulation on Microfinance. World Development Report: Improving the Investment Climate for Growth and Poverty Reduction, 1.

Hulme, D., & Mosley, P. (1996). Finance Against Poverty (Vol. 2). Psychology Press.

Ikeanyibe, O. M. (2009). Human resource management for sustainable microfinance institutions in Nigeria. *Global Journal of Social Sciences, 8*(1), 119. doi:10.4314/gjss.v8i1.48915

Insights, M. (2008). Human Resource Challenges and Solutions in Microfinance: Survey Report. New Delhi: Academic Press.

Jha, J. K., & Singh, M. (2015). Human resource (HR) & social challenges faced by microfinance in India: A framework. *Indian Journal of Industrial Relations, 50*(3), 494–505.

Krumm, D. (2007). *Open and Distance Leaning in Microfinance, Planet Finance, Morocco*. Available at http:// www.microfinancegateway.org/p/site/m//template.rc/1.9.29005 accessed on 27/12/2016

Lakwo, A. (2006). *Microfinance, rural livelihoods, and women's empowerment in Uganda* (Ph.D. thesis). Radboud Universiteit, Nijmegen.

Lascelles, D., Mendelson, S., & Rozas, D. (2012). *Microfinance Banana Skins 2012. In The CSFI survey of microfinance risk*. London: Centre for the Study of Financial Innovation.

Mbeba, R. D. (2007). *MFI Internal Audit and Controls Trainer's Manual*. Available at http://www.meda.org

Morduch, J. (1999). The microfinance promise. *Journal of Economic Literature, 37*(4), 1569–1614. doi:10.1257/jel.37.4.1569

Mubarik, Z. A. (2008). *Human Resource development in Microfinance Institutions*. Available at: www.microfinance gateway.org/gm/document-1.9.30202/23.pdf

NABARD. (2015). Status of Microfinance in India National Bank of Agriculture and Rural Development. Mumbai: NABARD.

Nasir, S. (2013). Microfinance in India: Contemporary issues and challenges. *Middle East Journal of Scientific Research, 15*(2), 191–199.

Orrick, Herrington & Sutcliffe. (2012). *Microfinance legal guide*. Author.

Otero, M. (1999). Bringing Development into Microfinance. *Journal of Microfinance, 1*(1), 8–19.

Pityn, K., & Helmuth, J. (2007). *Human Resorce Management: Toolkit*. Microsaves.

Raghav, N. (2012). A study of qualified HR practices among micro finance institution in Northern states in India. *Asian Journal of Research in Social Sciences and Humanities, 2*(4), 8–31.

Rashid, A., & Twaha, K. (2013). Exploring the determinants of the productivity of indian microfinance institutions. *Theoretical and Applied Economics, 18*(12), 83–96.

Rhyne, E. (1998). The yin and yang of microfinance: Reaching the poor and sustainability. *MicroBanking Bulletin, 2*(1), 6–8.

Robinson, M. (2001). *The microfinance revolution: Sustainable finance for the poor*. World Bank Publications. doi:10.1596/0-8213-4524-9

Sa-Dhan. (2015). *Bharat Microfinance Report-2015*. New Delhi: The Association of Community Development Finance Institutions.

Sar, A. L., Garth, L. M., & Ray, M. (1972). *Human resources and labour markets*. New York: Horper and Row Publishers.

Schreiner, M., & Morduch, J. (2001). *Replicating microfinance in the United States: Opportunities and challenges*. Washington, DC: Fannie Mae Foundation.

Schreiner, M., & Morduch, J. (2001). *Replicating microfinance in the United States: Opportunities and challenges*. Washington, DC: Fannie Mae Foundation.

Sector Report- Microfinance India: 2009. (2009). Available at http://www.microfinanceindia.com

Selvaraj, S.N. (2012). Challenging tasks of human resource department in Microfinance Institutions. *A Journal of Economics and Management, 1*(5).

Shastry, V. (2014). *Human Resource Management Practices among MFI's in India*. Available at http://indiamicrofinance.com/human-resource-management-mfi-india.html

Som, C. V. (2007). Exploring the human resource implications of clinical governance. *Health Policy (Amsterdam)*, *80*(2), 281–296. doi:10.1016/j.healthpol.2006.03.010 PMID:16678293

Stambor, Z. (2006). Employees: A company's best asset. *Monitor on Psychology*, *37*(3), 28.

United Nations, Department of Economic and United Nations Capital Development Fund. (2006). Building inclusive financial sectors for development. United Nations Publications.

Wakoko, F. (2004). *Microfinance and women's empowerment in Uganda: A socioeconomic approach* (Doctoral dissertation). The Ohio State University.

World Bank. (2013). *Historic Goals to End Extreme Poverty: Endorsed by World Bank Governors*. Press Release. Available at http://www.worldbank.org/en/news/press-release/2013/04/20/historic-goals-to-end-extreme-poverty-endorsed-by-world-bank-governors accessed on 07/08/2016

World Health Organization. (2007). *Knowledge Management Strategy*. World Health Organization Press.

Related References

To continue our tradition of advancing operations research, we have compiled a list of recommended IGI Global readings. These references will provide additional information and guidance to further enrich your knowledge and assist you with your own research and future publications.

Aboutalebi, R. (2016). Strategies for Effective Worldwide Supply Chains. In B. Christiansen (Ed.), *Handbook of Research on Global Supply Chain Management* (pp. 1–14). Hershey, PA: IGI Global. doi:10.4018/978-1-4666-9639-6.ch001

Adhikari, A., Biswas, I., & Avittathur, B. (2016). Green Retailing: A New Paradigm in Supply Chain Management. In N. Kamath & S. Saurav (Eds.), *Handbook of Research on Strategic Supply Chain Management in the Retail Industry* (pp. 290–307). Hershey, PA: IGI Global. doi:10.4018/978-1-4666-9894-9.ch016

Akkucuk, U. (2016). SCOR Model and the Green Supply Chain. In U. Akkucuk (Ed.), *Handbook of Research on Waste Management Techniques for Sustainability* (pp. 108–124). Hershey, PA: IGI Global. doi:10.4018/978-1-4666-9723-2.ch006

Anwar, H., Shibli, M. A., & Habiba, U. (2016). An Extensible Identity Management Framework for Cloud-Based E-Government Systems. In Z. Mahmood (Ed.), *Cloud Computing Technologies for Connected Government* (pp. 163–187). Hershey, PA: IGI Global. doi:10.4018/978-1-4666-8629-8.ch007

Bahr, W., & Price, B. (2016). Radio Frequency Identification and Its Application in E-Commerce. In I. Lee (Ed.), *Encyclopedia of E-Commerce Development, Implementation, and Management* (pp. 1841–1857). Hershey, PA: IGI Global. doi:10.4018/978-1-4666-9787-4.ch130

Baig, V. A., & Akhtar, J. (2016). Supply Chain Process Efficiency (SCPE) and Firm's Financial Efficiency (FFE): A Study of Establishing Linkages. In A. Dwivedi (Ed.), *Innovative Solutions for Implementing Global Supply Chains in Emerging Markets* (pp. 49–70). Hershey, PA: IGI Global. doi:10.4018/978-1-4666-9795-9.ch003

Basu, P., & Adhikari, A. (2016). Pricing Strategies in Multi-Channel Retailing of Seasonal Goods. In I. Lee (Ed.), *Encyclopedia of E-Commerce Development, Implementation, and Management* (pp. 639–652). Hershey, PA: IGI Global. doi:10.4018/978-1-4666-9787-4.ch047

Batten, L. M., & Savage, R. (2006). Information Sharing in Supply Chain Systems. In Y. Lan & B. Unhelkar (Eds.), *Global Integrated Supply Chain Systems* (pp. 67–82). Hershey, PA: IGI Global. doi:10.4018/978-1-59140-611-2.ch005

Boyce, W. S. (2016). Supply Chain Relationships: From Conflict to Collaboration. In B. Christiansen (Ed.), *Handbook of Research on Global Supply Chain Management* (pp. 227–239). Hershey, PA: IGI Global. doi:10.4018/978-1-4666-9639-6.ch013

Brahmia, Z., Grandi, F., Oliboni, B., & Bouaziz, R. (2014). Schema Change Operations for Full Support of Schema Versioning in the τXSchema Framework. *International Journal of Information Technology and Web Engineering*, 9(2), 20–46. doi:10.4018/ijitwe.2014040102

Carbonneau, R., Vahidov, R., & Laframboise, K. (2009). Forecasting Supply Chain Demand Using Machine Learning Algorithms. In V. Sugumaran (Ed.), *Distributed Artificial Intelligence, Agent Technology, and Collaborative Applications* (pp. 328–365). Hershey, PA: IGI Global. doi:10.4018/978-1-60566-144-5.ch018

Castelló, J., de Castro, R., & Bikfalvi, A. (2016). Hybrid Supply Chain Strategies in Wind Business. In R. Addo-Tenkorang, J. Kantola, P. Helo, & A. Shamsuzzoha (Eds.), *Supply Chain Strategies and the Engineer-to-Order Approach* (pp. 201–223). Hershey, PA: IGI Global. doi:10.4018/978-1-5225-0021-6.ch010

Cedillo-Campos, M. G., Bueno-Solano, A., González-Ramírez, R. G., Jiménez-Sánchez, E., & Pérez-Salas, G. (2016). Supply Chains under Security Threat: The First National Exploratory Study in Mexico. In A. Ochoa-Zezzatti, J. Sánchez, M. Cedillo-Campos, & M. de Lourdes (Eds.), *Handbook of Research on Military, Aeronautical, and Maritime Logistics and Operations* (pp. 32–55). Hershey, PA: IGI Global. doi:10.4018/978-1-4666-9779-9.ch003

Chan, P. Y., & Shi, X. (2006). Evaluation of the SCM Performances in Using of Global Logistics Information Technologies: A Research Study in Hong Kong. In Y. Lan & B. Unhelkar (Eds.), *Global Integrated Supply Chain Systems* (pp. 139–156). Hershey, PA: IGI Global. doi:10.4018/978-1-59140-611-2.ch009

Chandan, H. C. (2016). Implementation of Green Supply Chain Management in a Globalized Economy. In B. Christiansen (Ed.), *Handbook of Research on Global Supply Chain Management* (pp. 402–418). Hershey, PA: IGI Global. doi:10.4018/978-1-4666-9639-6.ch023

Chao, C. (2006). Inter-Enterprise Process Integration for E-Supply Chain Business Practices. In Y. Lan & B. Unhelkar (Eds.), *Global Integrated Supply Chain Systems* (pp. 183–199). Hershey, PA: IGI Global. doi:10.4018/978-1-59140-611-2.ch012

Conesa, J., Olive, A., & Caballé, S. (2011). Refactoring and its Application to Ontologies. In M. Lytras, P. Ordóñez de Pablos, & E. Damiani (Eds.), *Semantic Web Personalization and Context Awareness: Management of Personal Identities and Social Networking* (pp. 107–136). Hershey, PA: IGI Global. doi:10.4018/978-1-61520-921-7.ch010

Cox, S. A., & Perkins, J. S. (2008). Factors for Effective E-Collaboration in the Supply Chain. In N. Kock (Ed.), *Encyclopedia of E-Collaboration* (pp. 279–285). Hershey, PA: IGI Global. doi:10.4018/978-1-59904-000-4.ch043

Dima, I. C., Grabara, J., & Nowicka-Skowron, M. (2012). Equipment Replacement Decisions Models with the Context of Flexible Manufacturing Cells. In V. Modrák & R. Pandian (Eds.), *Operations Management Research and Cellular Manufacturing Systems: Innovative Methods and Approaches* (pp. 401–411). Hershey, PA: IGI Global. doi:10.4018/978-1-61350-047-7.ch019

Dima, I. C., & Modrák, V. (2013). The Management of Basic Production Functions. In I. Dima (Ed.), *Industrial Production Management in Flexible Manufacturing Systems* (pp. 110–175). Hershey, PA: IGI Global. doi:10.4018/978-1-4666-2818-2.ch004

Dragan, D., Kramberger, T., & Topolšek, D. (2016). Efficiency and Travel Agencies: Bayesian Structural Equation Model. In T. Kramberger, V. Potočan, & V. Ipavec (Eds.), *Sustainable Logistics and Strategic Transportation Planning* (pp. 211–235). Hershey, PA: IGI Global. doi:10.4018/978-1-5225-0001-8.ch010

Duan, F., Tan, J. T., Kato, R., Zhu, C., & Arai, T. (2012). Multi-Modal Assembly-Support System for Cellular Manufacturing. In V. Modrák & R. Pandian (Eds.), *Operations Management Research and Cellular Manufacturing Systems: Innovative Methods and Approaches* (pp. 412–427). Hershey, PA: IGI Global. doi:10.4018/978-1-61350-047-7.ch020

Dubey, R., & Gunasekaran, A. (2016). *Strategic Management of Sustainable Manufacturing Operations* (pp. 1–380). Hershey, PA: IGI Global. doi:10.4018/978-1-5225-0350-7

Durmusoglu, M. B., & Kaya, G. (2012). Lean Thinking Based Investment Planning at Design Stage of Cellular/Hybrid Manufacturing Systems. In V. Modrák & R. Pandian (Eds.), *Operations Management Research and Cellular Manufacturing Systems: Innovative Methods and Approaches* (pp. 342–365). Hershey, PA: IGI Global. doi:10.4018/978-1-61350-047-7.ch016

Eryılmaz, M. E., Erdur, D. A., Bektaş, O., Kara, E., & Aydoğan, E. (2016). The Case of ISO 9000 Quality Management System Certification in a Faculty of a Turkish Public University: Triggers, Processes, and Consequences. In W. Nuninger & J. Châtelet (Eds.), *Handbook of Research on Quality Assurance and Value Management in Higher Education* (pp. 257–278). Hershey, PA: IGI Global. doi:10.4018/978-1-5225-0024-7.ch010

Fayezi, S., & Zomorrodi, M. (2016). Supply Chain Management: Developments, Theories and Models. In B. Christiansen (Ed.), *Handbook of Research on Global Supply Chain Management* (pp. 313–340). Hershey, PA: IGI Global. doi:10.4018/978-1-4666-9639-6.ch018

Fernando, Y., & Wah, W. X. (2016). Moving forward a Parsimonious Model of Eco-Innovation: Results from a Content Analysis. In S. Dinda (Ed.), *Handbook of Research on Climate Change Impact on Health and Environmental Sustainability* (pp. 619–631). Hershey, PA: IGI Global. doi:10.4018/978-1-4666-8814-8.ch030

Furlong, S. (2016). What is Needed to Advance Transformational E-Government and Why: A Different Approach to Project Management. In Politics and Social Activism: Concepts, Methodologies, Tools, and Applications (pp. 1302-1322). Hershey, PA: IGI Global. doi:10.4018/978-1-4666-9461-3.ch067

Gackowski, Z. J. (2007). Purpose-Focused View of Information Quality: Telelogical Operations Research-Based Approach. In L. Al-Hakim (Ed.), *Challenges of Managing Information Quality in Service Organizations* (pp. 277–309). Hershey, PA: IGI Global. doi:10.4018/978-1-59904-420-0.ch012

Galup, S. D., Dattero, R., & Quan, J. (2016). The Compensation Benefit of ITIL® Skills and Certifications. *International Journal of Service Science, Management, Engineering, and Technology*, 7(2), 1 15. doi:10.4018/IJSSMET.2016040101

Gencer, Y. G., & Akkucuk, U. (2016). Reverse Logistics: Automobile Recalls and Other Conditions. In U. Akkucuk (Ed.), *Handbook of Research on Waste Management Techniques for Sustainability* (pp. 125–154). Hershey, PA: IGI Global. doi:10.4018/978-1-4666-9723-2.ch007

Ghezavati, V., Saidi-Mehrabad, M., Jabal-Ameli, M. S., Makui, A., & Sadjadi, S. J. (2012). Optimization and Mathematical Programming to Design and Planning Issues in Cellular Manufacturing Systems under Uncertain Situations. In V. Modrák & R. Pandian (Eds.), *Operations Management Research and Cellular Manufacturing Systems: Innovative Methods and Approaches* (pp. 298–316). Hershey, PA: IGI Global. doi:10.4018/978-1-61350-047-7.ch014

Gibson, P. R., & Edwards, J. (2005). The Strategic Importance of E-Commerce in Modern Supply Chains. In M. Khosrow-Pour (Ed.), *Advanced Topics in Electronic Commerce* (Vol. 1, pp. 266–286). Hershey, PA: IGI Global. doi:10.4018/978-1-59140-819-2.ch014

Grover, N. (2016). Performance Measurement: Measuring Retail Supply Chain Performance. In A. Dwivedi (Ed.), *Innovative Solutions for Implementing Global Supply Chains in Emerging Markets* (pp. 212–241). Hershey, PA: IGI Global. doi:10.4018/978-1-4666-9795-9.ch015

Guo, Z., Yang, J., Chen, L., & Guo, R. (2016). An Information System Framework and Prototype for Collaboration and Standardization in Chinese Liquor Production. *International Journal of Enterprise Information Systems, 12*(1), 38–58. doi:10.4018/IJEIS.2016010103

Gupta, A. (2016). Customer Service: A Key Differentiator in Retailing. In N. Kamath & S. Saurav (Eds.), *Handbook of Research on Strategic Supply Chain Management in the Retail Industry* (pp. 75–86). Hershey, PA: IGI Global. doi:10.4018/978-1-4666-9894-9.ch005

Gwangwava, N., Mpofu, K., & Mhlanga, S. (2016). Big Data and Data Modelling for Manufacturing Information Systems. In I. Management Association (Ed.), *Big Data: Concepts, Methodologies, Tools, and Applications* (pp. 116-138). Hershey, PA: IGI Global. doi:10.4018/978-1-4666-9840-6.ch007

Hadaya, P., & Pellerin, R. (2009). Determinants of Manufacturing Firms' Intent to Use Web Based Systems to Share Inventory Information with their Key Suppliers. In N. Kock (Ed.), *E-Collaboration: Concepts, Methodologies, Tools, and Applications* (pp. 1267–1288). Hershey, PA: IGI Global. doi:10.4018/978-1-60566-652-5.ch096

Haverkamp, R., & de Vries, H. J. (2016). Managing In-Company Standardisation while Avoiding Resistance: A Philosophical-Empirical Approach. In K. Jakobs (Ed.), *Effective Standardization Management in Corporate Settings* (pp. 184–213). Hershey, PA: IGI Global. doi:10.4018/978-1-4666-9737-9.ch009

Related References

Hsu, H. Y., & Shih, S. C. (2008). Strategic Alliances of Information Technology Among Channel Members. In H. Nemati (Ed.), *Information Security and Ethics: Concepts, Methodologies, Tools, and Applications* (pp. 1080–1095). Hershey, PA: IGI Global. doi:10.4018/978-1-59904-937-3.ch074

Huang, Z., & Gangopadhyay, A. (2006). Information Sharing in Supply Chain Management with Demand Uncertainty. In M. Khosrow-Pour (Ed.), *Advanced Topics in Information Resources Management* (Vol. 5, pp. 44–62). Hershey, PA: IGI Global. doi:10.4018/978-1-59140-929-8.ch003

Hurriyet, H., & Nakandala, D. (2016). Lean Thinking and the Innovation Process. In L. Al-Hakim, X. Wu, A. Koronios, & Y. Shou (Eds.), *Handbook of Research on Driving Competitive Advantage through Sustainable, Lean, and Disruptive Innovation* (pp. 39–58). Hershey, PA: IGI Global. doi:10.4018/978-1-5225-0135-0.ch002

Janczewski, L. J., & Colarik, A. M. (2005). Operations Management. In L. Janczewski & A. Colarik (Eds.), *Managerial Guide for Handling Cyber-Terrorism and Information Warfare* (pp. 175–198). Hershey, PA: IGI Global. doi:10.4018/978-1-59140-583-2.ch012

Jiao, J., You, X., & Kumar, A. (2006). An Agent-Based Collaborative Negotiation System for Global Manufacturing Supply Chain Management. In Y. Lan & B. Unhelkar (Eds.), *Global Integrated Supply Chain Systems* (pp. 243–271). Hershey, PA: IGI Global. doi:10.4018/978-1-59140-611-2.ch015

John, J., & Kumar, S. (2016). A Locational Decision Making Framework for Shipbreaking under Multiple Criteria. *International Journal of Strategic Decision Sciences*, *7*(1), 76–97. doi:10.4018/IJSDS.2016010104

Karaosman, H., & Brun, A. (2016). The Myth of Sustainability in Fashion Supply Chains. In A. Vecchi & C. Buckley (Eds.), *Handbook of Research on Global Fashion Management and Merchandising* (pp. 481–508). Hershey, PA: IGI Global. doi:10.4018/978-1-5225-0110-7.ch020

Kasemsap, K. (2015). The Role of Total Quality Management Practices on Quality Performance. In A. Moumtzoglou, A. Kastania, & S. Archondakis (Eds.), *Laboratory Management Information Systems: Current Requirements and Future Perspectives* (pp. 1–31). Hershey, PA: IGI Global. doi:10.4018/978-1-4666-6320-6.ch001

Kasemsap, K. (2016). Applying Lean Production and Six Sigma in Global Operations. In U. Akkucuk (Ed.), *Handbook of Research on Waste Management Techniques for Sustainability* (pp. 44–74). Hershey, PA: IGI Global. doi:10.4018/978-1-4666-9723-2.ch003

Kasemsap, K. (2016). Encouraging Supply Chain Networks and Customer Loyalty in Global Supply Chain. In N. Kamath & S. Saurav (Eds.), *Handbook of Research on Strategic Supply Chain Management in the Retail Industry* (pp. 87–112). Hershey, PA: IGI Global. doi:10.4018/978-1-4666-9894-9.ch006

Kasemsap, K. (2016). Fostering Supply Chain Management in Global Business. In B. Christiansen (Ed.), *Handbook of Research on Global Supply Chain Management* (pp. 45–71). Hershey, PA: IGI Global. doi:10.4018/978-1-4666-9639-6.ch003

Kasemsap, K. (2016). The Role of Cloud Computing in Global Supply Chain. In Web-Based Services: Concepts, Methodologies, Tools, and Applications (pp. 1556-1583). Hershey, PA: IGI Global. doi:10.4018/978-1-4666-9466-8.ch069

Kasemsap, K. (2016). The Role of Electronic Commerce in the Global Business Environments. In Web Design and Development: Concepts, Methodologies, Tools, and Applications (pp. 1014-1034). Hershey, PA: IGI Global. doi:10.4018/978-1-4666-8619-9.ch046

Kasemsap, K. (2016). The Role of Strategic Outsourcing in Global Business. In G. Alor-Hernández, C. Sánchez-Ramírez, & J. García-Alcaraz (Eds.), *Handbook of Research on Managerial Strategies for Achieving Optimal Performance in Industrial Processes* (pp. 325–357). Hershey, PA: IGI Global. doi:10.4018/978-1-5225-0130-5.ch016

Kasemsap, K. (2016). Promoting Service Quality and Customer Satisfaction in Global Business. In U. Panwar, R. Kumar, & N. Ray (Eds.), *Handbook of Research on Promotional Strategies and Consumer Influence in the Service Sector* (pp. 247–276). Hershey, PA: IGI Global. doi:10.4018/978-1-5225-0143-5.ch015

Khanam, S., Siddiqui, J., & Talib, F. (2016). A DEMATEL Approach for Prioritizing the TQM Enablers and IT Resources in the Indian ICT Industry. *International Journal of Applied Management Sciences and Engineering, 3*(1), 11–29. doi:10.4018/IJAMSE.2016010102

Klein, A. Z., Gomes da Costa, E., Vieira, L. M., & Teixeira, R. (2016). The Use of Mobile Technology in Management and Risk Control in the Supply Chain: The Case of a Brazilian Beef Chain. In I. Management Association (Ed.), International Business: Concepts, Methodologies, Tools, and Applications (pp. 646-666). Hershey, PA: IGI Global. doi:10.4018/978-1-4666-9814-7.ch031

Kong, E., & Lien, C. (2016). Impact of Social Media in Service Innovations: An Empirical Study on the Australian Hotel Industry. In Social Media and Networking: Concepts, Methodologies, Tools, and Applications (pp. 978-993). Hershey, PA: IGI Global. doi:10.4018/978-1-4666-8614-4.ch044

Related References

Kozlenkov, A., Spanoudakis, G., Zisman, A., Fasoulas, V., & Sanchez, F. (2007). Architecture-Driven Service Discovery for Service Centric Systems. *International Journal of Web Services Research, 4*(2), 82–113. doi:10.4018/jwsr.2007040104

Kristafor, Z. (2014). Simultaneous Operations. In D. Matanovic, N. Gaurina-Medjimurec, & K. Simon (Eds.), *Risk Analysis for Prevention of Hazardous Situations in Petroleum and Natural Gas Engineering* (pp. 96–114). Hershey, PA: IGI Global. doi:10.4018/978-1-4666-4777-0.ch005

Kumar, M., Raman, J., & Singh, P. (2015). An Unified Analytical Network Process (ANP) and Data Envelopment Analysis (DEA) Approach for Manufacturing Strategy Decision. *International Journal of Strategic Decision Sciences, 6*(2), 57–82. doi:10.4018/ijsds.2015040104

LaForge, R. L. (2009). Teaching Operations Management with Enterprise Software. In P. Tiako (Ed.), *Software Applications: Concepts, Methodologies, Tools, and Applications* (pp. 1798–1812). Hershey, PA: IGI Global. doi:10.4018/978-1-60566-060-8.ch106

Lan, Y., & Unhelkar, B. (2006). A Methodology for Developing Integrated Supply Chain Management System. In Y. Lan & B. Unhelkar (Eds.), *Global Integrated Supply Chain Systems* (pp. 1–13). Hershey, PA: IGI Global. doi:10.4018/978-1-59140-611-2.ch001

Lechuga, G. P., Martínez, F. V., & Ramírez, E. P. (2016). Stochastic Optimization of Manufacture Systems by Using Markov Decision Processes. In P. Vasant, G. Weber, & V. Dieu (Eds.), *Handbook of Research on Modern Optimization Algorithms and Applications in Engineering and Economics* (pp. 185–208). Hershey, PA: IGI Global. doi:10.4018/978-1-4666-9644-0.ch007

Lee, I. (2016). A Conceptual Framework of the Internet of Things (IoT) for Smart Supply Chain Management. In I. Lee (Ed.), *Encyclopedia of E-Commerce Development, Implementation, and Management* (pp. 1177–1189). Hershey, PA: IGI Global. doi:10.4018/978-1-4666-9787-4.ch084

Lee, I. (2016). Valuation Methods for RFID Investments. In I. Lee (Ed.), *Encyclopedia of E-Commerce Development, Implementation, and Management* (pp. 522–534). Hershey, PA: IGI Global. doi:10.4018/978-1-4666-9787-4.ch038

Liu, H., Ke, W., Wei, K. K., & Lu, Y. (2016). The Effects of Social Capital on Firm Substantive and Symbolic Performance: In the Context of E-Business. *Journal of Global Information Management, 24*(1), 61–85. doi:10.4018/JGIM.2016010104

Liu, Z. (2016). Structuring and Managing Supply Network: A Review of Current Literature and Conceptual Framework. In B. Christiansen (Ed.), *Handbook of Research on Global Supply Chain Management* (pp. 341–353). Hershey, PA: IGI Global. doi:10.4018/978-1-4666-9639-6.ch019

Liu, Z., Kim, H. M., & Zhang, K. (2016). Manufacturing and Logistics Networks of Korean Firms in China: A Case Study of Suzhou Industrial Park. In U. Aung & P. Ordoñez de Pablos (Eds.), *Managerial Strategies and Practice in the Asian Business Sector* (pp. 193–219). Hershey, PA: IGI Global. doi:10.4018/978-1-4666-9758-4.ch011

Lu, Y., Liu, Z., & Ma, L. (2016). Competing Through Logistics Management: Studies on E-Retailing in China. In S. Dixit & A. Sinha (Eds.), *E-Retailing Challenges and Opportunities in the Global Marketplace* (pp. 256–275). Hershey, PA: IGI Global. doi:10.4018/978-1-4666-9921-2.ch014

Maiga, A. S. (2016). Assessing the Impact of Supply Chain Integration on Firm Competitive Capability. *International Journal of Operations Research and Information Systems*, 7(1), 1–21. doi:10.4018/IJORIS.2016010101

Mangalaraj, G., & Amaravadi, C. S. (2016). The B2B Market Place: A Review and a Typology. In I. Lee (Ed.), *Encyclopedia of E-Commerce Development, Implementation, and Management* (pp. 905–915). Hershey, PA: IGI Global. doi:10.4018/978-1-4666-9787-4.ch064

Manotas-Duque, D. F., Osorio-Gómez, J. C., & Rivera, L. (2016). Operational Risk Management in Third Party Logistics (3PL). In G. Alor-Hernández, C. Sánchez-Ramírez, & J. García-Alcaraz (Eds.), *Handbook of Research on Managerial Strategies for Achieving Optimal Performance in Industrial Processes* (pp. 218–239). Hershey, PA: IGI Global. doi:10.4018/978-1-5225-0130-5.ch011

Manthou, V., Bialas, C., & Stefanou, C. J. (2016). Benefits and Barriers of E-Sourcing and E-Purchasing in the Healthcare Sector: A Case Study. In P. Papajorgji, F. Pinet, A. Guimarães, & J. Papathanasiou (Eds.), *Automated Enterprise Systems for Maximizing Business Performance* (pp. 71–87). Hershey, PA: IGI Global. doi:10.4018/978-1-4666-8841-4.ch005

Manzini, R., Accorsi, R., & Bortolini, M. (2012). Similarity-Based Cluster Analysis for the Cell Formation Problem. In V. Modrák & R. Pandian (Eds.), *Operations Management Research and Cellular Manufacturing Systems: Innovative Methods and Approaches* (pp. 140–163). Hershey, PA: IGI Global. doi:10.4018/978-1-61350-047-7.ch007

Marwah, A. K., Thakar, G., & Gupta, R. C. (2016). A New Approach to Supply Chain Performance Measurement: An Empirical Study of Manufacturing Organizations. In A. Dwivedi (Ed.), *Innovative Solutions for Implementing Global Supply Chains in Emerging Markets* (pp. 111–128). Hershey, PA: IGI Global. doi:10.4018/978-1-4666-9795-9.ch007

Modrák, V., Pandian, R. S., & Semanco, P. (2012). Alternative Heuristic Algorithm for Flow Shop Scheduling Problem. In V. Modrák & R. Pandian (Eds.), *Operations Management Research and Cellular Manufacturing Systems: Innovative Methods and Approaches* (pp. 277–297). Hershey, PA: IGI Global. doi:10.4018/978-1-61350-047-7.ch013

Modrák, V., & Semanco, P. (2012). Developments in Modern Operations Management and Cellular Manufacturing. In V. Modrák & R. Pandian (Eds.), *Operations Management Research and Cellular Manufacturing Systems: Innovative Methods and Approaches* (pp. 1–20). Hershey, PA: IGI Global. doi:10.4018/978-1-61350-047-7.ch001

Monios, J., & Bergqvist, R. (2016). A Life Cycle Framework for Governance of Intermodal Terminals: Planning, Operations, and Strategic Management. In T. Kramberger, V. Potočan, & V. Ipavec (Eds.), *Sustainable Logistics and Strategic Transportation Planning* (pp. 24–45). Hershey, PA: IGI Global. doi:10.4018/978-1-5225-0001-8.ch002

Nambiar, A. N., Imaev, A., Judd, R. P., & Carlo, H. J. (2012). Production Planning Models using Max-Plus Algebra. In V. Modrák & R. Pandian (Eds.), *Operations Management Research and Cellular Manufacturing Systems: Innovative Methods and Approaches* (pp. 227–257). Hershey, PA: IGI Global. doi:10.4018/978-1-61350-047-7.ch011

Narkhede, B. E. (2016). Linkages in Advanced Manufacturing Strategy: A Literature Review. *International Journal of Applied Management Sciences and Engineering*, *3*(1), 30–55. doi:10.4018/IJAMSE.2016010103

Ndede-Amadi, A. A. (2016). Student Interest in the IS Specialization as Predictor of the Success Potential of New Information Systems Programmes within the Schools of Business in Kenyan Public Universities. *International Journal of Information Systems and Social Change*, *7*(2), 63–79. doi:10.4018/IJISSC.2016040104

Ngai, E. W., Lam, S., Poon, J., Shen, B., & Moon, K. K. (2016). Design and Development of Intelligent Decision Support Prototype System for Social Media Competitive Analysis in Fashion Industry. *Journal of Organizational and End User Computing*, *28*(2), 13–32. doi:10.4018/JOEUC.2016040102

Orski, D. (2012). Application of Uncertain Variables to Knowledge-Based Resource Distribution. In Machine Learning: Concepts, Methodologies, Tools and Applications (pp. 928-950). Hershey, PA: IGI Global. doi:10.4018/978-1-60960-818-7.ch412

Panwar, N., Uniyal, D., & Rautela, K. S. (2016). Mapping Sustainable Tourism into Emergency Management Structure to Enhance Humanitarian Networks and Disaster Risk Reduction using Public-Private Partnerships (PPP) Initiatives in Himalayan States: The Global Supply Chain Issues and Strategies. In S. Joshi & R. Joshi (Eds.), *Designing and Implementing Global Supply Chain Management* (pp. 129–151). Hershey, PA: IGI Global. doi:10.4018/978-1-4666-9720-1.ch007

Polin, B. A., Troutt, M. D., & Acar, W. (2008). Supply Chain Globalization and the Complexities of Cost-Minimization Strategies. In F. Tan (Ed.), *Global Information Technologies: Concepts, Methodologies, Tools, and Applications* (pp. 2889–2904). Hershey, PA: IGI Global. doi:10.4018/978-1-59904-939-7.ch206

Priyan, S., & Uthayakumar, R. (2016). Operations Research in Healthcare Supply Chain Management Under Fuzzy-Stochastic Environment: Operations Research in Healthcare. In N. Anbazhagan (Ed.), *Stochastic Processes and Models in Operations Research* (pp. 271–314). Hershey, PA: IGI Global. doi:10.4018/978-1-5225-0044-5.ch016

Rangel, A. C., & Saucedo, I. J. (2016). A Review of the Main Options of Tools for Optimizing Operations (in Companies, Manufacturing, and Supply Chains). In A. Ochoa-Zezzatti, J. Sánchez, M. Cedillo-Campos, & M. de Lourdes (Eds.), *Handbook of Research on Military, Aeronautical, and Maritime Logistics and Operations* (pp. 408–421). Hershey, PA: IGI Global. doi:10.4018/978-1-4666-9779-9.ch021

Renna, P., & Ambrico, M. (2012). Performance Comparison of Cellular Manufacturing Configurations in Different Demand Profiles. In V. Modrák & R. Pandian (Eds.), *Operations Management Research and Cellular Manufacturing Systems: Innovative Methods and Approaches* (pp. 366–384). Hershey, PA: IGI Global. doi:10.4018/978-1-61350-047-7.ch017

Reza, J. R., Gayosso, D. G., Fernández, J. B., Macías, E. J., & Muro, J. C. (2016). SMED: A Literature Review from 1985 to 2015. In G. Alor-Hernández, C. Sánchez-Ramírez, & J. García-Alcaraz (Eds.), *Handbook of Research on Managerial Strategies for Achieving Optimal Performance in Industrial Processes* (pp. 386–404). Hershey, PA: IGI Global. doi:10.4018/978-1-5225-0130-5.ch018

Ribeiro, J. F. (2012). Design of Manufacturing Cells Based on Graph Theory. In V. Modrák & R. Pandian (Eds.), *Operations Management Research and Cellular Manufacturing Systems: Innovative Methods and Approaches* (pp. 53–67). Hershey, PA: IGI Global. doi:10.4018/978-1-61350-047-7.ch004

Ruhi, U., & Turel, O. (2006). Enabling the Glass Pipeline: The Infusion of Mobile Technology Applications in Supply Chain Management. In Y. Lan & B. Unhelkar (Eds.), *Global Integrated Supply Chain Systems* (pp. 291–309). Hershey, PA: IGI Global. doi:10.4018/978-1-59140-611-2.ch017

Sakaguchi, T., Nicovich, S. G., & Dibrell, C. C. (2006). Empirical Evaluation of an Integrated Supply Chain Model for Small and Medium Sized Firms. In M. Khosrow-Pour (Ed.), *Advanced Topics in Information Resources Management* (Vol. 5, pp. 211–231). Hershey, PA: IGI Global. doi:10.4018/978-1-59140-929-8.ch010

Sarang, J. P., Bhasin, H. V., Verma, R., & Kharat, M. G. (2016). Critical Success Factors for Supplier Development and Buyer Supplier Relationship: Exploratory Factor Analysis. *International Journal of Strategic Decision Sciences*, 7(1), 18–38. doi:10.4018/IJSDS.2016010102

Sarma, M., & Yen, D. C. (2007). Using SA for SAM Applications and Design: A Study of the Supply Chain Management Process. In A. Targowski & J. Tarn (Eds.), *Enterprise Systems Education in the 21st Century* (pp. 152–176). Hershey, PA: IGI Global. doi:10.4018/978-1-59904-349-4.ch010

Savita, K., Dominic, P., & Ramayah, T. (2016). The Drivers, Practices and Outcomes of Green Supply Chain Management: Insights from ISO14001 Manufacturing Firms in Malaysia. *International Journal of Information Systems and Supply Chain Management*, 9(2), 35–60. doi:10.4018/IJISSCM.2016040103

Shaikh, S. (2015). Sales and Operations Management in Contemporary Organizations. In E. Sabri (Ed.), *Optimization of Supply Chain Management in Contemporary Organizations* (pp. 176–197). Hershey, PA: IGI Global. doi:10.4018/978-1-4666-8228-3.ch007

Sharma, M., & Kumar, J. (2016). Operational Efficacy of 3PL in Reverse Logistics and Closed Loop Supply Chain: Service Quality Challenges in Emerging Markets. In S. Joshi & R. Joshi (Eds.), *Designing and Implementing Global Supply Chain Management* (pp. 106–128). Hershey, PA: IGI Global. doi:10.4018/978-1-4666-9720-1.ch006

Shaverdi, M., Ramezani, I., & Rostamy, A. A. (2016). Multi-Criteria Decision Making Models for Sustainable and Green Supply Chain Management Based on Fuzzy Approach. In A. Kumar & M. Dash (Eds.), *Fuzzy Optimization and Multi-Criteria Decision Making in Digital Marketing* (pp. 291–307). Hershey, PA: IGI Global. doi:10.4018/978-1-4666-8808-7.ch013

Shou, Y., Li, Y., & Wu, L. (2016). Antecedents of Collaborative Arrangements in the Innovation and Production System. In L. Al-Hakim, X. Wu, A. Koronios, & Y. Shou (Eds.), *Handbook of Research on Driving Competitive Advantage through Sustainable, Lean, and Disruptive Innovation* (pp. 534–558). Hershey, PA: IGI Global. doi:10.4018/978-1-5225-0135-0.ch022

Slomp, J., & Bokhorst, J. A. (2012). Decision Support Framework for the Selection of a Layout Type. In V. Modrák & R. Pandian (Eds.), *Operations Management Research and Cellular Manufacturing Systems: Innovative Methods and Approaches* (pp. 21–36). Hershey, PA: IGI Global. doi:10.4018/978-1-61350-047-7.ch002

Smith, A. D. (2016). Exploring RFID Healthcare Operational Strategies. In I. Lee (Ed.), *Encyclopedia of E-Commerce Development, Implementation, and Management* (pp. 1813–1824). Hershey, PA: IGI Global. doi:10.4018/978-1-4666-9787-4.ch128

Smith, A. D. (2016). Inventory Shrinkage and Corrective RFID and Management Strategies. In I. Lee (Ed.), *Encyclopedia of E-Commerce Development, Implementation, and Management* (pp. 1825–1840). Hershey, PA: IGI Global. doi:10.4018/978-1-4666-9787-4.ch129

Sood, T. (2016). Trimming Safety Stock: Empirically, Realizing Working Capital Gains. In N. Kamath & S. Saurav (Eds.), *Handbook of Research on Strategic Supply Chain Management in the Retail Industry* (pp. 250–268). Hershey, PA: IGI Global. doi:10.4018/978-1-4666-9894-9.ch014

Süer, G. A., & Alhawari, O. (2012). Operator Assignment Decisions in a Highly Dynamic Cellular Environment. In V. Modrák & R. Pandian (Eds.), *Operations Management Research and Cellular Manufacturing Systems: Innovative Methods and Approaches* (pp. 258–276). Hershey, PA: IGI Global. doi:10.4018/978-1-61350-047-7.ch012

Süer, G. A., & Lobo, R. (2012). Comparison of Connected vs. Disconnected Cellular Systems: A Case Study. In V. Modrák & R. Pandian (Eds.), *Operations Management Research and Cellular Manufacturing Systems: Innovative Methods and Approaches* (pp. 37–52). Hershey, PA: IGI Global. doi:10.4018/978-1-61350-047-7.ch003

Susanto, H., & Almunawar, M. N. (2016). Security and Privacy Issues in Cloud-Based E-Government. In Z. Mahmood (Ed.), *Cloud Computing Technologies for Connected Government* (pp. 292–321). Hershey, PA: IGI Global. doi:10.4018/978-1-4666-8629-8.ch012

Tambo, T., & Mikkelsen, O. E. (2016). Fashion Supply Chain Optimization: Linking Make-to-Order Purchasing and B2B E-Commerce. In S. Joshi & R. Joshi (Eds.), *Designing and Implementing Global Supply Chain Management* (pp. 1–21). Hershey, PA: IGI Global. doi:10.4018/978-1-4666-9720-1.ch001

Truong, D., & Jitbaipoon, T. (2016). How Can Agile Methodologies Be Used to Enhance the Success of Information Technology Projects? *International Journal of Information Technology Project Management*, 7(2), 1–16. doi:10.4018/IJITPM.2016040101

Udomleartprasert, P., & Jungthirapanich, C. (2006). The Critical Success Factors in Supply Chain Implementation. In Y. Lan & B. Unhelkar (Eds.), *Global Integrated Supply Chain Systems* (pp. 272–290). Hershey, PA: IGI Global. doi:10.4018/978-1-59140-611-2.ch016

Van Eenoo, C. (2006). A Framework for Analyzing Information Systems in an Integrated Supply Chain Environment: The Interaction Approach. In Y. Lan & B. Unhelkar (Eds.), *Global Integrated Supply Chain Systems* (pp. 125–138). Hershey, PA: IGI Global. doi:10.4018/978-1-59140-611-2.ch008

Venkumar, P., & Sekar, K. (2012). Design of Cellular Manufacturing System Using Non-Traditional Optimization Algorithms. In V. Modrák & R. Pandian (Eds.), *Operations Management Research and Cellular Manufacturing Systems: Innovative Methods and Approaches* (pp. 99–139). Hershey, PA: IGI Global. doi:10.4018/978-1-61350-047-7.ch006

Verbraeck, A., Tewoldeberhan, T., & Janssen, M. (2006). E-Supply Chain Orchestration. In M. Khosrow-Pour (Ed.), *Encyclopedia of E-Commerce, E-Government, and Mobile Commerce* (pp. 457–463). Hershey, PA: IGI Global. doi:10.4018/978-1-59140-799-7.ch075

Wagner, C., & Ryan, C. (2016). Physical and Digital Integration Strategies of Electronic Device Supply Chains and Their Applicability to ETO Supply Chains. In R. Addo-Tenkorang, J. Kantola, P. Helo, & A. Shamsuzzoha (Eds.), *Supply Chain Strategies and the Engineer-to-Order Approach* (pp. 224–245). Hershey, PA: IGI Global. doi:10.4018/978-1-5225-0021-6.ch011

Wan, Y. (2016). Designing and Managing ERP Systems for Virtual Enterprise Strategy: A Conceptual Framework for Innovative Strategic Thinking. In C. Graham (Ed.), *Strategic Management and Leadership for Systems Development in Virtual Spaces* (pp. 160–195). Hershey, PA: IGI Global. doi:10.4018/978-1-4666-9688-4.ch010

Wang, X., & Wood, L. C. (2016). The Influence of Supply Chain Sustainability Practices on Suppliers. In B. Christiansen (Ed.), *Handbook of Research on Global Supply Chain Management* (pp. 531–544). Hershey, PA: IGI Global. doi:10.4018/978-1-4666-9639-6.ch030

Yaokumah, W. (2016). Investigation into the State-of-Practice of Operations Security Management Based on ISO/IEC 27002. *International Journal of Technology Diffusion*, 7(1), 51–70. doi:10.4018/IJTD.2016010104

Zailani, S., & Rajagopal, P. (2007). The Effects of Information Quality on Supply Chain Performance: New Evidence from Malaysia. In L. Al-Hakim (Ed.), *Information Quality Management: Theory and Applications* (pp. 275–291). Hershey, PA: IGI Global. doi:10.4018/978-1-59904-024-0.ch012

Compilation of References

Abramson, J. S. (1990). Making teams works. *Social Work with Groups*, *12*(4), 45–63. doi:10.1300/J009v12n04_04

Abramson, J. S., & Bronstein, L. R. (2004). Group Process Dynamics & Skills in Interdisciplinary Teamwork. In C. Garvin, M. Galinsky, & L. Gutierrez (Eds.), *Group Work Handbook*. Guilford Press.

Accenture too drops bell shaped curve appraisals. (2015). Retrieved on May 20, 2017, from http://economictimes.indiatimes.com/news/international/business/accenture-too-drops-bell-curve-appraisals/articleshow/48230902.cms

Adams, R. B., & Ferreira, D. (2009). Women in the boardroom and their impact on governance and performance. *Journal of Financial Economics*, *94*(2), 291–309.

African Development Bank. (2015). *Where are the women:Inclusive Boardrooms in Africa'stop listed companies?* Author.

Afzalur, R. M. (2010). *Managing conflict in organizations*. Transaction Publishers.

Ahadi, S., & Suandi, T. (2014). Structural Empowerment and Organizational Commitment: The Mediating Role of Psychological Empowerment in Malaysian Research Universities. *Journal of Asian Development Studies*, *3*(1), 44–65.

Ahern, K. R., & Dittmar, A. K. (2012). The changing of the boards: The impact on firm valuation of mandated female board representation. *The Quarterly Journal of Economics*, *127*(1), 137–197. doi:10.1093/qje/qjr049

Ahmad, N., & Oranye, N. O. (2010). Empowerment, Job Satisfaction and Organizational Commitment: A Comparative Analysis of Nurses Working In Malaysia and England. *Journal of Nursing Management*, *18*(5), 582–591. doi:10.1111/j.1365-2834.2010.01093.x PMID:20636507

Ahmadreza, I., Ebraza, A., & Afsar, K. M. A. (2014). Analysis of different HRM policies Effect on Organization Knowledge Level. *Research Journal of Recent Sciences*, *3*(3), 12–22.

Ahmed, S. M., Petzold, M., Kabir, Z. N., & Tomson, G. (2006). Targeted intervention for the ultra poor in rural Bangladesh: Does it make any difference in their health-seeking behaviour? *Social Science & Medicine*, *63*(11), 2899–2911. doi:10.1016/j.socscimed.2006.07.024 PMID:16954049

Alas, R. (2006). Ethics in countries with different cultural dimensions. *Journal of Business Ethics*, *69*(3), 237–247. doi:10.1007/s10551-006-9088-3

Alas, R., & Vadi, M. (2006). The impact of organisational culture on organisational learning and attitudes concerning change from an institutional perspective. *International Journal of Strategic Change Management*, *1*(1-2), 155–170. doi:10.1504/IJSCM.2006.011109

Albanese, J. (2017). *What You Need to Know About AL in the Workplace*. Retrieved April, 2017, from http//:www.inc.org

Alderfer, C. P. (1977). *"Groups and Intergroup Relations," Improving Life at Work* (J. R. Hackman & J. L. Suttle, Eds.). Santa Monica, CA: Goodyear.

Ali, H.M., &Yangaiya, S.A. (2015). Distributed Leadership and Empowerment Influence on Teachers Organizational Commitment. *Academic Journal of Interdisciplinary Studies*, *4*(1).

Allen, R. E. (2008). Predictors of Organizational Commitment in College Students. *Dissertation Abstracts International*, *68*(7).

Allen, R. S., Dawson, G., Wheatley, K., & White, C. S. (2007). Perceived diversity and organisational performance. *Employee Relations*, *30*(1), 20–33. doi:10.1108/01425450810835392

Allen, T. D. (2001). Family-supportive work environments: The role of organizational perceptions. *Journal of Vocational Behavior*, *58*(3), 414–435. doi:10.1006/jvbe.2000.1774

Amagoh, F. (2009). Leadership development and leadership effectiveness. *Management Decision*, *47*(6), 989–999. doi:10.1108/00251740910966695

Amaram, D. I. (2011). Cultural diversity: Implications for workplace management. *Journal of Diversity Management*, *2*(4), 1–6. doi:10.19030/jdm.v2i4.5017

Ambler, T., & Barrow, S. (1996). The Employer Brand. *Journal of Brand Management*, *4*(3), 185–206. doi:10.1057/bm.1996.42

American Society for Training and Development (ASTD). (1996a). *ASTD buyer's guide &consultant directory*. Alexandria, VA: Author.

Anand, N. (2016). *Axis bank moves away from bell curve system*. Retrieved on May 21, 2017, from http://www.business-standard.com/article/economy-policy/axis-bank-moves-away-from-bell-curve-system-116021700035

Anand, R. (2013, February 26). *How Diversity and Inclusion Drive Employee Engagement*. Princeton, NJ: Academic Press.

Anaza, N. A., Anaza, N. A., Nowlin, E. L., Nowlin, E. L., Wu, G. J., & Wu, G. J. (2016). Staying engaged on the job: The role of emotional labor, job resources, and customer orientation. *European Journal of Marketing*, *50*(7/8), 1470–1492. doi:10.1108/EJM-11-2014-0682

Anderson, W., & Bostian, B. (2001). *Minority Employment Trends*. St. Petersburg, FL: Human Resource Institute.

Annual Report of Torrent Pharmaceuticals. (2016) Retrieved on May 14, 2017, from http://www.torrentpharma.com/download/financials/annual_report/AR-2015-16.pdf

AON. (2017). *Insights from Best Employers 2016*. Retrieved from http://aonhewitt.co.in/Home/Aon-Best-Employers-India/insights/Insights-from-2016/Case-studies

Apple. (2017). *Inclusion and Diversity*. Retrieved 08 14, 2017, from https://www.apple.com/diversity/: https://www.apple.com/diversity/

Appraisals: Companies across sectors on what they did to make performance appraisal a win-win process. (2017). Retrieved on May 10, 2017, from http://economictimes.indiatimes.com/jobs/appraisals-companies-across-sectors-on-what-they-did-to-make-performance-appraisal-a-win-win-process/articleshow/58056096.cms

April, K., & Blass, E. (2010). Measuring Diversity Practice And Developing Inclusion. *Dimensions*, *1*(1), 59–66.

April, K., & Shockley, M. (2007). *Diversity: New Realities in a Changing World*. Basingstoke, UK: Palgrave Macmillan. doi:10.1057/9780230627529

Arakawa, D., & Greenberg, M. (2007). Optimistic managers and the influence on productivity and employee engagement in a technology organization: Implications for coaching psychologists. *International Coaching Psychology Review*, *2*(1), 78–89.

Ararat, M., Alkan, S., & Aytekin, B. (2016). *Women on Board Turkey*. doi:10.5900/SU_SOM_WP.2016.29132

Armendáriz, B., & Morduch, J. (2010). *The economics of microfinance*. MIT Press.

Arnott, D. H. (1995). The five lenses of leadership. *The Journal of Leadership Studies*, *2*(1), 137–141. doi:10.1177/107179199500200112

Arntz, M., Gregory, T., & Zierahn, U. (2016). *The Risk of Automation for Jobs in OECD Countries: A Comparative Analysis*. OECD Social, Employment and Migration Working Papers, 189. OECD Publishing. 10.1787/5jlz9h56dvq7-en

Aronson, E., Vilson, T., & Akert, R. (2013). *Socijalna psihologija, peto izdanje*. Zagreb: Mate.

Arredondo, P. (1996). *Successful diversity management initiatives: A blueprint for planning and implementation*. Thousand Oaks, CA: Sage.

Arvey, R., McCall, T., & Bouchard, T. (1997). Genetic Influences on Job Satisfaction and Work Values. *Personality and Individual Differences*, *7*(2).

Aryee, S. (1992). Antecedents and outcomes of work-family conflict among married professional women: Evidence from Singapore. *Human Relations*, *45*(8), 813–837. doi:10.1177/001872679204500804

ASTD. (1996b). *National report on human resources*. Alexandria, VA: Author.

Avery, D. R., McKay, P. F., & Wilson, D. C. (2007). Engaging the aging workforce: The relationship between perceived age similarity, satisfaction with coworkers, and employee engagement. *The Journal of Applied Psychology*, *92*(6), 25–42. doi:10.1037/0021-9010.92.6.1542 PMID:18020795

Avigdor, A., Deborah, B., Jennifer, K., Daniel, K., & Bernardo, M. F. (2007). Workgroup inclusion, diversity, and performance. *Gender and Diversity in Organizations Division Academy of Management*, *2007*, 1–24.

Avruch, K. (1998). *Culture & conflict resolution* (Vol. 31). US Institute of Peace Press.

Avruch, K., Black, P., & Scimecca, J. (Eds.). (1998). *Conflict Resolution: Cross-Cultural Perspectives*. New York: Praeger.

Badal, S., & Harter, J. K. (2013). Gender Diversity, Business-Unit Engagement, and Performance. *Journal of Leadership & Organizational Studies*, *21*(4), 354–365. doi:10.1177/1548051813504460

Baer, M., Kempf, A., & Ruenzi, S. (2006). *Determinants and consequences of team management in the mutual fund industry*. Working Paper.

Baker, E. L. (1980). Managing organizational culture. *Management Review*, *69*(7), 8–13.

Bakhtiari, S. (2006). Microfinance and poverty reduction: Some international evidence. *International Business & Economics Research Journal*, *5*(12).

Bakker, A. B., Demerouti, E., Taris, T. W., Schaufeli, W. B., & Schreurs, P. J. (2003). A multigroup analysis of the job demands-resources model in four home care organizations. *International Journal of Stress Management*, *10*(1), 16–38. doi:10.1037/1072-5245.10.1.16

Bakker, A., & Demerouti, E. (2008). Towards a model of work engagement. *Career Development International*, *13*(3), 209–223. doi:10.1108/13620430810870476

Bani, M., Yasoureini, M., & Mesgarpour, A. (2014). A Study on Relationship between Employees' Psychological Empowerment and Organizational Commitment. *Management Science Letters*, *4*(6), 1197–1200. doi:10.5267/j.msl.2014.5.007

Banking sector in India. (2017). Retrieved on May 29, 2017, from https://www.ibef.org/industry/banking-india.aspx

Barber, A. E., & Daly, C. L. (1996). Compensation and diversity: new pay for a new workforce? In E. E. Kossek & S. A. Lobel (Eds.), *Managing Diversity: Human Resource Strategies for Transforming the Workplace*. Cambridge, UK: Blackwell.

Barna, G. (1994). Virtual America. *Regal*, *83*, 283.

Barrow, S., & Mosley, R. (2011). *The employer brand: Bringing the best of brand management to people at work*. John Wiley & Sons.

Basargekar, P. (2013). Can Human Resource challenges halt the growth of Microfinance in India. *Indian Journal of Management Science*, *3*(1).

Batra, V. (2012). The State of Microfinance in India: Emergence, Delivery Models and Issues. *Journal of International Economics, 3*(1).

Baumruk, R. (2004). The missing link: The role of employee engagement in business success. *Workspan, 47*, 48–52.

Bear, D., & Bostian, B. (2002). *The Generations at Work.* St Petersburg, FL: Human Resource Institute.

Becker, E. (2015, April 8). *Team Building and Group Dynamics.* Retrieved from https://www.td.org/Publications/Magazines/TD/TD-Archive/2015/04/Team-Building-and-Group-Dynamics

Becker, H., & Fritzsche, D. J. (1987). A comparison of ethical behaviour of American, French and German managers. *The Columbia Journal of World Business, 22*(4), 87–95.

Beilinson, J. (1991). How one company invites workforce 2000 to its door. *Management Review, 5*(3), 1–3.

Bennett, R. J., & Robinson, S. L. (2000). Development of a measure of workplace deviance. *The Journal of Applied Psychology, 85*(3), 349–360. doi:10.1037/0021-9010.85.3.349 PMID:10900810

Benschop, Y. (2001). Pride, prejudice and performance: Relations between HRM, diversity and performance. *International Journal of Human Resource Management, 12*(7), 1166–1181. doi:10.1080/09585190110068377

Berg, P., Kalleberg, A. L., & Appelbaum, E. (2003). Balancing Work and Family: The Role of High Commitment Environments. *Industrial Relations, 42*(2), 168–188. doi:10.1111/1468-232X.00286

Berry, L. L., & Parasuraman, A. (2004). Marketing services: Competing through quality. Simon and Schuster.

Berry, M. L., & Morris, M. L. (2008). The impact of employee engagement factors and job satisfaction on turnover intent. In T. J. Chermack (Ed.), *Academy of Human Resource Development International Research Conference in the Americas* (pp. 1-3). Panama City, FL: AHRD.

Berthon, P., Ewing, M., & Hah, L. L. (2005). Captivating company: Dimensions of attractiveness in employer branding. *International Journal of Advertising, 24*(2), 151–172. doi:10.1080/02650487.2005.11072912

Bertrand, M., Black, S. E., Jensen, S., & Lleras-Muney, A. (2014). *Breaking the glass ceiling? The effect of board quotas on female labor market outcomes in Norway.* National Bureau of Economic Research. Retrieved from http://www.nber.org/papers/w20256

Best practices: Talent assessment methodologies by Cadila healthcare. (2016). Retrieved on April 21, 2017, from https://www.peoplematters.in/article/talent-acquisition/best-practices-talent-assessment-methodologies-cadila-healthcare-12765

Bezrukova, K., Jehn, K. A., & Spell, C. S. (2012). Reviewing diversity training: Where we have been and where we should go. *Academy of Management Learning & Education, 11*(2), 207–227. doi:10.5465/amle.2008.0090

Bhadoria, V., Bhajanka, A., Chakraborty, K., & Mitra, P. (2012). *India pharma 2020: Propelling access and acceptance, realizing true potential.* McKinsey & Co.

Bilkis, A., Habib, S. B., & Sharmin, T. (2010). A review of discrimination in employment and workplace. *ASA University Review,* 137-150.

Black, B., & Holden, W. (1998). The Impact of gender on Productivity and Satisfaction Among Medical School Psychologist. *Journal of Clinical Psychology in Medical Settings, 3*(1).

BlackRock. (2015). *Achieving Gender Diversity in Australia: The Ugly.* The Bad and The Good.

Blanding, M. (2013). *How Cultural Conflict undermines workplace creativity.* Retrieved from https://www.forbes.com/sites/hbsworkingknowledge/2013/12/09/how-cultural-conflict-undermines-workplace-creativity/#367bbfb6214f

Blasco, M., Feldt, L. E., & Jakobsen, M. (2012). If only cultural chameleons could fly too: A critical discussion of the concept of cultural intelligence. *International Journal of Cross Cultural Management, 12*(2), 229–245. doi:10.1177/1470595812439872

Boal, K. B., & Hooijberg, R. (2001). Strategic leadership research: Moving on. *The Leadership Quarterly, 11*(4), 515–549. doi:10.1016/S1048-9843(00)00057-6

Bock, H., & Greco, C. (2002). *Implementing a Beneficially Diverse Organization.* Academic Press.

Bojanović, R. (1999). *Psihologija međuljudskih odnosa.* Centar za primenjenu psihologiju.

Bordin, C., & Casinir, T. B. G. (2007). The Antecedents and Consequences of Psychological Empowerment among Singaporean IT Employees. *Management Research News, 30.*

Bozionelos, N., & Nikolaou, I. (2010). Does treating the permanent workforce well matter to temporary employees? *The Academy of Management Perspectives, 24*(1), 84–86. doi:10.5465/AMP.2010.50304422

Branson, D. M. (2006). *No seat at the table: How corporate governance and law keep women out of the boardroom.* New York: NYU Press.

Brieger, S. A., Francoeur, C., Welzel, C., & Ben-Amar, W. (2017). Empowering Women: The Role of Emancipative Forces in Board Gender Diversity. *Journal of Business Ethics,* 1–17.

Broek, M. (2015). *From employer attractiveness to employer branding: Results of a mixed methods research.* Retrieved on August 15, 2017 from http://essay.utwente.nl/66622/7/Broek_BA_MB.pdf

Brondolo, E., Rahim, R., Grimaldi, S. J., Ashraf, A., Bui, N., & Schwartz, J. C. (2015). Place of birth effects on self reported discrimination: Variations by type of discrimination. *International Journal of Intercultural Relations, 49,* 212–222. doi:10.1016/j.ijintrel.2015.10.001 PMID:27647943

Brooks, S. (2015). *A Brief History of Performance Management*. Retrieved on May 22, 2017, from https://www.peoplehr.com/blog/index.php/2015/03/25/a-brief-history-of-performance-management/

Brown, S. P., & Leigh, T. W. (1996). A new look at psychological climate and its relationship to job involvement, effort, and performance. *The Journal of Applied Psychology*, *81*(4), 359–368. doi:10.1037/0021-9010.81.4.358 PMID:8751453

Brynjolfsson, E., & McAfee, A. (2011). *Race against the machine: How the digital revolution is accelerating innovation, driving productivity, and irreversibly transforming employment and the economy*. Lexington, MA: Digital Frontier Press.

Buchwald, A., & Hottenrott, H. (2015). Women on the Board and Executive Duration–Evidence for European Listed Firms. *ZEW, 178*. Retrieved from https://ssrn.com/abstract=2580776

Buckingham, M., & Coffiman, C. (2003). *First, Break All the Rules: What the Worlds Greates managers Do Differentialy*. New York: Simon & Schuster.

Bunny. (2007, September 13). *Bunny's Story. Starbucks Barista Victimized by Age Discrimination. Industrial Workers of the World*. Retrieved 04 12, 2017, from http://www.iww.org/node/3649

Burke, P. J., & Reitzes, D. C. (1991). An identity theory approach to commitment. *Social Psychology Quarterly*, 239–251.

Burke, R. J. (1996). Why aren't more women on corporate boards?: Views of women directors. *Psychological Reports*, *79*(3), 840–842. doi:10.2466/pr0.1996.79.3.840

Burke, R. J. (2003). Women on corporate boards of directors: The timing is right. *Women in Management Review*, *18*(7), 346–348. doi:10.1108/09649420310498966

Burpitt, W. J., & Bigoness, W. J. (1997). Leadership and innovation among teams: The impact of empowerment. *Small Group Research*, *28*(3), 414–423. doi:10.1177/1046496497283005

Bush, T., & Glover, D. (2003). *Leadership development: A literature review*. Nottingham, UK: National College for School Leadership.

Businesstoday. (2014a). *Microsoft is the most attractive employer in India, finds Randstad survey*. Retrieved on June 28, 2017, from http://www.businesstoday.in/current/corporate/microsoft-is-most-attractive-employer-in-india-randstad-survey/story/205253.html

Businesstoday. (2014b). *The best companies to work for.* Retrieved on May 25, 2017, from http://www.businesstoday.in/magazine/cover-story/business-today-peoplestrong-best-companies-to-work-for-2013/story/208130.html

Butt, J., & Neil, A. O. (2004). *'Let's Move On' Black and Minority Ethnic older people's views on research findings*. Layerthorpe: Joseph Rowntree Foundation.

Caligiuri, P., & Tarique, I. (2012). Dynamic cross-cultural competencies and global leadership effectiveness. *Journal of World Business*, *47*(4), 612–622. doi:10.1016/j.jwb.2012.01.014

Campbell-Kelly, M. (2009). Origin of computing. *Scientific American Magazine*, *301*(3), 62–69. doi:10.1038/scientificamerican0909-62 PMID:19708529

Cappelli, P., Singh, H., Singh, J. V., & Useem, M. (2010). Leadership lessons from India. *Harvard Business Review*, *88*(3), 90–97. PMID:20402052

Carlson, D. S., Kacmar, K. M., & Williams, L. J. (2000). Construction and initial validation of a multidimensional measure of work-family conflict. *Journal of Vocational Behavior*, *56*(2), 249–276.

Carnevale, A. P., & Stone. (1994). Diversity beyond the golden rule. *Training & Development*, *49*(10), 22–39.

Carnevale, A. P., & Stone, S. C. (1995). *The American mosaic*. New York: McGraw-Hill.

Caroselli, M. (2015). *Leadership Skills For Managers*. Zagreb: Mate.

Carr, C. (1993). Diversity and performance: A shotgun marriage? *Performance Improvement Quarterly*, (6): 115–126.

Carter, D. A., D'Souza, F., Simkins, B. J., & Simpson, W. G. (2010). The gender and ethnic diversity of US boards and board committees and financial performance. *Corporate Governance*, *18*(5), 396–414. doi:10.1111/j.1467-8683.2010.00809.x

Cascio, W. F. (1998). *Managing human resources*. Boston: McGraw Hill.

Catalyst. (2011). *2011 Catalyst Census: Fortune 500 Women Board Directors*. Author.

Caudron, S. (1990). Monsanto responds to diversity. *The Personnel Journal*, *69*(11), 71–77.

Caudron, S. (1992). U.S. West finds strength in diversity. *The Personnel Journal*, *71*(3), 40–44.

Certo, S., & Certo, T. (2008). *Modern management* (10th ed.). MATE.

CGAP. (2009). *Microfinance and the Financial Crisis*. Retrieved from http://www.cgap.org/gm/document1.9.7439/CGAP%20Virtual%20Conference%202008%20Summary.pdf

Chalofsky, N., & Krishna, V. (2009). Meaningfulness, commitment, and engagement: The intersection of a deeper level of intrinsic motivation. *Advances in Developing Human Resources*, *11*(2), 189–203. doi:10.1177/1523422309333147

Chan, D. K. S., & Goto, S. G. (2003). Conflict resolution in the culturally diverse workplace: Some data from Hong Kong employees. *Applied Psychology*, *52*(3), 441–460. doi:10.1111/1464-0597.00143

Chandhana, K., & Easow, D. T. (2015). Performance Appraisal Method Used in Top 10 IT Companies-360 Degree Feedback & Balanced Score Card: A Review. *Bonfring International Journal of Industrial Engineering and Management Science*, *5*(2), 73.

Chaput, A. (2012). *The impact of the use of favoritism on work groups*. Schmidt Labor Research Center Seminar Series.

Chatman, J. A., & Flynn, F. J. (2001). The influence of demographic heterogeneity on the emergence and consequences of cooperative norms in work teams. *Academy of Management Journal*, *44*(5), 956–974. doi:10.2307/3069440

Chaudhary, N. S. (2017). *Cross Cultural Diversity Boon or Bane?* Retrieved August, 23, 2017 from https://www.peoplematters.in/article/culture/cross-cultural-diversity-boon-or-bane-16070

Chelliah, J., & Chelliah, J. (2017). Will artificial intelligence usurp white collar jobs? *Human Resource Management International Digest*, *25*(3), 1–3. doi:10.1108/HRMID-11-2016-0152

Chen, Y., Tjosvold, D., & Fang, S. S. (2005). Working with foreign managers: Conflict management for effective leader relationships in China. *International Journal of Conflict Management*, *16*(3), 265–286. doi:10.1108/eb022932

Chew, E. W., Lee, K. M., Tan, S. C., & Tee, S. F. (2011). *The effects of workforce diversity towards the employee performance in an organization* (Doctoral dissertation). UTAR.

Chhabra, T. N. (2008). *Human resource management: concepts and issues*. Delhi: Dhanpat Rai & Co.

Chitramani, P., & Deepa, S. (2013). Employer Branding: A Case on Selected Indian IT companies. *Asia Pacific Journal of Marketing & Management Review*, *2*(5), 133–141.

Choan, P. S. (2003). *Value leadership: The seven principles that drive corporate value in any economic*. Academic Press.

Cho, J., Laschinger, H. K. S., & Wong, C. (2006). Workplace Empowerment, Work Engagement and Organizational Commitment of New Graduate Nurses. *Canadian Journal of Nursing Leadership*, *19*(3), 43–60. doi:10.12927/cjnl.2006.18368 PMID:17039996

Choudhary, A. I., Akhtar, S. A., & Zaheer, A. (2012). Impact of Transformational and Servant Leadership on Organizational Performance: A Comparative Analysis. *Journal of Business Ethics*, *116*(2), 433–440. doi:10.1007/s10551-012-1470-8

Chowdhury, T. G., & Coulter, R. A. (2006). Getting a "sense" of financial security for generation Y. *Marketing Theory and Applications*, 191-192.

Christian, M. S., Garza, A. S., & Slaughter, J. E. (2011). Work engagement: A quantitative review and test of its relations with and contextual performance. *Personnel Psychology*, *64*(1), 89–136. doi:10.1111/j.1744-6570.2010.01203.x

Christiansen, L., Lin, H., Pereira, J., Topalova, P. B., & Turk, R. (2016). Gender diversity in senior positions and firm performance: Evidence from Europe. *IMF Working Papers*, 1-29.

Chrobot-Mason, D., & Aramovich, N. P. (2013). The psychological benefits of creating an affirming climate for workplace diversity. *Group & Organization Management*, *38*(6), 659–689. doi:10.1177/1059601113509835

Chuang, S. F. (2013). *Essential skills for leadership effectiveness in diverse workplace development.* Academic Press.

Chua, R. Y. (2013). The costs of ambient cultural disharmony: Indirect intercultural conflicts in social environment undermine creativity. *Academy of Management Journal, 56*(6), 1545–1577. doi:10.5465/amj.2011.0971

Churchard, C. (2011). Boardroom quotas fail to convince senior women. *People Management,* 6.

Churchill, C. (1997). Managing growth: The organizational architecture of microfinance institutions. *USAID Microenterprise Best Practices Project Paper, 7,* 26–81.

CIPD. (2016). *Chartered Institute of Personnel and Development.* Retrieved from http://www.cipd.co.uk

Coleman, B. E. (2006). Microfinance in Northeast Thailand: Who benefits and how much? *World Development, 34*(9), 1612–1638. doi:10.1016/j.worlddev.2006.01.006

Combs, J., Liu, Y., Hall, A., & Ketchen, D. (2006). How much do high-performance work practices matter? A meta-analysis of their effects on organizational performance. *Personnel Psychology, 59*(3), 501–528. doi:10.1111/j.1744-6570.2006.00045.x

Comi, S., Grasseni, M., Origo, F., & Pagani, L. (2016, September 30). Quotas have led to more women on corporate boards in Europe. *LSE Business Review.* Retrieved from http://blogs.lse.ac.uk

Comi, S., Grasseni, M., Origo, F., & Pagani, L. (2016a). *Where Women Make the Difference. The Effects of Corporate Board Gender-Quotas on Firms' Performance Across Europe.* ESPE. Retrieved from https://editorialexpress.com

Conlon, D. E., Porter, C. O., & Parks, J. M. (2004). The fairness of decision rules. *Journal of Management, 30*(3), 329–349.

Cook, M., & Jaggers, T. (2005). Strategies for staff retention. *Exchanging Views Series, 3.*

Cooper, K., & Lee, G. (2009). Managing the dynamics of projects and changes at Fluor. *Conference of the System Dynamics Society. In Proceedings from the 27th International Conference of the System Dynamics Society,* 1-27.

Corruption Perceptions Index. 2016. (n.d.). Retrieved from https://www.transparency.org/news/feature/corruption_perceptions_index_2016

Cortina, M., & Wasti, S. (2005). Profiles in Coping: Responses to Sexual Harassment Across Persons, Organizations and Cultures. *The Journal of Applied Psychology, 2*(8).

Cox Jr, T. (1991). The multicultural organization. *The Executive,* 34-47.

Cox, T. H., & Blake, S. (1991). Managing cultural diversity: Implications for organizational competitiveness. *The Executive,* 45-56.

Compilation of References

Cranford, S., & Glover, S. (2007). Challenge match: The stakes grow higher for global leaders. *Leadership in Action*, *27*(3), 9–14. doi:10.1002/lia.1207

Crawford, E. R., LePine, J. A., & Rich, B. L. (2010). *Linking job demands and resources to employee engagement and burnout: a theoretical extension and meta-analytic test*. Academic Press.

Cridland, C. (2014). *How You Can Build a Positive Workplace Culture*. Retrieved April, 2017, from http//:www.mindfulmeditation.com

Crook, C. R. (2010). Rethinking Civil Service Reform in African Islands of Effectiveness and Organizational Commitment. *Commonwealth and Comparative Politics*, *48*(4), 479–504. doi:10.1080/14662043.2010.522037

Cummins, P. G., & O'Boyle, I. (2014, Fall). Leading through others: Social identity theory in the organisational setting. *Organization Development Journal*.

Cunningham, G. B. (2009). The moderating effect of diversity strategy on the relationship between racial diversity and organisational performance. *Journal of Applied Social Psychology*, *39*(6), 1445–1460. doi:10.1111/j.1559-1816.2009.00490.x

Czarnowsky, M. (2008). *Learning's role in employee engagement: An ASTD research Study*. Alexandria, VA: American Society for Training & Development.

Daft, R. L. (2011). The Leadership Experience (5th ed.). Cengage Learning.

Dalton, D. R., & Dalton, C. M. (2008). On the progress of corporate women: less a glass ceiling than a bottleneck? In S. Vinnicombe, V. Singh, R. J. Burke, D. Bilimoria, & M. Huse (Eds.), *Women on Corporate Board of Directors International Research and Practice* (pp. 184–197). Cheltenham, UK: Edward Elgar. doi:10.4337/9781848445192.00025

Daniel, S., Agarwal, R., & Stewart, K. J. (2013). The effects of diversity in global, distributed collectives: A study of open source project success. *Information Systems Research*, *24*(2), 312–333. doi:10.1287/isre.1120.0435

Danserau, F., & Alluto, J. A. (1990). Level-of-analysis issues in climate and culture research. In B. Schneider (Ed.), *Organizational Climate and Culture* (pp. 193–236). San Francisco, CA: Jossey Bass.

Dansereau, F., Alluto, I. A., & Yammarino, F. J. (1984). *Theory testing in organizational behavior: The varient approach*. Englewood Cliffs, NJ: Prentice Hall.

Darden, C. (2004). Legacy leadership. *Executive Excellence*, *21*(5), 11–12.

Das, A. (2017). *Infosys releases 9,000 employees with automation in 2016*. Retrieved on August 13, 2017 from http://timesofindia.indiatimes.com/companies/infosys-releases-9000-employees-with-automation-in-2016/articleshow/56680094.cms

Dass, P., & Parker, B. (1999). Strategies for managing human resource diversity: From resistance to learning. *The Academy of Management Executive*.

Daum, J. (2002, December 28). *The New Economy Analyst Report*. Retrieved from http://www.juergendaum.com/news/12_28_2002.htm

Davenport, T., & Pearlson, K. (1998). Two cheers for the Virtual Office. *Sloan Management Review*, *2*(1).

David, H., & Dorn, D. (2013). The growth of low-skill service jobs and the polarization of the US labor market. *The American Economic Review*, *103*(5), 1553–1597. doi:10.1257/aer.103.5.1553

Davidson, M. N., & Ferdman, B. M. (2002). The experience of inclusion. In B. Parker, B. M. Ferdman, P. Dass (Orgs.), *Inclusive and effective networks: Linking diversity theory and practice*. Presented at All-Academy symposium presented at the annual conference of the Academy of Management, Denver, CO.

Davies, I. A., & Crane, A. (2010). Corporate social responsibility in small- and medium-size enterprises: Investigating employee engagement in fair trade companies. *Business Ethics (Oxford, England)*, *19*(2), 126–139. doi:10.1111/j.1467-8608.2010.01586.x

Dawn, S.K., & Biswas, S. (2010). Employer Branding: A New Strategic Dimension of Indian Corporations. *Asian Journal of Management Research*, 21-33.

Dawson, C. (2001). Japan: Work-Sharing Will Prolong the pain. *Business Week*, *12*(3).

De Boer, E. M., Bakker, A. B., Syroitt, J. E., & Schaufeli, W. B. (2002). Unfairness at work as a predictor of absenteeism. *Journal of Organizational Behavior*, *23*(2), 181–197. doi:10.1002/job.135

De Meuse, K. P., & Hostager, T. J. (2001). Developing an instrument for measuring attitudes toward and perceptions of workplace diversity: An initial report. *Human Resource Development Quarterly*, *12*(1), 33–51. doi:10.1002/1532-1096(200101/02)12:1<33::AID-HRDQ4>3.0.CO;2-P

Deal, T., & Kennedy, A. (1982). *Corporate Cultures*. Reading, MA: Addison-Wesley.

DeChurch, L. A., Hiller, N. J., Murase, T., Doty, D., & Salas, E. (2010). Leadership across levels: Levels of leaders and their levels of impact. *The Leadership Quarterly*, *21*(6), 1069–1085. doi:10.1016/j.leaqua.2010.10.009

Deepak, A. (2006). *HR Planning, recruitment and deployment: challenges related to recruitment policies, HR policies and practices*. Available at http://m2iconsulting.com/wp-content/uploads/2014/12/HR-Issues.pdf

Delery, J. E., & Doty, D. H. (1996). Modes of theorizing in strategic human resource management: Test of universalistic, contingency, and configurational performance predictions. *Academy of Management Journal*, *39*(4), 802–835. doi:10.2307/256713

Dell, D., Ainspan, A., Nathan, Bodenberg, A., & Thomas. (2001). Engaging Employees Through Your Brand. The Conference Board.

Deloitte. (2015). *Global Human Capital Trends 2015 Leading in the new world of work*. Deloitte University Press.

Deloitte. (2015). *Women in the boardroom A global perspective.* Deloitte Touche Tohmatsu Limited.

Demerouti, E., Bakker, A. B., Nachreiner, F., & Schaufeli, W. B. (2001). The job demands-resources model of burnout. *The Journal of Applied Psychology*, *86*(3), 499–512. doi:10.1037/0021-9010.86.3.499 PMID:11419809

Deshpandé, R., Farley, J. U., & Webster, F. E. Jr. (1993). Corporate culture, customer orientation, and innovativeness in Japanese firms: A quadrad analysis. *Journal of Marketing*, *57*(1), 23–37. doi:10.2307/1252055

Deshpande, R., & Webster, F. E. Jr. (1989). Organizational culture and marketing: Defining the research agenda. *Journal of Marketing*, *53*(1), 3–15. doi:10.2307/1251521

Dessler, G. (2011). *Fundamentals of human resource management.* Pearson Higher Ed.

Dessler, G. (2015). *Human Resource Management (12th ed.).* Zagreb: MATE.

Dewettinck, K., & Ameijde, M. (2011). Linking Leadership Empowerment Behavior to Employee Attitudes and Behavioral Intentions: Testing the Mediating Role of Psychological Empowerment. *Personnel Review*, *40*(3), 284–305. doi:10.1108/00483481111118621

DeYmaz, M., (2017). *Disruption: Repurposing the Church to Redeem the Community.* Nashville, TN: Thomas Nelson; HarperCollins Christian Publishing, Inc.

Diener, E., Sandvik, E., Seidlitz, L., & Diener, M. (1993). The Relationship between Income and Subjective Well-Being: Relative or Absolute? *Social Indicators Research*, *28*(1).

Digh, P. (1998). Coming to terms with diversity. *HRMagazine*, *43*(12), 117.

Dike, P. (2013). *The impact of workplace diversity on organizations.* Academic Press.

Dollard, M. F., & Bakker, A. B. (2010). Psychosocial safety climate as a precursor to conducive work environments, psychological health problems, and employee engagement. *Journal of Occupational and Organizational Psychology*, *83*(3), 579–599. doi:10.1348/096317909X470690

Donaldson, T. (1996). Values in tension: Ethics away from home. *Harvard Business Review*, *74*(5), 48–62.

Drago, R. (2000). *Work/family issues in flux: Watch for these upcoming trends.* Positive Leadership.

Drucker, P. (2004). *The Daily Drucker.* Harper Collins Publishers.

DuPraw, M. E., & Axner, M. (1997). Working on common cross-cultural communication challenges. In *Toward a More Perfect Union in an Age of Diversity: A Guide to Building Stronger Communities through Public Dialogue.* Academic Press.

Duxbury, L. E., & Higgins, C. A. (1991). Gender differences in work-family conflict. *The Journal of Applied Psychology*, *76*(1), 60–74. doi:10.1037/0021-9010.76.1.60

Duxbury, L., & Higgins, C. (2001). *Work-Life Balance in the New Millennium: Where Are We? Where Do We Need to Go?* Work Network, Canadian Policy Research Networks.

Edmondson, A. (2002). The local and variegated nature of learning in organizations: A group-level perspective. *Organization Science, 13*(2), 128–146. doi:10.1287/orsc.13.2.128.530

Edwards, J. R., & Rothbard, N. P. (2000). Mechanisms linking work and family: Clarifying the relationship between work and family constructs. *Academy of Management Review, 25*(1), 178–199.

Elder, S. D., Lister, J., & Dauvergne, P. (2014). Big retail and sustainable coffee: A new development studies research agenda. *Progress in Development Studies, 14*(1), 77–90. doi:10.1177/1464993413504354

Eluvangal, S. (2014). *Bots cut Wipro employee strength by 12,000.* Retrieved on August 13, 2017 from https://ultra.news/s-e/30972/bots-help-wipro-cut-employee-strength-12000

Ely, R. J. (2004). A field study by group diversity, participation in diversity education programmes, and performance. *Journal of Organizational Behavior, 25*(6), 755–780. doi:10.1002/job.268

Ely, R. J., & Thomas, D. A. (2001). Cultural diversity at work: The effects of diversity perspectives on work group processes and outcomes. *Administrative Science Quarterly, 46*.

Equilibria. (2017). *How a Monthly Meeting Changed From 'A Waste Of Time' to a Positive Collaboration.* Retrieved from http://www.equilibria.com/case-studies/communication-teamwork/case-study-2/

Erdem, A. P. D. R., & Keklik, A. P. D. B. (2013). Beyond Family-Friendly Organizations: Life-Friendly Organizations-Organizational Culture of Life-Friendly Organizations. *International Journal of Humanities and Social Science, 3*(4), 102–113.

Erickson, T. J. (2005, May). Testimony submitted before the US Senate Committee on Health. *Education, Labor and Pensions, 26*.

Esty, K. C., Griffin, R., & Hirsch, M. S. (1995). *Workplace diversity.* Adams Media.

Esty, K., Griffin, R., & Schorr-Hirsh, M. (1995). *Workplace diversity. A manager's guide to solving problems and turning diversity into a competitive advantage.* Avon, MA: Adams Media Corporation.

Ettorre, B. (1997). The Empowerment Gap: Hype vs. Reality. *BRFocus, 62*, 4–6.

European Commission. (2011). Strategy for equality between women and men 2010-2015. Author.

European Commission. (2014). *Gender balance on corporate boards: Europe is cracking the glass ceiling.* Author.

Evans, C., & Redfern, D. (2010). How can employee engagement be improved at RRG Group? *Industrial and Commercial Training, 42*(5), 265–269. doi:10.1108/00197851011057564

Facet5 Case Studies. (n.d.). *Facet5: The most versatile asset in your organisational toolbox.* Retrieved from http://www.facet5global.com/facet5-solutions-case-studies/facet5-the-most-versatile-asset-in-your-organisational-toolbox

Compilation of References

FedEx Express. (2007, March 5). *FedEx Express Names Beth Galetti, Vice President of Information Technology.* Retrieved from http://www.fedex.com/cgi-bin/content.cgi?template=gb_pr&content=about%2Fpressreleases%2Femea%2Fpr030507&cc=gb

Ferdman, B. M., Allen, A., Barrera, V., & Vuong, V. (2006). *The experience of inclusion and inclusive behavior.* Unpublished paper. Marshall Goldsmith School of Management, Alliant International University.

Ferdman, B. M., & Davidson, M. N. (2002). Inclusion: What can I and my organization do about it? *The Industrial-Organizational Psychologist*, *29*(4), 80–85.

Fernandez, J. P. (1993). *The diversity advantage.* New York: Lexington Books.

Fernando, M. A., Pedro, M. R., & Gonzalo, S. G. (2013). Workforce diversity in strategic human resource management models. *Cross Cultural Management*, *20*(1), 39–49. doi:10.1108/13527601311296247

Ferrell, O. C., Gresham, L., & Fraedrich, J. (1989). A synthesis of ethical decision making models for marketing. *Journal of Macromarketing*, *9*(2), 55–64. doi:10.1177/027614678900900207

Ferry, K. (2013). *Diversity and Inclusion Survey.* Haygroup.

Ferry, K. (2013). *Executive attitudes on diversity positive, but actions lagging, Korn Ferry Institute survey finds.* Los Angeles, CA: Korn Ferry Institute.

Fiddler, S. (1999, July 7). Defence contracts 'pervaded by graft'. *Financial Times.*

Figurska, I., & Matuska, E. (2013). Employer branding as a human resources management strategy. *Human Resources Management & Ergonomics*, *7*(2).

Finkelstein, S., & Hambrick, D. C. (1996). *Strategic leadership: Top executives and their effects on organizations.* West Publishing Company.

Fink, J. S., Pastore, D. L., & Riemer, H. A. (2003). Managing employee diversity: Perceived practices and organisational outcomes in NCAA Division III athletic departments. *Sport Management Review*, *6*(2), 147–168. doi:10.1016/S1441-3523(03)70057-6

Fiona, C. (2011). Equality, diversity and corporate responsibility. *Equality, Diversity and Inclusion. International Journal (Toronto, Ont.)*, *30*(8), 719–734.

Flanagan, J. C. (1954). The critical incident technique. *Psychological Bulletin*, *51*(4), 327–358. doi:10.1037/h0061470 PMID:13177800

Flaum, S. (2002). Six Ps of great leadership. *Executive Excellence*, *19*(8), 3–4.

Fleming, J. H., & Asplund, J. (2007). *Human sigma.* New York, NY: Gallup Press.

Fleming, J. H., Coffman, C., & Harter, J. K. (2005). Manage your human sigma. *Harvard Business Review*, *83*(7), 106. PMID:16028821

Fletcher, C. (2001). Performance appraisal and management: The developing research agenda. *Journal of Occupational and Organizational Psychology, 74*(4), 473–487. doi:10.1348/096317901167488

Fornes, S. L., Rocco, T. R., & Wollard, K. K. (2008). Workplace commitment: A conceptual model developed from integrative review of the research. *Human Resource Development Review, 7*(3), 339–357. doi:10.1177/1534484308318760

Forsyth, D. R., & O'Boyle, E. H. Jr. (2011). Rules, standards, and ethics: Relativism predicts cross-national differences in the codification of moral standards. *International Business Review, 20*(2), 353–361. doi:10.1016/j.ibusrev.2010.07.008

Forsyth, D. R., O'Boyle, E. H. Jr, & McDaniel, M. (2008). East meets west: A meta-analytic investigation of cultural variations in idealism and relativism. *Journal of Business Ethics, 83*(4), 813–833. doi:10.1007/s10551-008-9667-6

Forsythe, J. (2005). Starbucks Coffee Company. Leading with diversity. *The New York Times*.

Frank, R., & Burton, T. M. (1997, February 4). Pharmacia & Upjohn Faces Culture Clash; Europeans Chafe Under US Rules. *Wall Street Journal*.

Freeman, R. E., & Gilbert, D. R. (1988). *Corporate strategy and the search for ethics*. Englewood Cliffs, NJ: Prentice- Hall.

Frey, C. B., & Osborne, M. A. (2017). The future of employment: How susceptible are jobs to computerisation? *Technological Forecasting and Social Change, 114*, 254–280. doi:10.1016/j.techfore.2016.08.019

Frone, M. R., Russell, M., & Cooper, M. L. (1992). Prevalence of work-family conflict: Are work and family boundaries asymmetrically permeable? *Journal of Organizational Behavior, 13*(7), 723–729. doi:10.1002/job.4030130708

Frone, M. R., Yardley, J. K., & Markel, K. S. (1997). Developing and testing an integrative model of the work-family interface. *Journal of Vocational Behavior, 50*(2), 145–167. doi:10.1006/jvbe.1996.1577

Frost, J., & Walker, M. (2007). Cross cultural leadership. *Engineering Management, 17*(3), 27–29. doi:10.1049/em:20070303

Fulkerson, J. R., & Schuler, R. S. (1992). *Managing worldwide diversity at Pepsi-Cola International*. Academic Press.

Galinsky, E., Bond, J. T., & Friedman, D. E. (1996). The role of employers in addressing the needs of employed parents. *The Journal of Social Issues, 52*(3), 111–136. doi:10.1111/j.1540-4560.1996.tb01582.x

Gallup. (2006). Gallup study: Engaged employees inspire company innovation: national survey finds that passionate workers are most likely to drive organisations forward. *The Gallup Management Journal*.

Compilation of References

Ganesh, A., & Rao, A. (2012). Performance Appraisal an Integrated Process-A Case Study with Reference to Karnataka Bank LTD. *Abhigyan*, *29*(4), 23–37.

Gangestand, S., & Snyder, M. (2000). Self-monitoring: Appraisal and Reappraisal. *Psychological Bulletin*, *4*(5). PMID:10900995

Ganster, D. C., Fusilier, M. R., & Mayes, B. T. (1986). Role of social support in the experience of stress at work. *The Journal of Applied Psychology*, *71*(1), 102–110. doi:10.1037/0021-9010.71.1.102 PMID:3957849

General Electric. (2017). *Welcome to GE.COM*. Retrieved from https://www.ge.com

Gerbasi, M. E., & Prentice, D. A. (2013). The Self-and Other-Interest Inventory. *Journal of Personality and Social Psychology*, *105*(3), 495–514. doi:10.1037/a0033483 PMID:23795908

Germain, M. L., Herzog, M. J. R., & Hamilton, P. R. (2012). Women employed in male-dominated industries: Lessons learned from female aircraft pilots, pilots-in-training and mixed-gender flight instructors. *Human Resource Development International*, *15*(4), 435–453. doi:10.1080/13678868.2012.707528

Gibbons, D. S., & Meehan, J. W. (2002). *Financing microfinance for poverty reduction*. Retrieved from http://www.microcreditsummit.org/papers/financing.pdf

Gibson, C. B., & Birkinshaw, J. (2004). The antecedents, consequences, and mediating role of organizational ambidexterity. *Academy of Management Journal*, *47*(2), 209–226. doi:10.2307/20159573

Gilliland, S. W. (1993). The perceived fairness of selection systems: An organizational justice perspective. *Academy of Management Review*, *18*(4), 694–734.

Glavis, A., & Piderit, S. (2009). How does doing good matter? Effects of corporate citizenship on employees. *Journal of Corporate Citizenship*, *36*(36), 51–70. doi:10.9774/GLEAF.4700.2009.wi.00007

Glocalizing responsible banking: Mindshare and outcomes in India. (2016). Retrieved on April 13, 2017, from https://www.yesbank.in/pdf/glocalizing_responsible_banking_mind_share_outcomes_in_india.pdf

Godwin, K. (2005). Promoting diversity – The role of line managers. *Equal Opportunities Review*.

Golding, N. (2010). Strategic human resource management. In *Human Resource Management A Contemporary Approach* (6th ed.; pp. 30-82). Person Financial Times/Prentice Hall.

Goldsmith, A. H., Sedo, S. Jr, Darity, W. Jr, & Hamilton, D. (2004). The labor supply consequences of perceptions of employment discrimination during search and on the job: Integrating neoclassical theory and cognitive dissconance. *Journal of Economic Psychology*, *25*(1), 15–39. doi:10.1016/S0167-4870(02)00210-6

Gonzalez, J. A., & Denisi, A. S. (2009). Cross-level effects of demography and diversity climate on organisational attachment and firm effectiveness. *Journal of Organizational Behavior*.

Gonzalez, J. A., & DeNisi, A. S. (2009). Cross-level effects of demography and diversity climate on organizational attachment and firm effectiveness. *Journal of Organizational Behavior, 30*(1), 21–40. doi:10.1002/job.498

Goode, W. J. (1960). A theory of role strain. *American Sociological Review, 25*(4), 483–496. doi:10.2307/2092933

Goodstein, J. D. (1994). Institutional pressures and strategic responsiveness: Employer involvement in work-family issues. *Academy of Management Journal, 37*(2), 350–382. doi:10.2307/256833

Goos, M., & Manning, A. (2007). Lousy and lovely jobs: The rising polarization of work in Britain. *The Review of Economics and Statistics, 89*(1), 118–133. doi:10.1162/rest.89.1.118

Gottfredson, L. S. (1992). Dilemmas in developing diversity programs. In S. E. Jackson (Ed.), *Diversity in the workplace* (pp. 59–83). New York: Guilford Press.

Graves, L. M., Ohlott, P. J., & Ruderman, M. N. (2007). Commitment to family roles: Effects on managers' attitudes and performance. *The Journal of Applied Psychology, 92*(1), 44–56. doi:10.1037/0021-9010.92.1.44 PMID:17227150

Greene, A. M., Kirton, G., & Wrench, J. (2005). Trade union perspectives on diversity management: A comparison of the UK and Denmark. *European Journal of Industrial Relations, 11*(2), 179–196. doi:10.1177/0959680105053962

Green, F. (2012). Employee involvement, technology and evolution in job skills: A task-based analysis. *Industrial & Labor Relations Review, 65*(1), 36–67. doi:10.1177/001979391206500103

Greenhaus, J. H., & Beutell, N. J. (1985). Organizational and Family Social Support and Work-Family Conflict. *Academy of Management Journal, 10*, 76–88.

Grewe, A. (2005). *"I'm sick to death with you..." or External Character Conflicts in Fawlty Towers*. Munich: GRIN Verlag.

Griggs, L. B. (1995). Valuing diversity: Where from ...where to? In L. B. Griggs & L. L. Louw (Eds.), *Valuing diversity: New tools for a new reality* (pp. 1–14). New York: McGraw-Hill.

Grobler, B. R., Moloi, K. C., Loock, C. F., Bisschoff, T. C., & Mestry, R. J. (2006). Creating a school environment for the effective management of cultural diversity. *Educational Management Administration & Leadership, 34*(4), 449–472. doi:10.1177/1741143206068211

Groeneveld, S., & Verbeek, S. (2012). Diversity policies in public and private sector organisations: An empirical comparison of incidence and effectiveness. *Review of Public Personnel Administration*. doi:10.1177/0734371X11421497

Grover, S. L. (1991). Predicting the perceived fairness of parental leave policies. *The Journal of Applied Psychology, 76*(2), 247–255. doi:10.1037/0021-9010.76.2.247

Groves, K. S., & Feyerherm, A. E. (2011). Leader cultural intelligence in context: Testing the moderating effects of team cultural diversity on leader and team performance. *Group & Organization Management*, *36*(5), 535–566.

Guillaume, Y. R., Dawson, J. F., Otaye-Ebede, L., Woods, S. A., & West, M. A. (2017). Harnessing demographic differences in organizations: What moderates the effects of workplace diversity? *Journal of Organizational Behavior*, *38*(2), 276–303. doi:10.1002/job.2040 PMID:28239234

Gu, L., & Chen, S. (2010). A System Dynamics Approach to Human Resource Mangement. In *International conference on Management and Service Science*. IEEE.

Gutierrez, B., Spencer, S. M., & Zhu, G. (2012). Thinking globally, leading locally: Chinese, Indian, and Western leadership. *Cross Cultural Management*, *19*(1), 67–89. doi:10.1108/13527601211195637

Guttmann, H. M. (2007, June 1). *Teamwork and Empowerment*. Retrieved from http://guttmandev.com/news-detail/teamwork-and-empowermen

Haberfeld, Y. (1992). Employment Discrimination: An Organizational Model. *Academy of Management Journal*, *35*(1), 161–180. doi:10.2307/256476

Hackman, J., & Okdham, G. (1976). Motivation through thr Design of Work: Test od a Theory. *Organizational Behavior and Human Performance*, *8*(1).

Hackman, J., & Okdham, G. (1980). *Work Redesign*. Reading, MA: Adison Wesley.

Hallberg, U. E., & Schaufeli, W. B. (2006). "Same same" but different? Can work engagement be discriminated from job involvement and organizational commitment? *European Psychologist*, *11*(2), 119–127. doi:10.1027/1016-9040.11.2.119

Hambrick, D. C., & Mason, P. A. (1984). Upper echelons: The organization as a reflection of its top managers. *Academy of Management Review*, *9*(2), 193–206.

Harcourt, M., Lam, H., Harcourt, S., & Flynn, M. (2008). Discrimination in hiring against immigrants and ethnic minorities: The effect of unionization. *International Journal of Human Resource Management*, *19*(1), 98–115. doi:10.1080/09585190701763958

Harish, C. J., & Anil, V. (1996). Managing workforce diversity for competitiveness The Canadian experience. *International Journal of Manpower*, *17*(4/5), 14–29. doi:10.1108/01437729610127677

Harman, G. (1975). Moral relativism defended. *The Philosophical Review*, *84*(1), 3–22. doi:10.2307/2184078

Harrigan, K. R. (1981). Numbers and positions of women elected to corporate boards. *Academy of Management Journal*, *24*(3), 619–625. doi:10.2307/255580

Harrison, D. A., Newman, D. A., & Roth, P. L. (2006). How important are job attitudes? Meta-analytic comparisons of integrative behavioral outcomes and time sequences. *Academy of Management Journal*, *49*(2), 305–325. doi:10.5465/AMJ.2006.20786077

Harrison, D. A., Price, K. H., & Bell, M. P. (1998). Beyond relational demography: Time and the effects of surface- and deep-level diversity on work group cohesion. *Academy of Management Journal, 41*(1), 96–107. doi:10.2307/256901

Harrison, D. A., Price, K. H., Gavin, J. H., & Florey, A. T. (2002). Time, teams, and task performance: Changing effects of surface- and deep-level diversity on group functioning. *Academy of Management Journal*.

Harter, J. K., Schmidt, F. L., & Hayes, T. L. (2002). Business-unit-level relationship between employee satisfaction, employee engagement, and business outcomes: A meta-analysis. *The Journal of Applied Psychology, 87*(2), 268–279. doi:10.1037/0021-9010.87.2.268 PMID:12002955

Hart, R. K., Conklin, T. A., & Allen, S. J. (2008). Individual leader development: An appreciative inquiry approach. *Advances in Developing Human Resources, 10*(5), 632–650. doi:10.1177/1523422308321950

Hashmi, M.S., & Naqvi, I.H. (2012). Psychological Empowerment: A Key to Boost organizational Commitment, Evidence from Banking Sector of Pakistan. *International Journal of Human Resource Studies, 2*.

Hawley, S. (2000). *Exporting corruption - privatization, multinationals and bribery*. Retrieved from: http://www.eldis.org/vfile/upload/1/document/0708/DOC8375.pdf

Hayes, B. C., & Major, D. A. (2003). *Creating inclusive organizations: Its meaning and measurement*. Paper presented at the 18th annual conference of the Society for Industrial and Organizational Psychology, Orlando, FL.

Hayles, V. R. (1996). Diversity training and development. In The ASTD training and development handbook (pp. 104-123). New York: McGraw-Hill.

Hayles, V. R. (1992). Valuing diversity in the food industry. *Food Engineering, 64*(4), 186.

Hayman, J. (2005). Psychometric assessment of an instrument designed to measure work life balance. *Research and Practice in Human Resource Management, 13*(1), 85–91.

Hegar, K., & Hodgetts, R. M. (2007). *Modern Human Relation at Work* (9th ed.). Thomson South-Western.

Heibutzki, R. (2017). *God Working Conditions for Workers*. Retrieved April, 2017, from http//:www.inc.com

Helmuth, J., Parrot, L., & Cracknell, D. (2004). *Human Resource Management for Growing MFIs*. MicroSave Briefing Note – 53. Available at http://www.Microsave.org

Hemphill, H., & Haines, R. (1997). *Discrimination, Harassment, and the Failure of Diversity Training*. Santa Barbara, CA: ABC-CLIO.

Henderson, G. (1994a). *Cultural diversity in the workplace: Issues and strategies*. Westport, CT: Quorum Books.

Compilation of References

Herdman, A. O., & McMillan-Capehart, A. (2010). Establishing a diversity program is not enough: Exploring the determinants of diversity climate. *Journal of Business and Psychology*, *25*(1), 39–53. doi:10.1007/s10869-009-9133-1

Herodotus, . (2003). *The histories: Reissue edition (J. M. Marincola* (A. De Selincourt Trans. & Ed.). Penguin Classics.

Herzberg, F. (1987). One time: How do you motivate employees? *Harvard Business Review*, *5*(1).

Herzberg, F. (1959). *The motivation to work*. New York, NY: Wiley.

Herzberg, F. (1968). One more time: How do you motivate employees? *Harvard Business Review*, *46*(1), 53–62. PMID:12545925

Hewitt Associates LLC. (2005). *Employee engagement*. Retrieved May 17, 2016, from http://was4.hewitt.com/hewitt/services/talent/subtalent/ee_engagement.htm

He, Z. L., & Wong, P. K. (2004). Exploration vs. exploitation: An empirical test of the ambidexterity hypothesis. *Organization Science*, *15*(4), 481–494. doi:10.1287/orsc.1040.0078

Hiatt, S. R., & Woodworth, W. P. (2006). Alleviating poverty through microfinance: Village banking outcomes in Central America. *The Social Science Journal*, *43*(3), 471–477. doi:10.1016/j.soscij.2006.04.017

Hicks-Clarke, D., & Iles, P. (2000). Climate for diversity and its effects on career and organisational attitudes and perceptions. *Personnel Review*, *29*(3), 324–345. doi:10.1108/00483480010324689

Higgins, C., Duxbury, L., & Lyons, S. (2007). *Reducing work-life conflict: What works. What doesn't*. Retrieved from travail/balancing-equilibre/sum-res-eng.php

Higgins, C. A., & Duxbury, L. E. (1992, July). Dual-career and traditional-career men. *Journal of Organizational Behavior*, *13*(4), 389–411. doi:10.1002/job.4030130407

Hillman, A. J., Shropshire, C., & Cannella, A. A. (2007). Organizational predictors of women on corporate boards. *Academy of Management Journal*, *50*(4), 941–952. doi:10.5465/AMJ.2007.26279222

Hinkin, T. R., & Tracey, J. B. (2010). What makes is so great? An analysis of human resources practices amongst Fortune's best companies to work for. *Cornell Hospitality Quarterly*, *51*(2), 158–170. doi:10.1177/1938965510362487

Hitt, M. A., Ireland, R. D., & Rowe, G. W. (2005). Strategic leadership: Strategy, resources, ethics and succession. *Handbook on responsible leadership and governance in global business*, 19-41.

Hobman, E. V., Bordia, P., & Gallois, C. (2003). Consequences of feeling dissimilar from others in a work teams. *Journal of Business and Psychology*, *17*(3), 301–304. doi:10.1023/A:1022837207241

Hofstede, G. (2001). *Culture's consequences: Comparing values, behaviors, institutions, and organizations across nations*. Thousand Oaks, CA: Sage.

Hofstede, G. H. (2001). *Culture's consequences: Comparing values, behaviors, institutions and organizations across nations.* Thousand Oaks, CA: Sage.

Holland, J. L. (1985). *Making Vocational Choices* (2nd ed.). Englewood Cliffs, NJ: Prentice-Hall.

Holt, K., & Seki, K. (2012). Global leadership: A developmental shift for everyone. *Industrial and Organizational Psychology: Perspectives on Science and Practice, 5*(2), 196–215. doi:10.1111/j.1754-9434.2012.01431.x

Homan, A. C., van Knippenberg, D., Van Kleef, G. A., & De Dreu, C. K. W. (2007). Bridging faultlines by valuing diversity: Diversity beliefs, information elaboration, and performance in diverse work groups. *The Journal of Applied Psychology, 92*(5), 1189–1199. doi:10.1037/0021-9010.92.5.1189 PMID:17845079

Hope Pelled, L., Ledford Jr, G. E., & Albers Mohrman, S. (1999). Demographic dissimilarity and workplace inclusion. *Journal of Management Studies, 36*(7), 1013–1031. doi:10.1111/1467-6486.00168

Hopkins, K. M. (1997). Supervisor intervention with troubled workers: A social identity perspective. *Human Relations, 50*(10), 1215–1238. doi:10.1177/001872679705001002

Hosmer, L. T. (1987). *The ethics of management.* Homewood, IL: Irwin Management.

House, J. S., & Wells, J. A. (1978, April). Occupational stress, social support and health. In *Reducing occupational stress: Proceedings of a conference* (pp. 78-140). Washington, DC: DHEW (NIOSH).

How should my organization define diversity? (2007). Retrieved 05 11, 2017, from http://www.shrm.org/diversity/library_published/nonIC/CMS_011970.asp#TopOfPag

Hubka, A., & Zaidi, R. (2005). Impact of Government Regulation on Microfinance. World Development Report: Improving the Investment Climate for Growth and Poverty Reduction, 1.

Hughes, J., & Rog, E. (2008). Talent management: A strategy for improving employee recruitment, retention and engagement within hospitality organizations. *Human Resource Management International Digest, 16*(7), 12.

Hulme, D., & Mosley, P. (1996). Finance Against Poverty (Vol. 2). Psychology Press.

Hunt, S. (n.d.). *The Importance of Employer Branding.* Retrieved on May 28, 2013 from www.sunlife.ca/static/canada/Customer%20Solutions/.../chapter7.pdf

Hurn, B. J., & Tomalin, B. (2013). What is Cross-Cultural Communication? In Cross-Cultural Communication (pp. 1-19). Palgrave Macmillan UK.

Hurn, B., & Tomalin, B. (2013). *Cross-cultural communication: Theory and practice.* Springer. doi:10.1057/9780230391147

Huselid, M. A., & Becker, B. E. (2011). Bridging micro and macro domains: Workforce differentiation and strategic human resource management. *Journal of Management, 37*(2), 421–428. doi:10.1177/0149206310373400

Huse, M., Nielsen, S. T., & Hagen, I. M. (2009). Women and employee-elected board members, and their contributions to board control tasks. *Journal of Business Ethics, 89*(4), 581–597. doi:10.1007/s10551-008-0018-4

Ikeanyibe, O. M. (2009). Human resource management for sustainable microfinance institutions in Nigeria. *Global Journal of Social Sciences, 8*(1), 119. doi:10.4314/gjss.v8i1.48915

Indian economy overview, market size, growth, development and statistics. (2017). Retrieved on May 11, 2017, from https://www.ibef.org/economy/indian-economy-overview

Indian Pharmaceutical Industry. (2017). Retrieved on May 27, 2017 from https://www.ibef.org/industry/information-technology-india.aspx

Ingersoll, G., & Schmitt, M. (2004). *Home - PubMed - NCBI*. Retrieved from https://www.ncbi.nlm.nih.gov/pubmed

Insights, M. (2008). *Human Resource Challenges and Solutions in Microfinance: Survey Report*. New Delhi: Academic Press.

International Culture. (2008). *The Environment of International Business*. Retrieved from http://www.unice.fr/crookall-cours/iup_cult/_docs/_RUGM_Chapter-05.pdf

International Labour Organization Convention 111. (1958). *Discrimination (Employment and Occupation)*. Retrieved from http://www.ilo.org/global/standards/subjects-covered-by-international-labour-standards/equality-of-opportunity-and-treatment/lang--en/index.htm

Ireland, R. D., & Hitt, M. A. (1999). Achieving and maintaining strategic competitiveness in the 21st century: The role of strategic leadership. *The Academy of Management Executive, 13*(1), 43–57.

Ishaq, H. M., & Zuilfqar, A. (2014). To investigate the moderating role of favoritism on employees motivation. Sci. Int.(Lahore), 347-351.

IT industry in India. (2017). Retrieved on April 27, 2017, from https://www.ibef.org/industry/information-technology-india.aspx

Jackson, S. E., & Associates. (1992). Diversity in the workplace. In Society for Industrial and Organizational Psychology. New York: Guilford Press.

Jackson, S. E., May, K. E., & Whitney, K. (1995). Understanding the dynamics of diversity in decision-making teams. *Team Effectiveness and Decision Making in Organizations, 204*, 261.

Jafari, V., Moradi, M., & Ahanchi, M. (2013). An Examination of the Relationship between Empowerment and Organizational Commitment (Case Study Kurdistan Province Electric Staff). *Interdisciplinary Journal of Contemporary Research in Business, 4*(12).

Jamieson, D., & O'Mara, J. (1991). *Managing workforce 2000: Gaining the diversity advantage.* San Francisco, CA: Jossey-Bass.

Jansen, J. J., Vera, D., & Crossan, M. (2009). Strategic leadership for exploration and exploitation: The moderating role of environmental dynamism. *The Leadership Quarterly*, *20*(1), 5–18. doi:10.1016/j.leaqua.2008.11.008

Jansen, W. S., Otten, S., & van der Zee, K. I. (2015). Being part of diversity: The effects of an all-inclusive multicultural diversity approach on majority members' perceived inclusion and support for organisational diversity efforts. *Group Processes & Intergroup Relations*, *18*(6), 817–832. doi:10.1177/1368430214566892

Jansen, W. S., Otten, S., & van der Zee, K. I. (2016). Being different at work: How gender dissimilarity relates to social inclusion and absenteeism. *Group Processes & Intergroup Relations*.

Jansen, W. S., Vos, M. W., Otten, S., Podsiadlowski, A., & van der Zee, K. I. (2016). Colorblind or colorful? How diversity approaches affect cultural majority and minority employees. *Journal of Applied Social Psychology*, *46*(2), 81–93. doi:10.1111/jasp.12332

Jeong, M. y., & Won, S. y. (2013). Factors affecting female worker's perceived discrimination in the workplace: An analysis using the Korean longitudinal survey of women and family. *GSPR*, 71-103.

Jha, S. (2011). Influence of Psychological Empowerment on Affective, Normative and Continuance Commitment: A Study in the Indian IT Industry. *Journal of Indian Business Research, 3*.

Jha, J. K., & Singh, M. (2015). Human resource (HR) & social challenges faced by microfinance in India: A framework. *Indian Journal of Industrial Relations*, *50*(3), 494–505.

Johnson, J. P., III. (2003). *Creating a diverse workforce.* Retrieved 06 11, 2017, from http://www.shrm.org/hrresources/whitepapers_published/CMS_005379.asp#P-

Johnson, H. H. (2008). Mental models and transformative learning: The key to leadership development. *Human Resource Development Quarterly*, *19*(1), 85–89. doi:10.1002/hrdq.1227

Johnson, L. H. (1985). Bribery in international markets: Diagnosis, clarification and remedy. *Journal of Business Ethics*, *4*(6), 447–455. doi:10.1007/BF00382606

Johnson, S. J. (1995). The status of valuing and managing diversity in Fortune 500 service organizations: Perceptions of top human resource professionals. *Academy of Human Resource Development (AHRD) Conference Proceedings*.

Johnston, W. B., & Packer, A. E. (1987). *Workforce 2000: Work and workers for the 21st century.* Indianapolis, IN: Hudson Institute.

Jones, G. E. (1997). Advancement opportunity issues for persons with disabilities. *Human Resource Management Review*, *7*(1), 55–76. doi:10.1016/S1053-4822(97)90005-X

Jones, G. R., & George, J. M. (2014). *Contemporary Management* (8th ed.). New York: McGraw-Hill.

Jones, J. R., & Harter, J. K. (2005). Race effects on the employee engagement-turnover intention relationship. *Journal of Leadership & Organizational Studies, 11*(2), 78–88. doi:10.1177/107179190501100208

Jónsdóttir, T., Vinnicombe, S., Singh, V., Burke, R., Bilimoria, D., & Huse, M. (2008). Women on corporate boards of directors: The Icelandic perspective. *Women on corporate boards of directors: International Research and Practice*, 88-95.

Joplin, J. R., & Daus, C. S. (1997). Challenges of leading a diverse workforce. *The Academy of Management Executive, 11*(3), 32–47.

Joshi, A., Neely, B., Emrich, C., Griffiths, D., & George, G. (2015). Gender research in AMJ: An overview of five decades of empirical research and calls to action thematic issue on gender in management research. *Academy of Management Journal, 58*(5), 1459–1475. doi:10.5465/amj.2015.4011

Joyce, W. F., & Slocum, J. W. (1984). Strategic Context and Organizational Climate. In B. Schneider (Ed.), *Organizational Climate and Culture*. San Francisco, CA: Jossey-Bass.

Jr, M. B., Rodriguez, R. E., & Jayaraman, S. (2010). Employment Discrimination in upscale restaurants: Evidence from matched pair testing. *The Social Science Journal*, 802–818.

Judge, T. A., Van Vianen, A. E. M., & De Pater, I. (2004). Emotional stability, core self-evaluations, and job outcomes: A review of the evidence and an agenda for future research. *Human Performance, 17*(3), 325–346. doi:10.1207/s15327043hup1703_4

Judge, T., Thoresen, C., Bono, E., & Patton, G. (2001). The Job Satisfaction-Job Performance Realationship: A Qualitative and Quantitative Review. *Psychological Bulletin, 27*(1). PMID:11393302

Jyothi, P. (2004). Practice of HR Functions in a Small Scale Organization. *Sedme, 31*(4), 19–26.

Kahn, R. L., Wolfe, D. M., Quinn, R. P., Snoek, J. D., & Rosenthal, R. A. (1964). *Organizational Stress: Studies in Role Conflict and Ambiguity*. New York: Wiley.

Kahn, W. (1990). Psychological conditions of personal engagement and disengagement at work. *Academy of Management Journal, 33*(4), 692–724. doi:10.2307/256287

Kahn, W. A. (1992). To be fully there: Psychological presence at work. *Human Relations, 45*(4), 321–349. doi:10.1177/001872679204500402

Kaikati, J. G., Sullivan, G. M., Virgo, J. M., Carr, T. R., & Katherine, S. V. (2000). The price of international business morality: Twenty years under the Foreign Corrupt Practices Act. *Journal of Business Ethics, 26*(3), 213–222. doi:10.1023/A:1006015110422

Kassem, R., Ajmal, M. M., & Khan, M. (2017). The Relationship Between Organizational Culture and Business Excellence: Case Study from United Arab Emirates. In Organizational Culture and Behavior: Concepts, Methodologies, Tools, and Applications (pp. 732-751). IGI Global.

Katz, D., & Kahn, R. L. (1978). *The Social Psychology of Organizations* (Vol. 2). New York: Wiley.

Katzenbach, J., Oeischlegel, C., & Thomas, J. (2017). *Principles of Organizational Culture*. Retrieved April, 2017, from http//:www.strategy-business.com

Kazlauskaite, R., Buciuniene, I., & Turauskas, L. (2006). Building Employee Commitment in the Hospitality Industry. *Baltic Journal of Management*, 1.

Kearney, E., Gebert, D., & Voelpel, S. C. (2009). When and how diversity benefits teams: The importance of team members' need for cognition. *Academy of Management Journal*, *52*(3), 581–598. doi:10.5465/AMJ.2009.41331431

Kelly, D. (2001). *Ranstad Ranks Employee Wants by Age*. Available at: www.hr-esource.com

Ketter, P. (2008). What's the big deal about employee engagement? *T+D*, *62*(2), 44-49.

Khandawalla, P. N. (1974). Mass output orientation of operations technology and organization structure. *Administrative Science Quarterly*, *19*(1), 74–97. doi:10.2307/2391789

Khurana, A., & Goyal, K. (2010). *Performance appraisal: A key to HR assessment and Development*. Retrieved on January 21, 2015 from http://papers.ssrn.com/sol3/papers.cfm?abstract_id=1714151

Kilgour, M. (2006). Improving the creative process: Analysis of the effects of divergent thinking techniques and domain specific knowledge on creativity. *International Journal of Business and Society*, *7*(2), 79.

Kilmann, R. H., & Saxton, M. J. (1983). Kilmann-Saxton culture-gap survey. Pittsburgh, PA: Academic Press.

Kim, S., Whitehead, E. J., & Zhang, Y. (2008). Classifying software changes: Clean or buggy? *Software Engineering. IEEE Transactions*, *34*(2), 181–196.

King, C. I. (2001, December 22). Saudi Arabia's apartheid. *The Washington Post*. Retrieved from https://www.washingtonpost.com/archive/opinions/2001/12/22/saudi-arabias-apartheid/6dc54ab8-37bc-4a87-86f4-c0b489fc8b8e/?utm_term=.5417d2f31901

King, E. B., Dawson, J. F., Kravitz, D. A., & Gulick, L. (2012). A multilevel study of the relationships between diversity training, ethnic discrimination and satisfaction in organizations. *Journal of Organizational Behavior*, *33*(1), 5–20. doi:10.1002/job.728

Kinnie, N., Hutchinson, S., Purcell, J., Rayton, B., & Swart, J. (2005). Satisfaction with HR practices and commitment to the organisation: Why one size does not fit all. *Human Resource Management Journal*, *15*(4), 9–29. doi:10.1111/j.1748-8583.2005.tb00293.x

Kirkman, B. L., & Rosen, B. (1997). A model of work team empowerment. In R. W. Woodman & W. A. Pasmore (Eds.), *Research in organizational change and development* (Vol. 10, pp. 131–167). Greenwich, CT: JAI Press.

Kochan, T., Bezrukova, K., Ely, R., Jackson, S., Joshi, A., Jehn, K., & Thomas, D. et al. (2003). The effects of diversity on business performance: Report of the diversity research network. *Human Resource Management*, *42*(1), 3–21. doi:10.1002/hrm.10061

Konrad, A. M., Kramer, V., & Erkut, S. (2008). Critical Mass: The Impact of Three or More Women on Corporate Boards. *Organizational Dynamics*, *37*(2), 145–164. doi:10.1016/j.orgdyn.2008.02.005

Konrad, A. M., & Linnehan, F. (1995). Formalized HRM structures: Coordinating equal employment opportunity or concealing organizational practices? *Academy of Management Journal*, *38*(3), 787–820. doi:10.2307/256746

Koonce, R. (n.d.). *Redefining Diversity: It's Not Just the Right Thing to Do. It Also Makes Good Business Sense*. Retrieved on August 29, 2017 from https://www.questia.com/magazine/1G1-83045836/redefining-diversity-it-s-not-just-the-right-thing

Koonce, R. (2001). Redefining diversity: It's not just the right to do; it also makes good business sense. *Training & Development*, *12*(12), 22–32.

Korsgaard, M. A., Schweiger, D. M., & Sapienza, H. J. (1995). Building commitment, attachment, and trust in strategic decision-making teams: The role of procedural justice. *Academy of Management Journal*, *38*(1), 60–84. doi:10.2307/256728

Kossek, E. E., Lobel, S. A., & Brown, A. J. (2005). Human Resource Strategies to Manage Workforce Diversity. In Handbook of Workplace Diversity. Academic Press.

Kossek, E. E. (1990). Diversity in child care assistance needs: Employee problems, preferences, and work-related outcomes. *Personnel Psychology*, *43*(4), 769–791. doi:10.1111/j.1744-6570.1990.tb00682.x

Kossek, E. E., & Lobel, A. (1996). *Managing diversity*. Blackwell Publishers.

Kossek, E. E., & Lobel, S. A. (1996). *Managing Diversity: Human Resource Strategies for Transforming the Workplace*. Cambridge, UK: Blackwell.

Kossek, E. E., Lobel, S. A., & Brown, J. (2004). 'Human Resource Strategies to Management Workforce Diversity:Examining "The Business Case". In A. M. Konrad, P. Prasad, & J. K. Pringle (Eds.), *Handbook of Workplace Diversity*. Thousand Oaks, CA: Sage Publications.

Kossek, E. E., & Nichol, V. (1992). The effects of on site child care on employee attitudes and performance. *Personnel Psychology*, *45*(3), 485–509. doi:10.1111/j.1744-6570.1992.tb00857.x

Kotler, P. (1994). *Analysis, planning, implementation, and control*. Prentice Hall International.

Kotter, J. P., & Heskett, J. L. (1992). *Corporate Culture and Performance*. New York, NY: Free Press.

Kowske, B. J., & Anthony, K. (2007). Towards defining leadership competence around the world: What mid-level managers need to know in twelve countries. *Human Resource Development International, 10*(1), 21–41. doi:10.1080/13678860601170260

Kramer, V. W., Konrad, A. M., Erkut, S., & Hooper, M. J. (2006). *Critical mass on corporate boards: Why three or more women enhance governance*. Wellesley, MA: Wellesley Centers for Women.

Kreitz, P. A. (2008). Best practices for managing organizational diversity. *Journal of Academic Librarianship, 34*(2), 101–120. doi:10.1016/j.acalib.2007.12.001

Krohe, J. (1997). The Big Business Ethics, Across The Board. *Human Resource Management Review, 16*(10).

Kroth, M., & Keeler, C. (2009). Caring as a managerial strategy. *Human Resource Development Review, 8*(4), 506–531. doi:10.1177/1534484309341558

Krumm, D. (2007). *Open and Distance Leaning in Microfinance, Planet Finance, Morocco*. Available at http:// www.microfinancegateway.org/p/site/m//template.rc/1.9.29005 accessed on 27/12/2016

Kuleto, V. (2017). *Organizacija radnog mesta*. Retrieved April, 2017, from http//www.valentinculeto.com

Kulik, C. T. (2014). Working below and above the line: The research–practice gap in diversity management. *Human Resource Management Journal, 24*(2), 129–144. doi:10.1111/1748-8583.12038

Kumari, N. (2016). A study of performance management system in Wipro. *International Journal of Human Resource & Industrial Research, 3*(7), 37–45.

Kumari, P., & Priya, B. (2017, January). Organizational Commitment: A Comparative Study of Public and Private Sector Bank Managers. *International Journal of Business and Management Invention, 6*(1), 38–47. Retrieved from http://www.ijbmi.org/papers/Vol(6)1/Version-3/G0601033847.pdf

Kurian, V. (2015). *New appraisal system in the works at sbi*. Retrieved on May 21, 2017, from http://www.thehindubusinessline.com/money-and-banking/new-staff-appraisal-system-in-the-works-at-sbi/article6979003.ece

Kvedaraitė, N., & Jankauskienė, V. (2011). Intercultural competence as precondition for cultural diversity management. *Economics & Management, 16*.

Laffaldano, M., & Muchinski, M. (1985). Job Satisfaction and Job performance: A meta-analysis. *Psychological Bulletin, 3*(1).

Compilation of References

Lakwo, A. (2006). *Microfinance, rural livelihoods, and women's empowerment in Uganda* (Ph.D. thesis). Radboud Universiteit, Nijmegen.

Lappetito, J. (1994). Workplace diversity: A leadership challenge. Managing diversity is a social, financial, and moral imperative. *Health Progress (Saint Louis, Mo.), 75*(2), 22–27. PMID:10132109

LaRocco, J. M., House, J. S., & French, J. R. P. (1980). Social support, occupational stress, and health. *Journal of Health and Social Behavior, 21*(3), 202–218. doi:10.2307/2136616 PMID:7410798

Lascelles, D., Mendelson, S., & Rozas, D. (2012). *Microfinance Banana Skins 2012. In The CSFI survey of microfinance risk*. London: Centre for the Study of Financial Innovation.

Lau, C. M., & Ngo, H. Y. (2004). The HR system, organizational culture, and product innovation. *International Business Review, 13*(6), 685–703. doi:10.1016/j.ibusrev.2004.08.001

Lawler, E. E., Mohrman, S. A., & Benson, G. (2001). *Organizing for high performance: Employee Involvement, TQM, Reengineering, and Knowledge Management in the Fortune 1000*. San Francisco, CA: Jossey-Bass.

Lawrence, T. B., & Robinson, S. L. (2007). Ain't Misbehavin: Workplace Deviance as Organizational Resistance. *Journal of Management, 33*(3), 378–394. doi:10.1177/0149206307300816

Lee, Y.-K., Kim, S., & Kim, S. Y. (2013). *The Impact of Internal Branding on Employee Engagement and outcome variables in the Hotel Industry*. Asian Pacific Journal of Tourism Research.

Lehman, C., & DuFrene, D. (2015). *Poslovna komunikacija*. Beograd: BCOM, DataStatus.

Leung, K., & Chan, D. K. S. (1999). Conflict management across cultures. In J. Adamopoulos & Y. Kashima (Eds.), *Social psychology and cultural context: Essays in honor of Harry C. Triandis* (pp. 177–188). Thousand Oaks, CA: Sage. doi:10.4135/9781452220550.n13

Levinson, E. (2007). *Developing High Employee Engagement Makes Good Business Sense*. Retrieved on April 28, 2015, from www.interactionassociates.com/ideas/2007/05/developing_high_ employee_engagement_makes_good_business_sense.php

Lewis, S. (1997). 'Family friendly' employment policies: A route to changing organizational culture or playing about at the margins? *Gender, Work and Organization, 4*(1), 13–23. doi:10.1111/1468-0432.00020

Lewis, S. (2001). Restructuring workplace cultures: The ultimate work-family challenge? *Women in Management Review, 16*(1), 21–29. doi:10.1108/09649420110380256

Lewis, S., & Cooper, C. L. (1999). The work-family research agenda in change contexts. *Journal of Occupational Health Psychology, 4*(4), 382–393. doi:10.1037/1076-8998.4.4.382 PMID:10526842

Liedtka, M. (1996). Collaborating across Lines of Business for Competitive Advantage. *The Academy of Management Executive, 4*(1).

Lindorff, M., & Peck, J. (2010). Exploring Australian financial leaders' views of corporate social responsibility. *Journal of Management & Organization, 16*(01), 48–65. doi:10.1017/S1833367200002261

LineF.III. (Ed.). (n.d.). Available at: www.diversityinc.com

Livshits, B., & Zimmermann, T. (2005). DynaMine: finding common error patterns by mining software revision histories. ACM SIGSOFT Software Engineering Notes, 30(5), 296-305. doi:10.1145/1081706.1081754

Loden, M., & Rosener, J. B. (1991). *Workforce America! Managing Employee Diversity as a Vital Resource*. Business One Irwin.

Lok, P., Westwood, R., & Crawford, J. (2005). Perceptions of Organizational Subculture and Their Significance for Organizational Commitment. *The Journal of Applied Psychology, 54*(4), 490–514. doi:10.1111/j.1464-0597.2005.00222.x

Lombardo, J. (2017, February 5). *Ford Motor Company's Organizational Culture Analysis*. Retrieved from http://panmore.com/ford-motor-company-organizational-culture-analysis

Longenecker, J. G., McKinney, J. A., & Moore, C. W. (1988). The ethical issue of international bribery: A study of attitudes among US business professionals. *Journal of Business Ethics, 7*(5), 341–346. doi:10.1007/BF00382536

Louw, L. L. (1995). No potential lost: The valuing diversity journeyan integrated approach to systemic change. In L. B. Griggs & L. L. Louw (Eds.), *Valuing diversity: New tools for a new reality* (pp. 15–58). New York: McGraw-Hill.

Lovvorn, A. S., & Chen, J. S. (2011). Developing a global mindset: The relationship between an international assignment and cultural intelligence. *International Journal of Business and Social Science, 2*(9).

Lundrigan, M., Tangsuvanich, V. L., Wu, S., & Mujtaba, B. (2012). Coaching a diverse workforce: The impact of changing demographics for modern leaders. *International Journal of Humanities and Social Science, 2*(3), 40–48.

Lundrigan, M., Tangsuvanich, V. L., Wu, S., & Mujtaba, B. G. (2012). Coaching a diverseworkforce: The impact of changing demographics for modern leaders. *International Journal of Humanities and Social Science, 2*(3), 40–48.

Lussier, R. (2012). *Human relations in organizations: Applications and skill building*. McGraw-Hill Higher Education.

Luthans, F., & Jensen, S. M. (2002). Hope: A new positive strength for human resource development. *Human Resource Development Review, 1*(3), 304–322. doi:10.1177/1534484302013003

Macey, W. H., & Schneider, B. (2008). The meaning of employee engagement. *Industrial and Organizational Psychology: Perspectives on Science and Practice, 1*(1), 3–30. doi:10.1111/j.1754-9434.2007.0002.x

MacLeod, D., & Clarke, N. (2009). *Engaging for Success: enhancing performance through employee engagement*. London: Department of Business, Innovation and Skills.

Macnamara, F. K. (2011). *Strategic Role of Performance Appraisal*. Retrieved on June 22, 2014 from https://www.academia.edu/ 707671/ Strategic _Role _of_ Performance_ Appraisals

Makwana, K., & Dave, G. (2014). Employer Branding: A Case of Infosys. *International Journal of Humanities and Social Science Invention*, *3*(6), 42–49.

Malhotra, A., Majchzak, A., & Rosen, B.(2007). Leading Virtual Teams. *Perspectives*, *21*(1).

Malone, M. (2017, July 5). *Consequences of Discrimination in the Workplace*. Retrieved from http://oureverydaylife.com/consequences-discrimination-workplace-3934.html

Marjoribanks, T. (2000). *News Corporation, Tehnology and the workplace*. Cambridge University Press. doi:10.1017/CBO9780511552137

Markus, H. R., & Kitayama, S. (1991). Culture and the self: Implications for cognition, emotion, and motivation. *Psychological Review*, *98*(2), 224–253. doi:10.1037/0033-295X.98.2.224

Marques, J. F. (2008). Spiritual performance from an organizational perspective: The Starbucks way. *Corporate Governance*, *8*(3), 248–257. doi:10.1108/14720700810879141

Marquis, B. K., & Huston, C. J. (1996). *Leadership Roles and Managers Function in Nursing* (2nd ed.). Philadelphia, PA: Lippincott.

Martin, G., Beaumont, P., Doig, R., & Pate, J. (2005). Branding: A new performance discourse for HR? *European Management Journal*, *23*(1).

Martin, J., & Siehl, C. (1983). Organizational culture and counterculture: An uneasy symbiosis. *Organizational Dynamics*, *12*(2), 52–64. doi:10.1016/0090-2616(83)90033-5

Martins, N. (1987). *Elandsrand Gold-mine: Organisational culture survey*. Unpublished report, Johannesburg.

Maslach, C., & Leiter, M. P. (1997). *The truth about Burnout*. New York: Jossey-Bass.

Maslach, C., & Leiter, M. P. (1997). *The truth about burnout: How organizations cause personal stress and what to do about it*. San Francisco, CA: Jossey-Bass.

Maslach, C., & Leiter, M. P. (2008). Early predictors of job burnout and engagement. *The Journal of Applied Psychology*, *93*(3), 498–512. doi:10.1037/0021-9010.93.3.498 PMID:18457483

Maslach, C., Schaufeli, W. B., & Leiter, M. P. (2001). Job burnout. *Annual Review of Psychology*, *52*(1), 397–422. doi:10.1146/annurev.psych.52.1.397 PMID:11148311

Maslow, A. (2004). *Psychology in Management*. Adizes.

Masson, R. C., Royal, M. A., Agnew, T. G., & Fine, S. (2008). Leveraging employee engagement: The practical implications. *Industrial and Organizational Psychology: Perspectives on Science and Practice*, *1*(1), 56–59. doi:10.1111/j.1754-9434.2007.00009.x

Mathis, R. L., & Jackson, J. H. (2008). *Human resource management*. Mason, OH: South-Western Cengage Leaning.

Maurer, T. J., & Rafuse, N. E. (2001). Learning, not litigating: Managing employee development and avoiding claims of age discrimination. *The Academy of Management Executive*, *15*(4), 110–121. doi:10.5465/AME.2001.5898395

May, D. R., Gilson, R. L., & Harter, L. M. (2004). The psychological conditions of meaningfulness, safety and availability and the engagement of the human spirit at work. *Journal of Occupational and Organizational Psychology*, *77*(1), 11–37. doi:10.1348/096317904322915892

Mayhew, R. (n.d.). *How does diversity affect HR functions?* Retrieved on August 28, 2017 from http://smallbusiness.chron.com/diversity-affect-hr-functions-59653.html

Mazur, B. (2010). Cultural Diversity in Organisational Theory and Practice. *Journal of Intercultural Management*, *2*(2), 5–15.

Mbeba, R. D. (2007). *MFI Internal Audit and Controls Trainer's Manual*. Available at http://www.meda.org

McCain, B. (1996). Multicultural team learning: An approach towards communication competency. *Management Decision*, *34*(6), 65–68. doi:10.1108/00251749610121498

Mccormack, J. (2011, November 18). Paul Ryan: The biggest problem in America isn't debt, it's moral relativism. *The Weekly Standard*, (Nov): 18.

McCuiston, V. E., Ross Wooldridge, B., & Pierce, C. K. (2004). Leading the diverse workforce: Profit, prospects and progress. *Leadership and Organization Development Journal*, *25*(1), 73–92. doi:10.1108/01437730410512787

McDonald, P., Brown, K., & Bradley, L. (2005). Explanations for the provision-utilisation gap in work-life policy. *Women in Management Review*, *20*(1), 37–55. doi:10.1108/09649420510579568

McKay, P. F., Avery, D. R., Tonidandel, S., Morris, M. A., Hernandez, M., & Hebl, M. R. (2007). Racial differences in employee retention: Are diversity climate perceptions the key? *Personnel Psychology*, *60*(1), 35–62. doi:10.1111/j.1744-6570.2007.00064.x

McKay, P., Avery, D. R., & Morris, M. (2009). A tale of two climates: Diversity climate from subordinates' and managers' perspectives and their role in store unit sales. *Personnel Psychology*, *62*(4), 767–791. doi:10.1111/j.1744-6570.2009.01157.x

Mclean, A. (2017, February 20). Emotional intelligence is the future of artificial intelligence: Fjord. *Zdnet.com*. Retrieved August 13, 2017, from http://www.zdnet.com/article/emotional-intelligence-is-the-future-of-artificial-intelligence-fjord/

McMahon, A. M. (2010). Does workplace diversity matter? A survey of empirical studies on diversity and firm performance, 2000-09. *Journal of Diversity Management*, *5*(2), 37.

Meglino, B. M., & Korsgaard, A. (2004). Considering rational self-interest as a disposition: Organizational implications of other orientation. *The Journal of Applied Psychology*, *89*(6), 946–959. doi:10.1037/0021-9010.89.6.946 PMID:15584834

Mendez-Russell, A. (2001). Diversity leadership. *Executive Excellence*, *18*(12), 16.

Mesmer-Magnus, J., & Viswesvaran, C. (2006). How family-friendly work enviroments affect work/family conflict: A Meta-analytic examination. *Journal of Labor Research*, *27*(4).

MGI. (2013). *Disruptive technologies: Advances that will transform life, business, and the global economy*. Tech. Rep., McKinsey Global Institute. Retrieved on August 13, 2017 from http://www.mckinsey.com/business-functions/digital-mckinsey/our-insights/disruptive-technologies

Miesing, P., & Preble, J. F. (1985). A comparison of five business philosophies. *Journal of Business Ethics*, *4*(6), 465–476. doi:10.1007/BF00382609

Miller, D. T. (1999). The norm of self-interest. *The American Psychologist*, *54*(12), 1053–1060. doi:10.1037/0003-066X.54.12.1053 PMID:15332526

Miller, F. A. (1998). 'Strategic culture change: The door to achieving high performance and inclusion'. *Public Personnel Management*, *27*(2), 151–160. doi:10.1177/009102609802700203

Milliken, F. J., Martins, L. L., & Morgan, H. (1998). Explaining organizational responsiveness to work-family issues: The role of human resource executives as issue interpreters. *Academy of Management Journal*, *41*(5), 580–592. doi:10.2307/256944

Milne, J. (2015). *Behavioural benefits from employee feedback at GlaxoSmithKline*. Retrieved on May 15, 2017, from http://diginomica.com/2015/06/29/behavioral-benefits-from-employee-feedback-at-glaxosmithkline/

Mims, C. (2010). AI that picks stocks better than the pros. *MIT Technology Review*. Retrieved on August 13, 2017 from https://www.technologyreview.com/s/419341/ai-that-picks-stocks-better-than-the-pros/

Mínguez-Vera, A., & Martin, A. (2011). Gender and management on Spanish SMEs: An empirical analysis. *International Journal of Human Resource Management*, *22*(14), 2852–2873. doi:10.1080/09585192.2011.599948

Mirage, L. (1994). Development of an instrument measuring valence of ethnicity and perception of discrimination. *Journal of Multicultural Counseling and Development*, 49–59.

Mitra, P. P. (2017, June 20). Watch: A 14-feet robocop directs traffic in Indore, makes commuters obey rules. *Hindustan Times*. Retrieved June 28, 2017, from http://www.hindustantimes.com/india-news/watch-a-14-feet-robocop-directs-traffic-in-indore-makes-commuters-obey-rules/story-rStGTxxsfCQgTOJV8kUzlO.html

Mogheli, A., Hasanpour, A., & Hasanpour, M. (2009). The Relationship between Employee Empowerment and Organizational Commitment. *Public Administration Publication*, *1*(2), 119–132.

Moira, A. (2000). Here comes the bribe. *Entrepreneur, 28*(10), 48.

Moore, S. (1999). Understanding and managing diversity among groups at work: Key issues for organizational training and development. *Journal of European Industrial Training, 23*(4/5), 208–218. doi:10.1108/03090599910272086

Mor Barak, M. E. (2014). *Managing diversity: Toward a globally inclusive workplace* (3rd ed.). Thousand Oaks, CA: Sage.

Mor Barak, M. E. (2015). *Inclusion is the key to diversity management, but what is inclusion? Human Service Organisations: Management, Leadership & Governance.*

Mor Barak, M. E., Cherin, D. A., & Berkman, S. (1998). Organizational and personal dimensions in diversity climate: Ethnic and gender differences in employee perceptions. *The Journal of Applied Behavioral Science, 34*(1), 82–104. doi:10.1177/0021886398341006

Morais, U. P., Jacqueline, P., Kevin, S., Lucien, S., Roiner, R., & Yesenia Rivera, M. B. (2014). Managing Diverse Employees at Starbucks: Focusing on Ethics and Inclusion. *International Journal of Learning & Development, 4*(3), 35–50. doi:10.5296/ijld.v4i3.5994

Mor-Barak, M. E., & Cherin, D. A. (1998). A tool to expand organizational understanding of workforce diversity: Exploring a measure of inclusion-exclusion. *Administration in Social Work, 22*(1), 47–64. doi:10.1300/J147v22n01_04

Morduch, J. (1999). The microfinance promise. *Journal of Economic Literature, 37*(4), 1569–1614. doi:10.1257/jel.37.4.1569

Moroko, L., & Uncles, M. D. (2008). Characteristics of successful employer brands. *Journal of Brand Management, 16*(3), 160–175. doi:10.1057/bm.2008.4

Morris, M. W., Williams, K. Y., Leung, K., Larrick, R., Mendoza, M. T., Bhahtnagar, D., & Hu, J. C. et al. (1998). Conflict management style: Accounting for cross-national differences. *Journal of International Business Studies, 29*(4), 729–747. doi:10.1057/palgrave.jibs.8490050

Morrison, A. M. (1992). The New Leaders: Guidelines on Leadership Diversity in America. Jossey-Bass, Inc.

Morrison, A. M. (1992). *The new leaders: Guidelines on leadership diversity in America*. San Francisco, CA: Jossey-Bass.

Mossevelde, C. V. (2010). *Employer branding five reasons why it matters five step to action*. Retrieved on May 20, 2017, from http://www.employerbrandingtoday.com/uk/2010/03/25/employer-branding-five-reasons-why-it-matters-five-steps-to-action/

Muafi. (2011). Causes and Consequence Deviant Workplace Behavior. *International Journal of Innovation, Management and Technology*, 123-126.

Mubarik, Z. A. (2008). *Human Resource development in Microfinance Institutions*. Available at: www.microfinance gateway.org/gm/document-1.9.30202/23.pdf

Mujtaba, B. G., & Cavico, F. J. (2013). Corporate Social Responsibility and Sustainability Model for Global Firms. *Journal of Leadership, Accountability and Ethics*, *10*(1), 58–75.

Mullins, L. J. (2002). *Management organizational behavior*. Harlow: Pearson Education Limited.

Murphy, K. R., & Cleveland, J. N. (1995). *Understanding performance appraisal: Social, organizational and goal-based perspectives*. Thousand Oaks, CA: Sage Publications.

NABARD. (2015). Status of Microfinance in India National Bank of Agriculture and Rural Development. Mumbai: NABARD.

Nakui, T., Paulus, P. B., & van der Zee, K. I. (2011). The role of attitudes in reactions toward diversity in workgroups. *Journal of Applied Social Psychology*, *41*(10), 2327–2351. doi:10.1111/j.1559-1816.2011.00818.x

Nasir, S. (2013). Microfinance in India: Contemporary issues and challenges. *Middle East Journal of Scientific Research*, *15*(2), 191–199.

Newman, D. A., & Harrison, D. A. (2008). Been there bottle that: Are state and behavior work engagement and useful construct "wines"? *Industrial and Organizational Psychology: Perspectives on Science and Practice*, *1*(1), 31–35. doi:10.1111/j.1754-9434.2007.00003.x

Ng, E. S., & Sears, G. J. (2012). CEO leadership styles and the implementation of organizational diversity practices: Moderating effects of social values and age. *Journal of Business Ethics*, *105*(1), 41–52. doi:10.1007/s10551-011-0933-7

Nicholson, M. W. (2009). *Leadership practices, organizational commitment and turnover intentions: A correlational study in a call centre* (Ph.D Thesis). University of Phoenix.

Nimon, K., Zigarmi, D., Houson, D., Witt, D., & Diehl, J. (2011). The Work Cognition Inventory: Initial evidence of construct validity. *Human Resource Development Quarterly*, *22*(1), 7–35. doi:10.1002/hrdq.20064

Nishii, L. H., & Mayer, D. M. (2009). Do inclusive leaders help to reduce turnover in diverse groups? The moderating role of leader-member exchange in the diversity to turnover relationship. *The Journal of Applied Psychology*, *94*(6), 1412–1426. doi:10.1037/a0017190 PMID:19916652

Nkomo, S. M., & Cox, T., Jr. (1996). Diverse identities in organisations. In S. R. Clegg, C. Hardy, & W. R. Nord (Eds.), Handbook of organisation studies. Academic Press.

Noland, M., Moran, T., & Kotschwar, B. R. (2016). *Is gender diversity profitable? Evidence from a global survey*. Peterson Institute for International Economics Working Paper. Retrieved from 10.2139/ssrn.2729348

Novartis annual report. (2016). Retrieved on April 21, 2017, from https://www.novartis.com/sites/www.novartis.com/files/novartis-annual-report-2016-en.pdf

Nowack, K. M. (1993). 360-degree feedback: The whole story. *Training & Development*, *47*, 69–72.

Nyab, N. (2010, September 21). *What are the Effects of Workplace Discrimination?* Retrieved from http://www.brighthub.com/office/human-resources/articles/87966.aspx

O'Reilly, C. A., Chatman, J., & Caldwell, D. F. (1991). People and organizational culture: A profile comparison approach to assessing person-organization fit. *Academy of Management Journal, 34*(3), 487–516. doi:10.2307/256404

Ohlott, P., Ruderman, M., & McCauley, C. (1994). Gender differences in managers' development job experiences. *Academy of Management Journal, 37*(1), 46–67. doi:10.2307/256769

Okoro, E. (2012). Cross-cultural etiquette and communication in global business: Toward a strategic framework for managing corporate expansion. *International Journal of Business and Management, 7*(16), 130. doi:10.5539/ijbm.v7n16p130

Olsen, J. E., & Martins, L. L. (2012). Understanding organisational diversity management programmes: A theoretical framework and directions for future research. *Journal of Organizational Behavior, 33*(8), 1168–1187. doi:10.1002/job.1792

OMRON Global. (2017). Retrieved September 28, 2017, from https://www.omron.com/

Orme, J. (2008). *CIPD Annual conference & exhibition.* Retrieved on January 29, 2013 from http://www.cipd.co.uk/pm/peoplemanagement/b/weblog/archive/2013/01/29/jackie-ormes-speech-to-the-cipds-annual-conference-and-exhibition-2008-09.aspx

Orrick, Herrington & Sutcliffe. (2012). *Microfinance legal guide.* Author.

Otero, M. (1999). Bringing Development into Microfinance. *Journal of Microfinance, 1*(1), 8–19.

Oumlil, A. B., & Balloun, J. L. (2009). Ethical decision-making differences between American and Moroccan managers. *Journal of Business Ethics, 84*(4), 457–478. doi:10.1007/s10551-008-9719-y

Pachucki, M. A., & Breiger, R. L. (2010). Cultural holes: Beyond relationality in social networks and culture. *Annual Review of Sociology, 36*(1), 205–224. doi:10.1146/annurev.soc.012809.102615

Pager, D., Bonikowski, B., & Western, B. (2009). Race at Work: Results from a Field Experiment of Discrimination in a Low Wage Labor Market. *American Sociological Review, 74*(5), 777–799. doi:10.1177/000312240907400505 PMID:20689685

Palmquist, M. (2003). *Relational analysis.* Retrieved from http://writing.colostate.edu/guides/research/content/com2b2.cfm

Parmar, A. (2017). *A study on team climate its relationship with team effectiveness for organisational development in manufacturing sectors of central Gujarat* (Unpublished Ph.D. thesis). The Maharaja Sayajirao University of Baroda, Vadodara.

Parrey, A. H., & Bhasin, J. (2013). Gender Discrimination in workforce and discretionary work effort-A prospective approach. *International Monthly Refereed Journal of Research in Management & Technology*, 114-121.

Parvis, L. (2003). Diversity and effective leadership in multicultural workplaces. *Journal of Environmental Health, 65*(7), 37.

Patten, T. H. (1977). *Pay: Employee compensation and incentive plans*. Free Press.

Pavlović, N. (2013). *Kriza u društvu znanja,Ključne kompetencije u obrazovanju odraslih, Zbornik radova;Međunarodna konferencija u Hrvatskoj*. Vodice.

Pavlović, N. (2013). *Savremene koncepcije liderstva i organizacione kulture,Srednja škola „Đura Jakšić*. Rača.

Pavlović, N. (2015). *Nove uloge menadžmenta ljudskih resursa, SŠ Đura Jakšić*. Rača.

Pavlovic, N. (2016). *Poslovna kultura i etika, Univerzitet u Kragujevcu, Fakultet za hotelijerstvo I turizam u Vrnjačkoj Banji*. Vrnjačka Banja.

Pavlović, N., & Krstić, J. (2016). *Preduzetništvo i menadžment. Univerzitet u Kragujevcu, Fakultet za hotelijerstvo i turizam u Vrnjačkoj Banji*. Vrnjačka Banja.

Pech, R., & Slade, B. (2006). Employee disengagement: is there evidence of a growing problem? Handbook of Business Strategy, 7(1), 21-25.

Pendry, L., Driscoll, D., & Field, S. (2007). Diversity training: Putting theory into practice. *Journal of Occupational and Organizational Psychology, 80*(1), 27–50. doi:10.1348/096317906X118397

Peoplematters. (2015). *Best People Practices – Part 4: Employer Branding Initiatives*. Retrieved on August 14, 2017 from https://www.peoplematters.in/article/employer-branding/best-people-practices-part-4-employer-branding-initiatives-11731

Peoplematters. (2016). *Best Practices: Employer Branding by Hindustan Unilever*. Retrieved on June 27, 2017, from https://www.peoplematters.in/article/employer-branding/best-practices-employer-branding-hindustan-unilever-12782

Perry, E. L., & Finkelstein, L. M. (1999). Toward a broader view of age discrimination in employment related decisions: A joint consideration of organizational factors and cognitive processes. *Human Resource Management Review, 9*(1), 21–49. doi:10.1016/S1053-4822(99)00010-8

Peters, T. (1999). *The brand you 50: Fifty ways to transform yourself from an employee into a brand that shouts distinction*. New York, NY: Knopf Publishers.

Pfeiffer, S., & Suphan, A. (2015). *The Labouring Capacity Index: Living Labouring Capacity and Experience as Resources on the Road to Industry 4.0*. Retrieved on August 13, 2017 from https://www.sabine-pfeiffer.de/files/downloads/2015-Pfeiffer-Suphan-EN.pdf

Picard, R. W. (2004). Toward Machines with Emotional Intelligence. In *ICINCO (Invited Speakers)* (pp. 29-30). Retrieved on August 13, 2017 from https://dam-prod.media.mit.edu/x/files/pdfs/07.picard-EI-chapter.pdf

Pityn, K., & Helmuth, J. (2007). *Human Resource Management: Toolkit*. Microsaves.

Plakhotnik, M., Rocco, T. S., & Roberts, N. (2011). Increasing retention and success of f first time managers: A model of three integral processes for the transition to management. *Human Resource Development Review, 10*(1), 26–45. doi:10.1177/1534484310386752

Plato. (1926). Laws, Volume II: Books 7-12 (R. G. Bury, Trans.). Loeb Classical Library 192. Cambridge, MA: Harvard University Press.

Pohlman, R. A., & Gardiner, G. S. (2000). *Value Driven Management, How to Create and Maximize Value Over Time for Organizational Success*. New York: Amacom.

Pojman, P. L. (1955). *Ethics: Discovering right and wrong (3rd ed.)*. Belmont, CA: Wadsworth Publishing Company.

Poorkyani, M., Abayi, N.H., & Zareie, F. (2015). An Investigation on the Relationship between Psychological Empowerment and Organizational commitment (A Case Study of the Employees of Public Organizations in Kerman). *International Journal of Scientific Management and Development, 3*(1), 757-766.

Porter, M. E. (1980). Competitive strategy: Techniques for analyzing industries and competition. Academic Press.

Prasad, L. M. (2006). *Organisational Behaviour* (4th ed.). New Delhi: Sultan Chand & Sons.

Prendergast, C., & Topel, R. H. (1996). Favoritism in Organizations. *Journal of Political Economy, 104*(5), 958–978. doi:10.1086/262048

Procter & Gamble. (1998). *Diversity*. Retrieved from http://www.pg.com/content/pdf/01_about_pg/01_about_pg_homepage/about_pg_toolbar/download_report/diversity.pdf

Purcell, J., & Hutchinson, S. (2007). Front-line managers as agents in the HRM-performance causal chain: Theory, analysis and evidence. *Human Resource Management Journal, 17*(1), 3–20. doi:10.1111/j.1748-8583.2007.00022.x

Quick, J.C., Piotrkowski, C., Jenkins, L., & Brooks, Y.B. (2004). *Four dimensions of healthy work: Stress, work-family relations, violence prevention, and relationships at work*. Academic Press.

Quick, J. C., Quick, J. D., Nelson, D. L., & Hurrell, J. J. Jr. (1997). *Preventive stress management in organizations*. American Psychological Association. doi:10.1037/10238-000

Quinn, R. E., & Spreitzer, G. M. (1991). The psychometrics of the competing values culture instrument and an analysis of the impact of organizational culture on quality of life. *Emerald.*, 5, 115–142.

Raghav, N. (2012). A study of qualified HR practices among micro finance institution in Northern states in India. *Asian Journal of Research in Social Sciences and Humanities, 2*(4), 8–31.

Rajarshi. (2016). *How organizations have changed their Performance Reviews*. Retrieved on May 22, 2017, from https://grosum.com/blog/how_organizations_have_changed_their_performance_reviews/

Compilation of References

Randstad. (2015). *Google India wins the Randstad Award 2015 for the 'Most Attractive Employer' in India*. Retrieved on June 25, 2015, from https://www.randstad.in/about-us/press-releases/press-releases/google-india-wins-the-randstad-award-2015-for-the-most-attractive-employer-in-india/

Randstad. (2016). *International Report Randstad Award Results*. Retrieved on June 28, 2017, from file:///C:/Users/acer/Downloads/Employer%20Branding%20-%20international%20insights%20Randstad%20Award%20research%202016%20(2).pdf

Randstad. (2017). *Employer branding for organizational change*. Retrieved on June 30, 2017, from https://www.randstad.in/workforce360/archives/employer-branding-as-an-instrument-of-organisational-change_82/

Randstad. (2017). *Google India emerges as India's most 'attractive employer' Randstad Employer Brand Research 2017*. Retrieved on June 25, 2017, from https://www.randstad.in/about-us/press-releases/press-releases/google-india-emerges-as-indias-most-attractive-employer-randstad-employer-brand-research-2017/

Rani, L., Kumar, N., & Kumar, S. (2012). Performnce appraisals research: A study of performance appraisals practicies in private bank. *ABHINAV National Monthly Refreed Journal of Research in Commerce & Management, 3*(2), 108–113.

Rao, V. (2016). *Employee Value Proposition: A key to creating a Great Workforce*. Retrieved on August 15, 2017 from https://www.linkedin.com/pulse/employee-value-proposition-key-creating-great-workforce-vivek-rao

Rao, T. V. (2004). *Performance Management and Appraisal Systems: HR tools for global competitiveness*. SAGE Publications India.

Rashid, A., & Twaha, K. (2013). Exploring the determinants of the productivity of indian microfinance institutions. *Theoretical and Applied Economics, 18*(12), 83–96.

Rausch, E., Halfhill, S. M., Sherman, H., & Washbush, J. B. (2001). Practical leadership-in-management education for effective strategies in a rapidly changing world. *Journal of Management Development, 20*(3), 245–258. doi:10.1108/02621710110386381

Ravichandran, K. K., Arasu, R. R., & Arun Kumar, S. S. (2011). The Impact of Emotional Intelligence on Employee Work Engagement Behavior: An Empirical Study. *International Journal of Business and Management, 6*(11), 157–169. doi:10.5539/ijbm.v6n11p157

Raychoudhri, S. (2013). *India's best employer: Branding initiative*. Retrieved on June 26, 2017, from http://www.greatplacetowork.in/storage/documents/Publications_Documents/Conference_presentations/Whirlpool-_Sarthak_Raychouduri.pdf

Reddin, B. (1988). *The output oriented organization*. Gower Publishing Company Limited.

Rees, F. (1997). *Teamwork from start to finish*. San Francisco, CA: Jossey-Bass.

Reeves, B., & Nass, C. (1996). *The Media Equation*. New York, NY: Cambridge University Press.

Reio, T. G. Jr, & Callahan, J. (2004). Affect, curiosity, and socialization-related learning: A pathanalysis of antecedents to job performance. *Journal of Business and Psychology, 18*, 35–50.

Reio, T. G. Jr, Petrosko, J. M., Wiswell, A. K., & Thongsukmag, J. (2006). The measurement and conceptualization of curiosity. *The Journal of Genetic Psychology, 167*(2), 117–135. doi:10.3200/GNTP.167.2.117-135 PMID:16910206

Reskin, B. F. (2000). The Proximate Causes of Employment Discrimination. *Contemporary Sociology, 29*(2), 319–328. doi:10.2307/2654387

Rhyne, E. (1998). The yin and yang of microfinance: Reaching the poor and sustainability. *MicroBanking Bulletin, 2*(1), 6–8.

Richard, O. C., Ford, D., & Ismail, K. (2006). Exploring the performance effects of visible attribute diversity: The moderating role of span of control and organizational life cycle. *International Journal of Human Resource Management, 17*(12), 2091–2109. doi:10.1080/09585190601000246

Richard, O. C., & Johnson, N. B. (2001). Understanding the impact of human resource diversity practices on firm performance. *Journal of Managerial Issues, 2*, 177–195.

Richard, O., & Johnson, N. B. (1991). Making the connection between formal human resource diversity practices and organizational effectiveness: Beyond management fashion. *Performance Improvement Quarterly, 12*(1), 77–96. doi:10.1111/j.1937-8327.1999.tb00116.x

Richardson, M. W. (1949). Forced-choice performance reports: A modern merit-rating method. *Personnel, 26*, 205–212.

Rich, B. L., Lepine, J. A., & Crawford, E. R. (2010). Job engagement: Antecedents and effects on job performance. *Academy of Management Journal, 53*(3), 617–635. doi:10.5465/AMJ.2010.51468988

Richman, A. (2006). Everyone wants an engaged workforce how can you create it? *Workspan, 49*, 36–39.

Riffkin, R., & Harter, J. (2016). *Using Employee Engagement to Build a Diverse Workforce*. Gallup Inc.

Riordan, C. M. (2000). Relational demography within groups: Past developments, contradictions, and new directions. In *Research in personnel and human resources management* (pp. 131–173). Emerald Group Publishing Limited. doi:10.1016/S0742-7301(00)19005-X

Robbins, S. P. (2003). *Organizational Behaviour*. Prentice Hall.

Robbins, S. P., & Judge, T. A. (2007). *Organizational Behavior* (12th ed.). Pearson Education, Inc.

Robbins, S., & Coulter, M. (2008). *Management* (8th ed.). Belgrade: DataStatus.

Robbins, S., & Judge, T. (2009). *Organizacijsko ponašanje (12th ed.)*. Zagreb: MATE.

Robbins, T. L., Crino, M. D., & Fredendall, L. D. (2002). An Integrative Model of the Empowerment Process. *Human Resource Management, 12*(1), 419–443. doi:10.1016/S1053-4822(02)00068-2

Roberge, M. É., Lewicki, R. J., Hietapelto, A., & Abdyldaeva, A. (2011). From theory to practice: Recommending supportive diversity practices. *Journal of Diversity Management, 6*(2), 1. doi:10.19030/jdm.v6i2.5481

Roberson, Q. M. (2006). Disentangling the meanings of diversity and inclusion in organizations. *Group & Organization Management, 31*(2), 212–236. doi:10.1177/1059601104273064

Robinson, D., Perryman, S., & Hayday, S. (2004). *The drivers of employee engagement.* Report-Institute for Employment Studies.

Robinson, D., Perryman, S., & Hayday, S. (2004). *The Drivers of Employee Engagement Report 408.* Institute for Employment Studies.

Robinson, M. (2001). *The microfinance revolution: Sustainable finance for the poor.* World Bank Publications. doi:10.1596/0-8213-4524-9

Robinson, S. L., & Benett, R. J. (1995). A typology of Deviant workplace behaviors: A multidimensional scaling study. *Academy of Management Journal, 38*(2), 555–572. doi:10.2307/256693

Robotics-VO. (2013). *A Roadmap for US Robotics: From Internet to Robotics.* Retrieved on August 13, 2017 from http://www.roboticscaucus.org/Schedule/2013/20March2013/2013%20Robotics%20Roadmap-rs.pdf

Rocco, T., Stein, D., & Lee, C. (2003). An exploratory examination of the literature on age and HRD policy development. *Human Resource Development Review, 2*(2), 155–180. doi:10.1177/1534484303002002004

Rockstuhl, T., Seiler, S., Ang, S., Van Dyne, L., & Annen, H. (2011). Beyond general intelligence (IQ) and emotional intelligence (EQ): The role of cultural intelligence (CQ) on cross-border leadership effectiveness in a globalized world. *The Journal of Social Issues, 67*(4), 825–840. doi:10.1111/j.1540-4560.2011.01730.x

Rodan, S., & Galunic, C. (2004). More than network structure: How knowledge heterogeneity influences managerial performance and innovativeness. *Strategic Management Journal, 25*(6), 541–562. doi:10.1002/smj.398

Rodgers, C. (1993). The Flexible Workplace: What have We Learned? *Human Resource Management, 31*(1).

Roosevelt, T. R. Jr. (2001). *Elements of a successful diversity process.* The American Institute for Managing Diversity.

Rose, A. (2016). *Consequences of Discrimination in the Workplace.* Retrieved from http://woman.thenest.com/consequences-discrimination-workplace-15256.html

Rose, M. (2015). *The impact of board diversity in board compositions on firm financial performance of organizations in Germany.* Paper presented at the fifth IBA Bachelor Thesis Conference, Enschede, The Netherlands.

Rosenberg, S. Z. (2008, April 8). Why Aren't There More Women on Boards? Moving past tokenism and box checking opens doors to more diversity. *Bloomberg.* Retrieved from https://www.bloomberg.com

Rothbard, N. P. (2001). Enriching or depleting? The dynamics of engagement in work and family roles. *Administrative Science Quarterly, 46*(4), 655–684. doi:10.2307/3094827

Rothmann, S., & Storm, K. (2003, May). *Work engagement in the South African police service.* Paper presented at the 11th European Congress of Work and Organizational Psychology, Lisbon, Portugal.

Rowe, K., & Howell, P. (2014). *The positive work place.* ASTD, Human Capital Community. Retrieved April, 2017, from http//:www.td.org/publication

Roy, S. R. (2012). Digital mastery: The skills needed for effective virtual leadership. *International Journal of e-Collaboration, 8*(3), 56–66. doi:10.4018/jec.2012070104

Rozensky, R. H., Johnson, N. G., Goodheart, C. D., & Hammond, W. (2004). *Psychology builds a healthy world: Opportunities for research and practice.* American Psychological Association. doi:10.1037/10678-000

Rozovsky, J. (2015, November 17). *The five keys to a successful Google team.* Retrieved from https://rework.withgoogle.com/blog/five-keys-to-a-successful-google-team/

Sa-Dhan. (2015). *Bharat Microfinance Report-2015.* New Delhi: The Association of Community Development Finance Institutions.

Saks, A. (2008). The Meaning and Bleeding of Employee Engagement: How Muddy Is the Water? *Industrial and Organizational Psychology: Perspectives on Science and Practice, 1*(1), 40–43. doi:10.1111/j.1754-9434.2007.00005.x

Saks, A. M. (2006). Antecedents and consequences of employee engagement. *Journal of Managerial Psychology, 21*(7), 600–619. doi:10.1108/02683940610690169

Salanova, M., Agut, S., & Peiró, J. M. (2005). Linking organizational resources and work engagement to employee performance and customer loyalty: The mediation of service climate. *The Journal of Applied Psychology, 90*(6), 1217–1227. doi:10.1037/0021-9010.90.6.1217 PMID:16316275

Sanchez, J. I., & Brock, P. (1996). Outcomes of Perceived Discrimination among Hispanic Employees: Is Diversity Management A Luxury or A Necessity. *Academy of Management Journal, 39*(3), 704–719. doi:10.2307/256660

Sar, A. L., Garth, L. M., & Ray, M. (1972). *Human resources and labour markets.* New York: Horper and Row Publishers.

Sarkar, J., & Selarka, E. (2015). Women on board and performance of family firms: Evidence from India. *IGIDR,* 1-50.

Compilation of References

Sashkin, M. (1991). *Pillars of excellence: Organizational beliefs questionnaire*. Organization Design and Development.

Šator, G. (2011). *Harmonia zivota a byvania (2nd ed.)*. Bratislava: IKAR.

Sauceda, J. M. (2003). Managing intercultural conflict effectively. In L. A. Samovar & R. E. Porter (Eds.), *Intercultural communication: A reader* (pp. 385–405). Belmont, CA: Wadsworth.

Schaubroeck, J., Ganster, D. C., Sime, W. E., & Ditman, D. (1993). A field experiment testing supervisory role clarification. *Personnel Psychology*, *46*(1), 1–25. doi:10.1111/j.1744-6570.1993.tb00865.x

Schaufeli, W. B., & Bakker, A. B. (2004). Job demands, job resources, and their relationship with burnout and engagement: A multi-sample study. *Journal of Organizational Behavior*, *25*(3), 293–315. doi:10.1002/job.248

Schaufeli, W. B., Bakker, A. B., & Salanova, M. (2006). The measurement of work engagement with a short questionnaire: A cross-national study. *Educational and Psychological Measurement*, *66*(4), 701–716. doi:10.1177/0013164405282471

Schaufeli, W. B., & Salanova, M. (2010). Work engagement: On how to better catch a slippery concept. *European Journal of Work and Organizational Psychology*, *20*(1), 39–46. doi:10.1080/1359432X.2010.515981

Schaufeli, W. B., Salanova, M., González-Romá, V., & Bakker, A. B. (2002). The measurement of engagement and burnout: A two sample confirmatory factor analytic approach. *Journal of Happiness Studies*, *3*(1), 71–92. doi:10.1023/A:1015630930326

Schaufeli, W. B., Taris, T. W., & Van Rhenen, W. (2008). Workaholism, burnout, and work engagement: Three of a kind or three different kinds of employee well-being? *Applied Psychology*, *57*(2), 173–203. doi:10.1111/j.1464-0597.2007.00285.x

Schein, E.H. (1985). How culture forms, develops, and changes. *Gaining Control of the Corporate Culture*, 17-43.

Schein, E. (1992). *Organizational Culture and Leadership* (2nd ed.). San Francisco, CA: Jossey-Bass.

Schein, E. (2010). *Organizational Culture and leadership* (4th ed.). San Francisco, CA: Jossey-Bass.

Schneider, B., Bowen, D. E., Ehrhart, M. G., & Holcombe, K. M. (2000). The climate for service: Evolution of a construct. In N. M. Ashkanasy, C. P. Wilderom, & M. F. Peterson (Eds.), *Handbook of organizational culture and climate* (pp. 21–36). Thousand Oaks, CA: Sage.

Schreiner, M., & Morduch, J. (2001). *Replicating microfinance in the United States: Opportunities and challenges*. Washington, DC: Fannie Mae Foundation.

Schumann, P. (2004). A Moral Principles Framework for Human Resource Management Ethics. *Human Resource Mangement RE:view*, *11*(1).

Schwartz-Ziv, M. (2013). Does the gender of directors matter? *Edmond J. Safra Working Papers, 8.*

Scott, W. D., & Clothier, R. C. (1923). *Personnel Management: Principles, practices, and points of view.* New York: A.W. Shaw.

Scott, W. D., Clothier, R. C., & Spriegel, W. R. (1941). *Personnel management.* New York: McGraw-Hill.

Sector Report- Microfinance India: 2009. (2009). Available at http://www.microfinanceindia.com

Seierstad, C., Warner-Søderholm, G., Torchia, M., & Huse, M. (2017). Increasing the number of women on boards: The role of actors and processes. *Journal of Business Ethics, 141*(2), 289–315. doi:10.1007/s10551-015-2715-0

Seijts, G. H., & Crim, D. (2006). What engages employees the most or, the ten C's of employee engagement. *Ivey Business Journal, 70*(4), 1–5.

Selvaraj, S.N. (2012). Challenging tasks of human resource department in Microfinance Institutions. *A Journal of Economics and Management, 1*(5).

Sen, A. (2016). *Wipro sets stage for broad overhaul for appraisal system ditches bell curve as part of pilot.* Retrieved on March 5, 2017, from http://economictimes.indiatimes.com/tech/ites/wipro-sets-stage-for-broad-overhaul-of-appraisal-system-ditches-bell-curve-as-part-of pilot/articleshow/51216872.cms

Sen, A., & Alawadhi, N. (2016). *Good bye annual appraisals IBM says hello to checkpoint.* Retrieved on May 22, 2017, from http://tech.economictimes.indiatimes.com/news/corporate/good-bye-annual-appraisals-ibm-says-hello-to-checkpoint/50829448

Seppälä, P., Mauno, S., Feldt, T., Hakanen, J., Kinnunen, U., & Schaufeli, W. et al.. (2009). The Construct Validity of the Utrecht Work Engagement Scale: Multisample and Longitudinal Evidence. *Journal of Happiness Studies, 10*(4), 459–481. doi:10.1007/s10902-008-9100-y

Sessa, V. I. (1992). *Managing diversity at the Xerox Corporation: Balanced workforce goals and caucus groups.* Academic Press.

Shankar, B. (2016). *Infosys using new system icount assess employee performance.* Retrieved on May 27, 2017, from http://www.ibtimes.co.in/infosys-using-new-system-icount-assess-employee-performance-666114

Sharit, J., & Czaja, S. J. (1994). Ageing, computer-based task performance, and stress: Issues and challenges. *Ergonomics, 37*(4), 559–577. doi:10.1080/00140139408963674 PMID:8187745

Sharma, A., & Das, G. (2016). *Sustaining Employer Branding at Whirlpool of India Ltd.* Retrieved on June 30, 2017 from http://www.etcases.com/media/clnews/14732403033363365 02.pdf

Shastry, V. (2014). *Human Resource Management Practices among MFI's in India.* Available at http://indiamicrofinance.com/human-resource-management-mfi-india.html

Compilation of References

Shaw, K. (2005). An engagement strategy process for communicators. *Strategic Communication Management*, 9(3), 26–29.

Shaw, M. E. (1976). *Group dynamics*. New York: McGraw-Hill.

Sheridan, A., & Milgate, G. (2003). "She says, he says": Women's and men's views of the composition of boards. *Women in Management Review*, 18(3), 147–154. doi:10.1108/09649420310471109

Shirom, A. (2007). Explaining vigor: On the antecedents and consequences of vigor as a positive affect at work. In C. L. Cooper & D. Nelson (Eds.), *Positive organizational behavior* (pp. 86–100). London, UK: SAGE. doi:10.4135/9781446212752.n7

Shraga, O. (2007). *Vigor at work: Its construct validity, and its relations with job satisfaction and job characteristics: Triangulating qualitative and quantitative methodologies* (Unpublished doctoral dissertation). Tel Aviv University, Israel.

Shrivastava, P., & Rai, U. K. (2012). Performance appraisal practices in Indian banks. *Integral Review*, 5(2), 46.

SHRM. (2008). *The Employer Brand: A Strategic Tool to Attract, Recruit and Retain Talent*. Retrieved on May, 2013, from www.shrm.org/Research/Articles/Articles/Pages/TheEmployerBrandAStrategicTooltoAttract,RecruitandRetainTalent.aspx

SHRM. (2009). *Global Diversity and Inclusion- Perceptions, Practices and Attitudes*. Society for Human Resource.

SHRM. (2014). *Branding: What is an employer brand, and how can we develop an employment branding strategy?* Retrieved on June 29, 2017 from https://www.shrm.org/resourcesandtools/tools-and-samples/hr-qa/pages/cms_023007.aspx

Shuck, B., & Herd, A. (2011). Employee engagement and leadership: Exploring the conceptual convergence of two paradigms and implications for leadership development in HRD. In K. M. Dirani (Ed.), *Proceedings of the Academy of Human Resource Development, 2011 Annual Conference*. Chicago, IL: AHRD.

Shuck, M. B. (2010). *Employee Engagement: An examination of antecedent and outcome varaibles* (Doctoral Thesis). Florida International University.

Shuck, B. (2011). Four emerging perspectives of employee engagement: An integrative literature review. *Human Resource Development Review*, 10(3), 304–328. doi:10.1177/1534484311410840

Shuck, B., Reio, T., & Rocco, T. (2011). Employee engagement: An antecedent and outcome approach to model development. *Human Resource Development International*, 14, 427–445. doi:10.1080/13678868.2011.601587

Shuck, B., Rocco, T., & Albornoz, C. (2011). Exploring employee engagement from the employee perspective: Implications for HRD. *Journal of European Industrial Training*, 35(4), 300–325. doi:10.1108/03090591111128306

Shuck, B., & Wollard, K. (2010). Employee engagement & HRD: A seminal review of the foundations. *Human Resource Development Review*, *9*(1), 89–110. doi:10.1177/1534484309353560

Silverstein, S. (1995, May 5). Workplace diversity efforts thrive despite backlash. *Los Angeles Times*, p. A1.

Simard, M., & Marchand, A. (1995). A multilevel analysis of organisational factors related to the taking of safety initiatives by work groups. *Safety Science*, *21*(2), 113–129. doi:10.1016/0925-7535(95)00050-X

Simmons-Welburn, J. (1999). Diversity dialogue groups: A model for enhancing work place diversity. *Journal of Library Administration*, *27*(1-2), 111–121. doi:10.1300/J111v27n01_08

Simons, G. F. (1992). *The questions of diversity: Assessment tools for organizations and individuals* (4th ed.). Amherst, MA: ODT Incorporated.

Singh, A. (2010). A study on the perception of work-life balance policies among software professionals. *Journal of Management Research*, *9*(2), 51.

Sippola, A., & Smale, A. (2007). The global integration of diversity management: A longitudinal case study. *International Journal of Human Resource Management*, *18*(11), 1895–1916. doi:10.1080/09585190701638101

Sisson, E. D. (1948). Forced-choice: The new army rating. *Personnel Psychology*, *1*(3), 365–438. doi:10.1111/j.1744-6570.1948.tb01316.x

Skalsky, P., & McCarthy, G. (2009). *Diversity Management in Australia and its Impact on Employee Engagement*. World at Work.

Smith, L. M., Andrusyszyn, M. A., & Laschinger, H. K. S. (2010). Effects of Workplace Incivility and Empowerment on Newly-Graduated Nurses' Organizational Commitment. *Journal of Nursing Management*, *18*(8), 1004–1015. doi:10.1111/j.1365-2834.2010.01165.x PMID:21073572

Smith, N., Smith, V., & Verner, M. (2006). Do women in top management affect firm performance? A panel study of 2,500 Danish firms. *International Journal of Productivity and Performance Management*, *55*(7), 569–593. doi:10.1108/17410400610702160

Smith, P. C., & Kendall, L. M. (1963). Retranslation of expectations: An approach to the construction of unambiguous anchors for rating scale. *The Journal of Applied Psychology*, *47*(2), 149–155. doi:10.1037/h0047060

Society for Human Resource Management (SHRM). (1998). *SHRM survey explores the best in diversity practices. Fortune 500 firms outpace the competition with greater commitment to diversity*. Retrieved on August 28, 2017 from http://www.shrm.org/

Som, C. V. (2007). Exploring the human resource implications of clinical governance. *Health Policy (Amsterdam)*, *80*(2), 281–296. doi:10.1016/j.healthpol.2006.03.010 PMID:16678293

Song, J. H., Kim, H. M., & Kolb, J. A. (2009). The effect of learning organization culture on the relationship between interpersonal trust and organizational commitment. *Human Resource Development Quarterly*, *20*(2), 147–167. doi:10.1002/hrdq.20013

Soulat, A., & Nasir, N. (2017). Examining the Role of Employee Diversity Management and Employee Involvement Variation on Organizational Innovation: A Study from Pakistan. *Singaporean Journal of Business. Economics and Management Studies*, *5*(9), 62–69.

Soutar, S. (2004). Beyond the Rainbow Diversity extends beyond ethnicity, age, and gender. *Association Management-Washington*, *56*(4), 26–33.

Sparrow, P. R., & Balain, S. (2010). Engaging HR strategists: Do the logics match the realities? In S. Albrecht (Ed.), *The handbook of employee engagement: Models, measures and practice* (pp. 263–296). London, UK: Edward-Elgar. doi:10.4337/9781849806374.00033

Spector, E. (1997). *Job Satisfaction: Aplication, Assessment, Causes and Consequences*. Thousand Oaks, CA: SAGE.

Spreitzer, G. M. (1995). Psychological empowerment in the workplace: Dimensions, measurement, and validation. *Academy of Management Journal*, *38*(5), 1442–1465. doi:10.2307/256865

Spreitzer, G. M. (2007). *A Review of More Than Twenty Years of Research on Empowerment at Work. In The Handbook of Organizational Behavior*. Sage Publications.

Srivastava, M. (2015, January 4). *India set to increase tech start-ups base to 11,500: report*. Retrieved from http://www.livemint.com/Industry/JvotTawbmJzMVXyrKZ8CPM/India-set-to-increase-tech-startups-base-to-11500-report.html

Srivastava, P., & Bhatnagar, J. (2010). Employer brand for talent acquisition: An exploration towards its measurement. *Vision*, *14*(1-2), 25–34. doi:10.1177/097226291001400103

Stainback, K., Ratliff, T. N., & Roscigno, V. J. (2011). The context of workplace sex discrimination: Sex composition, Workplace Culture and Relative Power. *Social Forces*, *89*(4), 1165–1188. doi:10.1093/sf/89.4.1165

Stambor, Z. (2006). Employees: A company's best asset. *Monitor on Psychology*, *37*(3), 28.

Stanton, M. (2011). *Killer stuff and tons of money: An insider's look at the world of flea markets, antiques, and collecting*. Penguin Books.

Starbucks. (2003). *Living our values. Corporate Social Responsibility. Fiscal 2003*. Annual Report. Author.

Starbucks. (2011). *Business ethics and compliance*. Author.

Starbucks (2014). *Diversity and inclusion*. Author.

Steidlmeier, P. (1999). Gift giving, bribery and corruption: Ethical management of business relationships in China. *Journal of Business Ethics*, *20*(2), 121–133. doi:10.1023/A:1005960026519

Stephenson, C. (2004). Leveraging diversity to maximum advantage: The business case for appointing more women to boards. *Ivey Business Journal*, *69*(1), 1–5.

Stevens, M. J., & Campion, M. A. (1994). The knowledge, skills, and ability requirements for teamwork: Implications for human resource management. *Journal of Management*, *20*(2), 503–530. doi:10.1177/014920639402000210

Stockdale, M. S., & Crosby, F. (2004). *The Psychology and Management of Workplace Diversity*. Boston, MA: Blackwell.

Story, J. S., & Barbuto, J. E. Jr. (2011). Global mindset: A construct clarification and framework. *Journal of Leadership & Organizational Studies*, *18*(3), 377–384. doi:10.1177/1548051811404421

Strauss, G., & Sayles, L. (1971). *Personnel – The human problems in management*. New Delhi: Prentice Hall of India.

Sullivan, J. (2004). *Eight elements of a successful employment brand*. Retrieved on June 21, 2017, from https://www.eremedia.com/ere/the-8-elements-of-a-successful-employment-brand/

Sutherland, M. M., Torricelli, D. G., & Karg, R. F. (2002). Employer-of-choice branding for knowledge workers. *South African Journal of Business Management*, *33*(4), 13–20.

Taghipur, M., Mahboobi, M., Nikoefair, A., & Mowloodi, E. (2015). Analysing the Effect of Physical Conditions of the Workpalce on Employees Productivity. *International Journal of Environmental Protection and Policy*, *3*(4).

Tannen, D. (1995). *You Just Do not Understand: Women and Men in Conversation*. New York: Ballantine Books.

Tanzi, V. (1998). Corruption around the world - Causes, consequences, scope and cures. *IMF Staff Papers*, *45*(4), 559–594. doi:10.2307/3867585

Taylor, J. (2002, May). For workers, it's all about the balancing act. *Omaha World-Herald*, p. 1d.

Techniques for Assessment of Performance and the Factors Affecting Assessments. (n.d.). Retrieved on June 02, 2017, from http://www.managementstudyguide.com/performance-assessment-techniques.htm

Terjesen, S., Sealy, R., & Singh, V. (2009). Women directors on corporate boards: A review and research agenda. *Corporate Governance*, *17*(3), 320–337. doi:10.1111/j.1467-8683.2009.00742.x

Terrapin Adventures. (2016, February 29). *Case Study: How Teamwork, Competition Motivate Employees*. Retrieved from https://www.terrapinadventures.com/blog/case-study-how-teamwork-competition-motivate-employees/

Thomas, D. A., & Ely, R. (1996, September/October). Making differences matter: A new paradigm for managing diversity. *Harvard Business Review*, 79–90.

Thomas, K. W., & Kilmann, R. H. (1974). *Conflict Mode Instrument*. Sterling Forest, NY: Xicom Inc.

Thomas, R. R. (1990). From affirmative action to affirming diversity. *Harvard Business Review*, *68*(2), 107–117. PMID:10106515

Thomas, R. R. (1992). Managing diversity: A conceptual framework. In *Diversity in the workplace* (pp. 306–317). New York: Guilford Press.

Thonas, R.J. (2000). Irreconcilable Differences. *Accenture Outlook, 1*.

Ting-Toomey, S., & Kurogi, A. (1998). Facework competence in intercultural conflict: An updated face-negotiation theory. *International Journal of Intercultural Relations*, *22*(2), 187–225. doi:10.1016/S0147-1767(98)00004-2

Toegel, G., & Barsoux, J. L. (2016). *3 Situations where cross-cultural communication creaks down*. Retrieved from https://hbr.org/2016/06/3-situations-where-cross-cultural-communication-breaks-down

Tomervik, K. (1995). Workforce diversity in Fortune 500, corporations headquartered in Minnesota: Concepts and practices. *Academy of Human Resource Development (AHRD) Conference Proceedings*.

Torraco, R. (2005). Writing integrative literature reviews: Guidelines and examples. *Human Resource Development Review*, *4*(3), 356–367. doi:10.1177/1534484305278283

Townsend, A., DeMarie, S., & Hendrickson, A. (2017). *Virtual teams: Technology and the workplace of the future*. Retrieved April, 2017, from http//www.amp.aom.or/content

Triandis, H. C. (1994). *Culture and social behavior*. New York: McGraw-Hill.

Triandis, H. C., Kurowski, L. L., & Gelfand, M. J. (1994). Workplace diversity. In H. C. Triandis, M. Dunnette, & L. M. Hough (Eds.), *Handbook of industrial and organizational psychology* (pp. 770–827). Palo Alto, CA: Consulting PsychologistsPress.

Tsui, A. S., & Gutek, B. A. (1999). *Demographic differences in organizations: Current research and future directions*. Lexington Books.

Turner, J., & Tajfel, H. (1982). *Social identity and intergroup relations*. Academic Press.

TylerK. (2005). *Performance Art*. Retrieved from https://www.shrm.org/hr-today/news/hr-magazine/pages/0805tyler.aspx

Ugaz, J. (2016). *Corruption perceptions index 2016*. Retrieved from https://www.transparency.org/news/feature/corruption_perceptions_index_2016

Ulrich, D., & Smallwood, N. (2012). What is leadership? In *Advances in global leadership* (pp. 9–36). Emerald Group Publishing Limited. doi:10.1108/S1535-1203(2012)0000007005

UNESCO. (2001). *Universal declaration on cultural diversity*. Retrieved from: http://unesdoc.unesco.org/Images/0012/001271/127162e.pdf

Unicef CSR. (2017). Retrieved April, 2017, from http//:www.unicef.com/csr/235.htm

United Nations, Department of Economic and United Nations Capital Development Fund. (2006). Building inclusive financial sectors for development. United Nations Publications.

Upadhya, C., Gurumurthy, A., Singh, P. J., Mundkur, A., & Swamy, M. (2005). *Gender Issues in the Indian Software Outsourcing Industry.* Elsevier.

Vera, D., & Crossan, M. (2004). Strategic leadership and organizational learning. *Academy of Management Review, 29*(2), 222–240.

Vinnicombe, S., & Singh, V. (2003). Locks and keys to the boardroom. *Women in Management Review, 18*(6), 325–333. doi:10.1108/09649420310491495

Vujić, D. (2008). Menadžment ljudskih resursa i kvalitet. Centar za primenjenu psihologiju.

Wah, L. (1999). Engaging employees a big challenge. *Management Review, 88*(9), 10.

Wakoko, F. (2004). *Microfinance and women's empowerment in Uganda: A socioeconomic approach* (Doctoral dissertation). The Ohio State University.

Walden, M. (2017). *How Important is Your Work Environment?* ICS Insights. Retrieved April, 2017, from http//:www.infinity-cs.com

Waldman. (2016). *The Importance of Diversity and inclusion on Employee Engagement.* The Employee Engagement Blog.

WaldmanP. (n.d.). Retrieved from Linkedin: https://www.linkedin.com/pulse/promoting-equality-workplace-phillip-waldman

Walker, B. A. (1991). Valuing differences: The concept and a model. In M. A. Smith & S. J. Johnson (Eds.), *Valuing differences in the workplace* (pp. 23–44). Alexandria, VA: ASTD Press.

Walmart. (2015). *Diversity & Inclusion.* Global Office of Diversity and Inclusion.

Wang, M. (2011). Integrating organizational, social, and individual perspectives in Web 2.0-based workplace e-learning. *Information Systems Frontiers, 13*(2), 191–205. doi:10.1007/s10796-009-9191-y

Wanous, J., & Reichers, E., & Hudy. (1997). Overall Job Satisfaction: How good Are Single-Item Measures? *The Journal of Applied Psychology, 4*(2). PMID:9109282

Watkins, M. (2013). What is Organizational Culture? And Why Should We care? *Harvard Business Review, 5*(10).

Watt, J., & Piotrowski, C. (2008). Organizational change cynicism: A review of the literature and intervention strategies. *Organization Development Journal, 26*(3), 23.

Weaver, G. R. (2001). Ethics programs in global businesses: Culture's role in managing ethics. *Journal of Business Ethics, 30*(1), 3–15. doi:10.1023/A:1006475223493

Weinreb, L. (1990). *Natural Law and Justice.* Cambridge, MA: Harvard University Press.

Compilation of References

Weiss, W. H. (2004). Effective Leadership: What are the requisites? *Super Vision, 65*(1), 14–17.

Wentling, R. M., & Palma-Rivas, N. (2000). Current status of diversity initiatives in selected multinational corporations. *Human Resource Development Quarterly, 11*(1), 35–60. doi:10.1002/1532-1096(200021)11:1<35::AID-HRDQ4>3.0.CO;2-#

Wesley, J. R., & Muthuswamy, P. R. (2005). Work-family conflict in India-An empirical study. *SCMS Journal of Indian Management*, 95-102.

Wheeler, M. L. (1994). *Diversity training*. New York: The Conference Board.

Wheeler, M. L. (1995). *Diversity: Business rationale and strategies*. New York: The Conference Board.

Wiese, D. L., & Buckley, M. R. (1998). The evolution of the performance appraisal process. *Journal of Management History, 4*(3), 233–249. doi:10.1108/13552529810231003

Williams, C. (2010). *Principi menadžmenta*. Beograd: DataStatus.

Williams, R. J. (2003). Women on corporate boards of directors and their influence on corporate philanthropy. *Journal of Business Ethics, 42*(1), 1–10. doi:10.1023/A:1021626024014

Winter, M. (1992). Workforce diversity: Corporate challenges. New York: The Conference Board.

Wood, R. E. (1986). Task complexity: Definition of the construct. *Organizational Behavior and Human Decision Processes, 37*(1), 60–82. doi:10.1016/0749-5978(86)90044-0

Working at GSK. (n.d.). Retrieved on May 29, 2017, from http://www.gsk.com/en-gb/responsibility/our-people/working-at-gsk/

World Bank. (2013). *Historic Goals to End Extreme Poverty: Endorsed by World Bank Governors*. Press Release. Available at http://www.worldbank.org/en/news/press-release/2013/04/20/historic-goals-to-end-extreme-poverty-endorsed-by-world-bank-governors accessed on 07/08/2016

World Health Organization. (2007). *Knowledge Management Strategy*. World Health Organization Press.

Xanthopoulou, D., Bakker, A. B., Demerouti, E., & Schaufeli, W. B. (2007). The role of personal resources in the job demands-resources model. *International Journal of Stress Management, 14*(2), 121–141. doi:10.1037/1072-5245.14.2.121

Xanthopoulou, D., Bakker, A. B., Demerouti, E., & Schaufeli, W. B. (2009). Reciprocal relationships between job resources, personal resources, and work engagement. *Journal of Vocational Behavior, 74*(3), 235–244. doi:10.1016/j.jvb.2008.11.003

Yang, Y. (2005, August). Developing cultural diversity advantage: The impact of diversity management structures. In *Academy of Management Best Conference Paper* (pp. H1-H6). GDO.

Yukl, G. A. (1981). *Leadership in organizations*. Pearson Education India.

Zammuto, R. F., & Krakower, J. Y. (1991). *Quantitative and qualitative studies of organizational culture*. JAI Press Inc.

Zillman, C. (2016). *IBM is blowing up its Annual Performance Review*. Retrieved on May 25, 2017, from http://fortune.com/2016/02/01/ibm-employee-performance-reviews/

Zohar, D. (2000). A group-level model of safety climate: Testing the effect of group climate on microaccidents in manufacturing jobs. *The Journal of Applied Psychology, 85*(4), 587–596. doi:10.1037/0021-9010.85.4.587 PMID:10948803

Index

360 Degree Appraisal 261, 268, 278

A

age discrimination 73, 212
artificial intelligence 39-41, 43-45, 49-50, 72
Artificial Workforce 41, 43, 45, 49
Assessment Centres 270, 272, 278

B

Baby boomers 39-41, 43
Balance Scorecard 270, 279
banks 175, 182, 266, 268, 271, 281-282, 285, 291-292, 298-299, 301, 303
biasness 47, 211-212, 219
boardrooms 22-31, 34

C

CCOpex 131
cognitive 6, 8, 12, 44-45, 47, 49, 84, 134-136, 156, 159, 171, 298
communication 12-13, 57, 60, 62, 64-68, 72, 74, 82-83, 86, 88, 90-92, 100, 102-103, 111, 123, 127, 151, 154, 158, 161, 187, 190, 192-193, 197-199, 208, 265, 270, 281, 290, 304
competitiveness 10-11, 13, 18, 98, 100, 102-104, 161, 266
Conflicts 1-2, 10-11, 18, 21, 26, 42, 68, 70, 79-85, 88-93, 100, 102-103, 106, 141, 188, 192-193, 196, 200, 233, 239, 247, 281, 283-285

corporate governance 20-22, 24-25, 28, 30, 34
corporate leaders 98, 103-104
creativity and innovation 224, 229, 232, 234, 264
cross-cultural 6-7, 43, 79, 81-83, 88-89, 93, 98, 139, 236, 247, 253
cross-cultural conflict 79, 81, 88
Cross-cultural management 88
cultural differences 18, 83, 87, 89, 91-93, 100, 103-104, 250
cultural diversity 80, 85, 88, 90, 92-93, 109, 239-240
cultural quotient 103-104
Customer-Centred Operational Excellence (CCOpex) 131

D

demographic 3-4, 8-9, 13, 18, 42, 99, 101-102, 105, 111, 141, 152, 174, 177, 182, 207, 211, 264
diverse cultures 219
diversity 1-13, 19-23, 29, 32, 72, 80, 85, 88, 90, 92-93, 98-104, 106, 108-111, 132-133, 135, 149-155, 157-159, 161, 177, 186, 190, 202, 206-208, 216-217, 219, 239-240, 264-265, 271, 273, 279, 298
diversity management 1-5, 11, 13, 98, 100-102, 108-109, 151, 159, 206, 216, 219

E

emotional 7, 41, 46-47, 51, 100, 120, 135-137, 155-156, 159, 171, 174, 176, 282

Emotional Intelligence 51
employee engagement 132-141, 149, 151, 155-159, 171, 234
employee work engagement 135
employees' empowerment 172
employer brand 117-118, 122-123, 125, 128
employer branding 116-128, 131
Employer Value Proposition (EVP) 120, 131
employment discrimination 29, 211
equal employment opportunity 1, 3, 171
ethical relativism 236, 238-239, 241, 245-247, 249, 252-253
ethnicity 3, 8, 12-13, 18, 73, 80, 98, 100-101, 103-104, 150-151, 154, 209-211, 213, 264-265, 273

G

gender discrimination 21, 211
Generation X 39-40, 42-43
Generation Y 39-40, 42-43
globalization 12, 71, 79, 88, 98-99, 101, 103-104, 118, 151, 207, 213, 253, 264, 271-273
Graphic Rating Scale 261, 279

H

hiring discrimination 211
human resource management 98-99, 117, 139, 208, 297-298, 303-304, 306-307
human workforce 39-41, 50

I

Imaginativeness 11, 19, 102
inclusion 110-111, 149-155, 157-158, 161, 171, 190, 218, 281, 298, 301
India 32, 40, 50, 81, 84, 90, 122-123, 125-126, 131, 190, 226, 243, 253, 259, 266-269, 285, 289, 291-292, 297-302, 304-307
Indian economy 266-268
Indian organizations 116, 124, 224-225, 228, 232-233
intercultural 7, 67, 80-81, 158
international business 92, 99, 152, 249

IT industry 172, 211, 266

J

Job demands-resources model 135
job satisfaction 11, 55, 58, 61, 65, 68-69, 138, 140-141, 149, 157, 175-176, 200, 282-283

L

leaders 3, 7, 55, 57, 60, 98-100, 102-106, 109-111, 125, 161, 171, 187, 191, 198-199, 219, 224-229, 232, 234, 269, 304-306
leadership 6, 23, 32, 57, 60, 86, 98-100, 103-106, 109, 125-127, 150, 153, 156, 158, 160-161, 171, 175-176, 191, 193, 197-199, 202, 214, 224-229, 231-234, 290, 306
leadership competitiveness 100

M

management techniques 99
manager 12, 24, 31, 43, 45, 56, 58, 60, 65-68, 70-72, 74, 100, 103, 138, 158, 190-191, 213, 247, 265
manpower planning 304, 307
mediating 159
Microfinance Institutions 297-298, 300-301, 304
Millennials 40
moderating 159, 161
moral relativism 237-238
motivation 58, 64-65, 116, 120, 127, 138, 140, 155, 181, 194-197, 264, 271, 303
multinational business 250, 253

N

norms 74, 80-83, 90-91, 187-188, 193, 225, 236, 238, 249, 281-283, 292

O

organisational culture 280-281, 290-291
organizational climate 55, 57-58, 60, 62,

Index

92, 154, 158-159, 186-189, 191, 291
organizational commitment 128, 132-134, 140, 157, 172, 174-176, 178-183, 201
organizational culture 55-60, 62, 65-68, 70, 74, 93, 192, 200, 214, 225, 280-285, 288-292

P

performance appraisal 123, 125-126, 259-262, 264-265, 267-273, 278-279
performance assessment 158, 271, 278
performance evaluation 260, 268, 271-272
pharmaceuticals 248, 267, 270
Psychographics 7-8, 13, 19

R

Randstad 122-123, 128, 131
recruitment and selection 176

S

Self-Appraisal 268-269, 271, 279
social 5, 8-9, 11-13, 18-19, 22-24, 40-41, 43, 47, 62, 69, 74, 89, 104, 106, 117-118, 125-126, 135, 149, 152, 159, 186-188, 202, 207, 209, 212, 227, 236-238, 240, 249, 253, 282, 291, 297-298
social climate 186-187, 202
Socio-Economic Diversity 19
Starbucks 150, 153-154, 158, 244
strategic leadership 224, 226-229, 231-234, 290
support 3, 11, 26, 29, 136, 139, 153, 157, 176, 190-192, 194, 200-201, 208, 260, 280, 284-285, 289-291, 301, 303-304
sustainability 80, 92-93, 111, 226, 228, 232-233, 268, 298

T

talented workforce 103, 109
team climate 186-189, 191-193, 197, 201-202

Team Functioning and Team Empowerment 186, 191, 193
technology 39-40, 42, 44, 49-50, 57, 67, 70-71, 98-99, 103-104, 106, 150, 153, 174, 210, 238, 269-271, 281
training and development 118, 125-126, 176, 304-305, 307
trends 22, 39, 47, 116, 133, 159
Turkey 20, 22, 25, 30-31, 33-35

V

values 2, 7-10, 12, 19, 42, 59, 70, 80-82, 88-89, 106, 117-119, 131, 151, 154, 156, 158-159, 171, 176, 178, 188, 192, 194, 236-237, 240, 247-253, 260-261, 264, 270, 282-283, 298
values and beliefs 9, 19, 80-81, 88, 282

W

Walmart 153
women 9, 20-35, 40, 67, 73, 123, 126, 151, 153-154, 160, 211-212, 238, 240, 244-245, 248, 265, 298, 300-302, 306
work culture 8, 19, 91, 103-105, 152, 161, 218, 292
work environment 23, 26, 55-64, 66, 68-70, 72, 74-75, 80, 86, 100, 117-118, 135, 137, 189-190, 207, 216-218, 225, 271, 290
work force diversity 133, 186
workforce management 99, 158, 171
work-life balance 63, 123, 280-286, 288-291
workplace 1-3, 9, 11, 19, 50, 55, 57-58, 62-66, 68-69, 71, 73, 80, 85, 89-91, 93, 99-100, 102-105, 108, 136-139, 150, 152-159, 161, 173, 188, 190, 192-193, 195, 200, 206-219
workplace conflicts 102
workplace discrimination 206-210, 213-219

Purchase Print, E-Book, or Print + E-Book

IGI Global books can now be purchased from three unique pricing formats: Print Only, E-Book Only, or Print + E-Book. Shipping fees apply.

www.igi-global.com

Recommended Reference Books

Analyzing the Economics of Financial Market Infrastructures
ISBN: 978-1-4666-8745-5
© 2016; 410 pp.
List Price: $220

Strategic Approaches to Successful Crowdfunding
ISBN: 978-1-4666-9604-4
© 2016; 378 pp.
List Price: $205

Leadership and Personnel Management
ISBN: 978-1-4666-9624-2
© 2016; 2,266 pp.
List Price: $2,200

Economics
ISBN: 978-1-4666-8468-3
© 2015; 1,704 pp.
List Price: $2,395

Financial and Banking Crisis Prediction through Early Warning Systems
ISBN: 978-1-4666-9484-2
© 2016; 514 pp.
List Price: $265

Integrating Social Media into Strategic Marketing
ISBN: 978-1-4666-8353-2
© 2015; 438 pp.
List Price: $310

Looking for free content, product updates, news, and special offers?
Join IGI Global's mailing list today and start enjoying exclusive perks sent only to IGI Global members.
Add your name to the list at **www.igi-global.com/newsletters**.

Publishing Information Science and Technology Research Since 1988

IGI Global
DISSEMINATOR of KNOWLEDGE

www.igi-global.com Sign up at www.igi-global.com/newsletters facebook.com/igiglobal twitter.com/igiglobal

Stay Current on the Latest Emerging Research Developments

Become an IGI Global Reviewer for Authored Book Projects

The overall success of an authored book project is dependent on quality and timely reviews.

In this competitive age of scholarly publishing, constructive and timely feedback significantly decreases the turnaround time of manuscripts from submission to acceptance, allowing the publication and discovery of progressive research at a much more expeditious rate. Several IGI Global authored book projects are currently seeking highly qualified experts in the field to fill vacancies on their respective editorial review boards:

Applications may be sent to:
development@igi-global.com

Applicants must have a doctorate (or an equivalent degree) as well as publishing and reviewing experience. Reviewers are asked to write reviews in a timely, collegial, and constructive manner. All reviewers will begin their role on an ad-hoc basis for a period of one year, and upon successful completion of this term can be considered for full editorial review board status, with the potential for a subsequent promotion to Associate Editor.

If you have a colleague that may be interested in this opportunity, we encourage you to share this information with them.

InfoSci®-Books
A Database for Information Science and Technology Research

www.igi-global.com

Maximize Your Library's Book Collection!

Invest in IGI Global's InfoSci®-Books database and gain access to hundreds of reference books at a fraction of their individual list price.

The InfoSci®-Books database offers unlimited simultaneous users the ability to precisely return search results through more than 80,000 full-text chapters from nearly 3,900 reference books in the following academic research areas:

Business & Management Information Science & Technology • Computer Science & Information Technology
Educational Science & Technology • Engineering Science & Technology • Environmental Science & Technology
Government Science & Technology • Library Information Science & Technology • Media & Communication Science & Technology
Medical, Healthcare & Life Science & Technology • Security & Forensic Science & Technology • Social Sciences & Online Behavior

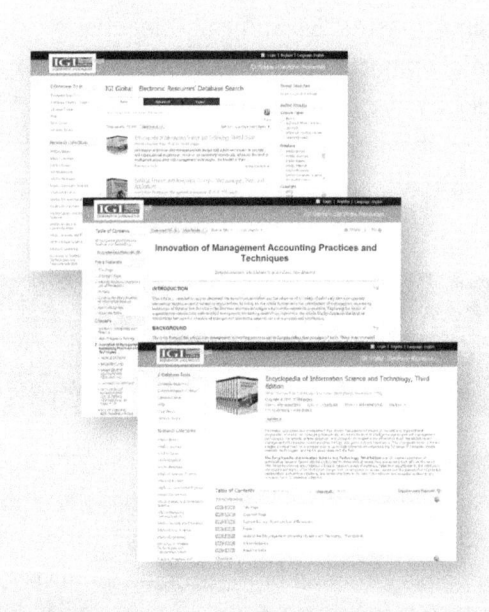

Peer-Reviewed Content:
- Cutting-edge research
- No embargoes
- Scholarly and professional
- Interdisciplinary

Award-Winning Platform:
- Unlimited simultaneous users
- Full-text in XML and PDF
- Advanced search engine
- No DRM

Librarian-Friendly:
- Free MARC records
- Discovery services
- COUNTER4/SUSHI compliant
- Training available

To find out more or request a free trial, visit:
www.igi-global.com/eresources

IGI Global
DISSEMINATOR OF KNOWLEDGE
www.igi-global.com

IGI Global Proudly Partners with eContent Pro International

Enhance Your Manuscript with eContent Pro International's Professional Copy Editing Service

Expert Copy Editing

eContent Pro International copy editors, with over 70 years of combined experience, will provide complete and comprehensive care for your document by resolving all issues with spelling, punctuation, grammar, terminology, jargon, semantics, syntax, consistency, flow, and more. In addition, they will format your document to the style you specify (APA, Chicago, etc.). All edits will be performed using Microsoft Word's Track Changes feature, which allows for fast and simple review and management of edits.

Additional Services

eContent Pro International also offers fast and affordable proofreading to enhance the readability of your document, professional translation in over 100 languages, and market localization services to help businesses and organizations localize their content and grow into new markets around the globe.

IGI Global Authors Save 25% on eContent Pro International's Services!

Scan the QR Code to Receive Your 25% Discount

The 25% discount is applied directly to your eContent Pro International shopping cart when placing an order through IGI Global's referral link. Use the QR code to access this referral link. eContent Pro International has the right to end or modify any promotion at any time.

Email: customerservice@econtentpro.com

econtentpro.com

www.igi-global.com

CPSIA information can be obtained
at www.ICGtesting.com
Printed in the USA
BVHW01*1254160918
R9085900001B/R90859PG526762BVX8B/3/P